C000151964

John Ruskin

SELECTED WRITINGS

MODERN PAINTERS

THE STONES OF VENICE

THE SEVEN LAMPS OF ARCHITECTURE

PRAETERITA

Edited by
PHILIP DAVIS
University of Liverpool

EVERYMAN
J. M. DENT · LONDON
CHARLES E. TUTTLE
VERMONT

Introduction, chronology and other critical material
© J. M. Dent 1995

This edition first published in Everyman in 1995

J. M. Dent
Orion Publishing Group
Orion House
5 Upper St Martin's Lane
London WC2H 9EA
and
Charles E. Tuttle Co. Inc.
28 South Main Street
Rutland, Vermont 05701, USA

Typeset in Sabon by Deltatype Ltd, Ellesmere Port, Cheshire
Printed in Great Britain by
The Guernsey Press Co. Ltd, Guernsey, C.I.

British Library Cataloguing-in-Publication Data
is available upon request.

ISBN 0 460 87460 8

CONTENTS

Editor's Acknowledgement

*I am grateful to Lucas Dietrich and Andrea Henry for their
helpful editorial guidance, and to Hilary Laurie
for encouraging the project.*

*I owe much to my colleague, Brian Nellist,
and to Sarah Coley.*

NOTE ON THE AUTHOR AND EDITOR

JOHN RUSKIN was born on 8 February 1819 in London, the son of John James Ruskin, a wine-merchant, and Margaret Ruskin (née Cox). His father's wealth enabled him to travel freely all over Europe between 1833 and 1888. He first became interested in the work of Turner in 1832, after receiving Samuel Rogers's *Italy*, illustrated with vignettes by Turner. In 1836 he wrote a defence of Turner in response to criticisms made in *Blackwood's Magazine*. He entered Christ Church, Oxford, in 1837 but had to suspend studies through illness, returning to take his degree in 1842. He met Turner for the first time in 1839 and began collecting his paintings. The five volumes of *Modern Painters* that grew out of his defence of Turner were published between 1843 and 1860. In 1857–8 he organized and catalogued the drawings in the Turner bequest. Ruskin's works on architecture, *The Seven Lamps of Architecture* and the three volumes of *The Stones of Venice*, appeared in 1848 and 1851–3 respectively. His social, economic and political writings include *Unto This Last* (1860), *Munera Pulveris* (1863) and *Fors Clavigera* (1871–1884). He carried out a number of social and environmental experiments in 1870–1876, including a drawing school at Oxford, road-building and diggings, a housing scheme in Marylebone, St George's Museum and St George's Farm in Sheffield. In 1871 he settled at Brantwood, overlooking Lake Coniston, and eventually he made a little world for himself there.

Ruskin married Effie Gray in 1848, but the marriage was annulled on the grounds of non-consummation in 1854. In 1858 he met the nine-year-old Rose La Touche, who became an inspiration to him: he proposed to her in 1866 and was turned down. After a series of reconciliations and partings she died in 1875. Ruskin suffered delirious visions in Venice in 1876, the first sign of his coming mental collapse. In 1858 Ruskin had experienced an 'unconversion' in Turin, which brought about his rejection of Evangelical Protestantism and put his Christianity in doubt. But Ruskin rediscovered his Christian faith in Assisi in 1874 while studying the frescoes of Giotto. In 1888 he proposed marriage to Kathleen Olander, an art student, but her parents separated them.

An outstanding watercolourist himself, Ruskin was appointed Slade Professor of Fine Art at Oxford in 1869. He suffered his first mental breakdown in 1878. In that year he was also fined a farthing damages for libelling James Abbott McNeill Whistler, whom he had accused of asking 'two hundred guineas for flinging a pot of paint in the public's face', and in protest resigned his professorship. He took up the professorship again in 1883 after a year without mental attacks (following a second breakdown in 1882), only to resign again in 1885 in protest against vivisection in the university. He suffered further attacks of madness in 1883, 1885 and 1887, but in 1884 he published *The Storm-Cloud of the Nineteenth Century*, describing environmental and climatic disorder in the modern world in prophetic terms. In 1889, after a further attack of madness, he prematurely concluded his autobiography *Praeterita* after four years of sporadic composition. He survived a further ten years, until his death on 20 January 1900, incapacitated and in almost total silence.

PHILIP DAVIS is senior lecturer in the English Department, University of Liverpool, and Director of the M.A. in Victorian Literature. He has published *Memory and Writing: from Wordsworth to Lawrence*; *In Mind of Johnson*; *The Experience of Reading*; and *Malamud's People*.

NOTE ON THE TEXT

The text used is that of the old standard edition, *The Library Edition of the Works of John Ruskin*, edited by E. T. Cook and Alexander Wedderburn, 39 vols. (London 1903–12).

Abbreviations

C&W: Cook and Wedderburn (eds), *Library Edition of the Works of John Ruskin*
MP: *Modern Painters*
SL: *The Seven Lamps of Architecture*
SV: *The Stones of Venice*
Sesame: *Sesame and Lilies*

CHRONOLOGY OF RUSKIN'S LIFE

Year	Age	Life
1817		Suicide of Ruskin's paternal grandfather (John Thomas), leaving debt of £5000. Ruskin senior takes on its repayment as a matter of honour and, when financially able to, marries his cousin Margaret, John Thomas's housekeeper
1819		Ruskin born 8 February in London, son of John James Ruskin and Margaret Ruskin (née Cox) who before his birth had devoted him to God
1823	4	Family moves to Herne Hill, Camberwell, south of London
1825	6	Family visit to Paris, Brussels, Waterloo
1830	11	First poem printed, 'On Skiddaw and Derwent Water', in *Spiritual Times*
1832	13	Receives birthday present of Samuel Rogers's *Italy* with vignettes after Turner
1833	14	Tour of Germany, Italy and especially Switzerland with Vale of Chamonix
1834	15	Studies in Alpine geology result in two articles published in *Magazine of National History*
1835	16	Tour of France, Switzerland and Italy, including Venice
1836	17	Writes essay defending Turner, who discourages its publication. Falls in love with Adèle Domecq on visit of his father's business partner

CHRONOLOGY OF HIS TIMES

Year	Literary Context	Historical Events
1819	Byron begins *Don Juan*	Peterloo Massacre
	Mary Ann Evans (George Eliot) born	Birth of Victoria
1820	Scott, *Ivanhoe*	Accession of George IV
1821	Death of Keats	Death of Napoleon
1822	Death of Shelley	
1823		War between France and Spain
1824	Death of Byron	
1830		Accession of William IV
		Reform Bill (1830–2)
1832	Death of Sir Walter Scott	
1833	Carlyle, *Sartor Resartus*	Oxford Movement
1834	Death of Coleridge	Abolition of slavery in British Empire
		Tolpuddle Martyrs transported
1835	Dickens, *Sketches by Boz* (1st series)	
1836	Dickens, *Sketches by Boz* (2nd series)	First train in London

Year	Age	Life
1837	18	Goes up to Christ Church, Oxford
1838	19	First book, *The Poetry of Architecture*, published in parts in *Architectural Magazine*
1839	20	Wins Oxford Newdigate Prize. Meets Turner, begins collecting Turner's works, financed by his father. Adèle Domecq marries. Suffering from depression and suspected consumption, goes on Italian tour (1840–1) with parents to recover health
1841	22	Meets thirteen-year-old Euphemia (Effie) Gray; writes *The King of the Golden River*, a fairy tale, for her
1842	23	Returns to Oxford to take B.A. Family moves to Denmark Hill, London
1843	24	Publishes first volume of *Modern Painters* begun the previous year
1845	26	First tour of Europe without parents, Tuscany, Florence, Alps. Discovers Tintoretto
1846	27	Takes parents over route of 1845. Publishes Vol. II of *Modern Painters*
1848	29	Marries Effie Gray, tours Normandy and studies Gothic architecture
1849	30	*The Seven Lamps of Architecture*. Winter in Venice, begins *The Stones of Venice*

Year	Literary Context	Historical Events
1837	Carlyle, *French Revolution* Dickens, *Oliver Twist*	Accession of Queen Victoria
1838		Beginnings of Chartism
1839	Carlyle, *Chartism* Turner, 'Fighting Téméraire'	Chartist riots Anglo-Chinese Opium War
1840		Queen's marriage to Prince Albert Great Irish Famine
1841	Carlyle, *Heroes and Hero Worship* Emerson, *Essays*	Peel P.M.
1842	Wordsworth, *Poems* Turner, 'Slavers'	Chartist riots Income tax introduced
1843	Wordsworth Poet Laureate J. S. Mill, *Logic* Dickens, *Christmas Carol*	
1844	Disraeli, *Coningsby*	Factory Act Royal Commission on Health of Towns
1845		Irish Potato Famine
1846	Brontës, *Poems*	Repeal of Corn Laws Railway boom
1847	Emily Brontë, *Wuthering Heights* Charlotte Brontë, *Jane Eyre*	
1848	Death of Emily Brontë Mrs Gaskell, *Mary Barton* Pre-Raphaelite Brotherhood	Revolution in Europe Communist Manifesto
1849	Charlotte Brontë, *Shirley* Froude, *Nemesis of Faith*	Christian Socialism of F.D. Maurice and Charles Kingsley

Year	Age	Life
1851	32	*The Stones of Venice* Vol. I. Defends Pre-Raphaelitism. Turner dies, Ruskin named as executor of his will. Winter in Venice
1853	34	*The Stones of Venice* Vols. II and III. Holidays at Glenfinlas with Effie and the painter Millais
1854	35	Effie leaves Ruskin for Millais, marriage annulled on grounds of non-consummation. *Lectures on Architecture and Painting.* Begins teaching at Working Men's College
1856	37	*Modern Painters* Vols. III and IV, *The Harbours of England*
1857	38	*The Elements of Drawing.* Lectures on *The Political Economy of Art* in Manchester. Sorts and catalogues drawings of Turner Bequest
1858	39	Meets nine-year-old Rose La Touche. In Turin undergoes 'unconversion' from Evangelical Protestantism; discovers Veronese
1859	40	*The Two Paths* (on applied art, design and craftsmanship), *The Elements of Perspective*
1860	41	*Modern Painters* Vol. V. Writes *Unto this Last* as essays for *Cornhill Magazine* but publication suspended due to political controversy: it appears in book form in 1862
1862	43	*Munera Pulveris* (essays in political economy) begin to appear in *Fraser's Magazine*, again publication suspended in 1863

Year	Literary Context	Historical Events
1850	Death of Wordsworth, *The Prelude* published Tennyson Poet Laureate, *In Memoriam* published Dickens, *David Copperfield*	
1851	Death of Turner	Great Exhibition in London
1853	Arnold, *Poems* Charlotte Brontë, *Villette*	Crimean War (1853–6)
1854	Dickens, *Hard Times* Holman Hunt, 'The Light of the World'	Battle of Balaclava
1856		Bessemer's Steel Process
1857	E. B. Browning, *Aurora Leigh*	National Portrait Gallery
1858	Carlyle, *Frederick the Great* Clough, *Amours de Voyage* George Eliot, *Scenes of Clerical Life*	
1859	Darwin, *Origin of Species* J. S. Mill, *On Liberty* Smiles, *Self-Help*	Franco-Austrian War over Italy
1860	Burckhardt, *Renaissance in Italy*	Italian Unification Lincoln U.S. President
1861	Mrs Browning, Clough die Arnold, *On Translating Homer*	American Civil War Death of Prince Consort
1862	Meredith, *Modern Love*	Colenso controversy on authenticity of books of Moses

Year	Age	Life
1864	45	Death of John James Ruskin. Joan Agnew (later Mrs Severn) comes to Denmark Hill to look after Ruskin and his mother. Gives lectures 'Traffic' and 'Of Kings' Treasuries'. *Cestus of Aglaia* (1864–5), on the enigmas of art and the use of myth
1865	46	*Sesame and Lilies*
1866	47	Proposes to Rose La Touche who puts off an answer. *The Ethics of the Dust* (on crystallography, written for pupils at the progressive girls' school Winnington Hall), *The Crown of Wild Olive* (lectures on labour and myth)
1867	48	*Time and Tide* (on the laws of work)
1869	50	*The Flamboyant Architecture of the Somme*, *The Queen of the Air* (lectures on classical mythology). Appointed first Slade Professor of Art at Oxford
1870	51	Founds Drawing School at Oxford. *Lectures on Art* at Oxford, *Verona and its Rivers*

Year	Literary Context	Historical Events
1863	Huxley, *Man's Place in Nature* Lyell, *Antiquity of Man* J. S. Mill, *Utilitarianism* Renan, *La Vie de Jésus*	
1864	Newman, *Apologia Pro Vita Sua*	Red Cross Geneva Convention
1865	Death of Mrs Gaskell Arnold, *Essays in Criticism* (1st series) Carroll, *Alice in Wonderland*	Abraham Lincoln assassinated End of American Civil War Ruskin and Carlyle form a Defence fund for Governor Eyre, accused of cruelly putting down a revolt in Jamaica
1866	Swinburne, *Poems and Ballads*	Riots in Ireland
1867	Bagehot, *English Constitution* Marx, *Das Kapital*, Vol. I	Disraeli P.M. Second Reform Bill
1868	Browning, *The Ring and the Book*	Gladstone P.M.
1869	Arnold, *Culture and Anarchy* J. S. Mill, *The Subjection of Women*	Suez Canal
1870	Death of Dickens Arnold, *St Paul and Protestantism* Newman, *Grammar of Assent*	Franco-Prussian War Elementary Education Act

Year	Age	Life
1871	52	Begins *Fors Clavigera: Letters to the Workmen and Labourers of Great Britain*. Founds Guild of St George for renewal of England. Mother dies; buys Brantwood by Lake Coniston
1872	53	*Aratra Pentelici* (lectures on sculpture), *The Eagle's Nest* (on science). Rose La Touche, physically and mentally ill, at last rejects proposal of marriage
1873	54	*Love's Meinie* (lectures on birds), *Ariadne Florentina* (lectures on wood and metal engravings)
1874	55	*Val d'Arno* (lectures on Tuscan art). Begins Hinksey diggings; opens Paddington tea-shop. In Italy studies Botticelli and Giotto frescoes in Rome and Assisi, respectively, and tomb of Ilaria di Caretto in Lucca
1875	56	Rose La Touche dies insane. Founds the St George's Museum at Walkley near Sheffield. *Mornings in Florence* (1875–7), *Deucalion* (1875–83, on geology), *Proserpina* (1875–86, on botany)
1876	57	First delirious visions, in Venice
1877	58	*St Mark's Rest* (1877–84, on Venice)
1878	59	First mental breakdown. Whistler libel case: Ruskin is fined a farthing for accusing Whistler of asking 'two hundred guineas for flinging a pot of paint in the public's face'
1879	60	Resigns Slade Professorship
1880	61	*Bible of Amiens* (1880–5, on Amiens Cathedral), *Fiction, Fair and Foul* (1880–1, literary criticism)
1882	63	Second attack of madness
1883	64	Resumes Slade Professorship amidst further mental disturbance
1884	65	*Storm-Cloud of the Nineteenth Century* (on sky and environmental conditions)

Year	Literary Context	Historical Events
1871	Darwin, *Descent of Man*	Trade Unions legalized
	George Eliot, *Middlemarch*	Abolition of religious tests at
	Carroll, *Through the Looking Glass*	Oxford and Cambridge
	Birth of Marcel Proust	
1872	Hardy, *Under the Greenwood Tree*	Secret Ballot
1873	Death of J. S. Mill, his *Autobiography* published	
	Tolstoy, *Anna Karenina*	
1874	Hardy, *Far from the Madding Crowd*	Disraeli P. M.
1875	Trollope, *The Way We Live Now*	Britain buys Suez Canal shares
1876	George Eliot, *Daniel Deronda*	Bulgarian atrocities
1877		Russo-Turkish War
1878	Hardy, *Return of the Native*	Eddystone Lighthouse
		Congress of Berlin
		Parnell's Irish Land League
1879	James Murray, editor of Oxford English Dictionary	Gladstone's Midlothian Campaign
1880	Death of George Eliot	Gladstone P.M.
1881	Deaths of Disraeli, Carlyle	Married Women's Property Act
	James, *Portrait of a Lady*	
1882	Deaths of Darwin, Trollope	Phoenix Park murders
1883	Nietzsche, *Thus Spake Zarathustra*	
1884	Oxford English Dictionary	Third Reform Bill

Year	Age	Life
1885	66	Resigns professorship again. Further breakdown. Begins autobiography, *Praeterita* (1885–9)
1887	68	Fifth breakdown
1888	69	Last tour of Europe
1900	81	After ten years' incapacity, dies 20 January at Brantwood and is buried in Coniston churchyard

Year	Literary Context	Historical Events
1885	Pater, *Marius the Epicurean* Birth of D. H. Lawrence	Salisbury P.M. Fall of Khartoum
1886	Nietzsche, *Beyond Good and Evil*	Gladstone and Salisbury P.M.s
1887		Queen's Jubilee
1888	Death of Matthew Arnold	Kodak box camera
1890	Morris, *News From Nowhere*	
1891		Free elementary education
1893		Independent Labour Party
1899	Tolstoy, *Resurrection*	Boer War begins
1900	Conrad, *Lord Jim*	Relief of Ladysmith and Mafeking

SUMMARY

Over the last ten years or so critical and biographical studies of Ruskin have tended to concentrate increasingly on his later writings, after 1860. In particular this includes his social and political writings, such as *Unto this Last* (begun in 1860) and *Fors Clavigera: Letters to the Workmen and Labourers of Great Britain* (from 1871), as well as the abstruse mythological and symbolic books including *The Queen of the Air* (1869, on classical mythology) and *Proserpina* (1875–86, on botany).

In contrast, the present *Selected Writings* begins where Ruskin himself did: not with politics but with art, not with mythology but with belief, not with social thinking but with seeing. The reader should be able to perceive, nonetheless, the seeds of the later interests already in the earliest ones. This selection therefore seeks to provide a renewed context for the classic writings of the period 1843 to 1864 that were traditionally considered to be at the centre of Ruskin's opus: *Modern Painters* above all, *The Stones of Venice*, *The Seven Lamps of Architecture* and *Sesame and Lilies*, as well as the late autobiographical work, *Praeterita* (1885–9).

The problem with any selection from Ruskin is the problem of length: his collected works take up thirty-nine volumes. Ruskin is a writer not only of long books of wandering argument but of long sentences within them – all demanding immersed attention. *Modern Painters* alone runs to over 600,000 words, *The Stones of Venice* to 450,000. Nor are these works what might be called formally systematic, despite the numbered divisions into parts and sections and chapters and paragraphs. His writings sprawl generously into matters large and small, they digress, they often seem to threaten to lose their way or contradict themselves. And yet as a whole they exist within an overall, indeed universal, purpose in creation.

Ruskin loathed the idea of what we might now call consumer-friendly selections: offering short-cuts to deep meaning, with purple passages for lazy aesthetes or aphoristic morals for busy philistines. But if *Modern Painters* is to become again a living classic for Everyman (and that is my aim in this edition), it will be by virtue of generous as well as rigorously discriminating selection. This selection has been built around the reproduction of seven more or less complete chapters that I take to be fundamental to the five volumes of *Modern Painters* ('Of the Truth of Space' in Volume I, 'Of Infinity' in Volume II, 'Of Greatness of Style' and 'Of the Use of Pictures' in Volume III, 'Of Turnerian Mystery: as Essential' Volume IV, and 'The Dark Mirror' and 'The Lance of Pallas' of Volume V), as well as 'The Nature of Gothic' from *The Stones of Venice*.

Around these central chapters I offer the amalgamated selection of certain topic areas (such as the idea of 'Finish' – of good and bad speed of execution in painting – in *Modern Painters*, or the uses of Imperfection in *The Stones of Venice*). In this way I have tried to show how the same concern can find different emphases, constellations and developments in Ruskin's varied and flexible thinking, while still remaining part of one all-encompassing view arising even out of scattered and tiny fragments. Indeed, Ruskin's holism is precisely what holds together this selection: the faith that wherever Ruskin travels, mentally as well as physically, he will find himself within a whole, ultimately theological, order of meaning.

Consequently, in addition to explanatory endnotes and a biographical glossary at the back of this volume, I have also incorporated footnotes, which are meant to provide living cross-references or echoes of Ruskin's views in other places without interfering with the forward movement of the main section. The method, adopted here in order to trace Ruskin's basic unity of mind across a wide range of years and topics, is essentially Marcel Proust's in his editing of Ruskin:

> I offer here a translation of *The Bible of Amiens* by John Ruskin. But it seemed to me that this was not enough for the reader. To read only one book by an author is to see the author only once. True in a single conversation with someone we can discern particular traits. But it is only through repeated encounters in varied circumstances that we can recognize these traits as characteristic and essential. For a writer, for a musician, or for a painter, this variation of circumstances that enables us to discern, by a sort of experimentation, the permanent features of character is found in the variety of the works themselves . . . By inserting a footnote to

the text of *The Bible of Amiens* each time this text evoked, through even remote analogies, the recollection of other works of Ruskin, and by translating in the note the passage which had come to my mind, I have tried to put the reader in the position of one who would not find himself in Ruskin's presence for the first time but who, having had previous conversations with Ruskin, would be able to recognize in his words what is permanent and fundamental in him. Thus I have tried to provide the reader with, so to speak, an improvised memory in which I have arranged recollections of other works of Ruskin – a kind of sounding board against which the words of *The Bible of Amiens* will be able to ring more deeply by awakening fraternal echoes.

The aim of the typographical lay-out in this selection is thus to give the reader easy and almost simultaneous access to another dimension of time and place in Ruskin's mind. For this method of reading fits with Ruskin's own sense of the overlap, in life and in thought, of different forces operating potentially in different directions at the same time. What interested Proust was this reading-experience of rich memory:

[Ruskin's] experience was so vast, that very often the most profound knowledge of which he gives evidence in one work is neither utilized nor mentioned, even by a mere allusion, in those other works of his where it would belong. He is so rich that he does not lend us his words; he gives them to us and does not take them back. . . . Generally, in a writer, the recurrence of certain favourite examples, if not even the repetition of certain developments, reminds you that you are dealing with a man who had a particular life, a particular body of knowledge as opposed to another, a limited experience from which he draws all the profit he can. The mere consultation of the indexes of Ruskin's various works, the perpetual newness of the works cited, and still more the disdain for the information of which he availed himself once and, very often, abandoned forever, give the idea of something more than human, or rather the impression that each book is by a new man, who has a different knowledge, not the same experience, another life.

On Reading Ruskin, translated and edited by J. Autret, W. Burford and P. J. Wolfe (Yale, 1987), pp. 5–6, 37–8 (Translator's Preface).

A parenthetical remark passed in a mere sentence inside one volume may become a whole chapter inside another, and vice versa. Yet although Ruskin is always different, he is also somehow always underlyingly the same. In this Ruskin resembles his beloved Turner, as Ruskin describes him in his analysis of the painting *Rouen from St Catherine's Hill* on page 56. If he is repetitive, he is so like nature itself: only in an infinitely varied way.

Thus, during the act of writing itself, revising and reassembling his work as he went along, as well as at regular intervals throughout his life, Ruskin thought of re-ordering the parts of *Modern Painters*. As late as 1883 he was still considering the impossible task of completely rearranging Volume II; in 1888, in an epilogue to Volume V, he expressed regret for the 'Protestant egotism and insolence' of the earlier volumes. As Ruskin put it in the preface to the final volume, 'Had I wished for future fame, I should have written one volume, not five.' This offers me some licence for a selective reassembling of my own, in seven separate but linked chapters, each with a brief explanatory introduction. They are largely but not invariably chronological and may also be read as semi-autonomous units.

Chapters One and Two begin the story by showing how Ruskin actually saw and 'read' paintings, in particular those of Turner. Here is Ruskin as the great teacher of art, of seeing. For as Charlotte Brontë wrote on first reading *Modern Painters* Vol. I, 'Hitherto I have only had instinct to guide me in judging art; I feel now as I had been walking blindfold – this book seems to give me eyes.' That is to say, Ruskin is the man from whom to *start* – even for those who think they know little about art, or come to Ruskin's writings more accustomed to the interpretation of written texts rather than pictures.

Chapter Three shows how Ruskin rewrote his particular analyses in *Modern Painters* Vol. I into the general principles of Volume II. Chapter Four similarly shows how the first half of *Modern Painters* Vol. III was a fresh attempt to regain hold of the inexhaustibly deep meaning of the first two volumes after the ten-year gap (1846–56) that followed the publication of *Modern Painters* Vol. II.

The Seven Lamps of Architecture and the three volumes of *The Stones of Venice* were published in 1848 and 1851–3 respectively. These architectural works form the subject of Chapter Five: it may be read independently of the other sections, but those readers who prefer a more chronological ordering may choose to read it after Chapter Three. It is placed where it is, however, in order that the central contrast between the old Gothic and the modern Renaissance ways of being may serve as an introduction to

Chapter Six, on the spiritual problems for the modern age discussed in the second half of *Modern Painters* Vol. III, and the fourth and final part (IX) of *Modern Painters* Vol. V.

As a postscript, Chapter Seven presents a variety of more personal or informal writings: public speeches and lectures, private diary workings, incidental literary criticism, as well as Ruskin's autobiography, *Praeterita*. These personal notes may help the reader to hear Ruskin's own voice, clinchingly, and experience the personal relevance of Ruskin's artistic concerns not only *to* him but *via* him. They may enable the reader to take away a final sense of the sheer embodiment of Ruskin's thinking in himself, in his life. Strong work, weak life – a large vision held in a man who increasingly felt himself to be small. Yet, even so, there is a sad, mortally chastened dignity in the anticlimax on which his life ends.

Wherever possible I have included Ruskin's more easily reproducible diagrams, drawings and engravings, so that the reader may be encouraged to take time to *see* what Ruskin was writing about.

INTRODUCTION

Work for Life

Looking through mists of indistinctness at the violently over-reaching and unnaturally restless colours, at the apparently unfocused washes of sheer paint, a critic of Turner's painting wrote in *Blackwood's Magazine* of 'a strange jumble', 'a kaleido-scopic power to patternize all confusion.' This was not untypical of the hostile reception Turner often suffered in his later life. It was in Ruskin's own home that Turner expressed his contempt for the critics who had dismissed his 'Snow storm – steam-boat off a harbour's mouth' as 'soapsuds and whitewash': 'Soapsuds and whitewash? What would they have? I wonder what the sea's like?' Then he added succinctly, 'I wish they'd been in it.'

In 1836 John Ruskin, aged seventeen, wrote an angry rejoinder to the *Blackwood's* critic, determined in Turner's defence to 'blow the critics out of the water'. He could not know at the time that he was making a commitment for life. But before he knew it, he had tied himself, eye and hand and soul, to following Turner and to trying to turn into words all that Turner had put into paint. He had set himself to try to catch up with a painter whom he had instinctively but deliberately chosen for being far ahead of all others.

It would have been far easier for Ruskin to devote himself to the realism of the contemporary Norwich School – of John Sell Cotman and John Crome. But Ruskin always chose to learn from those who knew more than he did, who would take him further through the mists or into the depths. In *Praeterita*, for example, Ruskin recalls how much his family admired Dickens, but added that Dickens 'taught us nothing with which we were not familiar, – only painted it perfectly for us ... so that he never became an educational element of my life, but only one of its chief comforts and restoratives' (Vol. II, Ch. IV, para. 64). Led beyond the familiar – that was Ruskin's sense of what a real education was.

And a real life was a career, following not fame but a project – a journeying out of the unknown into an ever-increasing realization of 'the unity and mystery' of the world. There is both in Ruskin himself and in reading Ruskin, 'the joy that the human mind has in contemplating any kind of maze and entanglement, so long as it can discern, through its confusion, any guiding clue or connecting plan' (*The Stones of Venice*, Vol. II, Ch. V, para. 22).

But to Ruskin, Turner was not just puzzlingly strange, fancifully fantastic or grotesque. Far from being a hopelessly unrealistic painter, Turner was in Ruskin's eyes the truest portrayer of realistic landscape – the whole of Volume I of *Modern Painters* was dedicated to establishing that realization. But beyond that, Turner was a deliverer not just of realistic but of visionary truth about the universe. 'He paints in colour, but he thinks in light and shade' (C&W III, p. 301). To know about Turner meant learning about virtually everything else – geology, botany, optics, anatomy, the history of painting, of architecture, history itself, and so on.

Indeed, that was why Turner was so important. Ruskin loved it when, even in the sheer shape of a stone or a tree, he could see the dynamic construction of apparently static things: it was as though their histories were written implicitly within them. Everything had a life, a story and a human meaning. Even a wall rising from rough foundations into final ornamentation showed different layers and levels in its making, like epochs in a human life. A cornice felt like a hand, which a wall used to bear the weight above it; a buttress bore and conveyed all the force of structural weight running through it. Buildings suddenly came to life when seen at the right distance. A Turner painting might seem to move in front of one's eyes, coming and going: 'its outlines perpetually melting and appearing again, – sharp here, vague there, – now lost altogether, now just hinted and still confused among each other; and so for ever in a state and necessity of change' (MP I, Pt. II, Sec. II, Ch. II, para. 16).

Everything came together, everything came to life – in Turner. There was so very much within and behind this taciturn artist, branching out from him. To follow Turner and to speak for him, to reconstruct what Turner stood for and represented, was for Ruskin an organic career.

Life for Work

Ruskin was more than devoted to Turner; to use Proust's word, he *sacrificed* his life for him. Says Proust, approvingly:

> The critic should then go further. He should try to reconstruct what the unique spiritual life of an artist haunted by such special realities could have been, the critic's inspiration being the measure of those realities, his talent the measure of his ability to recreate them in his work, his ethics, finally, the instinct which, making him consider them from a viewpoint of eternity (however particular these realities appear to us), impelled him to sacrifice to the need of perceiving them and to the necessity of reproducing them all his pleasures, all his duties, and even his own life which has no raison d'être except as the only possible way of entering into contact with those realities and has no value except that which an instrument indispensable to his experiments may have for a physicist. (Adapted from *On Reading Ruskin*, pp. 6–7)

That is the measure of Ruskin's sense of himself: as an instrument. For if, in the great hidden order of things in which Ruskin believed, one was really a second-rate person, then one should recognize the fact and subordinate oneself to one of the primary figures, such as Turner. One day, reports Ruskin in Letter 9 of *Fors Clavigera*, a man who was no more and no less than a good draughtsman said to him, 'Do you think, sir, that I shall ever draw as well as Turner?' Says Ruskin, 'Had he been taught early and thoroughly to know his place, and be content with his faculty, he would have been one of the happiest and most serviceable of men.'

Half interpreter, half prophet, Ruskin's own place was precisely to try to show the very order of things. He was to reveal the universe through Turner, the greater seer, so that Ruskin's sacrifice of himself to Turner mimed Turner's own self-sacrificing obedience to his vision of the world. As Proust writes, 'Among the ideas of Ruskin which may seem out of date to ordinary minds, incapable of understanding their true meaning and of feeling their truth, [is] that idea which holds freedom as fatal for the artist, and obedience and respect as essential, the idea that makes memory the most useful intellectual organ to the artist' (*On Reading Ruskin*, p. 95).

No sooner did Ruskin teach than he had to learn; no sooner did he write one volume of *Modern Painters* than he realized that he did not know enough. And in order to carry on, and to correct himself even as he went along, he would have to go off and travel and study more and look harder – at rocks or at early masters – and try to digest what he had learnt – all before he could write again. It was a manic race for Ruskin: from volume to volume he tried to turn seeing into writing, learning into teaching – even while hoping that the teaching was not too short of digested learning within it and that the very desire to learn did not itself harass and pre-empt the pure act of seeing.

It is clear from Ruskin's diaries that he suffered times of terrible anxiety when he could not integrate seeing with feeling, or when he scared himself out of the experience of the present by the very thought that he must afterwards remember it. 'I am gradually losing my zest for scenery and stood at the window to night (27 January 1841), while the sunset was touching the sprinkled snow on the lovely forms of the Mt. Angelo, rather with a sense of discharging a duty in drinking the draught of beauty than because it gave me pleasure.' He could not look at the scene 'without remembering Turner', yet still 'all this could not touch me' (*Diaries of John Ruskin*, Vol. I, pp. 145–6). 'I could not *feel* it.' Driving himself too often to utter exhaustion, Ruskin saw before him natural and cultural phenomena that he knew – perhaps too well – that he ought to love or remembered having loved but that now he could not love.

For someone who inherited a Romantic culture amid an encroaching industrialized society, the tensions were everywhere. Turner himself was almost over-full of paint and meaning and effort. Added to this, personal and family anxieties were not the least of Ruskin's problems for being shamefully smaller and more intimate. From the first, Ruskin's loving father, convinced of his son's genius, had wanted the boy to be a poet as great as Byron, only more pious, while rising in the Church to become at fifty the Archbishop of Canterbury no less. Instead, the father became increasingly convinced that he would be dead before the end of *Modern Painters* was ever in sight and begged piteously for its completion. His grown-up boy seemed to be wandering aimlessly in every possible field of study. To Ruskin himself, parental backing also felt like further pressure. D. H. Lawrence called Ruskin one of England's last generation of sons. The very strength he drew from his parents' support deprived him of a sense of independence.

All in all, there was almost too much for Ruskin in the world. It *was* too much for him. If you were Ruskin, there was no secure place to start from; wherever you started you would find out, even as part of your progress, that you had not known enough before. But Ruskin was, in the words of George Herbert that he himself quoted, 'full of himself' – not in the egotistical sense, but full of some big intuition that he trusted would unfold and be fundamentally right and about which he could not be silent, even when he felt less than fully prepared or competent to utter it.

Did Ruskin really sacrifice his own life, thus terrifyingly, to Turner's vision? Or, more disturbingly perhaps, did he have no real life of his own to sacrifice in the first place? Did he seek sacrifice in lieu of living himself? Or was it more that his commitment, made too early and too completely, reinforced itself as the only life he had?

Years after formal manhood, Ruskin remained a spoilt and repressed only child. 'I find myself in nothing changed . . . in the total of me, I am but the same youth, disappointed' (*Praeterita*, Vol. I, Ch. XII, para. 246). He failed to consummate his marriage. He often got on best with people when he could show them something of his collection of drawings, stones, coins – playfully pouring them all out in a mess of associations, saying only then, 'Now, we are comfortable.' More and more, Ruskin was subject to fits of mental depression, finally to periods of mental illness. He had strained his life towards the universe of things, as if he had no physical life of his own. The growing weariness, the loss of youthful Romantic intensity, haunted Ruskin and was echoed in Wordsworth's 'Ode: Intimations of Immortality':

> And custom lie upon thee with a weight
> Heavy as frost, and deep almost as life!

In our post-Freudian age we all too readily make our diagnoses for such disease – Turner as replacement father-figure; work as a sexual sublimation taking over the proper development from childishness to adulthood; the transference of body into mind inside and landscape without; nature, art and writing as the apparently impersonal forms of a personal compensation.

No wonder, we might think, that Ruskin never got the balance of things right, never had a fully adult sense of proportion – indeed had no real form or limit to his books as they took him over – but wrote too much as though he was actually in a world of his own. This is what ultimately worried Proust: that the man who put Art in the service of Life and Faith, put his own life and faith into the service of Art.

But perhaps, this is not really a contradiction. Because this man lacked a balance between life and work, and because he could not take things for granted like one adult among many others in a ready-made world, common truths came to Ruskin not as merely commonplace but as if for the first time. It is precisely his over-intensity we should value.

Do not just read books but *mine* them, he says in 'Of Kings' Treasuries' in *Sesame and Lilies*. Do not be merely cool; use your care and learning as pickaxes, use your thoughtful soul as a smelting furnace:

> Do not hope to get at any good author's meaning without those tools and that fire.

Be warmly attentive; melt the human ice. For over-intensity it is that registers in the individual the recognition of something so powerful as to be *more* than himself – something that bursting out of him *feels as though* it should connect with others and prevent the isolation of individualism. 'There is a crust about the impressible part of men's minds', writes Ruskin in 'The Lamp of Power' in *The Seven Lamps of Architecture*, 'which must be pierced through before they can be touched to the quick; and though we may prick at it in a thousand separate places, we might as well have let it alone if we do not come through somewhere with a deep thrust.' The extent and passion of Ruskin's knowledge seemed to isolate him from many other people in the world – unless he could teach them to know and feel what he himself had learnt. Ruskin may seem didactic in his search for a social unity to match the natural one he saw. But as Robert Harbison said of Ruskin in a book entitled *Eccentric Spaces*, 'He is one of those who take things hard, quarreling with all those who take them easy.'

There was a terrible personal cost for all this – which can be felt in the very language of Ruskin's autobiography, *Praeterita*. By trying to contain a universe of things within his mind, while beset from without by an uncongenial social world, Ruskin virtually broke and destroyed himself. There is no missing the terrible sense of decay, decline and disappointment in *Praeterita* at the end of his life. This autobiography is not a man's last effort at the end of his life to pull the meaning of his life together and give out a last, conclusive word. Ruskin's mental state was too perilous for that, even had it been possible. By 1885 he had become a man who, having tried to hold everything in his mind, now in his decline had to let go. No final system, no summation, there are instead apparently chance remarks, casual thoughts and memories. In writing *Praeterita*, Ruskin had to let in *time* itself – simply what occurred to him personally at the time of writing – in place of a whole lifetime's attempt at comprehensiveness. Yet here too there is something other than failure, something that is the fruit of failure, a virtue in necessity. So much of *Praeterita* gently exists in the remaining accidents of the present, in what seems like a final casual act of writing up a life:

> I was particularly fond of watching [my father] shave; and was always allowed to come into his room in the morning (under the one in which I am now writing), to be the motionless witness of that operation.
>
> > Vol. I, Ch. II, para. 42

> I have just opened my oldest (in use) Bible . . . My mother's list of the chapters with which, thus learned, she established my soul in life, has just fallen out of it.
>
> > ibid., para. 48

> I recollect that very evening bringing down my big geography book, still most precious to me; (I take it down now, and for the first time put my own initials under my father's name in it) –
>
> > Vol. I, Ch. IV, para. 88

As he writes up his autobiography, it is as though Ruskin is turning over old photographs, taking a last look at old diaries. It is a sort of peace in the passing presentness of life – if not quite the peace that Ruskin had always most admired and sought:

> And, in order to teach men how to be satisfied, it is necessary fully to understand the art and joy of humble life, – this, at present, of all arts and sciences being the one most needing study. Humble life, – that is to say, proposing to itself no future exaltation, but only a sweet continuance; not excluding the idea of foresight, but wholly of fore-sorrow, and taking no troublous thought for coming days; so also, not excluding the idea of providence, or provision, but wholly of accumulation; – the life of domestic affection and domestic peace, full of sensitiveness to all elements of costless and kind pleasure; – therefore, chiefly to the loveliness of the natural world.   *Modern Painters*, Vol. V, Pt. IX, Ch. XI, para. 21

In his prime Ruskin was probably what we should call a manic-depressive. In placing the value of the sheer state of being far above the activities of using or hurrying, he preached in part from the book of his own errors. But in *Praeterita* at least, when forced to slow down, when faced by a sense of a life's failure, proud Ruskin salvaged from near-humiliation something of a peaceful humility – even if when most short of an earthly future to worry about.

The Unifying Vision

'You must not follow Art without pleasure, nor must you follow it for the sake of pleasure.' Ruskin loved to set up sentences that sent you for their meaning through the eye of a needle, between two opposite mistakes for the sake of some carefully re-established unification.

Similarly, there never was a critic so for art who could also be so against it. And the two went together, the pro and the anti. But working out salvation meant knowing quite how. For Ruskin, accordingly, art was most important when it was not all-important. Art was important in itself only because it could point to something beyond itself. That was what Ruskin meant when he called it a language.

Truth is a biped, says Ruskin; it advances not on one foot but on two. We have to tread carefully, often between two seemingly opposite truths that contain, somewhere between them, the right way. It is especially like this in matters of religious faith. There is nothing you could say that could not be misrepresented, nothing you could assert that did not have another darker or mistaken side. What is so wonderful in Ruskin is to see him fitting his truths carefully together within a whole universe and composition of thought, not once as in stone, but again and again with sundry modifications. For Ruskin there is not simply a system of principles, but the right and wrong way of taking and applying them, the complex refinements involved in connecting them across pages or years or realms, the surrender of one to another that is suddenly seen to be higher. For sheer continuous thinking, with distinctions made in the very midst of connections, Ruskin represents one of the finest models.

'You must not follow Art for the sake of pleasure.' Art was no mere aesthetic pastime for odd hours. But neither was this puritan anti-aestheticism joyless. 'You must not follow Art without pleasure.' Art was praise and awe. Art's purpose was all for nothing if it was not ultimately visionary and religious. What is more, Ruskin sometimes dared to wonder if, after all, it *was* all for nothing.

Some commentators stress, quite reasonably, the many changes and developments in Ruskin's career. Much is often made of Ruskin's unconversion from orthodox Evangelicalism in 1858 and his alleged loss of belief in naturally grounded theology – in an intuition of the existence of God arising directly out of nature. Looking over his work, Ruskin himself came to regret the 'Protestant egoism and insolence' of the first two volumes of *Modern Painters*. In *Modern Painters* Vol. V in particular, what Ruskin calls mountain gloom threatens to eclipse mountain glory. But, for all the changes, Ruskin did not change essentially. That the sight and the smell of a rose was beautiful was to Ruskin throughout his life sheerly a *fact*. That it was a fact also told him something else: this was no valueless, inhospitable universe.

If Ruskin changed at all, it was the shift after 1860 to social and political writings. But it was a change that resulted from despair, signalled in *Modern Painters* Vol. V in the chapter 'The Two Boyhoods'. In loneliness Ruskin had recourse to a language of historical *explanation* for the loss of belief within nineteenth-century society. Ruskin himself was probably better off with a sense of mystery than with a sense of explanation, but he needed the language of explanation to back himself up in an unpropitious world, by showing how and why it became unpropitious. This shift took place not because social welfare became Ruskin's main concern, in place of belief in God, but because social conditions, in preventing belief, had themselves taken the place of true belief –even, symptomatically, in part of Ruskin's own mind. If socio-economic concerns had such an effect on the way people thought and felt as to replace faith, then a second-order concern for those socio-economic conditions threatened in Ruskin's later works to reduplicate that general loss of primary belief. He became in part a mental victim of what he felt he had to explain and protest against.

But the underlying continuity in Ruskin's career remained. As he puts it in the preface to the second edition of *Modern Painters* Vol. I in 1844:

> Thus it is in the progress of a painter's handling. We see the perfect child, the absolute beginner, using of necessity a broken, imperfect,

inadequate line, which, as he advances, becomes gradually firm, severe, and decided. Yet before he becomes a perfect artist, this severity and decision will again be exchanged for a light and careless stroke, which in many points will far more resemble that of his childhood than of his middle age, differing from it only by the consummate effect wrought out by the apparently inadequate means. So it is in many matters of opinion. Our first and last coincide, though on different grounds; it is the middle stage which is farthest from the truth.

It is to his credit that Ruskin never pretended that he had really left behind his first thoughts, the crude starting points of feeling and belief. He encourages us not to be ashamed of starting from what and from where we really are. 'It is necessary first to teach men to speak out, and say what they like truly.' So Ruskin had spoken out early and rashly for Turner.

Only then, 'in the second place', may men be taught 'which of their likings are ill set, and which justly' (*The Stones of Venice*, Vol. I, Ch. II, para. 12). So, in his own career, there is nothing that Ruskin initially finds to be strong in which, in the second place, he is afraid to detect weakness – be it in Turner, in landscape painting and the love of nature, in humanity, or in belief in God. This is what *strong* means for Ruskin: something that can stand to be tested, something that gives more, even out of the very challenge of opposition to it. For there is nothing so right that it cannot be made wrong. Indeed, the more valuable it is, the more dangerous it becomes to get it wrong, or use it wrongly, by a whisker or a tone. The closer you get to truth, the more the slightest error counts.

And yet Ruskin is never paralysed by the sense of human weakness in the midst of strength. In the lecture 'The Mystery of Life and its Arts' (see page 333ff.), Ruskin says that the better the work, the more it is the product of people who feel themselves wrong. And yet the better the work, the more it is also the product of people who know they are right. That is what the greatest ones do: they do not stop until they reach their point of failure. They even create their own failure by seeing more than the best they can do, which is why they feel wrong even through the very right they can imagine but not encompass.

In his felt mix of right and wrong, Ruskin was such a person. He always took risks, then tested them – in that order. He continually insisted upon registering the human meaning of non-human things – and then tested the dangers of what he calls 'pathetic fallacy', that is to say, the incontinent projection of human emotions.

Some might say that there is now no God – or if there is a God, God is no longer a 'He', as in the childhood of Man, but an 'It'. But for Ruskin, taking things humanly, even taking God humanly, as children do with God the Father, is not something we as humans should seek to transcend. We can only try to use the human mode rightly. 'This conception of God, which is the child's, is evidently the only one which *for us* can be true' (*Modern Painters*, Vol. IV, Pt. V, Ch. VI, para. 7). He stayed with this first thought through all the doubts, tests and modifications. At the personal level, Ruskin thought what he thought, unashamedly; likewise generically, humans had to think in the way they did, in human terms. Otherwise they would cease to be human.

The greatest of all differences between humans was the difference between those who believed and those who did not. Thinking of those exiled men who long ago, holding to their faith, had raised Venice itself out of nothing, in contrast to the men of his own day, Ruskin felt 'that difference which there is in the sight of God, in all ages'

> between the calculating, smiling, self-sustained, self-governed man, and the believing, weeping, wondering, struggling, Heaven-governed Man; – between the men who say in their hearts 'there is no God,' and those who acknowledge a God at every step, 'if haply they might feel after Him and find Him' [Psalms xiv. 1, liii. 1; Acts xvii. 27]. For that is indeed the difference which we shall find, in the end, between the builders of this day and the builders on that sand island long ago. They did honour something out of themselves; they did believe in spiritual presence judging, animating, redeeming them; they built to its honour and for its habitation.
>
> *The Stones of Venice*, Vol. II, Ch. III, para. 40

Art offered Ruskin the fullest picture of this humanly religious relation to the world, as something to honour out of himself. Hence in Ruskin we witness the natural extension of even the minutest analyses of art into large environmental, moral and religious concerns, on the planet and in the modern world. Accordingly, some present-day commentators, such as Peter Fuller in his book *Theoria*, have seen Ruskin as the first ecological critic, signalling the need for a new unifying synthesis between art, nature, science and faith. For above all Ruskin believed in the existence of one whole interrelated world. It is that faith, and no mere structure of their own, that holds his books together – just as surely as their subject matter is held together outside the books. In this way and in this faith, Ruskin is the true heir of both Wordsworth and Coleridge – and of whatever their Romantic way of seeing might still mean spiritually within the modern world.

People of a religious disposition who meditate in their closet, rather than go forth into the fields, mar their own happiness, believes Ruskin – for in struggling with fallen nature, they fail to seek aid from 'nature undestroyed':

> It seems to me that the real sources of bluntness in the feelings towards the splendour of the grass and glory of the flower, are less to be found in ardour of conception, in seriousness of compassion, or heavenliness of desire, than in the turning of the eye at intervals to rest too selfishly within; the want of power to shake off the anxieties of actual and near interest, and to leave results in God's hands; the scorn of all that does not seem immediately apt for our purposes, or open to our understanding, and perhaps something of pride, which desires rather to investigate than to feel.
>
> Modern Painters, Vol. II, Pt. III, Sec. I, Ch. XV, para. 10

That, with its echo of Wordsworth, is Ruskin's warning rebuke to narrowly human anxiety.

Yet in the end nature as such only gives Ruskin a language – a better language than that offered by contemporary human fashion or by any current economic system. The contemplation of creation's shapes and structures as of themselves forced out of Ruskin vital words, such as 'help' or 'architecture'. And so out of non-human forms human words were dynamically remembered and brought back to mind as if there were an ancient kinship – even here, still. For example, three mere tree buds in a cluster would all like to grow straight upright, towards the light, together:

> So far as they can, in kindness to each other, and by sufferance of external circumstances, work out that destiny they will. But their beauty will not result from their working it out, – only from their maintained purpose and resolve to do so, if it may be. They will fail – certainly two, perhaps all three of them: fail egregiously; – ridiculously; – it may be, agonizingly. Instead of growing up, they may be wholly sacrificed to happier buds above, and have to grow *down*, sideways, roundabout ways, all sorts of ways . . .
>
> Yet out of such sacrifice, gracefully made – such misfortune,

gloriously sustained — all their true beauty is to arise. Yes, and from more than sacrifice — more than misfortune: from *death*. Yes, and more than death: from the worst kind of death: not natural, coming to each in its due time; but premature, oppressed, unnatural, misguided — or so it would seem — to the poor dying sprays. Yet, without such death, no strong trunk were ever possible . . .

When a poor bough is gone, the one next above is left with greater freedom, and will shoot now from points of its sprays which were before likely to perish. Hence another condition of irregularity in form. But that bough also will fall in its turn, though after longer persistence. Gradually thus the central trunk is built, and the branches by whose help it was formed cast off, leaving here and there scars, which are all effaced by years, or lost sight of among the roughnesses and furrows of the aged surface. The work is continually advancing, and thus the head of foliage on any tree is not an expansion at a given height, like a flower-bell, but the collective group of boughs, or workmen, who have got up so far, and will get up higher next year, still losing one or two of their number underneath.

Modern Painters, Vol. V, Pt. VI, Ch. VII, paras. 7, 10

There is an active, mysteriously cooperative, whole 'life' here, 'a life of progress and will, — not a merely passive accumulation of substance' (Vol. V, Pt. VI, Ch. IV, para. 17). There is even a 'community' and a 'history' of purpose. The words, such as 'or workmen', seem not merely projected deliberately and anthropomorphically but *given* to thought suddenly and incidentally, and sanctioned in an instinctive mental pledge of the human bond with other created things. In the midst of his descriptive work, Ruskin excitedly rediscovers through the very act of writing something of the law by which all things were originally composed and connected, sees afresh the sources of linguistic analogy, and recalls the natural link between Earth and Human, as if he were God's memory. Ruskin is no mere nature-lover but a God-intoxicated man.

'The divisions of religious tenet and school to which I attached mistaken importance in my youth,' concluded Ruskin in 1888 in an epilogue to *Modern Painters* Vol. V, 'do not in the least affect the vital teaching and purpose of this book: the claim namely, of the Personal relation of God to man as the source of all human, as distinguished from brutal, virtue and art.'

The personal relation of God to man is the source of all human

xlii INTRODUCTION

virtue and art. Another nineteenth-century writer given to huge
and powerful claims, Leo Tolstoy, said of Ruskin, 'He was one of
those rare men who think with their hearts.' With their hearts
means something here, and is not sloppily Romantic. For Ruskin
was not interested in mere impersonal handwork or headwork:
'heartwork is the one work we want.' The reader will find
throughout these *Selected Writings* that Ruskin not only had
thoughts, but felt, personally, all they could mean. That is his
heartwork.

It would be nice if at the end of this book the reader feels like
that member of the audience who came up to Ruskin after a series
of lectures to say how much he had enjoyed them. But nice is not
enough with Ruskin, not at heart, for Ruskin replied to his
conventional admirer: 'I don't care whether you enjoyed them;
did they do you any good?'

PHILIP DAVIS

LIST OF ILLUSTRATIONS

SELECTED WRITINGS

CHAPTER I
How to Read a Painting

In the chapter 'Definition of Greatness in Art', near the very beginning of the first volume of Modern Painters, *Ruskin makes a basic distinction between the technical language of a painting and the thought that a painting thereby conveys:*

> Painting, or art generally, as such, with all its technicalities, difficulties, and particular ends, is nothing but a noble and expressive language, invaluable as the vehicle of thought, but by itself nothing. He who has learned what is commonly considered the whole art of painting, that is, the art of representing any natural object faithfully, has as yet only learned the language by which his thoughts are to be expressed. He has done just as much towards being that which we ought to respect as a great painter, as a man who has learnt how to express himself grammatically and melodiously has towards being a great poet ... It is not by the mode of representing and saying, but by what is represented and said, that the respective greatness either of the painter or the writer is to be finally determined. (MP I, Pt. I, Sec. I, Ch. II, para. 2)

More puritan than aesthete, Ruskin is in no doubt as to the priority of the meaning of the subject (thought) over its means of technical expression (language). He nonetheless admitted that it was not always easy 'to determine where the influence of language stops, and where that of thought begins' (para. 5). And in later life, typically, he felt he needed at once to modify what he had said in his youthful enthusiasm without losing his early definition of important relative priorities – as his editors Cook and Wedderburn explain in a footnote to the passage on language and thought:

> This is perhaps one of 'many passages' in the volume to which Ruskin afterwards referred as 'setting the subject or motive of the picture so much above the mode of its execution, that some of my more feebly gifted disciples supposed they were fulfilling my wishes by choosing exactly the subjects for painting which they

were least able to paint.' 'It was long,' he said elsewhere, 'before I myself understood the true meaning of the pride of the greatest men in their mere execution ... Inferior artists are continually trying to escape from the necessity of sound work, and either indulging themselves in their delights in subject, or pluming themselves on their noble motives for attempting what they cannot perform; ... whereas the great men always understand at once that the first morality of a painter, as of everybody else, is to know his business.' Yet though Ruskin felt that he had been 'provoked' too far into 'the exclusive assertion' of his proposition – that subject was principal, and technique the means of expression, yet to the truth of the proposition itself he constantly adhered. 'The principle itself,' he said, 'I maintain, now in advanced life, with more reverence and firmness than in earliest youth; and though I believe that among the teachers who have opposed its assertion, there are few who enjoy the mere artifices of composition or dexterities of handling so much as I, the time which I have given to the investigation of these has only farther assured me that the pictures were noblest which compelled me to forget them'. C&W III, p. 88

It remained vital to Ruskin throughout his life that there should be an almost visible distinction between the means and the end of a painting. A painter should not try merely to trick a spectator into the illusion of believing that a painting was itself the reality it portrayed. Art should not be an imitative deception, an act of what Ruskin called 'jugglery'. Instead, the viewer should be able to see an honest distinction between the language of the painting and the thought that that language tried to express. Accordingly, Ruskin wrote in his first defence of Turner against Blackwood's criticism: 'he can produce instantaneous effect by a roll of his brush, and, with a few dashes of mingled colour, will express the most complicated subject: the means employed appear more astonishingly inadequate to the effect produced than in any other master' (C&W III, p. 637). It is this very inadequacy expressed in the medium itself that induces the viewer to read and to interpret a painting's language rather than simply to take it at face value.

This chapter contains Ruskin's analysis of three of Turner's paintings, demonstrating how their visual language both produces and gives way to their thought. In the second and third examples he goes on to show how the reading of pictures has not only to do with the art of painting but with a recognition of what goes on within ordinary acts of seeing in life itself. The physical act of seeing, which implicitly involves the focusing of interpretation and imagination, is itself always an act of vision. Looking at Turner makes us see how we really see.

The Task of the Least

The reader has probably been surprised at my assertions made often before now, and reiterated here, that the *minutest* portion of a great composition is helpful to the whole. It certainly does not seem easily conceivable that this should be so. I will go farther, and say that it is inconceivable. But it is the fact.

We shall discern it to be so by taking one or two compositions to pieces, and examining the fragments. In doing which, we must remember that a great composition always has a leading emotional purpose, technically called its motive, to which all its lines and forms have some relation. Undulating lines, for instance, are expressive of action; and would be false in effect if the motive of the picture was one of repose. Horizontal and angular lines are expressive of rest and strength; and would destroy a design whose purpose was to express disquiet and feebleness. It is therefore necessary to ascertain the motive before descending to the detail.

One of the simplest subjects, in the series of the Rivers of France, is 'Reitz, near Saumur.' The published Plate gives a better rendering than usual of its tone of light; and my rough etching, Plate 1, sufficiently shows the arrangement of its lines. What is their motive?

To get at it completely, we must know something of the Loire.

The district through which it here flows is, for the most part, a low place, yet not altogether at the level of the stream, but cut into steep banks of chalk or gravel, thirty or forty feet high, running for miles at about an equal height above the water.

These banks are excavated by the peasantry, partly for houses, partly for cellars, so economizing vineyard space above; and thus a kind of continuous village runs along the river-side, composed half of caves, half of rude buildings, backed by the cliff, propped against it, therefore always leaning away from the river; mingled with overlappings of vineyard trellis from above, and little towers or summerhouses for outlook, when the grapes are ripe, or for gossip over the garden wall.

It is an autumnal evening, then, by this Loire side. The day has

Plate 1 *Loire Side*

been hot, and the air is heavy and misty still; the sunlight warm, but dim; the brown vine-leaves motionless: all else quiet. Not a sail in sight on the river, its strong noiseless current lengthening the stream of low sunlight.

The motive of the picture, therefore, is the expression of rude but perfect peace, slightly mingled with an indolent languor and despondency; the space between intervals of enforced labour; happy, but listless, and having little care or hope about the future; cutting its home out of this gravel bank, and letting the vine and the river twine and undermine as they will; careless to mend or build, so long as the walls hold together, and the black fruit swells in the sunshine.

To get this repose, together with rude stability, we have therefore horizontal lines and bold angles. The grand horizontal space and sweep of Turner's distant river show perhaps better in the etching than in the Plate; but depend wholly for value on the piece of near wall. It is the vertical line of its dark side which drives the eye up into the distance, right against the horizontal, and so makes it felt, while the flatness of the stone prepares the eye to understand the flatness of the river. Farther: hide with your finger the little ring on that stone, and you will find the river has stopped flowing. That ring is to repeat the curved lines of the river bank, which express its line of current, and to bring the feeling of them down near us. On the other side of the road the horizontal lines are taken up again by the dark pieces of wood, without which we should still lose half our space.

Next: The repose is to be not only perfect, but indolent: the repose of out-wearied people; not caring much what becomes of them.

You see the road is covered with litter. Even the crockery is left outside the cottage to dry in the sun, after being washed up. The steps of the cottage door have been too high for comfort originally, only it was less trouble to cut three large stones than four or five small. They are now all aslope and broken, not repaired for years. Their weighty forms increase the sense of languor throughout the scene, and of stability also, because we feel how difficult it would be to stir them. The crockery has its work to do also; – the arched door on the left being necessary to show the great thickness of walls and the strength they require to prevent falling in of the cliff above; – as the horizontal lines must be diffused on the right, so this arch must be diffused on the left;

and the large round plate on one side of the steps, with the two small ones on the other, are to carry down the element of circular curvature. Hide them, and see the result.

As they carry the arched group of forms down, the arched window-shutter diffuses it upwards, where all the lines of the distant buildings suggest one and the same idea of disorderly and careless strength, mingling masonry with rock.

So far of the horizontal and curved lines. How of the radiating ones? What has the black vine trellis got to do?

Lay a pencil or ruler parallel with its lines. You will find that they point to the massive building in the distance. To which, as nearly as is possible without at once showing the artifice, every other radiating line points also; almost ludicrously when it is once pointed out; even the curved line of the top of the terrace runs into it, and the last sweep of the river evidently leads to its base. And so nearly is it in the exact centre of the picture, that one diagonal from corner to corner passes through it, and the other only misses the base by the twentieth of an inch.

If you are accustomed to France, you will know in a moment by its outline that this massive building is an old church.

Without it, the repose would not have been essentially the labourer's rest — rest as of the Sabbath. Among all the groups of lines that point to it, two are principal: the first, those of the vine trellis: the second, those of the handles of the saw left in the beam: the blessing of human life, and its labour. (MP V, Pt. VIII, Ch. II, paras. 1–5)

Of Truth of Space

First, then, it is to be noticed, that the eye, like any other lens, must have its focus altered, in order to convey a distinct image of objects at different distances; so that it is totally impossible to see distinctly, at the same moment, two objects, one of which is much farther off than another. Of this, any one may convince himself in an instant. Look at the bars of your window-frame, so as to get a clear image of their lines and form, and you cannot, while your eye is fixed on them, perceive anything but the most indistinct and shadowy images of whatever objects may be visible beyond. But fix your eyes on those objects, so as to see them clearly, and though they are just beyond and apparently beside the window-frame, that frame will only be felt or seen as a vague, flitting, obscure interruption to whatever is perceived beyond it. A little attention directed to this fact will convince every one of its universality, and prove beyond dispute that objects at unequal distances cannot be seen together, not from the intervention of air or mist, but from the impossibility of the rays proceeding from both converging to the same focus, so that the whole impression, either of one or the other, must necessarily be confused, indistinct, and inadequate.

But, be it observed (and I have only to request that whatever I say may be tested by immediate experiment), the difference of focus necessary is greatest within the first five hundred yards; and therefore, though it is totally impossible to see an object ten yards from the eye, and one a quarter of a mile beyond it, at the same moment, it is perfectly possible to see one a quarter of a mile off, and one five miles beyond it, at the same moment. The consequence of this is, practically, that in a real landscape, we can see the whole of what would be called the middle distance and distance together, with facility and clearness; but while we do so, we can see nothing in the foreground beyond a vague and indistinct arrangement of lines and colours; and that if, on the contrary, we look at any foreground object, so as to receive a distinct impression of it, the distance and middle distance become all disorder and mystery.

And therefore, if in a painting our foreground is anything, our distance must be nothing, and *vice versâ* . . . Turner introduced a new era in landscape art, by showing that the foreground might be sunk for the distance, and that it was possible to express immediate proximity to the spectator, without giving anything like completeness to the forms of the near objects. This, observe, is not done by slurred or soft lines (always the sign of vice in art), but by a decisive imperfection, a firm, but partial assertion of form, which the eye feels indeed to be close home to it, and yet cannot rest upon, nor cling to, nor entirely understand, and from which it is driven away of necessity to those parts of distance on which it is intended to repose.' (MP I, Pt. II, Sec. II, Ch. IV, paras. 2–4)

*   *   *

We have seen how indistinctness of individual distances becomes necessary in order to express the adaptation of the eye to one or other of them; we have now to examine that kind of indistinctness which is dependent on real retirement of the object, even when the focus of the eye is fully concentrated upon it. The first kind of indecision is that which belongs to all objects which the eye is not adapted to, whether near or far off: the second is that consequent upon the want of power in the eye to receive a clear image of objects at a great distance from it, however attentively it may regard them.

Draw on a piece of white paper a square and a circle, each about a twelfth or eighth of an inch in diameter, and blacken them so that their forms may be very distinct; place your paper against the wall at the end of the room, and retire from it a greater or less distance accordingly as you have drawn the figures larger or smaller. You will come to a point where, though you can see both the spots with perfect plainness, you cannot tell which is the square and which the circle.

Now this takes place of course with every object in a landscape, in proportion to its distance and size. The definite forms of the leaves of a tree, however sharply and separately they may appear to come against the sky, are quite indistinguishable at fifty yards off, and the form of everything becomes confused before we finally lose sight of it. Now if the character of an object, say the front of a house, be explained by a variety of forms in it, as the shadows in the tops of the windows, the lines of the architraves, the seams of the masonry, etc.; these lesser details, as the object falls into distance, become confused and undecided, each of them losing its definite form, but all being perfectly visible as something, a white or a dark spot or stroke, not lost sight of, observe, but yet so seen that we cannot tell what they are. As the distance increases, the confusion becomes greater, until at last the whole front of the house becomes merely a flat pale space, in which, however, there is still observable a kind of richness and chequering, caused by the details in it, which, though totally merged and lost in the mass, have still an influence on the texture of that mass; until at last the whole house itself becomes a mere light or dark spot which we can plainly see, but cannot tell what it is, nor distinguish it from a stone or any other object.

Now what I particularly wish to insist upon, is the state of vision in which all the details of an object are seen, and yet seen in such confusion and disorder that we cannot in the least tell what they are, or what they mean. It is not mist between us and the object, still less is it shade, still less is it want of character; it is a confusion, a mystery, an interfering of undecided lines with each other, not a diminution of their number; window and door, architrave and frieze, all are there: it is no cold and vacant mass, it is full and rich and abundant, and yet you cannot see a single form so as to know what it is. Observe your friend's face as he is coming up to you. First it is nothing more than a white spot; now it is a face, but you cannot see the two eyes, nor the mouth, even as spots; you see a confusion of lines, a something which you know from experience to be indicative of a face, and yet you cannot tell how it is so. Now he is nearer, and you can see the spots for the eyes and mouth, but they are not blank spots neither; there is detail in them; you cannot see the lips, nor the teeth, nor the brows, and yet you see more than mere spots; it is a mouth and an eye, and there is light and sparkle and expression in them, but nothing distinct. Now he is nearer still, and you can see that he is like your friend, but you cannot tell whether he is, or not; there is a vagueness and indecision of the line still. Now you are sure, but even yet there are a thousand things in his face which have their effect in inducing the recognition, but which you cannot see so as to know what they are.

Changes like these, and states of vision corresponding to them, take place with each and all of the objects of nature, and two great principles of truth are deducible from their observation. First, place an object as close to the eye as you like, there is always something in it which you *cannot* see, except in the hinted and mysterious manner above described. You can see the texture of a piece of dress, but you cannot see the individual threads which compose it, though they are all felt, and have each of them influence on the eye. Secondly, place an object as far from the eye as you like, and until it becomes itself a mere spot, there is always something in it which you *can* see, though only in the hinted manner above described. Its shadows and lines and local colours are not lost sight of as it retires; they get mixed and indistinguishable, but they are still there, and there is a difference always perceivable between an object possessing such details and a flat or vacant space. The grass blades of a meadow a mile off, are so far discernible that there will be a marked difference between its appearance and that of a piece of wood painted green. And thus nature is never distinct and never vacant, she is always mysterious, but always abundant; you always see something, but you never see all.

And thus arise that exquisite finish and fulness which God has appointed to be the perpetual source of fresh pleasure to the cultivated and observant eye; a finish which no distance can render invisible, and no nearness comprehensible; which in every stone, every bough, every cloud, and every wave is multiplied around us, for ever presented, and for ever exhaustless. And hence in art, every space or touch in which we can see everything, or in which we can see nothing, is false. Nothing can be true which is either complete or vacant; every touch is false which does not suggest more than it represents, and every space is false which represents nothing.

Now, I would not wish for any more illustrative or marked examples of the total contradiction of these two great principles, than the landscape works of the old masters, taken as a body; the Dutch masters furnishing the cases of seeing everything, and the Italians of seeing nothing. The rule with both is indeed the same, differently applied – 'You shall see the bricks in the wall, and be able to count them, or you shall see nothing but a dead flat:' but the Dutch give you the bricks, and the Italians the flat. Nature's rule being the precise reverse – 'You shall never be able to count the bricks, but you shall never see a dead space.'

Take, for instance, the street in the centre of the really great landscape of Poussin (great in feeling at least) marked 260 in the Dulwich Gallery. The houses are dead square masses with a light side and a dark side, and black touches for windows. There is no suggestion of anything in any of the spaces; the light wall is dead grey, the dark wall dead grey, and the windows dead black. How differently would nature have treated us! She would have let us see the Indian corn hanging on the walls, and the image of the Virgin at the angles, and the sharp, broken, broad shadows of the tiled eaves, and the deep-ribbed tiles with the doves upon them, and the carved Roman capital built into the wall, and the white and blue stripes of the mattresses stuffed out of the windows, and the flapping corners of the mat blinds. All would have been there; not as such, not like the corn, or blinds or tiles, not to be comprehended or understood, but a confusion of yellow and black spots and strokes, carried far too fine for the eye to follow, microscopic in its minuteness, and filling every atom and part of space with mystery, out of which would have arranged itself the general impression of truth and life.

Again, take the distant city on the right bank of the river in

Claude's Marriage of Isaac and Rebecca, in the National Gallery. I have seen many cities in my life, and drawn not a few; and I have seen many fortifications, fancy ones included, which frequently supply us with very new ideas indeed, especially in matters of proportion; but I do not remember ever having met with either a city or a fortress *entirely* composed of round towers of various heights and sizes, all facsimiles of each other, and absolutely agreeing in the number of battlements. I have, indeed, some faint recollection of having delineated such a one in the first page of a spelling book when I was four years old; but, somehow or other, the dignity and perfection of the ideal were not appreciated, and the volume was not considered to be increased in value by the frontispiece. Without, however, venturing to doubt the entire sublimity of the same ideal as it occurs in Claude, let us consider how nature, if she had been fortunate enough to originate so perfect a conception, would have managed it in its details. Claude has permitted us to see every battlement, and the first impulse we feel upon looking at the picture is to count how many there are. Nature would have given us a peculiar confused roughness of the upper lines, a multitude of intersections and spots, which we should have known from experience was indicative of battle-ments, but which we might as well have thought of creating as of counting. Claude has given you the walls below in one dead void of uniform grey. There is nothing to be seen, or felt, or guessed at in it; it is grey paint or grey shade, whichever you may choose to call it, but it is nothing more. Nature would have let you see, nay, would have compelled you to see, thousands of spots and lines, not one to be absolutely understood or accounted for, but yet all characteristic and different from each other; breaking lights on shattered stones, vague shadows from waving vegetation, irregular stains of time and weather, mouldering hollows, sparkling casements; all would have been there; none indeed, seen as such, none comprehensible or like themselves, but all visible; little shadows and sparkles, and scratches, making that whole space of colour a transparent, palpitating, various infinity . . .

Now it is, indeed, impossible for the painter to follow all this; he cannot come up to the same degree and order of infinity, but he can give us a lesser kind of infinity. He has not one thousandth part of the space to occupy which nature has; but he can, at least, leave no part of that space vacant and unprofitable. If nature carries out her minutiæ over miles, he has no excuse for generalizing in inches. And if he will only give us all he can, if he will give us a fulness as complete and as mysterious as nature's, we will pardon him for its being the fulness of a cup instead of an ocean. But we will not pardon him, if, because he has not the mile to occupy, he will not occupy the inch, and because he has fewer means at his command, will leave half of those in his power unexerted. Still less will we pardon him for mistaking the sport of nature for her labour, and for following her only in her hour of rest, without observing how she has worked for it. After spending centuries in raising the forest, and guiding the river, and modelling the mountain, she exults over her work in buoyancy of spirit, with playful sunbeam and flying cloud; but the painter must go through the same labour, or he must not have the same recreation. Let him chisel his rock faithfully, and tuft his forest delicately, and then we will allow him his freaks of light and shade, and thank him for them; but we will not be put off with the play before the lesson, with the adjunct instead of the essence, with the illustration instead of the fact . . .

We might go through every part and portion of the works of the old masters, showing throughout, either that you have every leaf and blade of grass staring defiance at the mystery of nature, or that you have dead spaces of absolute vacuity, equally determined in their denial of her fulness. And even if we ever find (as here and there, in their better pictures, we do) changeful passages of agreeable playing colour, or mellow and transparent modulations of mysterious atmosphere, even here the touches, though satisfactory to the eye, are suggestive of nothing; they are characterless; they have none of the peculiar expressiveness and meaning by which nature maintains the variety and interest even of what she most conceals. She always tells a story, however hintedly and vaguely; each of her touches is different from all the others; and we feel with every one, that though we cannot tell what it is, it cannot be *any* thing; while even the most dexterous distances of the old masters pretend to secrecy without having anything to conceal, and are ambiguous, not from the concentration of meaning, but from the want of it.

And now, take up one of Turner's distances, it matters not which or of what kind, drawing or painting, small or great, done thirty years ago or for last year's Academy, as you like; say that of the Mercury and Argus [Plate 2];[a] and look if every fact which I

[a] It will be found in this picture (and I am now describing nature's work and

have just been pointing out in nature be not carried out in it. Abundant beyond the power of the eye to embrace or follow, vast and various beyond the power of the mind to comprehend, there is yet not one atom in its whole extent and mass which does not suggest more than it represents; nor does it suggest vaguely, but in such a manner as to prove that the conception of each individual inch of that distance is absolutely clear and complete in the master's mind, a separate picture fully worked out: but yet, clearly and fully as the idea is formed, just so much of it is given, and no more, as nature would have allowed us to feel or see; just so much as would enable a spectator of experience and knowledge to understand almost every minute fragment of separate detail, but appears, to the unpractised and careless eye, just what a distance of nature's own would appear, an unintelligible mass. Not one

Turner's with the same words) that the whole distance is given by retirement of solid surface; and that if ever an edge is expressed, it is only felt for an instant, and then lost again; so that the eye cannot stop at it and prepare for a long jump to another like it, but is guided over it, and round it into the hollow beyond; and thus the whole receding mass of ground, going back for more than a quarter of a mile, is made completely *one*, no part of it is separated from the rest for an instant, it is all united, and its modulations are *members*, not divisions of its mass. But these modulations are countless; heaving here, sinking there; now swelling, now mouldering; now blending, now breaking . . .

It is not until we have made ourselves acquainted with these simple facts of form as they are illustrated by the slighter works of Turner, that we can become at all competent to enjoy the combination of all, in such works as the Mercury and Argus, or Bay of Baiæ. in which the mind is at first bewildered by the abundant outpouring of the master's knowledge. Often as I have paused before these noble works, I never felt on returning to them as if I had ever seen them before; for their abundance is so deep and various, that the mind, according to its own temper at the time of seeing, perceives some new series of truths rendered in them, just as it would on revisiting a natural scene; and detects new relations and associations of these truths which set the whole picture in a different light at every return to it. And this effect is especially caused by the management of the foreground: for the more marked objects of the picture may be taken one by one, and thus examined and known; but the foregrounds of Turner are so united in all their parts that the eye cannot take them by divisions, but is guided from stone to stone and bank to bank, discovering truths totally different in aspect according to the direction in which it approaches them, and approaching them in a different direction, and viewing them as part of a new system every time that it begins its course at a new point. ('On Mercury and Argus', MP II, Pt. II, Sec. IV, Ch. IV, paras. 19, 29)

Plate 2 *Mercury and Argus*

line out of the millions there is without meaning, yet there is not one which is not affected and disguised by the dazzle and indecision of distance. No form is made out, and yet no form is unknown.

Perhaps the truth of this system of drawing is better to be understood by observing the distant character of rich architecture, than of any other object.[b] Go to the top of Highgate Hill on a

[b] *Compare Ruskin on reading the sculpture of architecture*:

For all good architecture depends upon the adaptation of its chiselling to the effect at a certain distance from the eye; and to render the peculiar confusion in the midst of order, and uncertainty in the midst of decision, and mystery in the midst of trenchant lines, which are the result of distance, together with perfect expression of the peculiarities of the design, requires the skill of the most admirable artist, devoted to the work with the most severe conscientiousness ...

It is foolish to carve what is to be seen forty feet off with the delicacy which the eye demands within two yards; not merely because such delicacy is lost in the distance, but because it is a great deal worse than lost: – the delicate work has actually worse effect in the distance than rough work. This is a fact well known to painters, and, for the most part, acknowledged by the critics of painting, namely, that there is a certain distance for which a picture is painted; and that the finish, which is delightful if that distance be small, is actually injurious if the distance be great: and, moreover, that there is a particular method of handling which none but consummate artists reach, which has its effect at the intended distance, and is altogether hieroglyphical and unintelligible at any other. This, I say, is acknowledged in painting, but it is not practically acknowledged in architecture ... It may be asked whether, in advocating this adaptation to the distance of the eye, I obey my adopted rule of observance of natural law. Are not all natural things, it may be asked, as lovely near as far away? Nay, not so. Look at the clouds, and watch the delicate sculpture of their alabaster sides, and the rounded lustre of their magnificent rolling. They were meant to be beheld far away; they were shaped for their place, nigh above your head; approach them, and they fuse into vague mists, or whirl away in fierce fragments of thunderous vapour. Look at the crest of the Alp, from the far-away plains over which its light is cast, whence human souls have communion with it by their myriads. The child looks up to it in the dawn, and the husbandman in the burden and heat of the day [Matthew xx. 12], and the old man in the going down of the sun [Daniel vi. 14] and it is to them all as the celestial city on the world's horizon; dyed with the depth of heaven, and clothed with the calm of eternity. There was it set, for holy dominion, by Him who marked for the sun his journey, and bade the moon know her going down [Psalms civ. 19]. It was built for its place in the far-off sky; approach it, and,

clear summer morning at five o'clock, and look at Westminster Abbey. You will receive an impression of a building enriched with multitudinous vertical lines. Try to distinguish one of those lines all the way down from the one next to it: You cannot. Try to count them: You cannot. Try to make out the beginning or end of any

as the sound of the voice of man dies away about its foundation, and the tide of human life, shallowed upon the vast aërial shore, is at last met by the Eternal 'Here shall thy waves be stayed' [Job xxxviii. 11], the glory of its aspect fades into blanched fearfulness; its purple walls are rent into grisly rocks, its silver fretwork saddened into wasting snow: the storm-brands of ages are on its breast, the ashes of its own ruin lie solemnly on its white raiment.

Nor in such instances as these alone, though, strangely enough, the discrepancy between apparent and actual beauty is greater in proportion to the unapproachableness of the object, is the law observed. For every distance from the eye there is a peculiar kind of beauty, or a different system of lines of form; the sight of that beauty is reserved for that distance, and for that alone. If you approach nearer, that kind of beauty is lost, and another succeeds, to be disorganised and reduced to strange and incomprehensible means and appliances in its turn. If you desire to perceive the great harmonies of the form of a rocky mountain, you must not ascend upon its sides. All is there disorder and accident, or seems so; sudden starts of its shattered beds hither and thither; ugly struggles of unexpected strength from under the ground; fallen fragments, toppling one over another into more helpless fall. Retire from it, and, as your eye commands it more and more, as you see the ruined mountain world with a wider glance, behold! dim sympathies begin to busy themselves in the disjointed mass; line binds itself into stealthy fellowship with line; group by group, the helpless fragments gather themselves into ordered companies; new captains of hosts and masses of battalions become visible, one by one, and far away answers of foot to foot, and of bone to bone, until the powerless chaos is seen risen up with girded loins, and not one piece of all the unregarded heap could now be spared from the mystic whole.

Now it is indeed true that where nature loses one kind of beauty, as you approach it, she substitutes another; this is worthy of her infinite power: and, as we shall see, art can sometimes follow her even in doing this; but all I insist upon at present is, that the several effects of nature are each worked with mea\s referred to a particular distance, and producing their effect at that distance only. Take a singular and marked instance: When the sun rises behind a ridge of pines, and those pines are seen from a distance of a mile or two, against his light, the whole form of the tree, trunk, branches, and all, becomes one frostwork of intensely brilliant silver, which is relieved against the clear sky like a burning fringe, for some distance on either side of the sun. Now suppose that a person who had never seen pines were, for the first time in his life, to see them under this strange aspect, and, reasoning as to the means by which such effect could be produced, laboriously to approach the eastern ridge, how would he be amazed to find that

one of them: You cannot. Look at it generally, and it is all symmetry and arrangement. Look at it in its parts, and it is all inextricable confusion. Am not I, at this moment, describing a piece of Turner's drawing, with the same words by which I describe nature? And what would one of the old masters have done with such a building as this in the distance? Either he would

the fiery spectres had been produced by trees with swarthy and grey trunks, and dark green leaves! We, in our simplicity, if we had been required to produce such an appearance, should have built up trees of chased silver, with trunks of glass, and then been grievously amazed to find that, at two miles off, neither silver nor glass was any more visible; but nature knew better, and prepared for her fairy work with the strong branches and dark leaves, in her own mysterious way.

Now this is exactly what you have to do with your good ornament. It may be that it is capable of being approached, as well as likely to be seen far away, and then it ought to have microscopic qualities, as the pine leaves have, which will bear approach. But your calculation of its purpose is for a glory to be produced at a given distance; it may be here or may be there, but it is a *given* distance; and the excellence of the ornament depends upon its fitting that distance, and being seen better there than anywhere else, and having a particular function and form which it can only discharge and assume there. You are never to say that ornament has great merit because 'you cannot see the beauty of it here:' but it has great merit because 'you *can* see its beauty *here only*.' . . .

How are we to manage this?

As nature manages it. I said above, that for every distance from the eye there was a different system of form in all natural objects: this is to be so then in architecture. The lesser ornament is to be grafted on the greater, and third or fourth orders of ornaments upon this again, as need may be, until we reach the limits of possible sight; each order of ornament being adapted for a different distance: first, for example, the great masses, – the buttresses and stories and black windows and broad cornices of the tower, which give it make and organism, as it rises over the horizon, half a score of miles away: then the traceries and shafts and pinnacles, which give it richness as we approach: then the niches and statues and knobs and flowers, which we can only see when we stand beneath it. At this third order of ornament, we may pause, in the upper portions; but on the roofs of the niches, and the robes of the statues, and the rolls of the mouldings, comes a fourth order of ornament, as delicate as the eye can follow, when any of these features may be approached.

All good ornamentation is thus arborescent, as it were, one class of it branching out of another and sustained by it; and its nobility consists in this, that whatever order or class of it we may be contemplating, we shall find it subordinated to a greater, simpler, and more powerful; and if we then contemplate the greater order, we shall find it again subordinated to a greater

only have given the shadows of the buttresses, and the light and
dark sides of the two towers, and two dots for the windows; or if,
more ignorant and more ambitious, he had attempted to render
some of the detail, it would have been done by distant lines, would
have been broad caricature of the delicate building, felt at once to
be false, ridiculous, and offensive. His most successful effort
would only have given us, through his carefully toned atmosphere, the effect of a colossal parish church, without one line of
carving on its economic sides. Turner, and Turner only, would
follow and render on the canvas that mystery of decided line, that
distinct, sharp, visible but unintelligible and inextricable richness,
which, examined part by part, is to the eye nothing but confusion

still; until the greatest can only be quite grasped by retiring to the limits of
distance commanding it.

It is nevertheless evident, that, however perfect this distribution, there cannot be
orders adapted to *every* distance of the spectator. Between the ranks of ornament
there must always be a bold separation: and there must be many intermediate
distances, where we are too far off to see the lesser rank clearly, and yet too near
to grasp the next higher rank wholly: and at all these distances the spectator will
feel himself ill-placed, and will desire to go nearer or farther away. This must be
the case in all noble work, natural or artificial. It is exactly the same with respect
to Rouen Cathedral or the Mont Blanc. We like to see them from the other side of
the Seine, or of the Lake of Geneva: from the Marché aux Fleurs, or the Valley of
Chamouni; from the parapets of the apse, or the crags of the Montagne de la
Côte: but there are intermediate distances which dissatisfy us in either case, and
from which one is in haste either to advance or to retire.

Directly opposed to this ordered, disciplined, well officered, and variously ranked
ornament, this type of divine, and therefore of all good human government, is the
democratic ornament, in which all is equally influential, and has equal office and
authority; that is to say, none of it any office nor authority . . .

The eye is continually influenced by what it cannot detect; nay, it is not going
too far to say, that it is most influenced by what it detects least. Let the painter
define, if he can, the variations of lines on which depend the changes of
expression in the human countenance. The greater he is, the more he will feel
their subtlety, and the intense difficulty of perceiving all their relations, or
answering for the consequences of a variation of a hair's breadth in a single
curve. Indeed, there is nothing truly noble either in colour or in form, but its
power depends on circumstances infinitely too intricate to be explained, and
almost too subtle to be traced. And as for these Byzantine buildings, we only do
not feel them because we do not *watch* them; otherwise we should as much
enjoy the variety of proportion in their arches, as we do at present that of the
natural architecture of flowers and leaves. (SV, Vol. II, Ch. IV, para. 48; Vol. I,
Ch. XXI, paras. 15, 17–19, 26–9; Vol. II, Ch. V, para. 12.)

and defeat, which, taken as a whole, is all unity, symmetry, and truth.

Nor is this mode of representation true only with respect to distances. Every object, however near the eye, has something about it which you cannot see, and which brings the mystery of distance even into every part and portion of what we suppose ourselves to see most distinctly. Stand in the Piazza di San Marco, at Venice, as close to the church as you can, without losing sight of the top of it. Look at the capitals of the columns on the second story. You see that they are exquisitely rich, carved all over. Tell me their patterns: You cannot. Tell me the direction of a single line in them: You cannot. Yet you see a multitude of lines, and you have so much feeling of a certain tendency and arrangement in those lines, that you are quite sure the capitals are beautiful, and that they are all different from each other. But I defy you to make out one single line in any one of them. Now go to Canaletto's painting of this church, in the Palazzo Manfrini, taken from the very spot on which you stood. How much has he represented of all this? A black dot under each capital for the shadow, and a yellow one above it for the light. There is not a vestige nor indication of carving or decoration of any sort or kind.

Very different from this, but erring on the other side, is the ordinary drawing of the architect, who gives the principal lines of the design with delicate clearness and precision, but with no uncertainty or mystery about them; which mystery being removed, all space and size are destroyed with it, and we have a drawing of a model, not of a building. (MP I, Pt. II, Sec. II, Ch. V, paras. 1–7, 9–14)

Of Water, As Painted By Turner

I believe it is a result of the experience of all artists, that it is the easiest thing in the world to give a certain degree of depth and transparency to water; but that it is next to impossible, to give a full impression of surface. If no reflection be given, a ripple being supposed, the water looks like lead: if reflection be given, it, in nine cases out of ten, looks *morbidly* clear and deep, so that we always go down *into* it, even when the artist most wishes us to glide *over* it. Now, this difficulty arises from the very same circumstance which occasions the frequent failure in effect of the best-drawn foregrounds, noticed in Section II, Chapter IV (above

p. 9), the change, namely, of focus necessary in the eye in order to receive rays of light coming from different distances.

Go to the edge of a pond in a perfectly calm day, at some place where there is duckweed floating on the surface, not thick, but a leaf here and there. Now, you may either see in the water the reflection of the sky, or you may see the duckweed; but you cannot, by any effort, see both together. If you look for the reflection, you will be sensible of a sudden change or effort in the eye, by which it adapts itself to the reception of the rays which have come all the way from the clouds, have struck on the water, and so been sent up again to the eye. The focus you adopt is one fit for great distance; and, accordingly, you will feel that you are looking down a great way under the water, while the leaves of the duckweed, though they lie upon the water at the very spot on which you are gazing so intently, are felt only as a vague uncertain interruption, causing a little confusion in the image below, but entirely undistinguishable as leaves, and even their colour unknown and unperceived. Unless you think of them, you will not even feel that anything interrupts your sight, so excessively slight is their effect. If, on the other hand, you make up your mind to look for the leaves of the duckweed, you will perceive an instantaneous change in the effort of the eye, by which it becomes adapted to receive near rays, those which have only come from the surface of the pond. You will then see the delicate leaves of the duckweed with perfect clearness, and in vivid green; but, while you do so, you will be able to perceive nothing of the reflections in the very water on which they float, nothing but a vague flashing and melting of light and dark hues, without form or meaning, which to investigate, or find out what they mean or are, you must quit your hold of the duckweed, and plunge down.

Hence it appears, that whenever we see plain reflections of comparatively distant objects, in near water, we cannot possibly see the surface, and *vice versâ*; so that when in a painting we give the reflections with the same clearness with which they are visible in nature, we presuppose the effort of the eye to look under the surface, and, of course, destroy the surface, and induce an effect of clearness which, perhaps, the artist has not particularly wished to attain, but which he has found himself forced into, by his reflections, in spite of himself. And the reason of this effect of clearness appearing preternatural is, that people are not in the habit of looking at water with the distant focus adapted to the

Plate 3 *Rosenau: Seat of Prince Albert*

reflections, unless by particular effort. We invariably, under ordinary circumstances, use the surface focus; and, in consequence, receive nothing more than a vague and confused impression of the reflected colours and lines, however clearly, calmly, and vigorously all may be defined underneath, if we choose to look for them. We do not look for them, but glide along over the surface, catching only playing light and capricious colour for evidence of reflection, except where we come to images of objects close to the surface, which the surface focus is of course adapted to receive; and these we see clearly, as of the weeds on the shore, or of sticks rising out of the water, etc. Hence, the ordinary effect of water is only to be rendered by giving the reflections of the *margin* clear and distinct (so clear they usually are in nature, that it is impossible to tell where the water begins); but the moment we touch the reflection of distant objects, as of high trees or clouds, that instant we must become vague and uncertain in drawing, and, though vivid in colour and light as the object itself, quite indistinct in form and feature.

If we take such a piece of water as that in the foreground of Turner's Château of Prince Albert [Plate 3], the first impression from it is, 'What a wide *surface!*' We glide over it a quarter of a mile into the picture before we know where we are, and yet the water is as calm and crystalline as a mirror; but we are not allowed to tumble into it, and gasp for breath as we go down, we are kept upon the surface, though that surface is flashing and radiant with every hue of cloud, and sun, and sky, and foliage. But the secret is in the drawing of these reflections. We cannot tell, when we look *at* them and *for* them, what they mean. They have all character, and are evidently reflections of something definite and determined; but yet they are all uncertain and inexplicable; playing colour and palpitating shade, which, though we recognize them in an instant for images of something, and feel that the water is bright, and lovely, and calm, we cannot penetrate nor interpret; we are not allowed to go down to them, and we repose, as we should in nature, upon the lustre of the level surface. It is in this power of saying everything, and yet saying nothing too plainly, that the perfection of art here, as in all other cases, consists. (MP I, Pt. II, Sec. V, Ch. III, paras. 1–4)

CHAPTER 2

Modern Painters, Volume I

Seeing the Truth

Ruskin's defence of Turner began in 1836 with a reply to adverse criticism of the painter made in Blackwood's Magazine. *On the advice of Turner himself, however, the essay was never sent for publication. The first volume of* Modern Painters, *published in 1843, continued the aborted defence of 1836. This time, in what Ruskin still intended to be a pamphlet, he would 'blow the critics out of the water'. In fact, it took him seventeen years to complete the five volumes of* Modern Painters. *As he put it in the preface to the first edition of* Modern Painters Vol. I, *1843:*

The work now laid before the public originated in indignation at the shallow and false criticisms of the periodicals of the day on the works of the great living artist to whom it principally refers. It was intended to be a short pamphlet, reprobating the manner and style of those critiques, and pointing out their perilous tendency, as guides of public feeling. But, as point after point presented itself for demonstration, I found myself compelled to amplify what was at first a letter to the editor of a Review, into something very like a treatise on art, to which I was obliged to give the more consistency and completeness, because it advocated opinions which, to the ordinary connoisseur, will sound heretical. I now scarcely know whether I should announce it as an Essay on Landscape Painting, and apologize for its frequent reference to the works of a particular master; or, announcing it as a critique on particular works, apologize for its lengthy discussion of general principles.

In 1844, in the preface to the second edition of the first volume of Modern Painters, *Ruskin makes it clear that the defence of Turner was intended first of all to challenge Turner's critics on their own terms:* 'For many a year we have heard nothing with respect to the works of Turner but accusations of their want of *truth*. To every observation on their power, sublimity, or beauty, there has been but one reply: They are not like nature. I therefore took my opponents on their ground, and demonstrated, by thorough investigation of actual facts, that Turner *is* like nature, and paints more of nature than any man who ever lived' (C&W III, pp. 51–2).

This chapter consists of Ruskin's defence of Turner's faithfulness in the light of Ruskin's own attempts to show us what sky, light, shadow, cloud, tree, mountain and sea are really like. Turner will help us to see nature truly; in turn, the right perception of nature will enable us to see the paintings of Turner. These are Ruskin's two purposes in one.

'Turner is like nature'

A man accustomed to the broad wild sea-shore, with its bright breakers, and free winds, and sounding rocks, and eternal sensation of tameless power, can scarcely but be angered when Claude bids him stand still on some paltry chipped and chiselled quay, with porters and wheelbarrows running against him, to watch a weak, rippling, bound and barriered water, that has not strength enough in one of its waves to upset the flowerpots on the wall, or even to fling one jet of spray over the confining stone. A man accustomed to the strength and glory of God's mountains, with their soaring and radiant pinnacles, and surging sweeps of measureless distance, kingdoms in their valleys, and climates upon their crests, can scarcely but be angered when Salvator bids him stand still under some contemptible fragment of splintery crag, which an Alpine snow-wreath would smother in its first swell, with a stunted bush or two growing out of it, and a volume of manufactory smoke for a sky. A man accustomed to the grace and infinity of nature's foliage, with every vista a cathedral, and every bough a revelation, can scarcely but be angered when Poussin mocks him with a black round mass of impenetrable paint, diverging into feathers instead of leaves, and supported on a stick instead of a trunk. The fact is, there is one thing wanting in all the doing of these men, and that is the very virtue by which the work of human mind chiefly rises above that of the daguerreotype or calotype, or any other mechanical means that ever have been or may be invented, Love. There is no evidence of their ever having gone to nature with any thirst, or received from her such emotion as could make them, even for an instant, lose sight of themselves; there is in them neither earnestness nor humility; there is no simple or honest record of any single truth; none of the plain words or straight efforts that men speak and make when they once feel. . . . It may be generally stated that Turner is the only painter, so far as I know, who has ever drawn the sky, not the clear sky, which we before saw belonged exclusively to the religious schools, but the various forms and phenomena of the cloudy heavens; all previous artists having only represented it typically or partially, but he absolutely and universally. He is the only painter who has ever drawn a mountain, or a stone; no other man ever having learned their organization, or possessed himself of their spirit, except in part and obscurely . . . He is the only painter who ever drew the stem of a tree, Titian having come the nearest before him, and excelling him in the muscular development of the larger trunks (though sometimes losing the woody strength in a serpent-like flaccidity), but missing the grace and character of the ramifications. He is the only painter who has ever represented the surface of calm, or the force of agitated water; who has represented the effects of space on distant objects, or who has rendered the abstract beauty of natural colour. These assertions I make deliberately, after careful weighing and consideration, in no spirit of dispute, or momentary zeal; but from strong and convinced feeling, and with the consciousness of being able to prove them. (MP I, Pt. II, Sec. I, Ch. VII, paras. 5, 46)

Sky

It is a strange thing how little in general people know about the sky. It is the part of creation in which nature has done more for the sake of pleasing man, more for the sole and evident purpose of talking to him and teaching him, than in any other of her works, and it is just the part in which we least attend to her. There are not many of her other works in which some more material or essential purpose than the mere pleasing of man is not answered by every part of their organization; but every essential purpose of the sky might, so far as we know, be answered, if once in three days, or thereabouts, a great, ugly, black rain-cloud were brought up over the blue, and everything well watered, and so all left blue again till next time, with perhaps a film of morning and evening mist for dew. And instead of this, there is not a moment of any day of our lives, when nature is not producing scene after scene, picture after picture, glory after glory, and working still upon such exquisite and constant principles of the most perfect beauty, that it is quite

certain it is all done for us, and intended for our perpetual
pleasure. And every man, wherever placed, however far from
other sources of interest or of beauty, has this doing for him
constantly. The noblest scenes of the earth can be seen and known
but by few; it is not intended that man should live always in the
midst of them; he injures them by his presence, he ceases to feel
them if he be always with them: but the sky is for all; bright as it is,
it is not

> Too bright or good
> For human nature's daily food;
> [Wordsworth, 'She was a phantom of delight']

it is fitted in all its functions for the perpetual comfort and exalting
of the heart, for soothing it and purifying it from its dross and
dust. Sometimes gentle, sometimes capricious, sometimes awful,
never the same for two moments together; almost human in its
passions, almost spiritual in its tenderness, almost divine in its
infinity, its appeal to what is immortal in us is as distinct, as its
ministry of chastisement or of blessing to what is mortal is
essential.

And yet we never attend to it, we never make it a subject of
thought, but as it has to do with our animal sensations: we look
upon all by which it speaks to us more clearly than to brutes, upon
all which bears witness to the intention of the Supreme that we are
to receive more from the covering vault than the light and the dew
which we share with the weed and the worm, only as a succession
of meaningless and monotonous accident, too common and too
vain to be worthy of a moment of watchfulness, or a glance of
admiration. If in our moments of utter idleness and insipidity, we
turn to the sky as a last resource, which of its phenomena do we
speak of? One says it has been wet; and another, it has been
windy; and another, it has been warm. Who, among the whole
chattering crowd, can tell me of the forms and the precipices of the
chain of tall white mountains that girded the horizon at noon
yesterday? Who saw the narrow sunbeam that came out of the
south and smote upon their summits until they melted and
mouldered away in a dust of blue rain? Who saw the dance of the
dead clouds when the sunlight left them last night, and the west
wind blew them before it like withered leaves? All has passed,
unregretted as unseen; or if the apathy be ever shaken off, even for
an instant, it is only by what is gross, or what is extraordinary;

and yet it is not in the broad and fierce manifestations of the elemental energies, not in the clash of the hail, nor the drift of the whirlwind, that the highest characters of the sublime are developed.

God is not in the earthquake, nor in the fire, but in the still, small voice. They are but the blunt and the low faculties of our nature, which can only be addressed through lamp-black and lightning. It is in quiet and subdued passages of unobtrusive majesty, the deep, and the calm, and the perpetual; that which must be sought ere it is seen, and loved ere it is understood; things which the angels work out for us daily, and yet vary eternally: which are never wanting, and never repeated; which are to be found always, yet each found but once; it is through these that the lesson of devotion is chiefly taught, and the blessing of beauty given. These are what the artist of highest aim must study; it is these, by the combination of which his ideal is to be created; these, of which so little notice is ordinarily taken by common observers, that I fully believe, little as people in general are concerned with art, more of their ideas of sky are derived from pictures than from reality; and that if we could examine the conception formed in the minds of most educated persons when we talk of clouds, it would frequently be found composed of fragments of blue and white reminiscences of the old masters.

I shall enter upon the examination of what is true in sky at greater length, because it is the only part of a picture of which all, if they will, may be competent judges. What I may have to assert respecting the rocks of Salvator, or the boughs of Claude, I can scarcely prove, except to those whom I can immure for a month or two in the fastnesses of the Apennines, or guide in their summer walks again and again through the ravines of Sorrento. But what I say of the sky can be brought to an immediate test by all, and I write the more decisively, in the hope that it may be so.

Let us begin then with the simple open blue of the sky. This is of course the colour of the pure atmospheric air, not the aqueous vapour, but the pure azote and oxygen, and it is the total colour of the whole mass of that air between us and the void of space. It is modified by the varying quantity of aqueous vapour suspended in it, whose colour, in its most imperfect and therefore most visible state of solution, is pure white (as in steam); which receives, like any other white, the warm hues of the rays of the sun, and, according to its quantity and imperfect solution, makes the sky paler, and at the same time more or less grey, by mixing warm tones with its blue. This grey aqueous vapour, when very decided, becomes mist, and when local, cloud. Hence the sky is to be considered as a transparent blue liquid, in which, at various elevations, clouds are suspended, those clouds being themselves only particular visible spaces of a substance with which the whole mass of this liquid is more or less impregnated.

Now, we all know this perfectly well, and yet we so far forget it in practice, that we little notice the constant connection kept up by nature between her blue and her clouds; and we are not offended by the constant habit of the old masters, of considering the blue sky as totally distinct in its nature, and far separated from the vapours which float in it. With them, cloud is cloud, and blue is blue, and no kind of connection between them is ever hinted at. The sky is thought of as a clear, high, material dome, the clouds as separate bodies suspended beneath it; and in consequence, however delicate and exquisitely removed in tone their skies may be, you always look *at* them, not *through* them.

Now if there be one characteristic of the sky more valuable or necessary to be rendered than another, it is that which Wordsworth has given in the [third] book of the Excursion:

> The chasm of sky above my head
> Is Heaven's profoundest azure; no domain
> For fickle, short-lived clouds, to occupy,
> Or to pass through; but rather an *abyss*
> In which the everlasting stars abide
> And whose soft gloom, and boundless depth, might tempt
> The curious eye to look for them by day.
>
> [III 94–100]

And in his American Notes, I remember Dickens notices the same truth, describing himself as lying drowsily on the barge deck, looking not at, but *through* the sky. And if you look intensely at the pure blue of a serene sky, you will see that there is a variety and fulness in its very repose. It is not flat dead colour, but a deep, quivering, transparent body of penetrable air, in which you trace or imagine short falling spots of deceiving light, and dim shades, faint veiled vestiges of dark vapour; and it is this trembling transparency which our great modern master [Turner] has especially aimed at and given.

His blue is never laid on in smooth coats, but in breaking, mingling, melting hues, a quarter of an inch of which, cut off from all the rest of the picture, is still *spacious*, still infinite and immeasurable in depth. It is a painting of the air, something into which you can see, through the parts which are near you, into those which are far off; something which has no surface and through which we can plunge far and farther, and without stay or end, into the profundity of space; – whereas, with all the old landscape painters except Claude, you may indeed go a long way before you come to the sky, but you will strike hard against it at last. A perfectly genuine and untouched sky of Claude is indeed most perfect, and beyond praise, in all qualities of air; though even with him, I often feel rather that there is a great deal of pleasant air between me and the firmament, than that the firmament itself is only air. (MP I, Pt. II, Sec. III, Ch. I, paras. 1–9)

Light and Colour

If we look at nature carefully, we shall find that her colours are in a state of perpetual confusion and indistinctness, while her forms, as told by light and shade, are invariably clear, distinct, and speaking. The stones and gravel of the bank catch green reflections from the boughs above; the bushes receive greys and yellows from the ground; every hair's breadth of polished surface gives a little bit of the blue of the sky, or the gold of the sun, like a star upon the local colour; this local colour, changeful and uncertain in itself, is again disguised and modified by the hue of the light, or quenched in the grey of the shadow; and the confusion and blending of tint are altogether so great, that were we left to find out what objects were by their colours only, we could scarcely in places distinguish the boughs of a tree from the air beyond them, or the ground beneath them. I know that people unpractised in art will not believe this at first; but if they have accurate powers of observation, they may soon ascertain it for themselves; they will find that while they can scarcely ever determine the *exact* hue of anything, except when it occurs in large masses, as in a green field or the blue sky, the form, as told by light and shade, is always decided and evident, and the source of the chief character of every object. (MP I, Pt. II, Sec. I, Ch. V, para. 8)

Shadow

Throughout the works of Claude, Poussin and Salvator, we shall find, especially in their conventional foliage, and unarticulated barbarisms of rock, that their whole sum and substance of chiaroscuro are merely the gradation and variation which nature gives in the *body* of her shadows, and that all which they do to express sunshine, she does to vary shade. They take only one step, while she always takes two; marking, in the first place, with violent decision, the great transition from sun to shade, and then varying the shade itself with a thousand gentle gradations and double shadows, in themselves equivalent, and more than equivalent, to all that the old masters did for their entire chiaroscuro.

Now, if there be one principle or secret more than another on which Turner depends for attaining brilliancy of light, it is his clear and exquisite drawing of the *shadows*. Whatever is obscure, misty, or undefined, in his objects or his atmosphere, he takes care that the shadows be sharp and clear; and then he knows that the light will take care of itself, and he makes them clear, not by blackness, but by excessive evenness, unity, and sharpness of edge. He will keep them clear and distinct, and make them felt as shadows, though they are so faint that, but for their decisive forms, we should not have observed them for darkness at all. He will throw them one after another like transparent veils along the earth and upon the air, till the whole picture palpitates with them, and yet the darkest of them will be a faint grey, imbued and penetrated with light . . .

Words are not accurate enough, nor delicate enough, to express or trace the constant, all-pervading influence of the finer and vaguer shadows throughout his works, that thrilling influence which gives to the light they leave its passion and its power. There is not a stone, not a leaf, not a cloud, over which light is not felt to be actually passing and palpitating before our eyes. There is the motion, the actual wave and radiation of the darted beam: not the dull universal daylight, which falls on the landscape without life, or direction, or speculation, equal on all things and dead on all things; but the breathing, animated, exulting light, which feels, and receives, and rejoices, and acts, – which chooses one thing, and rejects another, – which seeks, and finds, and loses again, – leaping from rock to rock, from leaf to leaf, from wave to wave – glowing, or flashing, or scintillating, according to what it strikes; or, in its holier moods, absorbing and enfolding all things in the deep fulness of its repose, and then again losing itself in bewilderment, and doubt, and dimness, – or perishing and passing away, entangled in drifting mist, or melted into melancholy air, but still, – kindling or declining, sparkling or serene, – it is the living light, which breathes in its deepest, most entranced rest, which sleeps, but never dies.

I need scarcely insist farther on the marked distinction between the works of the old masters and those of the great modern landscape painters in this respect. It is one which the reader can perfectly well work out for himself, by the slightest systematic attention; one which he will find existing, not merely between this work and that, but throughout the whole body of their productions, and down to every leaf and line. And a little careful watching of nature, especially in her foliage and foregrounds, and comparison of her with Claude, Gaspar Poussin, and Salvator, will soon show him that those artists worked entirely on conventional principles, not representing what they saw, but what they thought would make a handsome picture. (MP I, Pt. II, Sec. II, Ch. III, paras. 4–7)

Mountain and Cloud

Now if an artist, taking for his subject a chain of vast mountains several leagues long, were to unite all their varieties of ravine, crag, chasm, and precipice, into one solid unbroken mass, with one light side and one dark side, looking like a white ball or parallelopiped two yards broad, the words 'breadth,' 'boldness,' 'generalization,' would scarcely be received as a sufficient apology for a proceeding so glaringly false, and so painfully degrading. But when, instead of the really large and simple forms of mountains, united, as they commonly are, by some great principle of common organization, and so closely resembling each other as often to correspond in line and join in effect; when, instead of this, we have to do with spaces of cloud twice as vast, broken up into a multiplicity of forms necessary to, and characteristic of, their very nature, those forms subject to a thousand local changes, having no association with each other, and rendered visible in a thousand places by their own transparency or cavities, where the mountain forms would be lost in shade; that this far greater space, and this far more complicated arrangement, should be all summed up into one round mass, with one swell of white, and one flat side of unbroken grey, is considered an evidence of the sublimest powers in the artist of generalization and breadth. Now it may be broad, it may be grand, it may be beautiful, artistical, and in every way desirable. I don't say it is not: I merely say it is a concentration of every kind of falsehood; it is depriving heaven of its space, clouds of their buoyancy, winds of their motion, and distance of its blue.

This is done, more or less, by all the old masters, without an exception. Their idea of clouds was altogether similar; more or less perfectly carried out, according to their power of hand and accuracy of eye, but universally the same in conception. It was the idea of a comparatively small, round, puffed-up white body, irregularly associated with other round and puffed-up white bodies, each with a white light side, and a grey dark side, and a soft reflected light, floating a great way below a blue dome. Such is the idea of a cloud formed by most people; it is the first, general, uncultivated notion of what we see every day. (MP I, Pt. II, Sec. III, Ch. III, paras. 12–13)

Trees and Mountains

It ought farther to be observed respecting truths in general, that those are always most valuable which are most historical; that is, which tell us most about the past and future states of the object to which they belong. In a tree, for instance, it is more important to give the appearance of energy and elasticity in the limbs which is indicative of growth and life, than any particular character of leaf, or texture of bough. It is more important that we should feel that the uppermost sprays are creeping higher and higher into the sky, and be impressed with the current of life and motion which is animating every fibre, than that we should know the exact pitch of relief with which those fibres are thrown out against the sky. For the first truths tell us tales about the tree, about what it has been, and will be, while the last are characteristic of it only in its present state, and are in no way talkative about themselves. Talkative facts are always more interesting and more important than silent ones. So again the lines in a crag which mark its stratification, and how it has been washed and rounded by water, or twisted and drawn out in fire, are more important, because they tell more than the stains of the lichens which change year by year, and the accidental fissures of frost or decomposition; not but that both of these are historical, but historical in a less distinct manner, and for shorter periods. . . .

Now, it cannot be too carefully held in mind, in examining the principles of mountain structure, that nearly all the laws of nature with respect to external form are rather universal tendencies, evidenced by a plurality of instances, than imperative necessities complied with by all. For instance, it may be said to be a universal law with respect to the boughs of all trees, that they incline their extremities more to the ground in proportion as they are lower on the trunk, and that the higher their point of insertion is, the more they share in the upward tendency of the trunk itself. But yet there is not a single group of boughs in any one tree which does not show exceptions to the rule, and present boughs lower in insertion, and yet steeper in inclination, than their neighbours. Nor is this defect or deformity, but the result of the constant habit of nature to carry variety into her very principles, and make the symmetry and beauty of her laws the more felt by the grace and accidentalism with which they are carried out. No one familiar with foliage could doubt for an instant of the necessity of giving evidence of this downward tendency in the boughs; but it would be nearly as great an offence against truth to make the law hold good with every individual branch, as not to exhibit its influence on the majority. Now, though the laws of mountain form are more rigid and constant than those of vegetation, they are subject to the same species of exception in carrying out. Though every mountain has these great tendencies in its lines, not one in a thousand of those lines is absolutely consistent with, and obedient to, this universal tendency. There are lines in every direction, and of almost every kind, but the sum and aggregate of those lines will invariably indicate the *universal* force and influence to which they are all subjected; and of these lines there will, I repeat, be two principal sets or classes, pretty nearly at right angles with each other. When both are inclined, they give rise to peaks or ridges; when one is nearly horizontal and the other vertical, to table-lands and precipices.

This then is the broad organization of all hills, modified afterwards by time and weather, concealed by superincumbent soil and vegetation, and ramified into minor and more delicate details in a way presently to be considered, but nevertheless universal in its great first influence, and giving to all mountains a particular cast and inclination; like the exertion of voluntary power in a definite direction, an internal spirit, manifesting itself in every crag, and breathing in every slope, flinging and forcing the mighty mass towards the heaven with an expression and an energy like that of life.

Plate 4 *Loch Coriskin*

Now, as in the case of the structure of the central peaks described above, so also here, if I had to give a clear idea of this organization of the lower hills, where it is seen in its greatest perfection, with a mere view to geological truth, I should not refer to any geological drawings, but I should take the Loch Coriskin of Turner. It has been admirably engraved, and for all purposes of reasoning on form, is nearly as effective in the print as in the drawing. Looking at any group of the multitudinous lines which make up this mass of mountain, they appear to be running anywhere and everywhere; there are none parallel to each other, none resembling each other for a moment; yet the whole mass is felt at once to be composed with the most rigid parallelism, the surfaces of the beds towards the left, their edges or escarpments towards the right. In the centre, near the top of the ridge, the edge of a bed is beautifully defined, casting its shadow on the surface of the one beneath it; this shadow marking, by three jags, the chasms caused in the inferior one by three of its parallel joints. Every peak in the distance is evidently subject to the same great influence, and the evidence is completed by the flatness and evenness of the steep surfaces of the beds which rise out of the lake on the extreme right, parallel with those in the centre.[a] (MP I, Pt. II, Sec. I, Ch. VI, para. I; Sec. IV, Ch. III, paras. 4–5)

[a] *Cf Ruskin on mountain sympathy:*
[E]ach individual part and promontory, being compelled to assume the same symmetrical curves as its neighbours, and to descend at precisely the same slope to the valley, falls in with their prevailing lines, and becomes a part of a great and harmonious whole, instead of an unconnected and discordant individual. It is true that each of these members has its own touches of specific character, its own projecting crags, and peculiar hollows; but by far the greater portion of its lines will be such as unite with, though they do not repeat, those of its neighbours, and carry out the evidence of one great influence and spirit to the limits of the scene. This effort is farther aided by the original unity and connection of the rocks themselves, which, though it often may be violently interrupted, is never without evidence of its existence; for the very interruption itself forces the eye to feel that there is something to be interrupted, a sympathy and similarity of lines and fractures, which, however full of variety and change of direction, never lose the appearance of symmetry of one kind or another.

But, on the other hand, it is to be remembered that these great sympathizing masses are not one mountain, but a thousand mountains; that they are originally composed of a multitude of separate eminences, hewn and chiselled indeed into associating form, but each retaining still its marked points and features of character; that each of these individual members has, by the very

Sea

Of one thing I am certain; Turner never drew anything that could be *seen*, without having seen it. . . . He, in the year 1818, introduces a shipwreck; I am perfectly certain that, before the year 1818, he had *seen* a shipwreck; and, moreover, one of that horrible kind – a ship dashed to pieces in deep water, at the foot of an inaccessible cliff. Having once seen this, I perceive, also, that the image of it could not be effaced from his mind. It taught him two great facts, which he never afterwards forgot; namely, that both ships and sea were things that broke to pieces. *He never afterwards painted a ship quite in fair order.* There is invariably a feeling about his vessels of strange awe and danger; the sails are in some way loosening, or flapping as if in fear; the swing of the hull, majestic as it may be, seems more at the mercy of the sea than in triumph over it; the ship never looks gay, never proud, only warlike and enduring . . . and I am well persuaded that from that year 1818, when first he saw a ship rent asunder, he never beheld one at sea, without, in his mind's eye, at the same instant, seeing her skeleton.

I said that at this period he first was assured of another fact, namely, that the *Sea* also was a thing that broke to pieces. The sea up to that time had been generally regarded by painters as a liquidly composed, level-seeking consistent thing, with a smooth surface, rising to a watermark on sides of ships; in which ships

process which assimilated it to the rest, been divided and subdivided into equally multitudinous groups of minor mountains; finally, that the whole complicated system is interrupted for ever and ever by daring manifestations of the inward mountain will, by the precipice which has submitted to no modulation of the torrent, and the peak which has bowed itself to no terror of the storm. Hence we see that the same imperative laws which require perfect simplicity of mass, require infinite and termless complication of detail; that there will not be an inch nor a hair's-breadth of the gigantic heap which has not its touch of separate character, its own peculiar curve, stealing out for an instant and then melting into the common line; felt for a moment by the blue mist of the hollow beyond, then lost when it crosses the enlightened slope; that all this multiplicity will be grouped into larger divisions, each felt by its increasing aërial perspective, and its instants of individual form, these into larger, and these into larger still, until all are merged in the great impression and prevailing energy of the two or three vast dynasties which divide the kingdom of the scene. (MP. I, Pt. II, Sec. IV, Ch. III, paras. 13–14)

were scientifically to be embedded, and wetted, up to said water-mark, and to remain dry above the same. But Turner found during his Southern Coast tour that the sea was *not* this: that it was, on the contrary, a very incalculable and unhorizontal thing, setting its 'water-mark' sometimes on the highest heavens, as well as on sides of ships; – very breakable into pieces; half of a wave separable from the other half, and on the instant carriageable miles inland; – not in any wise limiting itself to a state of apparent liquidity, but now striking like a steel gauntlet, and now becoming a cloud, and vanishing, no eye could tell whither; one moment a flint cave, the next a marble pillar, the next a mere white fleece thickening the thundery rain. He never forgot those facts; never afterwards was able to recover the idea of positive distinction between sea and sky, or sea and land.[b] ('The Harbours of England' [1856], paras. 35, 37 [C&W XIII, pp. 42–4])

[b] *In 1856 Ruskin also admits the faults related to Turner's aims and strengths in his 'Notes on the Turner Collection of Oil-Pictures at the National Gallery' – on Turner's second, mature period (1820–35):*
Pictures belonging to the second period are technically distinguished from those of the first in three particulars:—

1. Colour takes the place of grey.
2. Refinement takes the place of force.
3. Quantity takes the place of mass.

First, Colour appears everywhere instead of grey. That is to say, Turner had discovered that the shaded sides of objects, as well as their illuminated ones, are in reality of different, and often brilliant colours. His shadow is, therefore, no longer of one hue, but perpetually varied; whilst the lights, instead of being subdued to any conventional level, are always painted as near the brightness of natural colour as he can.

Secondly, Refinement takes the place of force. He had discovered that it is much more difficult to draw tenderly than ponderously, and that all the most beautiful things in nature depended on definitely delicate lines. His effort is, therefore, always, now, to trace lines as finely, and shades as softly, as the point of the brush and feeling of hand are capable of doing; and the effects sought are themselves the most subtle and delicate which nature presents, rarely those which are violent. The change is the same as from the heavy touch and noisy preferences of a beginner in music, to the subdued and tender fingering or breathing of a great musician – rising, however, always into far more masterful stress when the occasion comes.

Thirdly, Quantity takes the place of mass. Turner had also ascertained, in the course of his studies, that nature was infinitely full, and that old painters had not only missed her pitch of hue, but her power of accumulation. He saw there were more clouds in any sky than ever had been painted; more trees in every

* * *

The Caudebec, in the Rivers of France, is a fine instance of almost
every fact which we have been pointing out [Plate 5]. We have in it,
first, the clear expression of what takes place constantly among hills;
that the river, as it passes through the valley, will fall backwards

forest, more crags on every hill side; and he set himself with all his strength to
proclaim this great fact of Quantity in the universe.

Now, so long as he introduced all these three changes in an instinctive and
unpretending way, his work was noble; but the moment he tried to idealize,
and introduced his principles for the sake of display, they led him into depths of
error proportioned exactly to the extent of effort. His painting, at this period,
of an English town, or a Welsh hill, was magnificent and faultless, but all his
idealism, mythology, romance, and composition in general, were more or less
wrong. He erred through all, and by reason of all – his great discoveries. He
erred in *colour*; because not content with discerning the brilliancy of nature, he
tried to enhance that brilliancy by every species of coloured accessary, until
colour was killed by colour, and the blue skies and snowy mountains, which
would have been lovely by themselves, were confused and vulgarized by the
blue dresses and white complexions of the foreground figures. He erred in
refinement, because, not content with the natural tenderness of tender things,
he strove to idealize even strong things into gentleness, until his architecture
became transparent, and his ground ghostly; and he erred finally, and chiefly, in
quantity, because, in his enthusiastic perception of the fulness of nature, he did
not allow for the narrowness of the human heart; he saw, indeed, that there
were no limits to creation, but forgot that there were many to reception; he
thus spoiled his most careful works by the very richness of invention they
contained, and concentrated the materials of twenty noble pictures into a single
failure.

In his third period (1835–45):
As Turner became more and more accustomed to, and satisfied in, the
principles of art he had introduced, his mind naturally dwelt upon them with
less of the pride of discovery, and turned more and more to the noble subjects
of natural colour and effect, which he found himself now able to represent. He
began to think less of showing or trying what he *could* do, and more of actually
doing this or that beautiful thing. It was no more a question with him how
many alternations of blue with gold he could crowd into a canvas, but how
nearly he could reach the actual blue of the Bay of Uri, when the dawn was on
its golden cliffs. I believe, also, that in powerful minds there is generally,
towards age, a return to the superstitious love of Nature which they felt in their
youth: and assuredly, as Turner drew towards old age, the aspect of mechanical
effort and ambitious accumulation fade from his work, and a deep imaginative
delight, and tender rest in the loveliness of what he had learned to see in
Nature, take their place. (C&W XIII, pp.128–30, 146)

Plate 5 *Caudebec*

and forwards from side to side, lying first, if I may so speak, with all its weight against the hills on the one side, and then against those on the other; so that, as here it is exquisitely told, in each of its circular sweeps the whole force of its current is brought deep and close to the bases of the hills, while the water on the side next the plain is shallow, deepening gradually. In consequence of this, the hills are cut away at their bases by the current, so that their slopes are interrupted by precipices mouldering to the water. Observe, first, how nobly Turner has given us the perfect unity of the whole mass of hill, making us understand that every ravine in it has been cut gradually by streams. The first eminence, beyond the city, is not disjointed from, nor independent of, the one succeeding, but evidently part of the same whole, originally united, separated only by the action of the stream between. The association of the second and third is still more clearly told, for we see that there has been a little longitudinal valley running along the brow of their former united mass, which, after the ravine had been cut between, formed the two jags which Turner has given us at the same point in each of their curves. This great triple group has, however, been originally distinct from those beyond it; for we see that these latter are only the termination of the enormous even slope, which appears again on the extreme right, having been interrupted by the rise of the near hills. Observe how the descent of the whole series is kept gentle and subdued, never suffered to become steep except where it has been cut away by the river, the sudden precipice caused by which is exquisitely marked in the last two promontories, where they are defined against the bright horizon; and, finally, observe how, in the ascent of the nearest eminence beyond the city, without one cast shadow or any division of distances, every yard of surface is felt to be retiring by the mere painting of its details, how we are permitted to walk up it, and along its top, and are carried, before we are half-way up, a league or two forward into the picture. The difficulty of doing this, however, can scarcely be appreciated except by an artist.

I do not mean to assert that this great painter is acquainted with the geological laws and facts he has thus illustrated; I am not aware whether he be or not; I merely wish to demonstrate, in points admitting of demonstration, that intense observation of, and strict adherence to, truth, which it is impossible to demonstrate in its less tangible and more delicate manifestations. However I may *feel* the truth of every touch and line, I cannot *prove* truth, except in large and general features; and I leave it to the arbitration of every man's reason, whether it be not likely that the painter who is thus so rigidly faithful in great things that every one of his pictures might be the illustration of a lecture on the physical sciences, is not likely to be faithful also in small. (MP I, Pt. II, Sec. III, Ch. III, paras. 20–1)

CHAPTER 3

From Modern Painters I to Modern Painters II

In the 10 February 1844 issue of the Athenaeum, *a reviewer of the first volume of* Modern Painters *complained that for the sake of truth Ruskin seemed to require landscape painters to be experts in each specialist science: 'Ancient landscapists,' the reviewer wrote, 'took a broader, deeper, higher view of their art: they neglected particular traits, and gave only general features.' Quoting this review in the preface to the second edition, Ruskin repeats his attack on generalization in painting:*

Thus we find ourselves unavoidably led to a conclusion directly opposed to that constantly enunciated dogma of the parrot-critic, that the features of nature must be 'generalized'; a dogma whose inherent and broad absurdity would long ago have been detected, if it had not contained in its convenient falsehood an apology for indolence, and a disguise for incapacity. Generalized! As if it were possible to generalize things generically different.

It is just as impossible to generalize granite and slate, as it is to generalize a man and a cow. An animal must be either one animal or another animal: it cannot be a general animal, or it is no animal; and so a rock must be either one rock or another rock; it cannot be a general rock, or it is no rock.

And so, if landscape painters choose, they may give us rocks which shall be half granite and half slate; but they cannot give us rocks which shall be either granite or slate, nor which shall be both granite and slate. Every attempt to produce that which shall be *any* rock, ends in the production of that which is *no* rock. (C&W III, pp. 34–5)

As Ruskin was to put it explicitly in Modern Painters *Vol. III:*

The more I think of it I find this conclusion more impressed upon me, – that the greatest thing a human soul ever does in this world is to *see* something, and tell what it *saw* in a plain way. Hundreds of people can talk for one who can think, but thousands can think for one who can see. To see clearly is poetry, prophecy, and religion – all in one.

Therefore, finding the world of Literature more or less divided into Thinkers and Seers, I believe we shall find also that the Seers are wholly the greater race of the two. A true Thinker who has practical purpose in his thinking, and is sincere, as Plato, or Carlyle, or Helps, becomes in some sort a seer, and must be always of infinite use in his generation; but an affected Thinker, who supposes his thinking of any other importance than as it tends to work, is about the vainest kind of person that can be found in the occupied classes. Nay, I believe that metaphysicians and philosophers are, on the whole, the greatest troubles the world has got to deal with; and that while a tyrant or bad man is of some use in teaching people submission or indignation, and a thoroughly idle man is only harmful in setting an idle example, and communicating to other lazy people his own lazy misunderstandings, busy metaphysicians are always entangling *good* and *active* people, and weaving cobwebs among the finest wheels of the world's business; and are as much as possible, by all prudent persons, to be brushed out of their way, like spiders, and the meshed weed that has got into the Cambridgeshire canals, and other such impediments to barges and business.[1] (MP III, Pt. IV, Ch. XVI, para. 28)

Nonetheless, Ruskin's defence of the particularity of real seeing, as opposed to the false suggestions of generalization, is still from the first, interestingly, also an argument for trust in the unity of all particular things on the planet:

I repeat then, generalization, as the word is commonly understood, is the act of a vulgar, incapable, and unthinking mind. To see in all mountains nothing but similar heaps of earth; in all rocks, nothing but similar concretions of solid matter; in all trees, nothing but similar accumulations of leaves, is no sign of high feeling or extended thought. The more we know and the more we feel, the more we separate; we separate to obtain a more perfect unity. Stones, in the thoughts of the peasant, lie as they do on his field; one is like another, and there is no connection between any of them. The geologist distinguishes, and in distinguishing connects them. Each becomes different from his fellow, but in differing from, assumes a relation to, his fellow; they are no more each the repetition of the other, they are parts of a system; and each implies and is connected with the existence of the rest. That generalization then is right, true, and noble, which is based on the knowledge of the distinctions and observance of the relations of individual kinds. That generalization is wrong, false, and contemptible, which is

based on ignorance of the one, and disturbance of the other. It is
indeed no generalization, but confusion and chaos; it is the
generalization of a defeated army into undistinguishable impotence, the generalization of the elements of a dead carcass into
dust. (C&W III, pp. 37–8)

In the second volume of Modern Painters *it becomes clear
that Ruskin's initial defence of Turner in terms of particular truth
is only part of a larger vision of unity and infinity in the created
world, which is too subtle and individualized to be merely man-
made.*

*Accordingly, this chapter offers a more explicit, abstract
account of the vision of a universe at once holistic and infinite. For*
Modern Painters Vol. II *spells out more systematically the work
that was done in* Modern Painters Vol. I *in more specific ways for
more ad hoc ends. In the first volume the purpose was the
temporary one of defending Turner from the charge of lack of
truthfulness, and the means of rebuttal were detailed in particular
analyses of 'obvious and visible facts' in nature and in Turner. In*
Modern Painters Vol. II *Ruskin takes his local thoughts on infinity
and unity and formalizes them, thus reviewing the work of the
earlier volume and bringing it back together at a higher and more
permanent level. The investigation now before us, says Ruskin
near the beginning of* Modern Painters Vol. II, *is no longer the
verification 'of things outward, and sensibly demonstrable' but
the deduction 'of the value and meaning of mental impressions'
involved in the very recognition of those outward things. Ruskin
moves from the external world to what is within the inner being of
humans in relation to that world. These inner faculties – of
contemplation and imagination – must be defended against the
utilitarian charge that they are merely impractical and useless.
They are not just arty concerns, they must be treated with a
'seriousness proportioned to the importance of rightly regarding
those faculties over which we have moral power, and therefore in
relation to which we assuredly incur a moral responsibility' (MP
II, Pt. III, Sec. I, Ch. I, para.1).*

*It was always Ruskin's nature not to repeat himself but to catch
up with himself. Thus, in this consolidation of the work of his first
volume, he concentrates on two main human powers – Contemplation or the Theoretic Faculty, and the Imaginative Faculty. The
emphasis on the Theoretic Faculty, or Theoria, owes much to
Aristotle, who saw in contemplation the highest form of human*

happiness, wherein human beings were closest to the viewpoint of the gods. With regard to imagination, Ruskin makes his own distinction between Imagination Associative (the form of imagination involved in first seeing and then producing the whole composition of a painting) and Imagination Penetrative (a mode of immediately grasping the full inner meaning of things). In later days Ruskin was often troubled by the classifications he had attempted to make in this volume, for fear that they were too clumsy or too rigid. But looking back in 1877, when considering a revision of the work, he concluded: 'I find now the main value of the book to be exactly in that schematic scheme of it which I had despised, and in the very adoption and insistence upon the Greek term Theoria, instead of sight and perception, in which I had thought myself perhaps uselessly or affectedly refined.' He had done more and better than he had realized. 'I had been a faithful scribe, writing words I knew not the force of or final intent' (C&W IV, p. xlix). For it was characteristic of Ruskin and of his belief in the power of truth that he would find he had laid hold of more than he quite knew the force of at the time. This overbrimming fullness made an intellectual future necessary for himself in his career-long quest for the development of the nascent truth he had first glimpsed in 1836.

'Useless' Faculties?

Art, properly so called, is no recreation; it cannot be learned at spare moments, nor pursued when we have nothing better to do. It is no handiwork for drawing-room tables, no relief of the ennui of boudoirs; it must be understood and undertaken seriously, or not at all. To advance it men's lives must be given, and to receive it, their hearts . . . But that this labour, the necessity of which, in all ages, has been most frankly admitted by the greatest men, is justifiable from a moral point of view, that it is not a vain devotion of the lives of men, that it has functions of usefulness addressed to the weightiest of human interests, and that the objects of it have calls upon us which it is inconsistent alike with our human dignity and our heavenward duty to disobey, has never been boldly asserted nor fairly admitted, least of all is it likely to be so in these days of despatch and display, where vanity, on the one side, supplies the place of that love of art which is the only effective patronage, and, on the other, that of *the incorruptible and earnest pride which no applause, no reprobation, can blind to its shortcomings, or beguile of its hope.*

And yet it is in the expectation of obtaining at least a partial acknowledgement of this, as a truth decisive both of aim and conduct, that I enter upon the second division of my subject. The time I have already devoted to the task I should have considered too great, and that which I fear may be yet required for its completion would have been cause to me of utter discouragement, but that the object I propose to myself is of no partial nor accidental importance. It is not now to distinguish between disputed degrees of ability in individuals, or agreeableness in canvases; it is not now to expose the ignorance or defend the principles of party or person; it is to summon the moral energies of the nation to a forgotten duty, to display the use, force, and function of a great body of neglected sympathies and desires, and to elevate to its healthy and beneficial operation that art which, being altogether addressed to them, rises or falls with their variableness of vigour, now leading them with Tyrtæan fire, now singing them to sleep with baby murmurings.

Because that with many of us the recommendation of our own favourite pursuits is, I fear, rooted more in conceit of ourselves, than in affection towards others, so that sometimes in our very pointing of the way we had rather that the intricacy of it should be admired than unfolded, whence a natural distrust of such recommendation may well have place in the minds of those who have not yet perceived any value in the thing praised; and because, also, men in the present century understand the word Useful in a strange way, or at least (for the word has been often so accepted from the beginning of time) since in these days they act its more limited meaning farther out, and give to it more practical weight and authority; it will be well in the outset that I define exactly what kind of Utility I mean to attribute to art, and especially to that branch of it which is concerned with those impressions of external Beauty, whose nature it is our present object to discover.

That is, to everything created pre-eminently useful, which enables it rightly and fully to perform the functions appointed to it by its Creator. Therefore, that we may determine what is chiefly useful to man, it is necessary first to determine the use of Man himself.

Man's use and function (and let him who will not grant me this follow me no farther, for this I purpose always to assume) are, to be the witness of the glory of God, and to advance that glory by his reasonable obedience and resultant happiness.

Whatever enables us to fulfil this function is, in the pure and first sense of the word, Useful to us: pre-eminently, therefore, whatever sets the glory of God more brightly before us. But things that only help us to exist are, (*only*) in a secondary and mean sense, useful; or rather, if they be looked for alone, they are useless, and worse, for it would be better that we should not exist, than that we should guiltily disappoint the purposes of existence.

And yet people speak in this working age, when they speak from their hearts, as if houses and lands, and food and raiment were alone useful, and as if Sight, Thought, and Admiration were all profitless, so that men insolently call themselves Utilitarians, who would turn, if they had their way, themselves and their race into vegetables; men who think, as far as such can be said to think, that the meat is more than the life, and the raiment than the body, who look to the earth as a stable, and to its fruit as fodder; vinedressers and husbandmen, who love the corn they grind, and the grapes they crush, better than the gardens of the angels upon the slopes of Eden; hewers of wood and drawers of water, who think that it is to give them wood to hew and water to draw, that the pine-forests cover the mountains like the shadow of God, and the great rivers move like His eternity. And so comes upon us that Woe of the preacher, that though God 'hath made everything beautiful in his time, also He hath set the world in their heart, so that no man can find out the work that God maketh from the beginning to the end.'[2]

This Nebuchadnezzar curse, that sends men to grass like oxen [Daniel iv. 25], seems to follow but too closely on the excess or continuance of national power and peace. In the perplexities of nations, in their struggles for existence, in their infancy, their impotence, or even their disorganization, they have higher hopes and nobler passions. Out of the suffering comes the serious mind; out of the salvation, the grateful heart; out of endurance, fortitude; out of deliverance, faith: but when they have learned to live under providence of laws and with decency and justice of regard for each other, and when they have done away with violent and external sources of suffering, worse evils seem to arise out of their rest; evils that vex less and mortify more, that suck the blood though they do not shed it, and ossify the heart though they do not torture it. And deep though the causes of thankfulness must be to every people at peace with others and at unity in itself, there are causes of fear, also, a fear greater than of sword and sedition: that dependence on God may be forgotten, because the bread is given and the water sure; that gratitude to Him may cease, because His constancy of protection has taken the semblance of a natural law; that heavenly hope may grow faint amidst the full fruition of the world; that selfishness may take place of undemanded devotion, compassion be lost in vainglory, and love in dissimulation [Romans xii. 9]; that enervation may succeed to strength, apathy to patience, and the noise of jesting words and foulness of dark thoughts, to the earnest purity of the girded loins and the burning lamp [Luke xii. 35]. About the river of human life there is a wintry wind, though a heavenly sunshine; the iris colours its agitation, the frost fixes upon its repose. Let us beware that our rest become not the rest of stones, which, so long as they are torrent-tossed and thunder-stricken, maintain their majesty, but when the stream is silent, and the storm passed, suffer the grass to cover them and the lichen to feed on them, and are ploughed down into dust.

And though I believe that we have salt enough of ardent and holy mind amongst us to keep us in some measure from this moral decay, yet the signs of it must be watched with anxiety, in all matters however trivial, in all directions however distant. And at this time, when the iron roads are tearing up the surface of Europe, as grapeshot do the sea; when their great net is drawing and twitching the ancient frame and strength together, contracting all its various life, its rocky arms and rural heart, into a narrow, finite, calculating metropolis of manufactures; when there is not a monument throughout the cities of Europe that speaks of old years and mighty people, but it is being swept away to build cafés and gaming-houses; when the honour of God is thought to consist in the poverty of His temple, and the column is shortened and the pinnacle shattered, the colour denied to the casement and the marble to the altar, while exchequers are exhausted in luxury of boudoirs and pride of reception-rooms; when we ravage without a pause all the loveliness of creation which God in giving pronounced Good [Genesis i. 10], and destroy without a thought all those labours which men have given their lives and their sons' sons' lives to complete, and have left for a legacy to all their kind, a legacy of more than their hearts' blood, for it is of their souls' travail; – there is need, bitter need, to bring back into men's minds, that to live is nothing, unless to live be to know Him by whom we live [John xvii. 3]; and that He is not to be known by marring His fair works, and blotting out the evidence of His influences upon His creatures; nor amidst the hurry of crowds and crash of innovation, but in solitary places, and out of the glowing intelligences which He gave to men of old. He did not teach them how to build for glory and for beauty; He did not give them the fearless, faithful, inherited energies that worked on and down from death to death, generation after generation, that we might give the work of their poured-out spirit to the axe and the hammer; He has not cloven the earth with rivers [Habbakkuk iii. 9], that their white wild waves might turn wheels and push paddles, nor turned it up under as it were fire [Job xxviii. 5], that it might heat wells and cure diseases; He brings not up His quails by the east wind only to let them fall in flesh about the camp of men [Numbers xi. 31]; He has not heaped the rocks of the mountain only for the quarry, nor clothed the grass of the field only for the oven [Matthew vi. 30].

Science and art are either subservient to life or the objects of it. As subservient to life, or practical, their results are, in the common sense of the word, Useful. As the object of life or theoretic, they are, in the common sense, Useless. And yet the step between practical and theoretic science is the step between the miner and the geologist, the apothecary and the chemist; and the step between practical and theoretic art is that between the builder and the architect, between the plumber and the artist; and this is a step allowed on all hands to be from less to greater. So that the so-called useless part of each profession does, by the authoritative and right instinct of mankind, assume the more noble place; even though books be sometimes written, and that by writers of no ordinary mind, which assume that a chemist is rewarded for the years of toil which have traced the greater part of the combinations of matter to their ultimate atoms, by discovering a cheap way of refining sugar; and date the eminence of the philosopher whose life has been spent in the investigation of the laws of light, from the time of his inventing an improvement in spectacles.

But the common consent of men admits that whatever branch of any pursuit ministers to the bodily comforts, and regards material uses, is ignoble, and whatever part is addressed to the mind only is noble; and that geology does better in reclothing dry bones and revealing lost creations, than in tracing veins of lead and beds of iron; astronomy better in opening to us the houses of heaven, than in teaching navigation; botany better in displaying structure than in expressing juices; surgery better in investigating organization than in setting limbs. Only it is ordained that, for our encouragement, every step we make in the more exalted range of science adds something also to its practical applicabilities; that all the great phenomena of nature, the knowledge of which is desired by the angels only, by us partly, as it reveals to farther vision the being and the glory of Him in whom they rejoice, and we live, dispense yet such kind influences, and so much of material blessing, as to be joyfully felt by all inferior creatures, and to be desired by them with such single desire as the imperfection of their nature may admit;[3] that the strong torrents which, in their own gladness, fill the hills with hollow thunder and the vales with winding light, have yet their bounden charge of field to feed, and barge to bear: that the fierce flames to which the Alp owes its upheaval, and the volcano its terror, temper for us the metal vein and warm the quickening spring; and that for our incitement, – I say not our reward, for knowledge is its own reward, – herbs have their healing, stones their preciousness, and stars their times.

It would appear, therefore, that those pursuits which are altogether theoretic, whose results are desirable or admirable in themselves and for their own sake, and in which no farther end to which their productions or discoveries are referred can interrupt the contemplation of things as they are, by the endeavour to discover of what selfish uses they are capable (and of this order are painting and sculpture), ought to take rank above all pursuits which have any taint[4] in them of subserviency to life, in so far as all such tendency is the sign of less eternal and less holy function. And such rank these two sublime arts would indeed assume in the minds of nations, and become objects of corresponding efforts, but for two fatal and widespread errors respecting the great faculties of mind concerned in them.

The first of these, or the Theoretic faculty, is concerned with the moral perception and appreciation of ideas of beauty. And the error respecting it is, the considering and calling it Æsthetic, degrading it to a mere operation of sense, or perhaps worse, of custom; so that the arts which appeal to it sink into a mere amusement, ministers to morbid sensibilities, ticklers and fanners of the soul's sleep.

The second great faculty is the Imaginative, which the mind

exercises in a certain mode of regarding or combining the ideas it has received from external nature, and the operations of which become in their turn objects of the theoretic faculty to other minds. And the error respecting this faculty is, in considering that its function is one of falsehood, that its operation is to exhibit things as they are *not*, and that in so doing it mends the works of God. (MP II, Pt. III, Sec. 1, Ch. 1, paras. 2–10)

Infinity and Unity: Modern Painters, Vol. I

As I before observed of mere execution, that one of the best tests of its excellence was the expression of *infinity*; so it may be noticed with respect to the painting of details generally, that more difference lies between one artist and another, in the attainment of this quality, than in any other of the efforts of art; and that if we wish, without reference to beauty of composition, or any other interfering circumstances, to form a judgment of the truth of painting, perhaps the very first thing we should look for, whether in one thing or another, – foliage, or clouds, or waves, – should be the expression of *infinity* always and everywhere, in all parts and divisions of parts. For we may be quite sure that what is not infinite cannot be true. It does not, indeed, follow that what is infinite is always true, but it cannot be altogether false; for this simple reason, that it is impossible for mortal mind to compose an infinity of any kind for itself, or to form an idea of perpetual variation, and to avoid all repetition, merely by its own combining resources. The moment that we trust to ourselves, we repeat ourselves, and therefore the moment we see in a work of any kind whatsoever the expression of infinity, we may be certain that the workman has gone to nature for it; while, on the other hand, the moment we see repetition, or want of infinity, we may be certain that the workman has *not* gone to nature for it.

When, on the other hand, we take up such a sky as that of Turner's Rouen seen from St Catherine's Hill, in the Rivers of France [Plate 6], and find, in the first place, that he has given us a distance over the hills in the horizon, into which when we are tired of penetrating, we must turn and come back again, there being not the remotest chance of getting to the end of it; and when we see that from this measureless distance up to the zenith, the whole sky is one ocean of alternate waves of cloud and light, so blended together that the eye cannot rest on any one without being guided

to the next, and so to a hundred more, till it is lost over and over
again in every wreath; that if it divides the sky into quarters of
inches, and tries to count or comprehend the component parts of
any single one of those divisions, it is still as utterly defied and
defeated by the part as by the whole; that there is not one line out
of the millions there which repeats another, not one which is
unconnected with another, not one which does not in itself convey
histories of distance and space, and suggest new and changeful
form; then we may be all but certain, though these forms are too
mysterious and too delicate for us to analyze, though all is so
crowded and so connected that it is impossible to test any single
part by particular laws, yet without any such tests we may be sure
that this infinity can only be based on truth, that it *must* be nature,
because man could not have originated it, and that every form
must be faithful, because none is like another. And therefore it is
that I insist so constantly on this great quality of landscape
painting, as it appears in Turner: because it is not merely a
constant and most important truth in itself, but it almost amounts
to a demonstration of every other truth. And it will be found a far
rarer attainment in the works of other men than is commonly
supposed, and the sign, wherever it is really found, of the very
highest art. For we are apt to forget that the greatest *number* is no
nearer infinity than the least, if it be definite number; and the
vastest bulk is no nearer infinity than the most minute, if it be
definite bulk; so that a man may multiply his objects for ever and
ever, and be no nearer infinity than he had reached with one, if he
do not vary them and confuse them; and a man may reach infinity
in every touch and line, and part, and unit, if in these he be
truthfully various and obscure. And we shall find, the more we
examine the works of the old masters, that always, and in all
parts, they are totally wanting in every feeling of infinity, and
therefore in *all* truth: and even in the works of the moderns,
though the aim is far more just, we shall frequently perceive an
erroneous choice of means, and a substitution of mere number or
bulk for real infinity.[a] (MP I, Pt. II, Sec. III, Ch. III paras. 22, 24–5)

---

[a] *Compare the following passage likewise against mechanical repetitiveness
and in favour of unpremeditated infinity*:
Though nature is constantly beautiful, she does not exhibit her highest powers
of beauty constantly, for then they would satiate us and pall upon our senses. It
is necessary to their appreciation that they should be rarely shown. Her finest
touches are things which must be watched for; her most perfect passages of

Plate 6 *Rouen from St Catherine's Hill*

Contemplation or Theoria: Infinity in Modern Painters Vol. II – 'the Type of Divine Incomprehensibility'

One, however, of these child instincts, I believe that few forget, the emotion, namely, caused by all open ground, or lines of any spacious kind against the sky, behind which there might be conceived the Sea. It is an emotion more pure than that caused by the sea itself, for I recollect distinctly running down behind the banks of a high beach to get their land line cutting against the sky, and receiving a more strange delight from this than from the sight of the ocean. I am not sure that this feeling is common to all children, (or would be common, if they were all in circumstances admitting it,) but I have ascertained it to be frequent among those who possess the most vivid sensibilities for nature; and I am certain that the modification of it which belongs to our after years is common to all, the love, namely, of a light distance appearing over a comparatively dark horizon. This I have tested too frequently to be mistaken, by offering to indifferent spectators forms of equal abstract beauty in half tint, relieved, the one

beauty are the most evanescent. She is constantly doing something beautiful for us, but it is something which she has not done before and will not do again; some exhibition of her general powers in particular circumstances, which, if we do not catch at the instant it is passing, will not be repeated for us. Now they are these evanescent passages of perfected beauty, these perpetually varied examples of utmost power, which the artist ought to seek for and arrest. No supposition can be more absurd than that effects or truths frequently exhibited are more characteristic of nature than those which are equally necessary by her laws, though rarer in occurrence. Both the frequent and the rare are parts of the same great system; to give either exclusively is imperfect truth, and to repeat the same effect or thought in two pictures is wasted life. What should we think of a poet who should keep all his life repeating the same thought in different words? and why should we be more lenient to the parrot painter, who has learned one lesson from the page of nature, and keeps stammering it out in eternal repetition, without turning the leaf? Is it less tautology to describe a thing over and over again with lines, than it is with words? The teaching of nature is as varied and infinite as it is constant; and the duty of the painter is to watch for every one of her lessons, and to give (for human life will admit of nothing more) those in which she has manifested each of her principles in the most peculiar and striking way. The deeper his research and the rarer the phenomena he has noted, the more valuable will his works be; to repeat himself, even in a single instance, is treachery to nature, for a thousand human lives would not be enough to give one instance of the perfect manifestation of each of her powers. (MP I, Pt. II, Sec. I, Ch. IV, paras. 2–4)

against dark sky, the other against a bright distance. The preference is invariably given to the latter; and it is very certain that this preference arises not from any supposition of there being greater truth in this than the other, for the same preference is unhesitatingly accorded to the same effect in Nature herself. Whatever beauty there may result from effects of light on foreground objects, – from the dew of the grass, the flash of the cascade, the glitter of the birch trunk, or the fair daylight hues of darker things (and joyfulness there is in all of them), there is yet a light which the eye invariably seeks with a deeper feeling of the beautiful, – the light of the declining or breaking day, and the flakes of scarlet cloud burning like watch-fires in the green sky of the horizon; a deeper feeling, I say, not perhaps more acute, but having more of spiritual hope and longing, less of animal and present life, more manifest, invariably, in those of more serious and determined mind, (I use the word serious, not as being opposed to cheerful, but to trivial and volatile,) but I think, marked and unfailing even in those of the least thoughtful dispositions. I am willing to let it rest on the determination of every reader, whether the pleasure which he has received from these effects of calm and luminous distance be not the most singular and memorable of which he has been conscious; whether all that is dazzling in colour, perfect in form, gladdening in expression, be not of evanescent and shallow appealing, when compared with the still small voice of the level twilight behind purple hills, or the scarlet arch of dawn over the dark troublous-edged sea.

Let us try to discover that which effects of this kind possess or suggest, peculiar to themselves, and which other effects of light and colour possess not. There *must* be something in them of a peculiar character, and that, whatever it be, must be one of the primal and most earnest motives of beauty to human sensation.

Do they show finer characters of form than can be developed by the broader daylight? Not so; for their power is almost independent of the forms they assume or display; it matters little whether the bright clouds be simple or manifold, whether the mountain line be subdued or majestic; the fairer forms of earthly things are by them subdued and disguised, the round and muscular growth of the forest trunks is sunk into skeleton lines of quiet shade, the purple clefts of the hill-side are labyrinthed in the darkness, the orbed spring and whirling wave of the torrent have given place to a white, ghastly, interrupted gleaming. Have they more perfection or fulness of colour? Not so; for their effect is oftentimes deeper when their hues are dim, than when they are blazoned with crimson and pale gold: and assuredly, in the blue of the rainy sky, in the many tints of morning flowers, in the sunlight on summer foliage and field, there are more sources of mere sensual colour-pleasure than in the single streak of wan and dying light. It is not then by nobler form, it is not by positiveness of hue, it is not by intensity of light (for the sun itself at noonday is effectless upon the feelings), that this strange distant space possesses its attractive power. But there is one thing that it has, or suggests, which no other object of sight suggests in equal degree, and that is – Infinity. It is of all visible things the least material, the least finite, the farthest withdrawn from the earth prison-house, the most typical of the nature of God, the most suggestive of the glory of His dwelling-place. For the sky of night, though we may know it boundless, is dark; it is a studded vault, a roof that seems to shut us in and down; but the bright distance has no limit, we feel its infinity, as we rejoice in its purity of light.

Now not only is this expression of infinity in distance most precious wherever we find it, however solitary it may be, and however unassisted by other forms and kinds of beauty, but it is of that value that no such other forms will altogether recompense us for its loss; and, much as I dread the enunciation of anything that may seem like a conventional rule, I have no hesitation in asserting that no work of any art, in which this expression of infinity is possible, can be perfect, or supremely elevated, without it, and that, in proportion to its presence, it will exalt and render impressive even the most tame and trivial themes. And I think if there be any one grand division, by which it is at all possible to set the productions of painting, so far as their mere plan or system is concerned, on our right and left hands, it is this of light and dark background, of *heaven light* or of *object light*.[5] For I know not any truly great painter of any time, who manifests not the most intense pleasure in the luminous space of his backgrounds, or who ever sacrifices this pleasure where the nature of his subject admits of its attainment; as, on the other hand, I know not that the habitual use of dark backgrounds can be shown as having ever been coexistent with pure or high feeling, and, except in the case of Rembrandt (and then under peculiar circumstances only), with any high power of intellect. It is, however, necessary carefully to observe the following modifications of this broad principle.

The absolute necessity, for such I indeed consider it, is of no more than such a mere luminous distant point as may give to the feelings a species of escape from all the finite objects about them. There is a spectral etching of Rembrandt, a Presentation of Christ in the Temple, where the figure of a robed priest stands glaring by its gems out of the gloom, holding a crozier. Behind it there is a subdued window-light, seen in the opening between two columns, without which the impressiveness of the whole subject would, I think, be incalculably brought down. I cannot tell whether I am at present allowing too much weight to my own fancies and predilections, but without so much escape into the outer air and open heaven as this, I can take permanent pleasure in no picture.

And I think I am supported in this feeling by the unanimous practice, if not the confessed opinion, of all artists. The painter of portrait is unhappy without his conventional white stroke under the sleeve, or beside the arm-chair; the painter of interiors feels like a caged bird, unless he can throw a window open, or set the door ajar; the landscapist dares not lose himself in forest without a gleam of light under its farthest branches, nor venture out in rain unless he may somewhere pierce to a better promise in the distance, or cling to some closing gap of variable blue above. Escape, Hope, Infinity, by whatever conventionalism sought, the desire is the same in all, the instinct constant: it is no mere point of light that is wanted in the etching of Rembrandt above instanced, a gleam of armour or fold of temple curtain would have been utterly valueless; neither is it liberty, for though we cut down hedges and level hills, and give what waste and plain we choose, on the right hand and the left, it is all comfortless and undesired, so long as we cleave not a way of escape forward; and however narrow and thorny and difficult the nearer path, it matters not, so only that the clouds open for us at its close. Neither will any amount of beauty in nearer form make us content to stay with it, so long as we are shut down to that alone; nor is any form so cold or so hurtful but that we may look upon it with kindness, so only that it rise against the infinite hope of light beyond. The reader can follow out the analogies of this unassisted.

But although this narrow portal of escape be all that is absolutely necessary, I think that the dignity of the painting increases with the extent and amount of the expression. With the earlier and mightier painters of Italy, the practice is commonly to leave their distance of pure and open sky, of such simplicity that it in nowise shall interfere with, or draw the attention from, the interest of the figures; and of such purity that, especially towards the horizon, it shall be in the highest degree expressive of the infinite space of heaven. I do not mean to say that they did this with any occult or metaphysical motives. They did it, I think, with the unpretending simplicity of all earnest men; they did what they loved and felt; they sought what the heart naturally seeks, and gave what it most gratefully receives; and I look to them as in all points of principle (not, observe, of knowledge or empirical attainment) as the most irrefragable authorities, precisely on account of the child-like innocence, which never deemed itself authoritative, but acted upon desire, and not upon dicta, and sought for sympathy, not for admiration . . .

Now although I doubt not that the general value of this treatment will be acknowledged by all lovers of art, it is not certain that the point to prove which I have brought it forward will be as readily conceded; namely, the inherent power of all representations of infinity over the human heart. For there are, indeed, countless associations of pure and religious kind, which combine with each other to enhance the impression when presented in this particular form, whose power I neither deny nor am careful to distinguish, seeing that they all tend to the same point, and have reference to heavenly hopes; delights they are in seeing the narrow, black, miserable earth fairly compared with the bright firmament; reaching forward unto the things that are before, and joyfulness in the apparent, though unreachable, nearness and promise of them. But there are other modes in which infinity may be represented, which are confused by no associations of the kind, and which would, as being in mere matter, appear trivial and mean, but for their incalculable influence on the forms of all that we feel to be beautiful.

The first of these is the curvature of lines and surfaces, wherein it at first appears futile to insist upon any resemblance or suggestion of infinity, since there is certainly, in our ordinary contemplation of it, no sensation of the kind. But I have repeated again and again that the ideas of beauty are instinctive, and that it is only upon consideration, and even then in doubtful and disputable way, that they appear in their typical character. Neither do I intend at all to insist upon the particular meaning which they appear to myself to bear, but merely on their actual and demonstrable agreeableness: so that in the present case, while I assert positively, and have no fear of being able to prove, that a curve of any kind is more beautiful than a right line, I leave it to the reader to accept or not, as he pleases, that reason of its agreeableness which is the only one that I can at all trace; namely, that every curve divides itself infinitely by its changes of direction . . .

What curvature is to lines, gradation is to shades and colours. It is their infinity, and divides them into an infinite number of degrees. Absolutely without gradation no natural surface can possibly be . . .

Gradation is so inseparable a quality of all natural shade, that the eye refuses in painting to understand a shadow which appears without it; while, on the other hand, nearly all the gradations of nature are so subtle, and between degrees of tint so slightly separated, that no human hand can in any wise equal, or do anything more than suggest the idea of them. In proportion to the space over which gradation extends, and to its invisible subtlety, is its grandeur: and in proportion to its narrow limits and violent degrees, its vulgarity. (MP II, Pt. III, Sec. I, Ch. V, paras. 3–9, 13–14, 16–17)

Contemplation or Theoria: Unity in Modern Painters Vol. II – 'the Type of Divine Comprehensiveness'

'All things,' says Hooker, 'God only excepted, besides the nature which they have in themselves, receive externally some perfection from other things' [Ecclesiastical Polity, Book I, Ch. XI, para. 1]. Hence the appearance of separation or isolation in anything, and of self-dependence, is an appearance of imperfection; and all appearances of connection and brotherhood are pleasant and right, both as significative of perfection in the things united, and as typical of that Unity which we attribute to God, and of which our true conception is rightly explained and limited by Dr Thomas Brown in his XCII.nd lecture [Lectures on the Philosophy of the Human Mind, 1820, 'On the Existence of the Deity']; that Unity which consists not in His own singleness or separation, but in the necessity of His inherence in all things that be, without which no creature of any kind could hold existence for a moment. Which necessity of divine essence I think it better to speak of as Comprehensiveness, than as Unity; because unity is often understood in the sense of oneness or singleness, instead of universality; whereas the only unity which by any means can become grateful or an object of hope to men, and whose types therefore in material things can be beautiful, is that on which turned the last words and prayer of Christ before His crossing of the Kedron brook, 'Neither pray I for these alone, but for them also which shall believe on Me through their word; that they all may be one, as Thou, Father, art in Me, and I in Thee.' [John xvii, 20]

And so there is not any matter, nor any spirit, nor any creature, but it is capable of a unity of some kind with other creatures; and in that unity is its perfection and theirs, and a pleasure also for the beholding of all other creatures that can behold. So the unity of spirits is partly in their sympathy, and partly in their giving and taking, and always in their love; and these are their delight and their strength; for their strength is in their co-working and army fellowship, and their delight is in the giving and receiving of alternate and perpetual good; their inseparable dependency on each other's being, and their essential and perfect depending on their Creator's. And so the unity of earthly creatures is their power and their peace; not like the dead and cold peace of undisturbed stones and solitary mountains; but the living peace of trust, and the living power of support; of hands that hold each other and are still [Ecclesiastes iv. 11] And so the unity of matter is, in its noblest form, the organization of it which builds it up into temples for the spirit; and in its lower form, the sweet and strange affinity which gives to it the glory of its orderly elements, and the fair variety of change and assimilation that turns the dust into the crystal, and separates the waters that be above the firmament from the waters that be beneath: and, in its lowest form, it is the working and walking and clinging together that gives their power to the winds, and its syllables and soundings to the air, and their weight to the waves, and their burning to the sunbeams, and their stability to the mountains, and to every creature whatsoever operation is for its glory and for others' good.

Now of that which is thus necessary to the perfection of all things, all appearance, sign, type, or suggestion must be beautiful, in whatever matter it may appear; and the appearance of some species of unity is, in the most determined sense of the word, essential to the perfection of beauty in lines, colours, or forms.

But of the appearances of unity, as of unity itself, there are several kinds, which it will be found hereafter convenient to consider separately. Thus there is the Unity of different and separate things, subjected to one and the same influence, which may be called Subjectional Unity; and this is the unity of the clouds, as they are driven by the parallel winds, or as they are ordered by the electric currents; this the unity of the sea-waves, this of the bending and undulation of the forest masses; and in creatures capable of will it is the unity of will or of impulse. And there is Unity of Origin, which we may call Original Unity; which is of things arising from one spring and source, and speaking always of this their brotherhood; and this in matter is the unity of the branches of the trees, and of the petals and starry rays of flowers, and of the beams of light; and in spiritual creatures it is their filial relation to Him from whom they have their being. And there is unity of Sequence, which is that of things that form links in chains, and steps in ascents, and stages in journeys; and this, in matter, is the unity of communicable forces in their continuance from one thing to another; and it is the passing upwards and downwards of beneficent effects among all things, the melody of sounds, the continuity of lines, and the orderly succession of motions and times; and in spiritual creatures it is their own constant building up, by true knowledge and continuous reasoning, to higher perfection, and the singleness and straightforwardness of their tendencies to more complete communion with God. And there is the unity of Membership, which we may call Essential Unity, which is the unity of things separately imperfect into a perfect whole; and this is the great unity of which other unities are but parts and means; it is in matter the harmony of sounds and consistency of bodies, and among spiritual creatures their love and happiness and very life in God.

Now of the nature of this last kind of unity, the most important whether in moral or in those material things with which we are at present concerned, there is this necessary to be observed; that it cannot exist between things similar to each other. Two or more equal and like things cannot be members one of another, nor can they form one, or a whole thing. Two they must remain, both in nature, and in our conception, so long as they remain alike, unless they are united by a third different from both. Thus the arms, which are like each other, remain two arms in our conception. They could not be united by a third arm; they must be united by something which is not an arm, and which, imperfect without them as they without it, shall form one perfect body. Nor is unity even thus accomplished, without a difference and opposition of direction in the setting on of the like members. Therefore, among all things which are to have unity of membership one with another, there must be difference of variety; and though it is possible that many like things may be made members of one body, yet it is remarkable that this structure appears characteristic of the lower creatures, rather than the higher, as the many legs of a caterpillar, and the many arms and suckers of the radiata; and that, as we rise in order of being, the number of similar members becomes less, and their structure commonly seems based on the principle of the unity of two things by a third, as Plato states it in the Timæus, § 11.[6]

Hence, out of the necessity of Unity, arises that of Variety; a necessity often more vividly, though never so deeply felt, because lying at the surface of things, and assisted by an influential principle of our nature, the love of change, and by the power of contrast. But it is a mistake which has led to many unfortunate results, in matters respecting art, to insist on any inherent agreeableness of variety, without reference to a farther end. For it is not even true that variety as such, and in its highest degree, is beautiful. A patched garment of many colours is by no means so agreeable as one of a single and continuous hue; the splendid colours of many birds are eminently painful from their violent separation, and inordinate variety, while the pure and colourless swan is, under certain circumstances, the most beautiful of all feathered creatures. A forest of all manner of trees is poor, if not disagreeable, in effect; a mass of one species of tree is sublime. It is therefore only harmonious and chordal variety, that variety which is necessary to secure and extend unity (for the greater the number of objects which by their differences become members of one another, the more extended and sublime is their unity), which is rightly agreeable; and so I name not Variety as essential to beauty, because it is only so in a secondary and casual sense.

Of the Love of Change as a principle of human nature, and the pleasantness of variety resulting from it, something has already been said (Ch. IV. § 4, see footnote p. 54ff.); only as there I was opposing the idea that our being familiar with objects was the cause of our delight in them, so here I have to oppose the contrary position that their strangeness is the cause of it. For neither familiarity nor strangeness has more operation on, or connection with, impressions of one sense than of another; and they have less power over the impressions of sense, generally, than over the intellect in its joyful accepting of fresh knowledge, and dull contemplation of that it has long possessed. Only in their operation on the senses they act contrarily at different times; as for instance, the newness of a dress, or of some kind of unaccustomed food, may make it for a time delightful, but as the novelty passes away, so also may the delight, yielding to disgust or indifference; which in their turn, as custom begins to operate, may pass into affection and craving, and that which was first a luxury, and then a matter of indifference, become a necessity: whereas in subjects of the intellect, the chief delight they convey is dependent upon their being newly and vividly comprehended; and as they become subjects of contemplation they lose their value, and become tasteless and unregarded, except as instruments for the reaching of others; only that though they sink down into the shadowy, effectless heap of things indifferent, which we pack, and crush down, and stand upon, to reach things new, they sparkle afresh at intervals as we stir them by throwing a new stone into the heap, and letting the newly admitted lights play upon them. And, both in subjects of the intellect and the senses, it is to be remembered that the love of change is a weakness and imperfection of our nature, (and implies in it the state of probation;)[7] and that it is to teach us that things about us here are not meant for our continual possession or satisfaction, that ever such passion of change was put in us at that 'custom lies upon us with a weight, heavy as frost, and deep almost as life' [Wordsworth, 'Intimations of Immortality']; and only such weak thews and baby grasp given to our intellect as that 'the best things we do are painful, and the exercise of them grievous, being continued without intermission, so as in those very actions whereby we are especially perfected in this life we are not able to persist.'[8] And so it will be found that they are the weakest-minded and the hardest-hearted men that most love variety and change. (MP II, Pt. III, Sec. 1, Ch. VI, paras. 1–7)

Imagination: From 'Of Imagination Associative'

It has been said that in composition the mind can only take cognizance of likeness or dissimilarity, or of abstract beauty among the ideas it brings together. But neither likeness nor dissimilarity secures harmony. We saw in the Chapter on Unity that likeness destroyed harmony or unity of membership; and that difference did not necessarily secure it, but only that particular *imperfection* in each of the harmonizing parts which can only be supplied by its fellow part. If, therefore, the combination made is to be harmonious, the artist must induce in each of its component parts (suppose two only, for simplicity's sake), such imperfection as that the other shall put it right. If one of them be perfect by itself, the other will be an excrescence. Both must be faulty when separate, and each corrected by the presence of the other. If he can accomplish this, the result will be beautiful; it will be a whole, an organized body with dependent members; — he is an inventor. If not, let his separate features be as beautiful, as apposite, or as resemblant as they may, they form no whole. They are two members glued together. He is only a carpenter and joiner.

Now, the conceivable imperfections of any single feature are infinite. It is impossible, therefore, to fix upon a form of imperfection in the one, and try with this all the forms of imperfection of the other until one fits; but the two imperfections must be co-relatively and simultaneously conceived.

This is Imagination, properly so called; imagination associative, the grandest mechanical power that the human intelligence possesses, and one which will appear more and more marvellous the longer we consider it. By its operation, two ideas are chosen out of an infinite mass (for it evidently matters not whether the imperfections be conceived out of the infinite number conceivable, or selected out of a number recollected), two ideas which are *separately wrong*, which together shall be right, and of whose unity, therefore, the idea must be formed at the instant they are seized, as it is only in that unity that either is good, and therefore only the *conception of that unity can prompt the preference*. Now, what is that prophetic action of mind, which out of an infinite mass of things that cannot be tried together, seizes, at the same instant, two that are fit for each other; together right, yet each disagreeable alone?

This operation of mind, so far as I can see, is absolutely inexplicable, but there is something like it in chemistry.

'The action of sulphuric acid on metallic zinc affords an instance of what was once called Disposing Affinity. Zinc decomposes pure water at common temperatures with extreme slowness; but as soon as sulphuric acid is added, decomposition of the water takes place rapidly, though the acid merely unites with oxide of zinc. The former explanation was, that the affinity of the acid for oxide of zinc disposed the metal to unite with oxygen, and thus enabled it to decompose water; that is, the oxide of zinc was supposed to produce an effect previous to its existence. The obscurity of this explanation arises from regarding changes as consecutive, which are in reality simultaneous. There is no succession in the process, the oxide of zinc is not formed previously to its combination with the acid, but at the same instant. There is, as it were, but one chemical change, which consists in the combination at one and the same moment, of zinc with oxygen, and of oxide of zinc with the acid; and this change occurs because these two affinities, acting together, overcome the attraction of oxygen and hydrogen for one another.' [*Elements of Chemistry*, by Edward Turner M.D., Part II, Sec. IV]

Now, if the imaginative artist will permit us, with all deference, to represent his combining intelligence under the figure of sulphuric acid; and if we suppose the fragment of zinc to be embarrassed among infinitely numerous fragments of diverse metals, and the oxygen dispersed and mingled among gases countless and indistinguishable; we shall have an excellent type, in material things, of the action of the imagination on the immaterial. Both actions are, I think, inexplicable; for, however simultaneous the chemical changes may be, yet the causing power is the affinity of the acid for what has no existence. It is neither to be explained how that affinity operates on atoms uncombined, nor how the artist's desire for an unconceived whole prompts him to the selection of necessary divisions.

This operation would be wonderful enough, if it were concerned with two ideas only. But a powerfully imaginative mind seizes and combines at the same instant, not only two, but all the important ideas of its poem or picture; and while it works with any one of them, it is at the same instant working with and modifying all in their relations to it, never losing sight of their bearings on each other; as the motion of a snake's body goes through all parts at once, and its volition acts at the same instant in coils that go contrary ways.

This faculty is indeed something that looks as if man were made after the image of God. It is inconceivable, admirable, altogether divine; and yet, wonderful as it may seem, it is palpably evident that no less an operation is necessary for the production of any great work: for, by the definition of Unity of Membership (the essential characteristic of greatness), not only certain couples or groups of parts, but *all* the parts of a noble work must be separately imperfect; each must imply, and ask for all the rest, and the glory of every one of them must consist in its relation to the rest; neither while so much as one is wanting can any be right. And it is evidently impossible to conceive, in each separate feature, a certain want or wrongness which can only be corrected by the other features of the picture (not by one or two merely, but by all), unless, together with the want, we conceive also of what is wanted, that is, of all the rest of the work or picture. Hence Fuseli (*Life and Writings*, 3 vols, 1831, Aphorisms 71–2, Vol. III, p. 85):–

'Second thoughts are admissible in painting and poetry only as dressers of the first conception; no great idea was ever formed in fragments.'

'He alone can conceive and compose, who sees the whole at once before him.'

There is, however, a limit to the power of all human imagination.[b] When the relations to be observed are *absolutely* necessary, and highly complicated, the mind cannot grasp them; and the result is a total deprivation of all power of imagination associative in such matter. (MP II, Pt. III, Sec. II, Ch. II, paras. 6–10)

Imagination Associative in Turner's Cephalus and Procris (*the whole not piecemeal vision*)

When an unimaginative painter is about to draw a tree, (and we will suppose him, for better illustration of the point in question, to have good feeling and correct knowledge of the nature of trees,)

[b] *Ruskin has already said that the operations of imagination cannot of themselves create something entirely new, only combine and re-combine what is already in the world:*

> Of which operations this much may be prematurely said, that they are not creative, that no new ideas are elicited by them, and that their whole function is only a certain dealing with, concentrating, or mode of regarding the impressions received from external things: that therefore, in the beauty to which they will conduct us, there will be found no new element, but only a peculiar combination or phase of those elements that we now know. (MP II, Pt. III, Sec. I, Ch. XV, para. 3)

he probably lays on his paper such a general form as he knows to be characteristic of the tree to be drawn, and such as he believes will fall in agreeably with the other masses in his picture, which we will suppose partly prepared. When this form is set down, he assuredly finds it has done something he did not intend it to do. It has mimicked some prominent line, or overpowered some necessary mass. He begins pruning and changing, and, after several experiments, succeeds in obtaining a form which does no material mischief to any other. To this form he proceeds to attach a trunk, and, working probably on a received notion or rule (for the unimaginative painter never works without a principle) that tree trunks ought to lean first one way and then the other as they go up, and ought not to stand under the middle of the tree, he sketches a serpentine form of requisite propriety; when it has gone up far enough, that is, till it looks disagreeably long, he will begin to ramify it; and if there be another tree in the picture with two large branches, he knows that this, by all laws of composition, ought to have three or four, or some different number; and because he knows that if three or four branches start from the same point they will look formal, therefore he makes them start from points one above another; and because equal distances are improper, therefore they shall start at unequal distances. When they are fairly started, he knows they must undulate or go backwards and forwards, which accordingly he makes them do at random; and because he knows that all forms ought to be contrasted, he makes one bend down while the other three go up. The three that go up he knows must not go up without interfering with each other, and so he makes two of them cross. He thinks it also proper that there should be variety of character in them; so he makes the one that bends down graceful and flexible, and, of the two that cross, he splinters one and makes a stump of it. He repeats the process among the more complicated minor boughs, until coming to the smallest, he thinks farther care unnecessary, but draws them freely, and by chance. Having to put on the foliage, he will make it flow properly in the direction of the tree's growth; he will make all the extremities graceful; but will be tormented by finding them come all alike, and at last will be obliged to spoil a number of them altogether, in order to obtain opposition. They will not, however, be united in this their spoliation, but will remain uncomfortably separate and individually ill-tempered. He consoles himself by the reflection that it is unnatural for all of them to be equally perfect.

Now, I suppose that through the whole of this process, he has been able to refer to his definite memory or conception of nature for every one of the fragments he has successively added; that the details, colour, fractures, insertions, etc., of his boughs, are all either actual recollections or based on secure knowledge of the tree (and herein I allow far more than is commonly the case with unimaginative painters). But, as far as the process of combination is concerned, it is evident that, from beginning to end, his laws have been his safety, and his plague has been his liberty. He has been compelled to work at random or under the guidance of feeling only, whenever there was anything left to his own decision. He has never been decided in anything except in what he *must* or *must not* do. He has walked as a drunken man on a broad road; his guides are the hedges; and, between these limits, the broader the way, the more difficult his progress.

The advance of the imaginative artist is precisely the reverse of this. He owns no laws. He defies all restraint, and cuts down all hedges. There is nothing within the limits of natural possibility that he dares not do, or that he allows the necessity of doing. The laws of nature he knows; these are to him no restraint. They are his own nature. All other laws or limits he sets at utter defiance; his journey is over an untrodden and pathless plain. But he sees his end over the waste from the first, and goes straight at it; never losing sight of it, nor throwing away a step. Nothing can stop him, nothing turn him aside; falcons and lynxes are of slow and uncertain sight compared with his. He saw his tree, trunk, boughs, foliage and all, from the first moment; not only the tree, but the sky behind it; not only that tree or sky, but all the other great features of his picture: by what intense power of instantaneous selection and amalgamation cannot be explained, but by this it may be proved and tested; that, if we examine the tree of the unimaginative painter, we shall find that on removing any part or parts of it, though the rest will indeed suffer, as being deprived of the proper development of a tree, and as involving a blank space that wants occupation, yet the portions left are not made discordant or disagreeable. They are absolutely and in themselves as valuable as they can be; every stem is a perfect stem, and every twig a graceful twig, or at least as perfect and as graceful as they were before the removal of the rest. But if we try the same experiment on the imaginative painter's work, and break off the merest stem or twig of it, it all goes to pieces . . .

Take it away, and the boughs will sing to us no longer. All is dead and cold . . .[c]

[c] *Ruskin returns to the topic of the artist's simultaneous grasp of the whole of what he is doing in the fifth volume of* Modern Painters

The degree in which the ground colours are extended over his picture, as he works, is to a great painter absolutely indifferent. It is all the same to him whether he grounds a head, and finishes it at once to the shoulders, leaving all round it white; or whether he grounds the whole picture. His harmony, paint as he will, never can be complete till the last touch is given; so long as it remains incomplete, he does not care how little of it is suggested, or how many notes are missing. All is wrong, till all is right; and he must be able to bear the all wrongness till his work is done, or he cannot paint at all. His mode of treatment will, therefore, depend on the nature of his subject, as is beautifully shown in the water-colour sketches by Turner in the National Gallery. His general system was to complete inch by inch; leaving the paper quite white all round, especially if the work was to be delicate. The most exquisite drawings left unfinished in the collection – those at Rome and Naples – are thus outlined accurately on pure white paper, begun in the middle of the sheet, and worked out to the side, finishing as he proceeds. If, however, any united effect of light or colour is to embrace a large part of the subject, he will lay it in with a broad wash over the whole paper at once; then paint into it, using it as a ground, and modifying it in the pure Venetian manner. His oil pictures were laid roughly with ground colours, and painted into with such rapid skill, that the artists who used to see him finishing at the Academy sometimes suspected him of having the picture finished underneath the colours he showed, and removing, instead of adding, as they watched.

But, whatever the means used may be, the certainty and directness of them imply absolute grasp of the whole subject, and without this grasp there is no good painting. This, finally, let me declare, without qualification – that partial conception is no conception. The whole picture must be imagined, or none of it is. And this grasp of the whole implies very strange and sublime qualities of mind. It is not possible, unless the feelings are completely under control; the least excitement or passion will disturb the measured equity of power; a painter needs to be as cool as a general; and as little moved or subdued by his sense of pleasure, as a soldier by the sense of pain. Nothing good can be done without intense feeling; but it must be feeling so crushed, that the work is set about with mechanical steadiness, absolutely untroubled, as a surgeon – not without pity, but conquering it and putting it aside – begins an operation. Until the feelings can give strength enough to the will to enable it to conquer them, they are not strong enough. If you cannot leave your picture at any moment; – cannot turn from it, and go on with another, while the colour is drying; – cannot work at any part of it you choose with equal contentment – you have not firm enough grasp of it . . .

I know not if the reader can understand, – I myself cannot, though I see it to

And now we find what noble sympathy and unity there are between the Imaginative and Theoretic faculties. Both agree in this, that they reject nothing, and are thankful for all; but the Theoretic faculty takes out of everything that which is beautiful, while the Imaginative faculty takes hold of the very imperfections which the Theoretic rejects; and, by means of these angles and roughnesses, it joints and bolts the separate stones into a mighty temple, wherein the Theoretic faculty, in its turn, does deepest homage. Thus sympathetic in their desires, harmoniously diverse in their operation, each working for the other with what the other needs not, all things external to man are by one or other turned to good . . .

But for immediate and close illustration, it is perhaps best to refer to a work more accessible, the Cephalus and Procris of Turner in the Liber Studiorum. I know of no landscape more purely or magnificently imaginative, or bearing more distinct evidence of the relative and simultaneous conception of the parts. Let the reader first cover with his hand the two trunks that rise against the sky on the right, and ask himself how any termination of the central mass so *ugly* as the straight trunk which he will then painfully see, could have been conceived or admitted without *simultaneous conception* of the trunks he has taken away on the right? Let him again conceal the whole central mass, and leave these two only, and again ask himself whether anything so ugly as that bare trunk in the shape of a Y, could have been admitted without reference to the central mass? Then let him remove from this trunk its two arms, and try the effect; let him again remove the

be demonstrable, – the simultaneous occurrence of idea which produces such a drawing as this: the grasp of the whole, from the laying of the first line, which induces continual modifications of all that is done, out of respect to parts not done yet. No line is ever changed or effaced: no experiment made; but every touch is placed with reference to all that are to succeed, as to all that have gone before; every addition takes its part, as the stones in an arch of a bridge; the last touch locks the arch. Remove that keystone, or remove any other of the stones of the vault, and the whole will fall.

I repeat – the power of mind which accomplishes this, is yet wholly inexplicable to me, as it was when first I defined it in the chapter on imagination associative, in the second volume. But the grandeur of the power impresses me daily more and more; and, in quitting the subject of invention, let me assert finally, in clearest and strongest terms, that no painting is of any true imaginative perfectness at all, unless it has been thus conceived. (MP V, Pt. VIII, Ch. IV, paras. 19–20, 15–16)

Plate 7 *Procris and Cephalus*

single trunk on the extreme right; then let him try the third trunk without the excrescence at the bottom of it; finally, let him conceal the fourth trunk from the right, with the slender boughs at the top: he will find, in each case, that he has destroyed a feature on which everything else depends; and if proof be required of the vital power of still smaller features, let him remove the sunbeam that comes through beneath the faint mass of trees on the hill in the distance. (MP II, Pt. III, Sec. II, Ch. II, paras. 11–13, 16, 20)

Imagination Associative: in Turner's reworking of a topography of the Pass of Faido

There is nothing in this scene, taken by itself, particularly interesting or impressive. The mountains are not elevated, nor particularly fine in form, and the heaps of stones which encumber the Ticino present nothing notable to the ordinary eye. But, in reality, the place is approached through one of the narrowest and most sublime ravines in the Alps, and after the traveller during the early part of the day has been familiarized with the aspect of the highest peaks of the Mont St Gothard. Hence it speaks quite another language to him from that in which it would address itself to an unprepared spectator: the confused stones, which by themselves would be almost without any claim upon his thoughts, become exponents of the fury of the river by which he has journeyed all day long; the defile beyond, not in itself narrow or terrible, is regarded nevertheless with awe, because it is imagined to resemble the gorge that had just been traversed above; and, although no very elevated mountains immediately overhang it, the scene is felt to belong to, and arise in its essential characters out of, the strength of those mightier mountains in the unseen north.

Any topographical delineation of the facts, therefore, must be wholly incapable of arousing in the mind of the beholder those sensations which would be caused by the facts themselves, seen in their natural relations to others. And the aim of the great inventive landscape painter must be to give the far higher and deeper truth of mental vision, rather than that of the physical facts, and to reach a representation which, though it may be totally useless to engineers or geographers, and, when tried by rule and measure, totally unlike the place, shall yet be capable of producing on the far-away beholder's mind precisely the impression which the

Plate 8 Pass of Faido (first simple topography)

reality would have produced, and putting his heart into the same state in which it would have been, had he verily descended into the valley from the gorges of Airolo.

Now observe; if in his attempts to do this the artist does not understand the sacredness of the truth of *Impression*, and supposes that, once quitting hold of his first thought, he may by Philosophy compose something prettier than he saw and mightier than he felt, it is all over with him. Every such attempt at composition will be utterly abortive, and end in something that is neither true nor fanciful; something geographically useless, and intellectually absurd.

But if, holding fast his first thought, he finds other ideas insensibly gathering to it, and, whether he will or not, modifying it into something which is not so much the image of the place itself, as the spirit of the place, let him yield to such fancies, and follow them wherever they lead. For, though error on this side is very rare among us in these days, it *is* possible to check these finer thoughts by mathematical accuracies, so as materially to impair the imaginative faculty. I shall be able to explain this better after we have traced the actual operation of Turner's mind on the scene under discussion.

Turner was always from his youth fond of stones . . . So that this great litter of fallen stones, which to any one else would have been simply disagreeable, was to Turner much the same as if the whole valley had been filled with plums and pineapples, and delighted him exceedingly, much more than even the gorge of Dazio Grande just above. But that gorge had its effect upon him also, and was still not well out of his head when the diligence stopped at the bottom of the hill, just at that turn of the road on the right of the bridge; which favourable opportunity Turner seized to make what he called a 'memorandum' of the place, composed of a few pencil scratches on a bit of thin paper, that would roll up with others of the sort and go into his pocket afterwards. These pencil scratches he put a few blots of colour upon (I suppose at Bellinzona the same evening, certainly *not* upon the spot), and showed me this blotted sketch when he came home. I asked him to make me a drawing of it, which he did, and casually told me afterwards (a rare thing for him to do) that he liked the drawing he had made. Of this drawing I have etched a reduced outline in Plate 9.

In which, primarily, observe that the whole place is altered in scale, and brought up to the general majesty of the higher forms of the Alps. It will be seen that, in my topographical sketch, there are a few trees rooted in the rock on this side of the gallery, showing, by comparison, that it is not above four or five hundred feet high. These trees Turner cuts away, and gives the rock a height of about a thousand feet, so as to imply more power and danger in the avalanche coming down the couloir.

Next, he raises, in a still greater degree, all the mountains beyond, putting three or four ranges instead of one, but uniting them into a single massy bank at their base, which he makes overhang the valley, and thus reduces it nearly to such a chasm as that which he had just passed through above, so as to unite the expression of this ravine with that of the stony valley. The few trees, in the hollow of the glen, he feels to be contrary in spirit to the stones, and fells them, as he did the others; so also he feels the bridge in the foreground, by its slenderness, to contradict the aspect of violence in the torrent; he thinks the torrent and avalanches should have it all their own way hereabouts; so he strikes down the nearer bridge, and restores the one farther off, where the force of the stream may be supposed less. Next, the bit of road on the right, above the bank, is not built on a wall, nor on arches high enough to give the idea of an Alpine road in general; so he makes the arches taller, and the bank steeper, introducing, as we shall see presently, a reminiscence from the upper part of the pass.

I say, he '*thinks*' this, and 'introduces' that. But, strictly speaking, he does not think at all. If he thought, he would instantly go wrong; it is only the clumsy and uninventive artist who thinks. All these changes come into his head involuntarily; an entirely imperative dream, crying, 'Thus it must be,' has taken possession of him; he can see, and do, no otherwise than as the dream directs.

This is especially to be remembered with respect to the next incident – the introduction of figures. Most persons to whom I have shown the drawing, and who feel its general character, regret that there is any living thing in it; they say it destroys the majesty of its desolation. But the dream said not so to Turner. The dream insisted particularly upon the great fact of its having come by the road. The torrent was wild, the storms were wonderful; but the most wonderful thing of all was how we ourselves, the dream and I, ever got here. By our feet we could not – by the clouds we could not – by any ivory gates we could not – in no other wise could we

Plate 9 *Pass of Faido (Turner)*

have come than by the coach road. One of the great elements of sensation, all the day long, has been that extraordinary road, and its goings on, and gettings about; here, under avalanches of stones, and among insanities of torrents, and overhangings of precipices, much tormented and driven to all manner of make-shifts and coils to this side and the other, still the marvellous road persists in going on, and that so smoothly and safely, that it is not merely great diligences, going in a caravannish manner, with whole teams of horses, that can traverse it, but little postchaises with small postboys, and a pair of ponies. And the dream declared that the full essence and soul of the scene, and consummation of all the wonderfulness of the torrents and Alps, lay in a postchaise with small ponies and post-boy, which accordingly it insisted upon Turner's inserting, whether he liked it or not, at the turn of the road.

Now, it will be observed by any one familiar with ordinary principles of arrangement of form (on which principles I shall insist at length in another place), that while the dream introduces these changes bearing on the expression of the scene, it is also introducing other changes, which appear to be made more or less in compliance with received rules of composition, rendering the masses broader, the lines more continuous, and the curves more graceful. But the curious part of the business is, that these changes seem not so much to be wrought by imagining an entirely new condition of any feature, as by *remembering* something which will fit better in that place. For instance, Turner felt the bank on the right ought to be made more solid and rocky, in order to suggest firmer resistance to the stream, and he turns it, as will be seen by comparing the etchings, into a kind of rock buttress to the wall, instead of a mere bank. Now the buttress into which he turns it is very nearly a facsimile of one which he had drawn on that very St Gothard road, far above, at the Devil's Bridge, at least thirty years before, and which he had himself etched and engraved for the Liber Studiorum, although the plate was never published. Plate 10 is a copy of the bit of the etching in question. Note how the wall winds over it, and observe especially the peculiar depression in the middle of its surface, and compare it in those parts generally with the features introduced in the later composition. Of course, this might be set down as a mere chance coincidence, but for the frequency of the cases in which Turner can be shown to have done the same thing, and to have

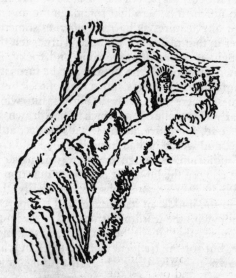

Plate 10 Detail from *Pass of Faido*

introduced, after a lapse of many years, memories of something which, however apparently small or unimportant, had struck him in his earlier studies. These instances, when I can detect them, I shall point out as I go on engraving his works; and I think they are numerous enough to induce a doubt whether Turner's composition was not universally an arrangement of remembrances, summoned just as they were wanted, and set each in its fittest place. It is this very character which appears to me to mark it as so distinctly an act of dream-vision; for in a dream there is just this kind of confused remembrance of the forms of things which we have seen long ago, associated by new and strange laws. That common dreams are grotesque and disorderly, and Turner's dream natural and orderly, does not, to my thinking, involve any necessary difference in the real species of act of mind. I think I shall be able to show in the course of the following pages, or elsewhere, that whenever Turner really tried to *compose*, and made modifications of his subjects on principle, he did wrong, and spoiled them; and that he only did right in a kind of passive obedience to his first vision, that vision being composed primarily of the strong memory of the place itself which he had to draw; and secondarily, of memories of other places (whether recognized as such by himself or not I cannot tell), associated, in a harmonious and helpful way, with the new central thought.

The kind of mental chemistry by which the dream summons and associates its materials, I have already endeavoured, not to explain, for it is utterly inexplicable, but to illustrate, by a well-ascertained though equally inexplicable fact in common chemistry. That illustration (§ 8 of chapter on Imagination Associative, Vol. II: above, p. 66) I see more and more ground to think correct. How far I could show that it held with all great inventors, I know not, but with all those whom I have carefully studied (Dante, Scott, Turner, and Tintoret) it seems to me to hold absolutely; their imagination consisting, not in a voluntary production of new images, but an involuntary remembrance, exactly at the right moment, of something they had actually seen.

Imagine all that any of these men had seen or heard in the whole course of their lives, laid up accurately in their memories as in vast storehouses, extending, with the poets, even to the slightest intonations of syllables heard in the beginning of their lives, and with the painters, down to minute folds of drapery, and shapes of leaves or stones; and over all this unindexed and immeasurable mass of treasure, the imagination brooding and wandering, but dream-gifted, so as to summon at any moment exactly such groups of ideas as shall justly fit each other: this I conceive to be the real nature of the imaginative mind, and this, I believe, it would be oftener explained to us as being, by the men themselves who possess it, but that they have no idea what the state of other persons' minds is in comparison; they suppose every one remembers all that he has seen in the same way, and do not understand how it happens that they alone can produce good drawings or great thoughts. (MP IV, Pt. V, Ch. II, paras. 10–17)

Imagination Associative: Modern Painters *Vol. V – simply called 'Help'*

Composition may be best defined as the help of everything in the picture by everything else.

I wish the reader to dwell a little on this word 'Help'. It is a grave one.

In substance which we call 'inanimate', as of clouds, or stones, their atoms may cohere to each other, or consist with each other, but they do not help each other. The removal of one part does not injure the rest.

But in a plant, the taking away of any one part does injure the rest. Hurt or remove any portion of the sap, bark, or pith, the rest is injured. If any part enters into a state in which it no more assists the rest, and has thus become 'helpless', we call it also 'dead'.

The power which causes the several portions of the plant to help each other, we call life. Much more is this so in an animal. We may take away the branch of a tree without much harm to it; but not the animal's limb. Thus, intensity of life is also intensity of helpfulness – completeness of depending of each part on all the rest. The ceasing of this help is what we call corruption; and in proportion to the perfectness of the help, is the dreadfulness of the loss. The more intense the life has been, the more terrible is its corruption . . .

Now invention in art signifies an arrangement, in which everything in the work is thus consistent with all things else, and helpful to all else.

It is the greatest and rarest of all the qualities of art. The power by which it is effected is absolutely inexplicable and incommunicable; but exercised with entire facility by those who possess it, in many cases even unconsciously.

In work which is not composed, there may be many beautiful things, but they do not help each other. They at the best only stand beside, and more usually compete with and destroy, each other. They may be connected artificially in many ways, but the test of there being no invention is, that if one of them be taken away, the others are no worse than before. But in true composition, if one be taken away, all the rest are helpless and valueless. Generally, in falsely composed work, if anything be taken away, the rest will look better; because the attention is less distracted. Hence the pleasure of inferior artists in sketching, and their inability to finish; all that they add destroys.

Also in true composition, everything not only helps everything else a *little*, but helps with its utmost power. Every atom is in full energy; and *all* that energy is kind. Not a line, nor spark of colour, but is doing its very best, and that best is aid. The extent to which this law is carried in truly right and noble work is wholly inconceivable to the ordinary observer, and no true account of it would be believed.

True composition being entirely easy to the man who can compose, he is seldom proud of it, though he clearly recognizes it. Also, true composition is inexplicable. No one can explain how the notes of a Mozart melody, or the folds of a piece of Titian's drapery, produce their essential effects on each other. If you do not feel it, no one can by reasoning make you feel it. And the highest composition is so subtle, that it is apt to become unpopular, and sometimes seem insipid.

The reader may be surprised at my giving so high a place to invention. But if he ever come to know true invention from false, he will find that it is not only the highest quality of art, but is simply the most wonderful act or power of humanity. It is preeminently the deed of human creation; ποίησις, otherwise, poetry.

If the reader will look back to my definition of poetry, he will find it is 'the suggestion by the imagination of noble grounds for noble emotion' amplified into 'assembling by help of the imagination'; that is to say, imagination associative, described at length in Vol. II., in the chapter just referred to. The mystery of the power is sufficiently set forth in that place. (MP V, Pt. VIII, Ch. 1, paras. 4, 10–13)

Imagination Penetrative

Thus far we have been defining that combining operation of the Imagination, which appears to be in a sort mechanical, yet takes place in the same inexplicable modes, whatever be the order of conception submitted to it, though I choose to illustrate it by its dealings with mere matter before taking cognizance of any nobler subjects of imagery. We must now examine the dealing of the Imagination with its separate conceptions, and endeavour to understand, not only its principles of selection, but its modes of apprehension with respect to what it selects.

When Milton's Satan first 'rears from off the pool his mighty stature,' the image of leviathan before suggested not being yet abandoned, the effect on the fire-wave is described as of the upheaved monster on the ocean-stream.

> On each hand the flames
> Driven backward, slope their pointed spires, and, rolled
> In billows, leave i' the midst a horrid vale.
> [Milton, *Paradise Lost*, I. 244ff]

And then follows a fiercely restless piece of volcanic imagery:

> As when the force
> Of subterranean wind transports a hill
> Torn from Pelorus, or the shattered side
> Of thundering Ætna, whose combustible
> And fuelled entrails, thence conceiving fire,
> Sublimed with mineral fury, aid the winds,
> And leave a singèd bottom all involved
> With stench and smoke: such resting found the sole
> Of unblest feet.

Yet I think all this is too far detailed, and deals too much with externals: we feel rather the form of the fire-waves than their fury; we walk upon them too securely; and the fuel, sublimation, smoke, and singeing seem to me images only of partial combustion; they vary and extend the conception, but they lower the thermometer. Look back, if you will, and add to the description the glimmering of the livid flames; the sulphurous hail and red lightning; yet all together, however they overwhelm us with horror, fail of making us thoroughly, unendurably *hot*. The essence of intense flame has not been given. Now hear Dante:

Feriami 'l Sole in su l' omero destro,
  Che già raggiando tutto l' Occidente
  Mutava in bianco aspetto di cilestro.
Ed io facea *con l'ombra più rovente*
  Parer la fiamma.[9]

That is a slight touch; he has not gone to Ætna or Pelorus for fuel; but we shall not soon recover from it, he has taken our breath away, and leaves us gasping. No smoke nor cinders there. Pure white, hurtling, formless flame; very fire-crystal, we cannot make spires nor waves of it, nor divide it, nor walk on it; there is no question about singeing soles of feet. It is lambent annihilation.

Such is always the mode in which the highest imaginative faculty seizes its materials. It never stops at crusts or ashes, or outward images of any kind; it ploughs them all aside, and plunges into the very central fiery heart; nothing else will content its spirituality; whatever semblances and various outward shows and phases its subject may possess go for nothing; it gets within all fence, cuts down to the root, and drinks the very vital sap of that it deals with: once therein, it is at liberty to throw up what new shoots it will, so always that the true juice and sap be in them, and to prune and twist them at its pleasure, and bring them to fairer fruit than grew on the old tree; but all this pruning and twisting is work that it likes not, and often does ill; its function and gift are the getting at the root, its nature and dignity depend on its holding things always by the heart. Take its hand from off the beating of that, and it will prophesy no longer; it looks not in the eyes, it judges not by the voice, it describes not by outward features; all that it affirms, judges, or describes, it affirms, from within.

It may seem to the reader that I am incorrect in calling this penetrating possession-taking faculty Imagination. Be it so; the name is of little consequence; the faculty itself, called by what name we will, I insist upon as the highest intellectual power of man. There is no reasoning in it; it works not by algebra, nor by integral calculus; it is a piercing pholas-like[10] mind's tongue, that works and tastes into the very rock heart; no matter what be the subject submitted to it, substance or spirit; all is alike divided asunder, joint and marrow, whatever utmost truth, life, principle it has, laid bare, and that which has no truth, life, nor principle, dissipated into its original smoke at a touch. The whispers at men's ears it lifts into visible angels. Vials that have lain sealed in the deep sea a thousand years it unseals, and brings out of them Genii.

Every great conception of poet or painter is held and treated by this faculty. Every character that is so much as touched by men like Æschylus, Homer, Dante, or Shakspeare, is by them held by the heart; and every circumstance or sentence of their being, speaking, or seeming, is seized by process from within, and is referred to that inner secret spring of which the hold is never lost for an instant; so that every sentence, as it has been thought out from the heart, opens for us a way down to the heart, leads us to the centre, and then leaves us to gather what more we may. It is the Open Sesame of a huge, obscure, endless cave, with inexhaustible treasure of pure gold scattered in it; the wandering about and gathering the pieces may be left to any of us, all can accomplish that; but the first opening of that invisible door in the rock is of the imagination only.

Hence there is in every word set down by the imaginative mind an awful under-current of meaning, and evidence and shadow upon it of the deep places out of which it has come. It is often obscure, often half-told; for he who wrote it, in his clear seeing of the things beneath, may have been impatient of detailed interpretation: but, if we choose to dwell upon it and trace it, it will lead us always securely back to that metropolis of the soul's dominion from which we may follow out all the ways and tracks to its farthest coasts.

I think the 'Quel giorno più non vi leggemmo avante' of Francesca di Rimini, and the 'He has no children' of Macduff,[11] are as fine instances as can be given; but the sign and mark of it are visible on every line of the four great men above instanced.

The unimaginative writer, on the other hand, as he has never pierced to the heart, so he can never touch it. If he has to paint a passion, he remembers the external signs of it, he collects expressions of it from other writers, he searches for similes, he composes, exaggerates, heaps term on term, figure on figure, till we groan beneath the cold disjointed heap: but it is all faggot and no fire; the life breath is not in it; his passion has the form of the leviathan, but it never makes the deep boil; he fastens us all at anchor in the scaly rind of it; our sympathies remain as idle as a painted ship upon a painted ocean [Coleridge, 'The Ancient Mariner'].

And that virtue of originality that men so strain after is not *newness*, as they vainly think (there is nothing new), it is only *genuineness*; it all depends on this single glorious faculty of getting to the spring of things and working out from that; it is the coolness, and clearness, and deliciousness of the water fresh from the fountain head, opposed to the thick, hot, unrefreshing drainage from other men's meadows.

This freshness, however, is not to be taken for an infallible sign of imagination, inasmuch as it results also from a vivid operation of fancy, whose parallel function to this division of the imaginative faculty it is here necessary to distinguish.

I believe it will be found that the entirely unimaginative mind *sees* nothing of the object it has to dwell upon or describe, and is therefore utterly unable, as it is blind itself, to set anything before the eyes of the reader.

The fancy sees the outside, and is able to give a portrait of the outside, clear, brilliant, and full of detail.

The imagination sees the heart and inner nature, and makes them felt, but is often obscure, mysterious, and interrupted, in its giving of outer detail . . .

This, then, is one essential difference between imagination and fancy; and another is like it and resultant from it, that the imagination being at the heart of things, poises herself there, and is still, quiet, and brooding, comprehending all around her with her fixed look; but the fancy staying at the outside of things cannot see them all at once; but runs hither and thither, and round and about to see more and more, bounding merrily from point to point, and glittering here and there, but necessarily always settling, if she settle at all, on a point only, never embracing the whole. And from these single points she can strike out analogies and catch resemblances, which, so far as the point she looks at is concerned, are true, but would be false, if she could see through to the other side. This, however, she cares not to do; the point of contact is enough for her, and even if there be a gap left between the two things and they do not quite touch, she will spring from one to the other like an electric spark, and be seen brightest in her leaping.

Now these differences between the imagination and the fancy hold not only in the way they lay hold of separate conceptions, but even in the points they occupy of time; for the fancy loves to run hither and thither in time, and to follow long chains of circumstances from link to link; but the imagination, if it may, gets hold of a moment or link in the middle that implies all the rest, and fastens there . . .

In Retsch's illustrations to Schiller's *Kampf mit dem Drachen*, we have an instance, miserably feeble indeed, but characteristic, and suited to our present purpose, of the detailing, finishing action of the fancy. The dragon is drawn from head to tail, vulture eyes, serpent teeth, forked tongue, fiery crest, armour, claws, and coils as grisly as may be; his den is drawn, and all the dead bones in it, and all the savage forest country about it far and wide; we have him, from the beginning of his career to the end, devouring, rampant, victorious over whole armies, gorged with death; we are present at all the preparations for his attack, see him receive his death-wound, and our anxieties are finally becalmed by seeing him lie peaceably dead on his back.

All the time we have never got into the dragon heart, we have never once felt real pervading horror, nor sense of the creature's being; it is throughout nothing but an ugly composition of claw and scale. Now take up Turner's Jason, Liber Studiorum, and observe how the imagination can concentrate all this, and infinitely more, into one moment. No far forest country, no secret path, nor cloven hills; nothing but a gleam of pale horizontal sky, that broods over pleasant places far away, and sends in, through the wild overgrowth of the thicket, a ray of broken daylight into the hopeless pit. No flaunting plumes nor brandished lances, but stern purpose in the turn of the crestless helmet, visible victory in the drawing back of the prepared right arm behind the steady point. No more claws, nor teeth, nor manes, nor stinging tails. We have the dragon, like everything else, by the middle. We need see no more of him. All his horror is in that fearful, slow, griding upheaval of the single coil. Spark after spark of it, ring after ring, is sliding into the light, the slow glitter steals along him step by step, broader and broader, a lighting of funeral lamps one by one, quicker and quicker; a moment more, and he is out upon us, all crash and blaze, among those broken trunks; — but he will be nothing then to what he is now.

Now it is necessary here very carefully to distinguish between that character of the work which depends on the imagination of the beholder, and that which results from the imagination of the artist; for a work is often called imaginative when it merely leaves room for the action of the imagination; whereas though nearly all imaginative works do this, yet it may be done also by works that have in them no imagination at all. A few shapeless scratches or accidental stains on a wall, or the forms of clouds, or any other

Plate 11 *Jason*

complicated accidents, will set the imagination to work to coin something out of them; and all paintings in which there is much gloom or mystery, possess therein a certain sublimity owing to the play given to the beholder's imagination, without, necessarily, being in the slightest degree imaginative themselves. The vacancy of a truly imaginative work results not from absence of ideas, or incapability of grasping and detailing them, but from the painter having told the whole pith and power of his subject and disdaining to tell more; and the sign of this being the case is, that the mind of the beholder is forced to act in a certain mode, and feels itself overpowered and borne away by that of the painter, and not able to defend itself, nor go which way it will: and the value of the work depends on the truth, authority, and inevitability of this suggestiveness. Now observe in this work of Turner that the whole value of it depends on the character of curve assumed by the serpent's body; for had it been a mere semicircle, or gone down in a series of smaller coils, it would have been in the first case, ridiculous, as unlike a serpent, or in the second, disgusting, nothing more than an exaggerated viper; but it is that *coming straight* at the right hand which suggests the drawing forth of an enormous weight, and gives the bent part its springing look, that frightens us. Again, remove the light trunk on the left, and observe how useless all the gloom of the picture would have been, if this trunk had not given it depth and *hollowness*. Finally and chiefly, observe that the painter is not satisfied even with all the suggestiveness thus obtained, but to make sure of us, and force us, whether we will or not, to walk his way, and not ours, the trunks of the trees on the right are all cloven into yawning and writhing heads and bodies, and alive with dragon energy all about us; note especially the nearest with its gaping jaws and claw-like branch at the seeming shoulder; a kind of suggestion which in itself is not imaginative, but merely fanciful . . .; but it is imaginative in its present use and application, for the painter addresses thereby that morbid and fearful condition of mind which he has endeavoured to excite in the spectator, and which in reality would have seen in every trunk and bough, as it penetrated into the deeper thicket, the object of its terror.

It is nevertheless evident, that however suggestive the work or picture may be, it cannot have effect unless we are ourselves both watchful of its every hint, and capable of understanding and carrying it out; and although I think that this power of continuing or accepting the direction of feeling given is less a peculiar gift, like that of the original seizing, than a faculty dependent on attention and improvable by cultivation; yet, to a certain extent, the imaginative work will not, I think, be rightly esteemed except by a mind of some corresponding power: not but that there is an intense enjoyment in minds of feeble yet right conception in the help and food they get from those of stronger thought; but a certain imaginative susceptibility is at any rate necessary, and above all things earnestness and feeling; so that assuredly a work of high conceptive dignity will be always incomprehensible and valueless except to those who go to it in earnest and give it time; and this is peculiarly the case when the imagination acts not merely on the immediate subject, nor in giving a fanciful and peculiar character to prominent objects, as we have just seen, but busies itself throughout in expressing occult and far-sought sympathies in every minor detail; of which action the most sublime instances are found in the works of Tintoret, whose intensity of imagination is such that there is not the commonest subject to which he will not attach a range of suggestiveness almost limitless; nor a stone, leaf, or shadow, nor anything so small, but he will give it meaning and oracular voice . . .[d]

[d] *Compare Ruskin's discovery of Tintoretto in company with his teacher in water-colour J. D. Harding:*

My companion, though by no means modest as to his own powers, was (partly for that very reason, his confidence in them being well grounded) quite frank and candid in his admiration of stronger painters; and when we had got through the upper gallery, and into the room of the Crucifixion, we both sate down and looked – not at it – but at each other, – literally the strength so taken out of us that we couldn't stand!

When we came away, Harding said that he felt like a whipped schoolboy. I, not having been at school so long as he, felt only that a new world was opened to me, that I had seen that day the Art of Man in its full majesty for the first time; and that there was also a strange and precious gift in myself enabling me to recognize it, and therein ennobling, not crushing me. That sense of my own gift and function as an interpreter strengthened as I grew older; and supports, and I believe justifies me now in accepting in this last cycle of life, the responsibilities lately once more offered to me in Oxford [Slade Professor, 1883].   (MP II, Epilogue (1883) para. 12 (C&W, p. 354))

But the most exquisite instance of this imaginative power occurs in an incident in the background of the Crucifixion. I will not insult this marvellous picture by an effort at a verbal account of it. I would not whitewash it with praise, and I refer to it only for the sake of two thoughts peculiarly illustrative of the intellectual faculty immediately under discussion. In the common and most Catholic treatment of the subject, the mind is either painfully directed to the bodily agony, coarsely expressed by outward anatomical signs, or else it is permitted to rest on that countenance inconceivable by man at any time, but chiefly so in this its consummated humiliation. In the first case, the representation is revolting; in the second, inefficient, false, and sometimes blasphemous. None even of the greatest religious painters have ever, so far as I know, succeeded here: Giotto and Angelico were cramped by the traditional treatment, and the latter especially, as before observed, is but too apt to indulge in those points of vitiated feeling which attained their worst development among the Byzantines; Perugino fails in his Christ in almost every instance: of other men than these, after them, we need not speak. But Tintoret here, as in all other cases, penetrating into the root and deep places of his subject, despising all outward and bodily appearances of pain, and seeking for some means of expressing, not the rack of nerve or sinew, but the fainting of the deserted Son of God before His Eloi cry, and yet feeling himself utterly unequal to the expression of this by the countenance, has, on the one hand, filled his picture with such various and impetuous muscular exertion, that the body of the Crucified is, by comparison, in perfect repose, and, on the other, has cast the countenance altogether into shade. But the Agony is told by this, and by this only; that, though there yet remains a chasm of light on the mountain horizon where the earthquake darkness closes upon the day, the broad and sunlike glory about the head of the Redeemer has become wan, *and of the colour of ashes*.

But the great painter felt he had something more to do yet. Not only that Agony of the Crucified, but the tumult of the people, that rage which invoked His blood upon them and their children. Not only the brutality of the soldier, the apathy of the Centurion, or any other merely instrumental cause of the Divine suffering, but the fury of His own people, the noise against Him of those for whom He died, were to be set before the eye of the understanding, if the power of the picture was to be complete. This rage, be it remembered, was one of disappointed pride; and the disappointment dated essentially from the time when, but five days before, the King of Zion came, and was received with hosannahs, riding upon an ass, and a colt the foal of an ass. To this time, then, it was necessary to direct the thoughts, for therein are found both the cause and the character, the excitement of, and the witness against, this madness of the people. In the shadow behind the cross, a man, riding on an ass colt, looks back to the multitude, while he points with a rod to the Christ crucified. The ass is feeding on the *remnants* of *withered palm-leaves*.

With this master-stroke, I believe, I may terminate all illustration of the peculiar power of the imagination over the feelings of the spectator, by the elevation into dignity and meaning of the smallest accessory circumstances. (MP II, Pt. III, Sec. II, Ch. III, paras. 1–7, 11–15, 20)

CHAPTER 4

Modern Painters III

In the ten years between Modern Painters Vol. II *(1846) and*
Modern Painters Vol. III *(1856), Ruskin wrote* The Seven Lamps
of Architecture *(1849) and the three volumes of* The Stones of
Venice *(1851, 1853).*

*The first ten chapters of volume III are in part an attempt to get
back in touch with the project of* Modern Painters *as a whole; in
particular the chapters 'Of the Real Nature of Greatness of Style'
and 'Of the Use of Pictures'.*

*'Of the Real Nature of Greatness of Style', with its emphasis on
making careful distinctions, is central to Ruskin's whole way of
thinking — in much the same way as was the idea in* Modern
Painters Vol. I *that separation was also the foundation of unity. It
has to do with what elsewhere Ruskin called one of 'the most
pitiable and practically hurtful weaknesses of the modern English
mind': namely, the 'inability to grasp the connection between any
two ideas which have elements of opposition of them, as well as
connection' (C&W VI, p. 482). In* Modern Painters Vol. II *the
painter's version of this capacity to see complex forms of unity lay
in the function of associative imagination; but as some pages of
unpublished manuscript make clear, what Ruskin learnt in
writing* The Stones of Venice *also provided a context for what
went into 'Of the Real Nature of Greatness of Style':*

> I believe it has been acutely felt by all men who have ever devoted
> themselves to the elucidation of abstract truth, that exactly in
> proportion to the scope, depth, and importance of any given
> principle was the difficulty of so expressing it as that it should not
> be capable of misapprehension, and of guarding it against certain
> forms of associated error. This is especially the case with the
> principles of religious faith which are so universally dependent
> upon two opposite truths (for truths may be and often are *opposite*
> though they cannot be contradictory), that it is physically impos-
> sible so to express them in brief form as that the adversary may not
> be able to misrepresent them, nor the simple run any risk of

misapprehending them. And this I have long felt to be also the case with every great principle of art which it has been my endeavour in this and my other writings to assert or defend. There is not any one but has, as it were, two natures in it – at least two different colours or sides – according to the things in connexion with which it is viewed; and therefore, exactly in proportion to the breadth and universality which I have endeavoured to give to all my statements, is their liability to appearances of contradiction, and the certainty of their being misunderstood by any person who does not take the pains to examine the connexion.

This is peculiarly the case with respect to the principle now under consideration [that is, the principle stated in § 6 of ch. iv. of *The Stones of Venice III* that art should express the soul of the artist], and some additional ambiguity may perhaps arise in the reader's mind from the difference between the senses in which I am now using the word 'modern,' and that which it bore in my first work upon painting. In *Modern Painters* our task was to compare the work of living artists with that of so-called 'old' masters of landscape, who flourished for the most part in the seventeenth and eighteenth centuries; but throughout the present volume I use the term 'modern' of all work whatsoever subsequent to the period of the Renaissance – that is to say, the middle of the fifteenth century, Claude, Salvator, and Poussin being in the larger view now taken of the history of art as much moderns as Turner and Stanfield. The recent – would that I could still say, living – school of landscape, is healthy and noble just because in many respects it has broken through the Renaissance systems, and returned in its study of external nature to the earnestness with which the great and, in the large sense, early schools studied men. And yet not enough; for in his necessary opposition to the rules of art which were established by the Renaissance formalists, the modern landscape painter has fallen too often into the same kind of error as the modern religious reformer. For though right in receiving the authority of the present truth and living impression upon the soul, rather than that of tradition and ordinance, he has [not] taken care to render such impressions accurate or profound: he does not take pains to increase the Perceptive power of his mind; but is content with first thoughts and outside visions of things; whereas the truly noble perceptive power is only attained by patience and watchfulness, always going on to see more and more, and helped by the Imagination to see rather the heart of things than their surface . . . But because the volume of *Modern Painters* was written in definite defence of a great artist against whom it was alleged by the commonality of critics that the only merit of his work – if it had merit at all – was in its imaginative power, and that there was no truth nor resemblance to Nature in his pictures, I met these persons first upon their own ground, and devoted that first volume to the demonstration that not only Turner *did* paint the material and actual truth of Nature, but that the truth had never in landscape been fully painted by any other man. And in doing this I had to meet two distinct classes of opponents, first and principally those who looked for nothing in art but a literal and painstaking imitation of the externals of Nature, as in the works of the Dutch school, against whom I had to prove that the truths thus sought were but a small part of the truth of Nature, and that there were higher and more occult kinds of truth which could not be rendered but by some sacrifice of imitative accuracy, and which Turner had by such sacrifice succeeded in rendering for the first time in the history of art. But in the second place and collaterally I had to meet those men who in their love of system or 'composition' disregarded or denied the truth of Nature altogether, and supposed that the Imagination was independent of truth. Against whom I had to assert the dignity and glory of Truth, and its necessity as the foundation of all art whatsoever. (C&W XI, pp. xvii–xviii, xx)

Ruskin was not interested in false clarity but in complex connections and distinctions to be made within the area that he described at the opening of Chapter II of The Seven Lamps of Architecture *as 'the debateable land':*

There is a marked likeness between the virtue of man and the enlightenment of the globe he inhabits – the same diminishing gradation in vigour up to the limits of their domains, the same essential separation from their contraries – the same twilight at the meeting of the two: a something wider belt than the line where the world rolls into night, that strange twilight of the virtues; that dusky debateable land, wherein zeal becomes impatience, and temperance becomes severity, and justice becomes cruelty, and faith superstition, and each and all vanish into gloom. ('The Lamp of Truth')

These connections and distinctions sometimes are held together within a single passage or chapter, as when Ruskin considers the difference between the right and wrong use of the ambition to produce great art. But sometimes, as with his scattered thoughts on what constitutes good and bad finish in a picture, they are split across hundreds of pages and only occasionally gathered into complex unity. For Ruskin there is no truth that does not have to be distinguished from closely allied falsehoods on either side of it: 'No principle can be simply enforced but it shall seem to countenance a vice' (MP I, Pt. II, Sec. I, Ch. VII, para. 10). And yet there is always an underlying, if scattered, unity to Modern Painters.

'Of the Use of Pictures' is a chapter that Ruskin himself judged to be a piece of work he could not better. It concerns the advantages and disadvantages that result from painting's inability to be a complete and perfect imitation of the external world. The very deficiencies in the power of literal representation leave room for the expression of the human spirit – its efforts to interpret the world, its feelings and beliefs in relation to it. The chapter should be read in the context of Ruskin's whole moral and spiritual concern about the history and development of painting as an honourable but compromised form of representing truth. As art moves beyond its infancy, its 'power of realization' must be seen as dependent on certain painterly conventions in order to achieve its approximations as truly as possible without disguised false-nesses. In this selection, 'Of The Use of Pictures' is introduced by means of an excerpt from 'Of the False Ideal', on the origins and development of painting, and with the aid of passages from both Modern Painters Vol. IV *(on 'Turnerian Light') and* Modern Painters vol. I *(on 'Truth of Tone' and 'Truth of Colour'), which stress the almost visibly expressive choices, compromises and sacrifices in honest representation.*

'Of the Use of Pictures' leads finally toward the celebration of 'Turnerian Mystery' to which Ruskin devotes two chapters of Modern Painters Vol. IV, *extracts from which are printed below. Drawing upon the implications of 'Of the Use of Pictures', Ruskin shows the use of Turner's painting, in particular, in volume four. Turner's pictures express the mind of a 'God-made great man', in whom there is revealed a sense of mystery intrinsic to the Creation and to the human relation with it.*

Of the Real Nature of Greatness of Style

Let us therefore look into the facts of the thing, not with any metaphysical, or otherwise vain and troublesome effort at acuteness, but in a plain way; for the facts themselves are plain enough, and may be plainly stated; only the difficulty is, that out of these facts, right and left, the different forms of misapprehension branch into grievous complexity, and branch so far and wide, that if once we try to follow them, they will lead us quite from our mark into other separate, though not less interesting discussions. The best way will be, therefore, I think, to sketch out at once in this chapter, the different characters which really constitute 'greatness' of style, and to indicate the principal directions of the outbranching misapprehensions of them; then, in the succeeding chapters, to take up in succession those which need more talk about them, and follow out at leisure whatever inquiries they may suggest.

1 CHOICE OF NOBLE SUBJECT — Greatness of style consists, then: first, in the habitual choice of subjects of thought which involve wide interests and profound passions, as opposed to those which involve narrow interests and slight passions. The style is greater or less in exact proportion to the nobleness of the interests and passions involved in the subject. The habitual choice of sacred subjects, such as the Nativity, Transfiguration, Crucifixion (if the choice be sincere), implies that the painter has a natural disposition to dwell on the highest thoughts of which humanity is capable; it constitutes him so far forth a painter of the highest order, as, for instance, Leonardo, in his painting of the Last Supper: he who delights in representing the acts or meditations of great men, as, for instance, Raphael painting the School of Athens, is, so far forth, a painter of the second order: he who represents the passions and events of ordinary life, of the third. And in this ordinary life, he who represents deep thoughts and sorrows, as, for instance, Hunt, in his Claudio and Isabella, and such other works, is of the highest rank in his sphere; and he who represents the slight malignities and passions of the drawing-room, as, for instance, Leslie, of the second rank: he who represents the sports of boys, or simplicities of clowns, as Webster or Teniers, of the third rank; and he who represents brutalities and vices (for delight in them, and not for rebuke of them), of no rank at all, or rather of a negative rank, holding a certain order in the abyss.

The reader will, I hope, understand how much importance is to be attached to the sentence in the first parenthesis, 'if the choice be sincere'; for choice of subject is, of course, only available as a criterion of the rank of the painter, when it is made from the heart. Indeed, in the lower orders of painting, the choice is always made from such a heart as the painter has; for his selection of the brawls of peasants or sports of children can, of course, proceed only from the fact that he has more sympathy with such brawls or pastimes than with nobler subjects. But the choice of the higher kind of subjects is often insincere; and may, therefore, afford no real criterion of the painter's rank. The greater number of men who have lately painted religious or heroic subjects have done so in mere ambition, because they had been taught that it was a good thing to be a 'high art' painter; and the fact is that in nine cases out of ten, the so-called historical or 'high art' painter is a person infinitely inferior to the painter of flowers or still life. He is, in modern times, nearly always a man who has great vanity without pictorial capacity, and differs from the landscape or fruit painter merely in misunderstanding and over-estimating his own powers. He mistakes his vanity for inspiration, his ambition for greatness of soul, and takes pleasure in what he calls 'the ideal,' merely because he has neither humility nor capacity enough to comprehend the real.

But also observe, it is not enough even that the choice be sincere. It must also be wise. It happens very often that a man of weak intellect, sincerely desiring to do what is good and useful, will devote himself to high art subjects because he thinks them the only ones on which time and toil can be usefully spent, or, sometimes, because they are really the only ones he has pleasure in contemplating. But not having intellect enough to enter into the minds of truly great men, or to imagine great events as they really happened, he cannot become a great painter; he degrades the subjects he intended to honour, and his work is more utterly thrown away, and his rank as an artist in reality lower, than if he had devoted himself to the imitation of the simplest objects of natural history. The works of Overbeck are a most notable instance of this form of error.

It must also be remembered, that in nearly all the great periods of art the choice of subject has not been left to the painter. His employer, – abbot, baron, or monarch, – determined for him whether he should earn his bread by making cloisters bright with choirs of saints, painting coats of arms on leaves of romances, or decorating presence-chambers with complimentary mythology; and his own personal feelings are ascertainable only by watching, in the themes assigned to him, what are the points in which he seems to take most pleasure. Thus, in the prolonged ranges of varied subjects with which Benozzo Gozzoli decorated the cloisters of Pisa, it is easy to see that love of simple domestic incident, sweet landscape, and glittering ornament, prevails slightly over the solemn elements of religious feeling which, nevertheless, the spirit of the age instilled into him in such measure as to form a very lovely and noble mind, though still one of the second order. In the work of Orcagna, an intense solemnity and energy in the sublimest groups of his figures, fading away as he touches inferior subjects, indicates that his home was among the archangels, and his rank among the first of the sons of men; while Correggio, in the sidelong grace, artificial smiles, and purple languors of his saints, indicates the inferior instinct which would have guided his choice in quite other directions, had it not been for the fashion of the age, and the need of the day.

It will follow, of course, from the above considerations that the choice which characterizes the school of high art is seen as much in the treatment of a subject as in its selection, and that the expression of the thoughts of the persons represented will always be the first thing considered by the painter who worthily enters that highest school. For the artist who sincerely chooses the noblest subject will also choose chiefly to represent what makes that subject noble, namely, the various heroism or other noble emotions of the persons represented. If, instead of this, the artist seeks only to make his picture agreeable by the composition of its masses and colours, or by any other merely pictorial merit, as fine drawing of limbs, it is evident, not only that any other subject would have answered his purpose as well, but that he is unfit to approach the subject he has chosen, because he cannot enter into its deepest meaning, and therefore cannot in reality have chosen it for that meaning. Nevertheless, while the expression is always to be the first thing considered, all other merits must be added to the utmost of the painter's power; for until he can both colour and draw beautifully he has no business to consider himself a painter at all, far less to attempt the noblest subjects of painting; and, when he has once possessed himself of these powers, he will naturally and fitly employ them to deepen and perfect the impression made by the sentiment of his subject.

The perfect unison of expression, as the painter's main purpose, with the full and natural exertion of his pictorial power in the details of the work, is found only in the old Pre-Raphaelite periods, and in the modern Pre-Raphaelite school. In the works of Giotto, Angelico, Orcagna, John Bellini, and one or two more, these two conditions of high art are entirely fulfilled, so far as the knowledge of those days enabled them to be fulfilled; and in the modern Pre-Raphaelite school they are fulfilled nearly to the uttermost. Hunt's Light of the World, is, I believe, the most perfect instance of expressional purpose with technical power, which the world has yet produced.

Now in the Post-Raphaelite period of ancient art and in the spurious high art of modern times, two broad forms of error divide the schools; the one consisting in (A) the superseding of expression by technical excellence, and the other in (B) the superseding of technical excellence by expression.

(A) Superseding expression by technical excellence. – This takes place most frankly, and therefore most innocently, in the work of the Venetians. They very nearly ignore expression altogether, directing their aim exclusively to the rendering of external truths of colour and form. Paul Veronese will make the Magdalene wash the feet of Christ with a countenance as absolutely unmoved as that of any ordinary servant bringing a ewer to her master, and will introduce the supper at Emmaus as a background to the portraits of two children playing with a dog. Of the wrongness or rightness of such a proceeding we shall reason in another place; at present we have to note it merely as displacing the Venetian work from the highest or expressional rank of art. But the error is generally made in a more subtle and dangerous way. The artist deceives himself into the idea that he is doing all he can to elevate his subject by treating it under rules of art, introducing into it accurate science, and collecting for it the beauties of (so called) ideal form; whereas he may, in reality, be all the while sacrificing his subject to his own vanity or pleasure, and losing truth, nobleness, and impressiveness for the sake of delightful lines or creditable pedantries.

(B) Superseding technical excellence by expression. – This is usually done under the influence of another kind of vanity. The artist desires that men should think he has an elevated soul, affects to despise the ordinary excellence of art, contemplates with separated egotism the course of his own imaginations or sensations, and refuses to look at the real facts round about him, in order that he may adore at leisure the shadow of himself. He lives in an element of what he calls tender emotions and lofty aspirations; which are, in fact, nothing more than very ordinary weaknesses or instincts, contemplated through a mist of pride. A large range of modern German art comes under this head.

A more interesting and respectable form of this error is fallen into by some truly earnest men, who, finding their powers not adequate to the attainment of great artistical excellence, but adequate to rendering, up to a certain point, the expression of the human countenance, devote themselves to that object alone, abandoning effort in other directions, and executing the accessories of their pictures feebly or carelessly. With these are associated another group of philosophical painters, who suppose the artistical merits of other parts *adverse* to the expression, as drawing the spectator's attention away from it, and who paint in grey colour, and imperfect light and shade, by way of enforcing the purity of their conceptions. Both these classes of conscientious but narrow-minded artists labour under the same grievous mistake of imagining that wilful fallacy can ever be either pardonable or helpful. They forget that colour, if used at all, must be either true or false, and that what *they* call chastity, dignity, and reserve is, to the eye of any person accustomed to nature, pure, bold, and impertinent falsehood. It does not in the eyes of any soundly minded man, exalt the expression of a female face that the cheeks should be painted of the colour of clay, nor does it in the least enhance his reverence for a saint to find the scenery around him deprived, by his presence, of sunshine. It is an important consolation, however, to reflect that no artist ever fell into any of these last three errors (under head B) who had really the capacity of becoming a great painter. No man ever despised colour who could produce it; and the error of these sentimentalists and philosophers is not so much in the choice of their manner of painting, as in supposing themselves capable of painting at all. Some of them might have made efficient sculptors, but the greater number had their mission in some other sphere than that of art, and would have found, in works of practical charity, better employment for their gentleness and sentimentalism, than in denying to human beauty its colour, and to natural scenery its light; in depriving heaven of its blue, and earth of its bloom, valour of its glow, and modesty of its blush.

2 LOVE OF BEAUTY — The second characteristic of the great school of art is, that it introduces in the conception of its subject as much beauty as is possible, consistently with truth.[1]

For instance, in any subject consisting of a number of figures, it will make as many of those figures beautiful as the faithful representation of humanity will admit. It will not deny the facts of ugliness or decrepitude, or relative inferiority and superiority of feature as necessarily manifested in a crowd, but it will, so far as it is in its power, seek for and dwell upon the fairest forms, and in all things insist on the beauty that is in them, not on the ugliness. In this respect, schools of art become higher in exact proportion to the degree in which they apprehend and love the beautiful. Thus, Angelico, intensely loving all spiritual beauty, will be of the highest rank; and Paul Veronese and Correggio, intensely loving physical and corporeal beauty, of the second rank; and Albert Dürer, Rubens, and in general the Northern artists, apparently insensible to beauty, and caring only for truth, whether shapely or not, of the third rank; and Teniers and Salvator, Caravaggio, and other such worshippers of the depraved, of no rank, or as we said before, of a certain order in the abyss.

The corruption of the schools of high art, so far as this particular quality is concerned, consists in the sacrifice of truth to beauty. Great art dwells on all that is beautiful; but false art omits or changes all that is ugly. Great art accepts Nature as she is, but directs the eyes and thoughts to what is most perfect in her; false art saves itself the trouble of direction by removing or altering whatever it thinks objectionable. The evil results of which proceeding are twofold.

First. That beauty deprived of its proper foils and adjuncts ceases to be enjoyed as beauty, just as light deprived of all shadow ceases to be enjoyed as light. A white canvas cannot produce an effect of sunshine; the painter must darken it in some places before he can make it look luminous in others; nor can an uninterrupted succession of beauty produce the true effect of beauty; it must be foiled by inferiority before its own power can be developed. Nature has for the most part mingled her inferior and noble elements as she mingles sunshine with shade, giving due use and influence to both, and the painter who chooses to remove the shadow, perishes in the burning desert he has created. The truly high and beautiful art of Angelico is continually refreshed and strengthened by his frank portraiture of the most ordinary features of his brother monks and of the recorded peculiarities of ungainly sanctity; but the modern German and Raphaelesque schools lose all honour and nobleness in barber-like admiration of handsome faces, and have, in fact, no real faith except in straight noses, and curled hair. Paul Veronese opposes the dwarf to the soldier, and the negress to the queen; Shakspeare places Caliban beside Miranda, and Autolycus beside Perdita; but the vulgar idealist withdraws his beauty to the safety of the saloon, and his innocence to the seclusion of the cloister; he pretends that he does this in delicacy of choice and purity of sentiment, while in truth he has neither courage to front the monster, nor wit enough to furnish the knave.

It is only by the habit of representing faithfully all things, that we can truly learn what is beautiful, and what is not. The ugliest objects contain some element of beauty; and in all it is an element peculiar to themselves, which cannot be separated from their ugliness, but must either be enjoyed together with it or not at all. The more a painter accepts nature as he finds it, the more unexpected beauty he discovers in what he at first despised; but once let him arrogate the right of rejection, and he will gradually contract his circle of enjoyment, until what he supposed to be nobleness of selection ends in narrowness of perception. Dwelling perpetually upon one class of ideas, his art becomes at once monstrous and morbid; until at last he cannot faithfully represent even what he chooses to retain; his discrimination contracts into darkness, and his fastidiousness fades into fatuity.

High art, therefore, consists neither in altering, nor in improving nature; but in seeking throughout nature for 'whatsoever things are lovely, and whatsoever things are pure' [Philippians iv.8]; in loving these, in displaying to the utmost of the painter's power such loveliness as is in them, and directing the thoughts of others to them by winning art or gentle emphasis. Of the degree in which this can be done, and in which it may be permitted to gather together, without falsifying, the finest forms or thoughts, so as to create a sort of perfect vision, we shall have to speak hereafter: at present, it is enough to remember that art (*cæteris paribus*) is great in exact proportion to the love of beauty shown by the painter, provided that love of beauty forfeit no atom of truth.

3 SINCERITY – The next characteristic of great art is that it includes the largest possible quantity of Truth in the most perfect possible harmony. If it were possible for art to give all the truths of nature it ought to do it. But this is not possible. Choice must always be made of some facts which *can* be represented, from among others which must be passed by in silence, or even, in some respects, misrepresented. The inferior artist chooses unimportant and scattered truths; the great artist chooses the most necessary first, and afterwards the most consistent with these, so as to obtain the greatest possible and most harmonious *sum*. For

instance, Rembrandt always chooses to represent the exact force with which the light on the most illumined part of an object is opposed to its obscurer portions. In order to obtain this, in most cases, not very important truth, he sacrifices the light and colour of five-sixths of his picture, and the expression of every character of objects which depends on tenderness of shape or tint. But he obtains his single truth, and what picturesque and forcible expression is dependent upon it, with magnificent skill and subtlety. Veronese, on the contrary, chooses to represent the great relations of visible things to each other, to the heaven above, and to the earth beneath them. He holds it more important to show how a figure stands relieved from delicate air, or marble wall; how as a red, or purple, or white figure, it separates itself, in clear discernibility, from things not red, nor purple, nor white; how infinite daylight shines round it; how innumerable veils of faint shadow invest it; how its blackness and darkness are, in the excess of their nature, just as limited and local as its intensity of light; all this, I say, he feels to be more important than showing merely the exact *measure* of the spark of sunshine that gleams on a dagger-hilt, or glows on a jewel. All this, moreover, he feels to be harmonious, – capable of being joined in one great system of spacious truth. And with inevitable watchfulness, inestimable subtlety, he unites all this in tenderest balance, noting in each hair's-breadth of colour, not merely what its rightness or wrongness is in itself, but what its relation is to every other on his canvas; restraining, for truth's sake, his exhaustless energy, reining back, for truth's sake, his fiery strength: veiling, before truth, the vanity of brightness; penetrating, for truth, the discouragement of gloom; ruling his restless invention with a rod of iron; pardoning no error, no thoughtlessness, no forgetfulness; and subduing all his powers, impulses, and imaginations, to the arbitrament of a merciless justice, and the obedience of an incorruptible verity.

I give this instance with respect to colour and shade: but, in the whole field of art, the difference between the great and inferior artists is of the same kind, and may be determined at once by the question, which of them conveys the largest sum of truth?

It follows from this principle, that in general all *great* drawing is *distinct* drawing; for truths which are rendered indistinctly might, for the most part, as well not be rendered at all. There are, indeed, certain facts of mystery, and facts of indistinctness, in all objects, which must have their proper place in the general harmony, and the reader will presently find me, when we come to that part of our investigation, telling him that all good drawing must in some sort be *in*distinct. We may, however, understand this apparent contradiction, by reflecting that the highest knowledge always involves a more advanced perception of the fields of the unknown; and, therefore, it may most truly be said, that to know anything well involves a profound sensation of ignorance, while yet it is equally true that good and noble knowledge is distinguished from vain and useless knowledge chiefly by its clearness and distinctness, and by the vigorous consciousness of what is known and what is not.

So in art. The best drawing involves a wonderful perception and expression of indistinctness; and yet all noble drawing is separated from the ignoble by its distinctness, by its fine expression and firm assertion of *Something;* whereas the bad drawing, without either firmness or fineness, expresses and asserts *Nothing.* The first thing, therefore, to be looked for as a sign of noble art, is a clear consciousness of what is drawn and what is not; the bold statement and frank confession — '*This* I know,' '*that* I know not'; and, generally speaking, all haste, slurring, obscurity, indecision, are signs of low art, and all calmness, distinctness, luminousness, and positiveness, of high art.

It follows, secondly, from this principle, that as the great painter is always attending to the sum and harmony of his truths rather than to one or the other of any group, a quality of Grasp is visible in his work, like the power of a great reasoner over his subject, or a great poet over his conception, manifesting itself very often in missing out certain details or less truths (which, though good in themselves, he finds are in the way of others), and in a sweeping manner of getting the beginnings and ends of things shown at once, and the squares and depths rather than the surfaces: hence, on the whole, a habit of looking at large masses rather than small ones; and even a physical largeness of handling, and love of working, if possible, on a large scale; and various other qualities, more or less imperfectly expressed by such technical terms as breadth, massing, unity, boldness, etc., all of which are, indeed, great qualities, when they mean breadth of truth, weight of truth, unity of truth, and courageous assertion of truth; but which have all their correlative errors and mockeries, almost universally mistaken for them, — the breadth which has no contents, the weight which has no value, the unity which plots deception, and the boldness which faces out fallacy.

And it is to be noted especially respecting largeness of scale, that though for the most part it is characteristic of the more powerful masters, they having both more invention wherewith to fill space (as Ghirlandajo wished that he might paint all the walls of Florence), and, often, an impetuosity of mind which makes them like free play for hand and arm (besides that they usually desire to paint everything in the foreground of their picture of the natural size), yet, as this largeness of scale involves the placing of the picture at a considerable distance from the eye, and this distance involves the loss of many delicate details, and especially of the subtle lines of expression in features, it follows that the masters of refined detail and human expression are apt to prefer a small scale to work upon; so that the chief masterpieces of expression which the world possesses are small pictures by Angelico, in which the figures are rarely more than six or seven inches high; in the best works of Raphael and Leonardo the figures are almost always less than life, and the best works of Turner do not exceed the size of 18 inches by 12.

As its greatness depends on the sum of truth, and this sum of truth can always be increased by delicacy of handling, it follows that all great art must have this delicacy to the utmost possible degree. This rule is infallible and inflexible. All coarse work is the sign of low art. Only, it is to be remembered, that coarseness must be estimated by the distance from the eye; it being necessary to consult this distance, when great, by laying on touches which appear coarse when seen near; but which, so far from being coarse, are, in reality, more delicate in a master's work than the finest close handling, for they involve a calculation of result, and are laid on with a subtlety of sense precisely correspondent to that with which a good archer draws his bow; the spectator seeing in the action nothing but the strain of the strong arm, while there is in reality, in the finger and eye, an ineffably delicate estimate of distance, and touch on the arrow plume. And, indeed, this delicacy is generally quite perceptible to those who know what the truth is, for strokes by Tintoret or Paul Veronese, which were done in an instant, and look to an ignorant spectator merely like a violent dash of loaded colour (and are, as such, imitated by blundering artists), are, in fact, modulated by the brush and finger to that degree of delicacy that no single grain of the colour could be taken from the touch without injury; and little golden particles of it, not the size of a gnat's head, have important share and function in the balances of light in a picture perhaps fifty feet long. Nearly *every* other rule applicable to art has some exception but this. This has absolutely none. All great art is delicate art, and all coarse art is bad art. Nay, even, to a certain extent, all *bold* art is bad art; for boldness is not the proper word to apply to the courage and swiftness of a great master, based on knowledge, and coupled with fear and love. There is as much difference between the boldness of the true and the false masters, as there is between the courage of a sure woman and the shamelessness of a lost one.

4 INVENTION – The last characteristic of great art is that it must be inventive, that is, be produced by the imagination. In this respect, it must precisely fulfil the definition . . . of poetry; and not only present grounds for noble emotion, but furnish these grounds by *imaginative power*. Hence there is at once a great bar fixed between the two schools of Lower and Higher art. The lower merely copies what is set before it, whether in portrait, landscape, or still-life; the higher either entirely imagines its subject, or arranges the materials presented to it, so as to manifest the imaginative power in all the three phases which have been already explained in the second volume.[2]

And this was the truth which was confusedly present in Reynolds's mind when he spoke . . . of the difference between Historical and Poetical Painting. *Every relation of the plain facts which the painter saw* is proper *historical* painting. If those facts are unimportant (as that he saw a gambler quarrel with another gambler, or a sot enjoying himself with another sot), then the history is trivial; if the facts are important (as that he saw such and such a great man look thus, or act thus, at such a time), then the history is noble: in each case perfect truth of narrative being supposed, otherwise the whole thing is worthless, being neither history nor poetry, but plain falsehood. And farther, as greater or less elegance and precision are manifested in the relation or painting of the incidents, the merit of the work varies; so that, what with difference of subject, and what with difference of treatment, historical painting falls or rises in changeful eminence, from Dutch trivialities to a Velasquez portrait, just as historical talking or writing varies in eminence, from an old woman's story-telling up to Herodotus. Besides which, certain operations of the imagination come into play inevitably, here and there, so as to touch the history with some light of poetry, that is, with some light shot forth of the narrator's mind, or brought out by the way he has put the accidents together: and wherever the imagination has thus had anything to do with the matter at all (and it must be somewhat cold work where it has not), then, the confines of the lower and higher schools touching each other, the work is coloured by both; but there is no reason why, therefore, we should in the least confuse the historical and poetical characters, any more than that we should confuse blue with crimson, because they may overlap each other, and produce purple.

Now, historical or simply narrative art is very precious in its proper place and way, but it is never *great* art until the poetical or imaginative power touches it; and in proportion to the stronger manifestation of this power, it becomes greater and greater, while the highest art is purely imaginative, all its materials being wrought into their form by invention; and it differs, therefore, from the simple historical painting, exactly as Wordsworth's stanza, above quoted,[3] differs from Saussure's plain narrative of the parallel fact; and the imaginative painter differs from the historical painter in the manner that Wordsworth differs from Saussure.

Farther, imaginative art always *includes* historical art; so that, strictly speaking, according to the analogy above used, we meet with the pure blue, and with the crimson ruling the blue and changing it into kingly purple, but not with the pure crimson: for all imagination must deal with the knowledge it has before accumulated; it never produces anything but by combination or contemplation. Creation, in the full sense, is impossible to it. And the mode in which the historical faculties are included by it is often quite simple, and easily seen. Thus, in Hunt's great poetical picture of the Light of the World, the whole thought and arrangement of the picture being imaginative, the several details of it are wrought out with simple portraiture; the ivy, the jewels, the creeping plants, and the moonlight being calmly studied or remembered from the things themselves. But of all these special ways in which the invention works with plain facts, we shall have to treat farther afterwards.

And now, finally, since this poetical power includes the historical, if we glance back to the other qualities required in great art, and put all together, we find that the sum of them is simply the sum of all the powers of man. For as (1) the choice of the high subject involves all conditions of right moral choice, and as (2) the love of beauty involves all conditions of right admiration, and as (3) the grasp of truth involves all strength of sense, evenness of judgment, and honesty of purpose, and as (4) the poetical power involves all swiftness of invention, and accuracy of historical memory, the sum of all these powers is the sum of the human soul. Hence we see why the word 'Great' is used of this art. It is literally great. It compasses and calls forth the entire human spirit, whereas any other kind of art, being more or less small or narrow, compasses and calls forth only *part* of the human spirit. Hence the idea of its magnitude is a literal and just one, the art being simply less or greater in proportion to the number of faculties it exercises and addresses. And this is the ultimate meaning of the definition I gave of it long ago, as containing the 'greatest number of the greatest ideas'.

Such, then, being the characters required in order to constitute high art, if the reader will think over them a little, and over the various ways in which they may be falsely assumed, he will easily perceive how spacious and dangerous a field of discussion they open to the ambitious critic, and of error to the ambitious artist; he will see how difficult it must be, either to distinguish what is truly great art from the mockeries of it, or to rank the real artists in anything like a progressive system of greater and less. For it will have been observed that the various qualities which form greatness are partly inconsistent with each other (as some virtues are, docility and firmness for instance), and partly independent of each other; and the fact is, that artists differ not more by mere capacity, than by the component *elements* of their capacity, each possessing in very different proportions the several attributes of greatness; so that, classed by one kind of merit, as, for instance, purity of expression, Angelico will stand highest; classed by another, sincerity of manner, Veronese will stand highest; classed by another, love of beauty, Leonardo will stand highest; and so on: hence arise continual disputes and misunderstandings among those who think that high art must always be one and the same, and that great artists ought to unite all great attributes in an equal degree . . .

The greatness or smallness of a man is, in the most conclusive sense, determined for him at his birth . . . Education, favourable circumstances, resolution, and industry can do much; in a certain sense they do *everything* . . . But great man out of small, did never yet art or effort make; and, in a general way, men have their excellence nearly fixed for them when they are born . . .[a]

Therefore it is, that every system of teaching is false which holds forth 'great art' as in any wise to be taught to students, or even to be aimed at by them. Great art is precisely that which never was, nor will be taught, it is pre-eminently and finally the expression of the spirits of great men[b], so that the only wholesome teaching is that which simply endeavours to fix those characters of nobleness in the pupil's mind, of which it seems easily susceptible; and without holding out to him, as a possible or even probable result, that he should ever paint like Titian, or carve like Michael Angelo, enforces upon him the manifest possibility, and assured duty, of endeavouring to draw in a manner at least honest and intelligible; and cultivates in him those general charities of heart, sincerities of thought, and graces of habit which are likely to lead him, throughout life, to prefer openness to affectation, realities to shadows, and beauty to corruption. (MP III, Pt. IV, Ch. III, paras. 4–25, 27–8)

[a] *On predestination of function see MP IV, Pt. V, Ch. II, para. 4:*
Nor let it be supposed that artists who possess minor degrees of imaginative gift need be embarrassed by the doubtful sense of their own powers. In general, when the imagination is at all noble, it is irresistible, and therefore those who can at all resist it *ought* to resist it. Be a plain topographer if you possibly can; if Nature meant you to be anything else, she will force you to it; but never try to be a prophet; go on quietly with your hard camp-work, and the spirit will come to you in the camp, as it did to Eldad and Medad [Numbers xi. 26–7], if you are appointed to have it; but try above all things to be quickly perceptive of the noble spirit in others, and to discern in an instant between its true utterance and the diseased mimicries of it. In a general way, remember it is a far better thing to find out other great men, than to become one yourself: for you can but become *one* at best, but you may bring others to light in numbers.

[b] *It is characteristic of Ruskin to seek the largest, most generous definition, refusing to hamper human power – compare his liberatingly inclusive account of the sublime:*
The fact is, that sublimity is not a specific term, – not a term descriptive of the effect of a particular class of ideas. Anything which elevates the mind is sublime, and elevation of mind is produced by the contemplation of greatness of any kind; but chiefly, of course, by the greatness of the noblest things. Sublimity is, therefore, only another word for the effect of greatness upon the feelings; – greatness, whether of matter, space, power, virtue, or beauty: and there is perhaps no desirable quality of a work of art, which, in its perfection, is not, in some way or degree, sublime. (MP I, Pt. I, Sec. II, Ch. III, para. 1)

Addendum:
On Finish

While qualification and explanation both weaken the force of what is said, and are not always likely to be with patience received; so also those who desire to misunderstand or to oppose have it always in their power to become obtuse listeners, or specious opponents. Thus I hardly dare insist upon the virtue of completion, lest I should be supposed a defender of Wouvermans or Gerard Dow; neither can I adequately praise the power of Tintoret, without fearing to be thought adverse to Holbein or Perugino. The fact is, that both finish and impetuosity, specific minuteness and large abstraction, may be the signs of passion, or of its reverse; may result from affection or indifference, intellect or dulness. Some men finish from intense love of the beautiful in the smallest parts of what they do; others in pure incapability of comprehending anything but parts; others to show their dexterity with the brush, and prove expenditure of time. Some are impetuous and bold in their handling, from having great thoughts to express which are independent of detail; others because they have bad taste or have been badly taught; others from vanity, and others from indolence. Now both the finish and incompletion are right where they are the signs of passion or of thought, and both are wrong, and I think the finish the more contemptible of the two, when they cease to be so. The modern Italians will paint every leaf of a laurel or rosebush, without the slightest feeling of their beauty or character; and without showing one spark of intellect or affection from beginning to end. Anything is better than this; and yet the very highest schools *do* the same thing, or nearly so, but with totally different motives and perceptions, and the result is divine. On the whole, I conceive that the extremes of good and evil lie with the finishers, and that whatever glorious power we may admit in men like Tintoret, whatever attractive-ness of method in Rubens, Rembrandt, or, though in far less degree, our own Reynolds, still the thoroughly great men are those who have done everything thoroughly, and who, in a word, have never despised anything, however small, of God's making. And this is the chief fault of our English landscapists, that they have not the intense all-observing penetration of well-balanced mind; they have not, except in one or two instances, anything of that feeling which Wordsworth shows in the following lines:—

So fair, so sweet, withal so sensitive;—
Would that the little flowers were born to live
Conscious of half the pleasure which they give.
That to this mountain daisy's self were known
The beauty of its star-shaped shadow, thrown
On the smooth surface of this naked stone.

That is a little bit of good, downright, foreground painting – no mistake about it; daisy, and shadow, and stone texture and all. Our painters must come to this before they have done their duty; and yet, on the other hand, let them beware of finishing, for the sake of finish, all over their picture. The ground is not to be all over daisies, nor is every daisy to have its star-shaped shadow; there is as much finish in the right concealment of things as in the right exhibition of them; and while I demand this amount of specific character where nature shows it, I demand equal fidelity to her where she conceals it. To paint mist rightly, space rightly, and light rightly, it may be often necessary to paint nothing else rightly, but the rule is simple for all that; if the artist is painting something that he knows and loves, as he knows it, because he loves it, whether it be the fair strawberry of Cima, or the clear sky of Francia, or the blazing incomprehensible mist of Turner, he is all right; but the moment he does anything as he thinks it ought to be, because he does not care about it, he is all wrong. He has only to ask himself whether he cares for anything except himself; so far as he does he will make a good picture; so far as he thinks of himself, a vile one.[c] (MP I, Pt. II, Sec. I, Ch. VII, para. 10)

[c]   *A footnote to* Modern Painters *vol. V goes thus, with additions from* Modern Painters *vol. III as suggested therein, marked in square brackets*

I do not wonder at people sometimes thinking I contradict myself when they come suddenly on any of the scattered passages, in which I am forced to insist on the opposite practical applications of subtle principles of this kind. It may amuse the reader, and be finally serviceable to him in showing him how necessary it is to the right handling of any subject, that these contrary statements should be made, if I assemble here the principal ones I remember having brought forward, bearing on this difficult point of precision in execution.

It would be well if you would first glance over the chapter on Finish in the third volume . . .

Viz:

[I propose therefore, in the present chapter, to examine as thoroughly as I can, the real signification of this word, Finish, as applied to art, and to see if in this, as in other matters, our almost tiresome test is not the right one: whether there be a *fallacious* finish and a *faithful* finish . . . In England, we seem at present to value highly the first sort of finish which belongs to work*manship*, in our manufactures and general doings of any kind, but to despise totally the impressive finish which belongs to work; and therefore we like smooth ivories better than rough ones, – but careless scrawls or daubs better than the most complete paintings. Now, I believe that we exactly reverse the fitness of judgment in this matter, and that we ought, on the contrary, to despise the finish of work*manship*, which is done for vanity's sake, and to love the finish of work, which is done for truth's sake, – that we ought, in a word, to finish our ivory toys more roughly, and our pictures more delicately . . .

In nearly all work this distinction will, more or less, take place between substantial finish and apparent finish, or what may be briefly characterized as 'Make' and 'Polish' . . . God alone can finish; and the more intelligent the human mind becomes, the more the infiniteness of interval is felt between human and divine work in this respect . . . I do not say that stone must not be cut; it needs to be cut for certain uses; only I say that the cutting is not 'finishing', but *un*finishing, it; and that so far as the mere fact of chiselling goes, the stone is ruined by the human touch. It is with it as with the stones of the Jewish altar; 'If thou lift up thy tool upon it, thou hast polluted it' [Exodus xx.25] . . .

[True] finish does not consist in smoothing or polishing, but in the *completeness of the expression of ideas*. And this sort of finish is not, properly speaking, so much *completing* the picture as *adding* to it. It is not that what is painted is more delicately done, but that infinitely more is painted . . .

All true finish is *added fact*; and Turner's word for finishing a picture was always this significant one, 'carry forward' . . . Take Leonardo, Michael Angelo, and Raphael for a triad, to begin with. *They* all completed their detail with such subtlety of touch and gradation, that, in a careful drawing by any of the three, you cannot see where the pencil ceased to touch the paper, the stroke of it is so tender . . .

Who shall gainsay these men? Above all, who shall gainsay them when they and Nature say precisely the same thing? for where does Nature pause in *her* finishing – that finishing which consists not in the smoothing of surface, but the filling of space, and the multiplication of life and thought?]

(MP III, Pt. IV, Ch. IX, paras. 2–3, 5–7, 15, 18)

[Everything imperfectly realised (as, for instance, by a mere outline of a tree) necessarily makes us think not only of the thing itself, but of the sort of stroke or mark which represents it. If art were perfect, so that it could not be distinguished from the reality, of course the idea of merit in execution would have no place in our minds; the picture would either deceive and be right, or not deceive and be wrong. But, imitation being necessarily imperfect, we habitually regard these means, by which it is effected, according to their success, and take pleasure in examining and inquiring into them. To do as

much as possible with small means, and other such excellence, becomes therefore an ideal aim with respect to execution.]
(Manuscript draft for opening of chapter, C&W V, p. 149)

The general conclusion reached in that chapter being that finish, for the sake of added truth, or utility, or beauty, is noble; but finish, for the sake of workmanship, neatness, or polish, ignoble, – turn to the fourth chapter of the *Seven Lamps*, where you will find the Campanile of Giotto given as the model and mirror of perfect architecture, just on account of its exquisite completion. Also, in the next chapter, I expressly limit the delightfulness of rough and imperfect work to developing and unformed schools; then turn to the [sixth chapter] of the *Stones of Venice*, Vol. II., and you will find this directly contrary statement:–

'No good work whatever can be perfect, and the demand for perfection is always a sign of a misunderstanding of the ends of art.' . . . 'The first cause of the fall of the arts in Europe was a relentless requirement of perfection'. By reading the intermediate text, you will be put in possession of many good reasons for this opinion; and, comparing it with that just cited about the Campanile of Giotto, will be brought, I hope, into a wholesome state of not knowing what to think.

Then turn to where the great law of finish is again maintained as strongly as ever: 'Delicate finish (finish – that is to say, up to the point possible) is always desirable from the greatest masters, and is always given by them.'

And lastly, if you look to the chapter on the Early Renaissance, Vol. III., you will find the profoundest respect paid to completion; and, at the close of that chapter, the principle is resumed very strongly. '*As ideals of executive perfection*, these palaces are most notable among the architecture of Europe, and the Rio façade of the Ducal palace, as an example of finished masonry in a vast building, is one of the finest things, not only in Venice, but in the world.'

Now all these passages are perfectly true; and, as in much more serious matters, the essential thing for the reader is to receive their truth, however little he may be able to see their consistency. If truths of apparently contrary character are candidly and rightly received, they will fit themselves together in the mind without any trouble. But no truth maliciously received will nourish you, or fit with others. The clue of connection may in this case, however, be given in a word. Absolute finish is always right; finish, inconsistent with prudence and passion, wrong. The imperative demand for finish is ruinous, because it refuses better things than finish. The stopping short of the finish, which is honourably possible to human energy, is destructive on the other side, and not in less degree. Err, of the two, on the side of completion. (MP V, Pt. IX, Ch. V, footnote to para. 22 [C&W VII, pp. 358–60])

*   *   *

Towards 'The Use of Pictures': early religious representation and the development of 'The False Ideal'

The imagination is chiefly warped and dishonoured by being allowed to create false images, where it is its duty to create true ones. And this most dangerously in matters of religion. For a long time when art was in its infancy, it remained unexposed to this danger, because it could not, with any power, realize or create *any* thing. It consisted merely in simple outlines and pleasant colours, which were understood to be nothing more than signs of the thing thought of, a sort of pictorial letter for it, no more pretending to represent it than the written characters of its name. Such art excited the imagination, while it pleased the eye. But it *asserted* nothing, for it could realize nothing. The reader glanced at it as a glittering symbol, and went on to form truer images for himself. This act of the mind may be still seen in daily operation in children, as they look at brightly coloured pictures in their story-books. Such pictures neither deceive them nor satisfy them; they only set their own inventive powers to work in the directions required.

But as soon as art obtained the power of realization, it obtained also that of *assertion*. As fast as the painter advanced in skill he gained also in credibility, and that which he perfectly represented was perfectly believed, or could be disbelieved only by an actual effort of the beholder to escape from the fascinating deception. What had been faintly declared, might be painlessly denied; but it was difficult to discredit things forcibly alleged; and representations, which had been innocent in discrepancy, became guilty in consistency.

For instance, when in the thirteenth century, the Nativity was habitually represented by such a symbol as that on this page, Plate 12, there was not the smallest possibility that such a picture could disturb, in the mind of the reader of the New Testament, the simple meaning of the words 'wrapped Him in swaddling clothes, and laid Him in a manger' [Luke ii. 7]. That this manger was typified by a trefoil arch would no more prevent his distinct understanding of the narrative, than the grotesque heads introduced above it would interfere with his firm comprehension of the words 'ox' or 'ass'; while if there were anything in the action of the principal figures suggestive of real feeling, that suggestion he

Plate 12 *Nativity*

would accept, together with the general pleasantness of the lines
and colours in the decorative letter; but without having his faith in
the unrepresented and actual scene obscured for a moment. But it
was far otherwise when Francia or Perugino, with exquisite
power of representing the human form, and high knowledge of
the mysteries of art, devoted all their skill to the delineation of an
impossible scene; and painted, for their subjects of the Nativity, a
beautiful and queenly lady, her dress embroidered with gold, and
with a crown of jewels upon her hair, kneeling, on a floor of inlaid
and precious marble, before a crowned child, laid under a portico
of Lombardic architecture,[4] with a sweet, verdurous, and vivid
landscape in the distance, full of winding rivers, village spires, and
baronial towers. It is quite true that the frank absurdity of the
thought prevented its being received as a deliberate contradiction
of the truths of Scripture; but it is no less certain, that the
continual presentment to the mind of this beautiful and fully
realized imagery more and more chilled its power of apprehend-
ing the real truth; and that when pictures of this description met
the eye in every corner of every chapel, it was physically
impossible to dwell distinctly upon facts the direct reverse of those
represented. The word 'Virgin' or 'Madonna', instead of calling
up the vision of a simple Jewish girl, bearing the calamities of
poverty, and the dishonours of inferior station, summoned
instantly the idea of a graceful princess, crowned with gems, and
surrounded by obsequious ministry of kings and saints. The
fallacy which was presented to the imagination was indeed
discredited, but also the fact which was *not* presented to the
imagination was forgotten; all true grounds of faith were
gradually undermined, and the beholder was either enticed into
mere luxury of fanciful enjoyment, believing nothing; or left, in
his confusion of mind, the prey of vain tales and traditions; while
in his best feelings he was unconsciously subject to the power of
the fallacious picture, and, with no sense of the real cause of his
error, bowed himself, in prayer or adoration, to the lovely lady on
her golden throne, when he would never have dreamed of doing
so to the Jewish girl in her outcast poverty, or, in her simple
household, to the carpenter's wife.

But a shadow of increasing darkness fell upon the human mind
as art proceeded to still more perfect realization. These fantasies
of the earlier painters, though they darkened faith, never
hardened *feeling*; on the contrary, the frankness of their

unlikelihood proceeded mainly from the endeavour on the part of the painter to express, not the actual fact, but the enthusiastic state of his own feelings about the fact; he covers the Virgin's dress with gold, not with any idea of representing the Virgin as she ever was, or ever will be seen, but with a burning desire to show what his love and reverence would think fittest for her. He erects for the stable a Lombardic portico, not because he supposes the Lombardi to have built stables in Palestine in the days of Tiberius, but to show that the manger in which Christ was laid is, in his eyes, nobler than the greatest architecture in the world. He fills his landscape with church spires and silver streams, not because he supposes that either were in sight at Bethlehem, but to remind the beholder of the peaceful course and succeeding power of Christianity. And, regarded with due sympathy and clear understanding of these thoughts of the artist, such pictures remain most impressive and touching, even to this day. I shall refer to them in future, in general terms, as the pictures of the 'Angelican Ideal' – Angelico being the central master of the school.

It was far otherwise in the next step of the Realistic progress. The greater his powers became, the more the mind of the painter was absorbed in their attainment, and complacent in their display. The early arts of laying on bright colours smoothly, of burnishing golden ornaments, or tracing, leaf by leaf, the outlines of flowers, were not so difficult as that they should materially occupy the thoughts of the artist, or furnish foundation for his conceit; he learned these rudiments of his work without pain, and employed them without pride, his spirit being left free to express, so far as it was capable of them, the reaches of higher thought. But when accurate shade, and subtle colour, and perfect anatomy, and complicated perspective, became necessary to the work, the artist's whole energy was employed in learning the laws of these, and his whole pleasure consisted in exhibiting them. His life was devoted, not to the objects of art, but to the cunning of it; and the sciences of composition and light and shade were pursued as if there were abstract good in them; – as if, like astronomy or mathematics, they were ends in themselves, irrespective of anything to be effected by them. And without perception, on the part of any one, of the abyss to which all were hastening, a fatal change of aim took place throughout the whole world of art. In early times *art was employed for the display of religious facts*; now, *religious facts were employed for the display of art*. The transition, though imperceptible, was consummate; it involved the entire destiny of painting. It was passing from the paths of life to the paths of death.

And this change was all the more fatal, because at first veiled by an appearance of greater dignity and sincerity than were possessed by the older art . . .

I suppose there is no event in the whole life of Christ to which, in hours of doubt or fear, men turn with more anxious thirst to know the close facts of it, or with more earnest and passionate dwelling upon every syllable of its recorded narrative, than Christ's showing Himself to His disciples at the lake of Galilee. There is something pre-eminently open, natural, full fronting our disbelief, in this manifestation. The others, recorded after the resurrection, were sudden, phantom-like, occurring to men in profound sorrow and wearied agitation of heart; not, it might seem, safe judges of what they saw. But the agitation was now over. They had gone back to their daily work, thinking still their business lay net-wards, unmeshed from the literal rope and drag. 'Simon Peter saith unto them, "I go a fishing." They say unto him, "We also go with thee." ' True words enough, and having far echo beyond those Galilean hills. That night they caught nothing; but when the morning came, in the clear light of it, behold, a figure stood on the shore. They were not thinking of anything but their fruitless hauls. They had no guess who it was. It asked them simply if they had caught anything. They said No; and it tells them to cast yet again. And John shades his eyes from the morning sun with his hand, to look who it is; and though the glinting of the sea, too, dazzles him, he makes out who it is, at last; and poor Simon, not to be outrun this time, tightens his fisher's coat about him, and dashes in, over the nets. One would have liked to see him swim those hundred yards, and stagger to his knees on the beach.

Well, the others get to the beach, too, in time, in such slow way as men in general do get, in this world, to its true shore, much impeded by that wonderful 'dragging the net with fishes'; but they get there – seven of them in all; – first the Denier, and then the slowest believer, and then the quickest believer, and then the two throne-seekers, and two more, we know not who.

They sit down on the shore face to face with Him and eat their broiled fish as He bids. And then, to Peter, all dripping still, shivering and amazed, staring at Christ in the sun, on the other side of the coal fire, – thinking a little, perhaps, of what happened by another coal fire, when it was colder, and having had no word once changed with him by his Master since that look of His, – to him, so amazed, comes the question, 'Simon, lovest thou Me?' Try to feel that a little, and think of it till it is true to you; and then, take up that infinite monstrosity and hypocrisy – Raphael's cartoon of the Charge to Peter [Plate 13]. Note, first, the bold fallacy – the putting *all* the Apostles there, a mere lie to serve the Papal heresy of the Petric supremacy, by putting them all in the background while Peter receives the charge, and making them all witnesses to it. Note the handsomely curled hair and neatly tied sandals of the men who had been out all night in the sea-mists and on the slimy decks. Note their convenient dresses for going a-fishing, with trains that lie a yard along the ground, and goodly fringes, – all made to match, an apostolic fishing costume. Note how Peter especially (whose chief glory was in his wet coat *girt* about him, and naked limbs) is enveloped in folds and fringes, so as to kneel and hold his keys with grace. No fire of coals at all, nor lonely mountain shore, but a pleasant Italian landscape, full of villas and churches, and a flock of sheep to be pointed at; and the whole group of Apostles, not round Christ, as they would have been naturally, but straggling away in a line, that they may all be shown.

The simple truth is, that the moment we look at the picture we feel our belief of the whole thing taken away. There is, visibly, no possibility of that group ever having existed, in any place, or on any occasion. It is all a mere mythic absurdity, and faded concoction of fringes, muscular arms, and curly heads of Greek philosophers.

Now, the evil consequences of the acceptance of this kind of religious idealism for true, were instant and manifold. So far as it was received and trusted in by thoughtful persons, it only served to chill all the conceptions of sacred history which they might otherwise have obtained. Whatever they could have fancied for themselves about the wild, strange, infinitely stern, infinitely tender, infinitely varied veracities of the life of Christ, was blotted out by the vapid fineries of Raphael: the rough Galilean pilot, the orderly custom receiver, and all the questioning wonder and fire of uneducated apostleship, were obscured under an antique mask of philosophical faces and long robes. The feeble, subtle, suffering, ceaseless energy and humiliation of St Paul were confused with an idea of a meditative Hercules leaning on a sweeping

Plate 13 *Christ's Charge to St Peter*

sword; and the mighty presences of Moses and Elias were softened by introductions of delicate grace, adopted from dancing nymphs and rising Auroras.

Now, no vigorously minded religious person could possibly receive pleasure or help from such art as this; and the necessary result was the instant rejection of it by the healthy religion of the world. Raphael ministered, with applause, to the impious luxury of the Vatican, but was trampled under foot at once by every believing and advancing Christian of his own and subsequent times; and thenceforward pure Christianity and 'high art' took separate roads, and fared on, as best they might, independently of each other.

But although Calvin, and Knox, and Luther, and their flocks, with all the hardest-headed and truest-hearted faithful left in Christendom, thus spurned away the spurious art, and all art with it, (not without harm to themselves, such as a man must needs sustain in cutting off a decayed limb,) certain conditions of weaker Christianity suffered the false system to retain influence over them; and to this day, the clear and tasteless poison of the art of Raphael infects with sleep of infidelity the hearts of millions of Christians. It is the first cause of all that pre-eminent *dulness* which characterises what Protestants call sacred art; a dulness not merely baneful in making religion distasteful to the young, but in sickening, as we have seen, all vital belief of religion in the old. A dim sense of impossibility attaches itself always to the graceful emptiness of the representation; we feel instinctively that the painted Christ and painted apostle are not beings that ever did or could exist; and this fatal sense of fair fabulousness, and well-composed impossibility, steals gradually from the picture into the history, until we find ourselves reading St Mark or St Luke with the same admiring, but uninterested, incredulity, with which we contemplate Raphael. (MP III, Pt. IV, Ch. IV, paras. 7–12, 16–18)

Representation: Of Turnerian Light

Make the sky calm and luminous, and raise against it dark trees, mountains, or towers, or any other substantial and terrestrial thing, in bold outline, and the mind accepts the assertion of this great and solemn truth with thankfulness.

But this may be done either nobly or basely, as any other solemn truth may be asserted. It may be spoken with true feeling of all that it means; or it may be declared, as a Turk declares that 'God is great,' when he means only that he himself is lazy. The 'heaven is bright', of many vulgar painters, has precisely the same amount of signification; it means that they know nothing, – will do nothing, are without thought – without care – without passion. They will not walk the earth, nor watch the ways of it, nor gather the flowers of it. They will sit in the shade, and only assert that very perceptible, long-ascertained fact, 'heaven is bright'. And as it may be *asserted* basely, so it may be *accepted* basely. Many of our capacities for receiving noblest emotion are abused, in mere idleness, for pleasure's sake, and people take the excitement of a solemn sensation as they do that of a strong drink. Thus the abandoned court of Louis xiv had on fast days its sacred concerts, doubtless entering in some degree into the religious expression of the music, and thus idle and frivolous women at the present day will weep at an oratorio. So the sublimest effects of landscape may be sought through mere idolence; and even those who are not ignorant, or dull, judge often erroneously of such effects of art because their very openness to all pleasant and sacred association instantly colours whatever they see, so that, give them but the feeblest shadow of a thing they love, they are instantly touched by it to the heart, and mistake their own pleasurable feelings for the result of the painter's power. Thus when, by spotting and splashing, such a painter as Constable reminds them somewhat of wet grass and green leaves, forthwith they fancy themselves in all the happiness of a meadow walk; and when Gaspar Poussin throws out his yellow horizon with black hills, forthwith they are touched as by the solemnity of a real Italian twilight, altogether forgetting that wet grass and twilight do not constitute the universe; and prevented by their joy at being pleasantly cool, or gravely warm, from seeking any of those more precious truths which cannot be caught by momentary sensation, but must be thoughtfully pursued.

I say 'more precious', for the simple fact that the sky is brighter than the earth is *not* a precious truth unless the earth itself be first understood. Despise the earth, or slander it; fix your eyes on its gloom, and forget its loveliness; and we do not thank you for your languid or despairing perception of brightness in heaven. But rise up actively on the earth, – learn what there is in it, know its colour and form, and the full measure and make of it, and if *after that* you can say 'heaven is bright', it will be a precious truth, but not till then . . .

Bring the edge of the paper against the thing to be drawn, and on that edge – as precisely as a lady would match the colours of two pieces of a dress – match the colour of the landscape (with a little opaque white mixed in the tints you use, so as to render it easy to lighten or darken them). Take care not to imitate the tint as you believe it to be, but accurately as it is; so that the coloured edge of the paper shall not be discernible from the colour of the landscape. You will then find (if before inexperienced) that shadows of trees, which you thought were dark green or black, are pale violets and purples; that lights, which you thought were green, are intensely yellow, brown, or golden, and most of them far too bright to be matched at all. When you have got all the imitable hues truly matched, sketch the masses of the landscape out completely in those true and ascertained colours; and you will find, to your amazement, that you have painted it in the colours of Turner, – in those very colours which perhaps you have been laughing at all your life, – the fact being that he, and he alone, of all men, *ever painted Nature in her own colours*.

'Well, but,' you will answer, impatiently, 'how is it, if they are the true colours, that they look so unnatural?'[d]

[d] *From 'Of Truth of Colour'*
What recollection have we of the sunsets which delighted us last year? We may know that they were magnificent, or glowing, but no distinct image of colour or form is retained – nothing of whose *degree* (for the great difficulty with the memory is to retain, not facts, but *degrees* of fact) we could be so certain as to say of anything now presented to us, that it is like it. If we did say so, we should be wrong; for we may be quite certain that the energy of an impression fades from the memory, and becomes more and more indistinct every day; and thus we compare a faded and indistinct image with the decision and certainty of one present to the senses. How constantly do we affirm that the thunderstorm of last week was the most terrible one we ever saw in our lives, because we compare it, not with the thunderstorm of last year, but with the faded and feeble recollection of it! And so, when we enter an Exhibition, as we have no definite standard of truth before us, our feelings are toned down and subdued to the quietness of colour, which is all that human power can ordinarily attain to; and when we turn to a piece of higher and closer truth, approaching the pitch of the colour of nature, but to which we are not guided, as we should be in nature, by corresponding gradations of light everywhere around us, but which is isolated and cut off suddenly by a frame and a wall, and surrounded by darkness and coldness, what can we expect but that it should surprise and shock the feelings?
Suppose where the 'Napoleon'[5] hung in the Academy, there could have been

Because they are not shown in true contrast to the sky, and to other high lights. Nature paints her shadows in pale purple, and then raises her lights of heaven and sunshine to such heights that the pale purple becomes, by comparison, a vigorous dark. But poor Turner has no sun at his command to oppose his pale colours. He follows Nature submissively as far as he can; puts

left, instead, an opening in the wall, and through that opening, in the midst of the obscurity of the dim room and the smoke-laden atmosphere, there could suddenly have been poured the full glory of a tropical sunset, reverberated from the sea; how would you have shrunk, blinded, from its scarlet and intolerable lightnings! What picture in the room would not have been blackness after it? And why then do you blame Turner because he dazzles you? Does not the falsehood rest with those who do *not?* There was not one hue in this whole picture which was not far below what nature would have used in the same circumstances, nor was there one inharmonious or at variance with the rest. The stormy blood-red of the horizon, the scarlet of the breaking sunlight, the rich crimson browns of the wet and illumined sea-weed, the pure gold and purple of the upper sky, and, shed through it all, the deep passage of solemn blue, where the cold moonlight fell on one pensive spot of the limitless shore, — all were given with harmony as perfect as their colour was intense; and if, instead of passing, as I doubt not you did, in the hurry of your unreflecting prejudice, you had paused but so much as one quarter of an hour before the picture, you would have found the sense of air and space blended with every line, and breathing in every cloud, and every colour instinct and radiant with visible, glowing, absorbing light.

It is to be observed, however, in general, that wherever in brilliant effects of this kind, we approach to anything like a true statement of nature's colour, there must yet be a distinct difference in the impression we convey, because we cannot approach her *light.* All such hues are usually given by her with an accompanying intensity of sunbeams which dazzles and overpowers the eye, so that it cannot rest on the actual colours, nor understand what they are; and hence in art, in rendering all effects of this kind, there must be a want of the ideas of *imitation,* which are the great source of enjoyment to the ordinary observer; because we can only give one series of truths, those of colour, and are unable to give the accompanying truths of light; so that the more true we are in colour, the greater, ordinarily, will be the discrepancy felt between the intensity of hue and the feebleness of light. But the painter who really loves nature will not, on this account, give you a faded and feeble image, which indeed may appear to you to be right, because your feelings can detect no discrepancy in its parts, but which he knows to derive its apparent truths from a systematized falsehood. No; he will make you understand and feel that art *cannot* imitate nature; that where it appears to do so, it must malign her and mock her. He will give you, or state to you, such truths as are in his power, completely and perfectly; and those which he cannot give, he will leave to your imagination. If

pale purple where she does, bright gold where she does; and then when, on the summit of the slope of light, she opens her wings and quits the earth altogether, burning into ineffable sunshine, what can he do but sit helpless, stretching his hands towards her in calm consent, as she leaves him and mocks at him!

you are acquainted with nature, you will know all he has given to be true, and you will supply from your memory and from your heart that light which he cannot give. If you are unacquainted with nature, seek elsewhere for whatever may happen to satisfy your feelings; but do not ask for the truth which you would not acknowledge and could not enjoy.

Nevertheless the aim and struggle of the artist must always be to do away with this discrepancy as far as the powers of art admit, not by lowering his colour, but by increasing his light. And it is indeed by this that the works of Turner are peculiarly distinguished from those of all other colourists, by the dazzling intensity, namely, of the light which he sheds through every hue, and which, far more than their brilliant colour, is the real source of their overpowering effect upon the eye, an effect so *reasonably* made the subject of perpetual animadversion; as if the sun which they represent, were quite a quiet, and subdued, and gentle, and manageable luminary, and never dazzled anybody, under any circumstances whatsoever. I am fond of standing by a bright Turner in the Academy, to listen to the unintentional compliments of the crowd – 'What a glaring thing!' 'I declare I can't look at it!' 'Don't it hurt your eyes?' – expressed as if they were in the constant habit of looking the sun full in the face with the most perfect comfort and entire facility of vision . . .

Every picture of this great colourist has, in one or two parts of it (keynotes of the whole), points where the system of each individual colour is concentrated by a single stroke, as pure as it can come from the pallet; but throughout the great space and extent of even the most brilliant of his works, there will not be found a raw colour; that is to say, there is no warmth which has not grey in it, and no blue which has not warmth in it; and the tints in which he most excels and distances all other men, the most cherished and inimitable portions of his colour, are, as with all perfect colourists they must be, his greys.

It is instructive in this respect, to compare the sky of the Mercury and Argus [Plate 2] with the various illustrations of the serenity, space, and sublimity naturally inherent in blue and pink, of which every year's Exhibition brings forward enough, and to spare. In the Mercury and Argus, the pale and vaporous blue of the heated sky is broken with grey and pearly white, the gold colour of the light warming it more or less as it approaches or retires from the sun; but, throughout, there is not a grain of pure blue; all is subdued and warmed at the same time by the mingling grey and gold, up to the very zenith, where, breaking through the flaky mist, the transparent and deep azure of the sky is expressed with a single crumbling touch; the keynote of the whole is given, and every part of it passes at once far into glowing and aërial space. The reader can scarcely fail to remember at once sundry works, in contradistinction to this, with great names

'Well,' but you will farther ask, 'is this right or wise? ought not the contrast between the masses to be given, rather than the actual hues of a few parts of them, when the others are inimitable?'

Yes, if this *were* possible, it ought to be done; but the true contrasts can NEVER be given. The whole question is simply whether you will be false at one side of the scale or at the other, – that is, whether you will lose yourself in light or in darkness. This

attached to them, in which the sky is a sheer piece of plumber's and glazier's work, and should be valued per yard, with heavy extra charge for ultramarine.

Throughout the works of Turner, the same truthful principle of delicate and subdued colour is carried out with a care and labour of which it is difficult to form a conception. He gives a dash of pure white for his highest light; but all the other whites of his picture are pearled down with grey or gold. He gives a fold of pure crimson to the drapery of his nearest figure, but all his other crimsons will be deepened with black, or warmed with yellow. In one deep reflection of his distant sea, we catch a trace of the purest blue, but all the rest is palpitating with a varied and delicate gradation of harmonized tint, which indeed looks vivid blue as a mass, but is only so by opposition. It is the most difficult, the most rare thing, to find in his works a definite space, however small, of unconnected colour; that is, either of a blue which has nothing to connect it with the warmth, or of a warm colour, which has nothing to connect it with the greys of the whole; and the result is, that there is a general system and under-current of grey pervading the whole of his colour, out of which his highest lights, and those local touches of pure colour, which are, as I said before, the keynotes of the picture, flash with the peculiar brilliancy and intensity in which he stands alone.

Intimately associated with this toning down and connection of the colours actually used, is his inimitable power of varying and blending them, so as never to give a quarter of an inch of canvas without a change in it, a melody as well as a harmony of one kind or another.

Observe, I am not at present speaking of this as artistical or desirable in itself, not as a characteristic of the great colourist, but as the aim of the simple follower of nature. For it is strange to see how marvellously nature varies the most general and simple of her tones. A mass of mountain seen against the light, may at first appear all of one blue; and so it is, blue as a whole, by comparison with other parts of the landscape. But look how that blue is made up. There are black shadows in it under the crags, there are green shadows along the turf, there are grey half-lights upon the rocks, there are faint touches of stealthy warmth and cautious light along their edges; every bush, every stone, every tuft of moss has its voice in the matter, and joins with individual character in the universal will. Who is there who can do this as Turner will? The old masters would have settled the matter at once with a transparent, agreeable, but monotonous grey. Many among the moderns would probably be equally monotonous with absurd and false colours. Turner only would give the uncertainty; the palpitating, perpetual change; the subjection of all to a great influence, without one part or portion being lost or merged in it; the unity of action with infinity of agent.

necessity is easily expressible in numbers. Suppose the utmost light you wish to imitate is that of serene, feebly lighted clouds in ordinary sky (not sun or stars, which it is, of course, impossible deceptively to imitate in painting by any artifice). Then, suppose the degrees of shadow between those clouds and Nature's utmost darkness accurately measured, and divided into a hundred degrees (darkness being zero). Next we measure our own scale, calling our utmost possible black, zero; and we shall be able to keep parallel with Nature, perhaps up to as far as her 40 degrees; all above that being whiter than our white paper. Well, with our power of contrast between zero and 40, we have to imitate her contrasts between zero and 100. Now, if we want true contrasts, we can first set our 40 to represent her 100, our 20 for her 80, and our zero for her 60; everything below her 60 being lost in blackness. This is, with certain modifications, Rembrandt's system. Or, secondly, we can put zero for her zero, 20 for her 20, and 40 for her 40; everything above 40 being lost in *white*ness. This is, with certain modifications, Paul Veronese's system. Or, finally, we can put our zero for her zero, and our 40 for her 100; our 20 for her 50, our 30 for her 75, and our 10 for her 25, proportioning the intermediate contrasts accordingly. This is, with certain modifications, Turner's system; the modifications, in each case, being the adoption, to a certain extent, of either of the

And I wish to insist on this the more particularly, because it is one of the eternal principles of nature, that she will not have one line or colour, nor one portion or atom of space, without a change in it. There is not one of her shadows, tints, or lines that is not in a state of perpetual variation: I do not mean in time, but in space. There is not a leaf in the world which has the *same colour* visible over its whole surface; it has a white high light somewhere; and in proportion as it curves to or from that focus, the colour is brighter or greyer. Pick up a common flint from the roadside, and count, if you can, its changes and hues of colour. Every bit of bare ground under your feet has in it a thousand such; the grey pebbles, the warm ochre, the green of incipient vegetation, the greys and blacks of its reflexes and shadows, might keep a painter at work for a month, if he were obliged to follow them touch for touch: how much more when the same infinity of change is carried out with vastness of object and space. The extreme of distance may appear at first monotonous; but the least examination will show it to be full of every kind of change; that its outlines are perpetually melting and appearing again, – sharp here, vague there, – now lost altogether, now just hinted and still confused among each other; and so for ever in a state and necessity of change. Hence, wherever in a painting we have unvaried colour extended even over a small space, there is falsehood. Nothing can be natural which is monotonous; nothing true which only tells one story. (MP I, Pt. II, Sec. II, Ch. II, paras. 8–11, 13–16)

other sytems. Thus, Turner inclines to Paul Veronese; liking, as
far as possible, to get his hues perfectly true up to a certain point, —
that is to say, to let his zero stand for Nature's zero, and his 10 for
her 10, and his 20 for her 20, and then to expand towards the light
by quick but cunning steps, putting 27 for 50, 30 for 70, and
reserving some force still for the last 90 to 100. So Rembrandt
modifies his system on the other side, putting his 40 for 100, his 30
for 90, his 20 for 80; then going subtly downwards, 10 for 50, 5
for 30; nearly everything between 30 and zero being lost in gloom,
yet so as still to reserve his zero for zero. The systems expressed in
tabular form will stand thus:—

NATURE	REMBRANDT	TURNER	VERONESE
0	0	0	0
10	1	10	10
20	3	20	20
30	5	24	30
40	7	26	32
50	10	27	34
60	13	28	36
70	17	30	37
80	20	32	38
90	30	36	39
100	40	40	40

Now it is evident that in Rembrandt's system, while the
contrasts are not more right than with Veronese, the *colours* are
all wrong, from beginning to end. With Turner and Veronese,
Nature's 10 is their 10, and Nature's 20 their 20; enabling them to
give pure truth up to a certain point. But with Rembrandt, *not one
colour* is absolutely true, from one side of the scale to the other;
only the contrasts are true at the top of the scale . . . Rembrandt
generally chose subjects in which the real colours were very nearly
imitable — as single heads with dark backgrounds, in which
Nature's honest light was little above his own; her 40 being then
truly representable by his 40, his picture became nearly an
absolute truth. But his system is only right when applied to such
subjects; clearly, when we have the full scale of natural light to
deal with, Turner's and Veronese's convey the greatest sum of
truth . . . Veronese confines himself to more imitable things, as
draperies, figures, and architecture, in which his exquisite truth at

the bottom of the scale tells on the eye at once; but Turner works a great deal also (see the table) at the *top* of the natural scale, dealing with effects of sunlight and other phases of the upper colours, more or less inimitable, and betraying therefore, more or less, the artifices used to express them. It will be observed, also, that in order to reserve some force for the top of his scale, Turner is obliged to miss his gradations chiefly in middle tints (see the table), where the feebleness is sure to be felt. His principal point for missing the midmost gradations is almost always between the earth and sky; he draws the earth truly as far as he can, to the horizon; then the sky as far as he can, with his 30 to 40 part of the scale. They run together at the horizon; and the spectator complains that there is no distinction between earth and sky, or that the earth does not *look solid enough* . . .

Now, from all the preceding inquiry, the reader must perceive more and more distinctly the great truth, that all forms of right art consist in a certain *choice* made between various classes of truths, a few only being represented, and others necessarily excluded; and that the excellence of each style depends first on its consistency with itself, – the perfect fidelity, as far as possible, to the truths it has chosen; and secondly, on the breadth of its harmony, or number of truths it has been able to reconcile, and the consciousness with which the truths refused are acknowledged, even though they may not be represented.[e] A great artist is

[e] *From* 'Of Truth of Tone'
Now the finely-toned pictures of the old masters are . . . some of the notes of nature played two or three octaves below her key; the dark objects in the middle distance having precisely the same relation to the light of the sky which they have in nature, but the light being necessarily infinitely lowered, and the mass of the shadow deepened in the same degree. I have often been struck, when looking at the image in a camera-obscura on a dark day, with the exact resemblance it bore to one of the finest pictures of the old masters; all the foliage coming dark against the sky, and nothing being seen in its mass but here and there the isolated light of a silvery stem or an unusually illumined cluster of leafage.

Now if this could be done consistently, and all the notes of nature given in this way an octave or two down, it would be right and necessary so to do: but be it observed, not only does nature surpass us in power of obtaining light as much as the sun surpasses white paper, but she also infinitely surpasses us in her power of shade. Her deepest shades are void spaces from which no light whatever is reflected to the eye; ours are black surfaces from which, paint as black as we may, a great deal of light is still reflected, and which, placed against

just like a wise and hospitable man with a small house: the large companies of truths, like guests, are waiting his invitation; he wisely chooses from among this crowd the guests who will be happiest with each other, making those whom he receives

one of nature's deep bits of gloom, would tell as distinct light. Here we are, then, with white paper for our highest light, and visible illumined surface for our deepest shadow, set to run the gauntlet against nature, with the sun for her light, and vacuity for her gloom. It is evident that *she* can well afford to throw her material objects dark against the brilliant aërial tone of her sky, and yet give in those objects themselves a thousand intermediate distances and tones before she comes to black, or to anything like it – all the illumined surfaces of her objects being as distinctly and vividly brighter than her nearest and darkest shadows, as the sky is brighter than those illumined surfaces. But if we, against our poor dull obscurity of yellow paint, instead of sky, insist on having the same relation of shade in material objects, we go down to the bottom of our scale at once; and what in the world are we to do then? Where are all our intermediate distances to come from? – how are we to express the aërial relations among the parts themselves; for instance, of foliage, whose most distant boughs are already almost black? – how are we to come up from this to the foreground; and when we have done so, how are we to express the distinction between its solid parts, already as dark as we can make them, and its vacant hollows, which nature has marked sharp and clear and black, among its lighted surfaces? It cannot but be evident at a glance, that if to any one of the steps from one distance to another, we give the same quantity of difference in pitch of shade which nature does, we must pay for this expenditure of our means by totally missing half a dozen distances, not a whit less important or marked, and so sacrifice a multitude of truths, to obtain one. And this accordingly was the means by which the old masters obtained their truth (?) of tone. They chose those steps of distance which are the most conspicuous and noticeable, that for instance from sky to foliage, or from clouds to hills; and they gave these their precise pitch of difference in shade with exquisite accuracy of imitation. Their means were then exhausted, and they were obliged to leave their trees flat masses of mere filled-up outline, and to omit the truths of space in every individual part of their picture by the thousand. But this they did not care for; it saved them trouble; they reached their grand end, imitative effect; they thrust home just at the places where the common and careless eye looks for imitation, and they attained the broadest and most faithful appearance of truth of tone which art can exhibit.

But they are prodigals, and foolish prodigals in art; they lavish their whole means to get one truth, and leave themselves powerless when they should seize a thousand. And is it indeed worthy of being called a truth, when we have a vast history given us to relate, to the fulness of which neither our limits nor our language are adequate, instead of giving all its parts abridged in the order of their importance, to omit or deny the greater part of them, that we may dwell with verbal fidelity on two or three? Nay, the very truth to which the rest are

thoroughly comfortable and kindly remembering even those whom he excludes; while the foolish host, trying to receive all, leaves a large part of his company on the staircase, without even knowing who is there, and destroys, by inconsistent fellowship, the pleasure of those who gain entrance.

sacrificed, is rendered falsehood by their absence; the relation of the tree to the sky is marked as an impossibility by the want of relation of its parts to each other.

Turner starts from the beginning with a totally different principle. He boldly takes pure white (and justly, for it is the sign of the most intense sunbeams) for his highest light, and lampblack for his deepest shade; and between these he makes every degree of shade indicative of a separate degree of distance, giving each step of approach, not the exact difference in pitch which it would have in nature, but a difference bearing the same proportion to that which his sum of possible shade bears to the sum of nature's shade; so that an object half-way between his horizon and his foreground, will be exactly in half tint of force, and every minute division of intermediate space will have just its proportionate share of the lesser sum, and no more. Hence where the old masters expressed one distance, he expresses a hundred, and where they said furlongs, he says leagues. Which of these modes of procedure be the more agreeable with truth, I think I may safely leave the reader to decide for himself. He will see, in this very first instance, one proof of what we above asserted, that the deceptive imitation of nature is inconsistent with real truth; for the very means by which the old masters attained the apparent accuracy of tone which is so satisfying to the eye, compelled them to give up all idea of real relations of retirement, and to represent a few successive and marked stages of distance, like the scenes of a theatre, instead of the imperceptible, multitudinous, symmetrical retirement of nature, who is not more careful to separate her nearest bush from her farthest one, than to separate the nearest bough of that bush from the one next to it.

Take, for instance, one of the finest landscapes that ancient art has produced – the work of a really great and intellectual mind, the quiet Nicholas Poussin in our own National Gallery, with the traveller washing his feet [Plate 14]. The first idea we receive from this picture is that it is evening, and all the light coming from the horizon. Not so. It is full noon, the light coming steep from the left, as is shown by the shadow of the stick on the right-hand pedestal; for if the sun were not very high, that shadow could not lose itself half-way down, and if it were not lateral, the shadow would slope, instead of being vertical. Now ask yourself, and answer candidly, if those black masses of foliage, in which scarcely any form is seen but the outline, be a true representation of trees under noon-day sunlight, sloping from the left, bringing out, as it necessarily would do, their masses into golden green, and marking every leaf and bough with sharp shadow and sparkling light. The only truth in the picture is the exact pitch of relief against the sky of both trees and hills; and to this the organization of the hills, the intricacy of the foliage, and everything indicative

Plate 14 *A Man Washing His Feet*

But even those hosts who choose well will be farther distinguished from each other by their choice of nobler or inferior
companies; and we find the greatest artists mainly divided into
two groups, – those who paint principally with respect to local
colour, headed by Paul Veronese, Titian, and Turner; and those
who paint principally with reference to light and shade irrespective of colour, headed by Leonardo da Vinci, Rembrandt, and
Raphael. The noblest members of each of these classes introduce
the element proper to the other class, in a subordinate way. Paul
Veronese introduces a subordinate light and shade, and Leonardo
introduces a subordinate local colour. The main difference is, that
with Leonardo, Rembrandt, and Raphael, vast masses of the
picture are lost in comparatively colourless (dark grey or brown)

either of the nature of the light, or the character of the objects, are
unhesitatingly sacrificed. So much falsehood does it cost to obtain two apparent
truths of tone! . . .

Compare . . . Turner's treatment of his materials in the Mercury and Argus
[Plate 2]. He has here his light actually coming from the distance, the sun being
nearly in the centre of the picture, and a violent relief of objects against it would
be far more justifiable than in Poussin's case. But this dark relief is used in its full
force only with the nearest *leaves* of the nearest group of foliage overhanging the
foreground from the left; and between these and the more distant members of the
same group, though only three or four yards separate, distinct aërial perspective
and intervening mist and light are shown; while the large tree in the centre, though
very dark, as being very near, compared with all the distance, is much diminished
in intensity of shade from this nearest group of leaves, and is faint compared with
all the foreground. It is true that this tree has not, in consequence, the actual pitch
of shade against the sky which it would have in nature; but it has precisely as
much as it possibly can have, to leave it the same proportionate relation to the
objects near at hand. And it cannot but be evident to the thoughtful reader, that
whatever trickery or deception may be the result of a contrary mode of treatment,
this is the only scientific or essentially truthful system, and that what it loses in
tone it gains in aërial perspective . . .

Now, as much of this kind of richness of tone is always given by Turner as is
compatible with truth of aërial effect; but he will not sacrifice the higher truths
of his landscape to mere pitch of colour, as Titian does. He infinitely prefers
having the power of giving extension of space, and fulness of form, to that of
giving deep melodies of tone; he feels too much the incapacity of art, with its
feeble means of light, to give the abundance of nature's gradations; and
therefore it is, that taking pure white for his highest expression of light, that
even pure yellow may give him one more step in the scale of shade, he becomes
necessarily inferior in richness of effect to the old masters of tone who always
used a golden highest light, but gains by the sacrifice a thousand more essential
truths. (MP I, Pt. II, Sec. II, Ch. I, paras. 4–9, 16–17)

shadow; these painters *beginning* with the *lights* and going *down* to blackness; but with Veronese, Titian, and Turner, the whole picture is like the rose, – glowing with colour in the shadows, and rising into paler and more delicate hues, or masses of whiteness, in the lights; they having *begun* with the *shadows*, and gone up *to* whiteness. (MP IV, Pt. V, Ch. III, paras. 5–7, 9–12, 17–18)

Of the Use of Pictures

I am afraid this will be a difficult chapter; one of drawbacks, qualifications, and exceptions. But the more I see of useful truths, the more I find that, like human beings, they are eminently biped; and, although, as far as apprehended by human intelligence, they are usually seen in a crane-like posture, standing on one leg, whenever they are to be stated so as to maintain themselves against all attack it is quite necessary they should stand on two, and have their complete balance on opposite fulcra.

I doubt not that one objection with which, as well as with another, we may begin, has struck the reader very forcibly, after comparing the illustrations above given from Turner, Constable, and Claude. He will wonder how it was that Turner, finishing in this exquisite way, and giving truths by the thousand, where other painters gave only one or two, yet, of all painters, seemed to obtain least acknowledgeable resemblance to nature, so that the world cried out upon him for a madman, at the moment when he was giving exactly the highest and most consummate truth that had ever been seen in landscape.

And he will wonder why still there seems reason for this outcry. Still, after what analysis and proof of his being right have as yet been given, the reader may perhaps be saying to himself: 'All this reasoning is of no use to me. Turner does *not* give me the idea of nature; I do not feel before one of his pictures as I should in a real scene. Constable takes me out into the shower, and Claude into the sun; and De Wint makes me feel as if I were walking in the fields; but Turner keeps me in the house, and I know always that I am looking at a picture.'

I might answer to this: Well, what else *should* he do? If you want to feel as if you were in a shower, cannot you go and get wet without help from Constable? If you want to feel as if you were walking in the fields, cannot you go and walk in them without help from De Wint? But if you want to sit in your room and look at a beautiful picture, why should you blame the artist for giving you one? This *was* the answer actually made to me by various journalists, when first I showed that Turner was truer than other painters: 'Nay,' said they, 'we do not want truth, we want something else than truth; we would not have nature, but something better than nature.'

I do not mean to accept that answer, although it seems at this moment to make for me: I have never accepted it. As I raise my eyes from the paper, to think over the curious mingling in it, of direct error, and far-away truth, I see upon the room-walls, first, Turner's drawing of the chain of the Alps from the Superga above Turin; then a study of a block of gneiss at Chamouni, with the purple Aiguilles Rouges behind it; another of the towers of the Swiss Fribourg, with a cluster of pine forest behind them; then another Turner, Isola Bella, with the blue opening to the St Gothard in the distance; and then a fair bit of thirteenth-century illumination, depicting, at the top of the page, the Salutation; and beneath, the painter who painted it, sitting in his little convent cell, with a legend above him to this effect:—

> *ego johes sepsi hunc librum*
> I, John, wrote this book.

None of these things are bad pieces of art; and yet, — if it were offered me to have, instead of them, so many windows, out of which I should see, first, the real chain of the Alps from the Superga; then the real block of gneiss, and Aiguilles Rouges; then the real towers of Fribourg, and pine forest; the real Isola Bella; and, finally, the true Mary and Elizabeth; and beneath them, the actual old monk at work in his cell, — I would very unhesitatingly change my five pictures for the five windows; and so, I apprehend, would most people, not, it seems to me, unwisely.

'Well, then,' the reader goes on to question me, 'the more closely the picture resembles such a window, the better it must be?'

Yes.

'Then, if Turner does not give me the impression of such a window, that is, of Nature, there must be something wrong in Turner?'

Yes.

'And if Constable and De Wint give me the impression of such a window, there must be something right in Constable and De Wint?'

Yes.

'And something more right than in Turner?'

No.

'Will you explain yourself?'

I *have* explained myself, long ago, and that fully; perhaps too fully for the simple sum of the explanation to be remembered. If the reader will glance back to, and in the present state of our inquiry, reconsider in the first volume, Part I. Sec. I, Ch. V., and Part II. Sec. I, Ch. VII., he will find our present difficulties anticipated.[6] There are some truths, easily obtained, which give a deceptive resemblance to Nature; others only to be obtained with difficulty, which cause no deception, but give inner and deeper resemblance. These two classes of truths cannot be obtained together; choice must be made between them. The bad painter gives the cheap deceptive resemblance. The good painter gives the precious non-deceptive resemblance. Constable perceives in a landscape that the grass is wet, the meadows flat, and the boughs shady; that is to say, about as much as, I suppose, might in general be apprehended, between them, by an intelligent fawn, and a sky-lark. Turner perceives at a glance the whole sum of visible truth open to human intelligence. So Berghem perceives nothing in a figure, beyond the flashes of light on the folds of its dress; but Michael Angelo perceives every flash of thought that is passing through its spirit: and Constable and Berghem may imitate windows; Turner and Michael Angelo can by no means imitate windows. But Turner and Michael Angelo are nevertheless the best.

'Well but,' the reader persists, 'you admitted just now that because Turner did not get his work to look like a window there was something wrong in him.'

I did so; if he were quite right he would have *all* truth, low as well as high; that is, he would be Nature and not Turner, but that is impossible to man. There is much that is wrong in him; much that is infinitely wrong in all human effort.[7] But, nevertheless, in some an infinity of Betterness above other human effort.

'Well, but you said you would change your Turners for windows; why not, therefore, for Constables?'

Nay, I did not say that I would change them for windows *merely*, but for windows which commanded the chain of the Alps and Isola Bella. That is to say, for all the truth that there is in Turner, and all the truth besides which is not in him; but I would not change them for Constables, to have a small piece of truth which is not in Turner, and none of the mighty truth which there is.

Thus far, then, though the subject is one requiring somewhat lengthy explanation, it involves no real difficulty. There is not the slightest inconsistency in the mode in which, throughout this work, I have desired the relative merits of painters to be judged. I have always said, he who is closest to Nature is best. All rules are useless, all genius is useless, all labour is useless, if you do not give facts; the more facts you give, the greater you are; and there is no fact so unimportant as to be prudently despised, if it be possible to represent it. Nor, but that I have long known the truth of Herbert's lines,

> Some men are
> Full of themselves, and answer their own notion,
> ['The Church Porch', liv]

would it have been without intense surprise that I heard querulous readers asking, 'how it was possible' that I could praise Pre-Raphaelitism and Turner also. For, from the beginning of this book to this page of it, I have never praised Turner highly for any other cause than that he *gave facts* more *delicately*, more Pre-Raphaelitically, than other men. Careless readers, who dashed at the descriptions and missed the arguments, took up their own conceptions of the cause of my liking Turner, and said to themselves: 'Turner cannot draw, Turner is generalizing, vague, visionary; and the Pre-Raphaelites are hard and distinct. How can any one like both?' But *I* never said that Turner could not draw. *I* never said that he was vague or visionary. What *I* said was, that nobody had ever drawn so well: that nobody was so certain, so *un*-visionary; that nobody had ever given so many hard and downright facts. Glance back to the first volume, and note the expression now. 'He is the only painter who ever drew a mountain or a stone; the only painter who can draw the stem of a tree; the only painter who has ever drawn the sky, previous artists having only drawn it typically or partially, but he absolutely and universally.' Note how he is praised in his rock drawing for 'not selecting a pretty or interesting morsel here or there, but giving the whole truth, with all the relations of its parts'. Observe how the *great virtue* of the landscape of Cima da Conegliano and the early sacred painters is said to be giving 'entire, exquisite, humble realization – a strawberry plant in the foreground with a blossom, *and a berry just set, and one half ripe, and one ripe*, all patiently and innocently painted from the *real thing, and therefore most divine*'. Then re-read the following paragraph carefully, and note its conclusion, that the thoroughly great men are those who have done everything thoroughly, and who have never despised anything, however small, of God's making; with the instance given of Wordsworth's daisy casting its shadow on a stone; and the following sentence, 'Our painters must come to this before they have done their duty.' And yet, when our painters *did* come to this, did do their duty, and did paint the daisy with its shadow (this passage having been written years before Pre-Raphaelitism was thought of), people wondered how I could possibly like what was neither more or less than the precise fulfilment of my own most earnest exhortations and highest hopes.[8]

Thus far, then, all I have been saying is absolutely consistent, and tending to one simple end. Turner is praised for his truth and finish; that truth of which I am beginning to give examples. Pre-Raphaelitism is praised for its truth and finish; and the whole duty inculcated upon the artist is that of being in all respects as like Nature as possible.

And yet this is not all I have to do. There is more than this to be inculcated upon the student, more than this to be admitted or established, before the foundations of just judgment can be laid.

For, observe, although I believe any sensible person would exchange his pictures, however good, for windows, he would not feel, and ought not to feel, that the arrangement was *entirely* gainful to him. He would feel it was an exchange of a less good of one kind, for a greater of another kind, but that it was definitely *exchange*, not pure gain, not merely getting more truth instead of less. The picture would be a serious loss; something gone which the actual landscape could never restore, though it might give something better in its place, as age may give to the heart something better than its youthful delusion, but cannot give again the sweetness of that delusion.

What is this in the picture which is precious to us, and yet is not natural? Hitherto our arguments have tended, on the whole, somewhat to the depreciation of art; and the reader may every now and then, so far as he has been convinced by them, have been inclined to say, 'Why not give up this whole science of Mockery at once, since its only virtue is in representing facts, and it cannot, at best, represent them completely, besides being liable to all manner of shortcomings and dishonesties, – why not keep to the facts, to real fields, and hills and men, and let this dangerous painting alone?'

No, it would not be well to do this. Painting has its peculiar virtues, not only consistent with, but even resulting from, its shortcomings and weaknesses. Let us see what these virtues are.

I must ask permission, as I have sometimes done before, to begin apparently a long way from the point.

Not long ago, as I was leaving one of the towns of Switzerland, early in the morning, I saw in the clouds behind the houses an Alp which I did not know, a grander Alp than any I knew, nobler than the Schreckhorn or the Mönch; terminated, as it seemed, on one side by a precipice of almost unimaginable height; on the other, sloping away for leagues in one field of lustrous ice, clear and fair and blue, flashing here and there into silver under the morning sun. For a moment I received a sensation of as much sublimity as any natural object could possibly excite; the next moment, I saw that my unknown Alp was the glass roof of one of the work-shops of the town rising above its nearer houses and rendered aerial and indistinct by some pure blue wood smoke which rose from intervening chimneys.

It is evident, that so far as the mere delight of the eye was concerned, the glass roof was here equal, or at least equal for a moment, to the Alp. Whether the power of the object over the heart was to be small or great, depended altogether upon what it was understood for, upon its being taken possession of and apprehended in its full nature, either as a granite mountain or a group of panes of glass; and thus, always, the real majesty of the appearance of the thing to us, depends upon the degree in which we ourselves possess the power of understanding it, – that penetrating, possession-taking power of the imagination, which has been long ago defined[9] as the very life of the man, considered as a *seeing* creature. For though the casement had indeed been an Alp, there are many persons on whose minds it would have produced no more effect than the glass roof. It would have been to them a glittering object of a certain apparent length and breadth, and whether of glass or ice, whether twenty feet in length, or twenty leagues, would have made no difference to them; or, rather, would not have been in any wise conceived or considered by them. Examine the nature of your own emotion (if you feel it) at the sight of the Alp, and you find all the brightness of that emotion hanging, like dew on gossamer, on a curious web of subtle fancy and imperfect knowledge. First, you have a vague idea of its size, coupled with wonder at the work of the great Builder of its walls and foundations, then an apprehension of its eternity, a pathetic sense of its perpetualness, and your own transientness, as of the grass upon its sides; then, and in this very sadness, a sense of strange companionship with past generations in seeing what they saw. They did not see the clouds that are floating over your head: nor the cottage wall on the other side of the field; nor the road by which you are travelling. But they saw *that*. The wall of granite in the heavens was the same to them as to you. They have ceased to look upon it; you will soon cease to look also, and the granite wall will be for others. Then, mingled with these more solemn imaginations, come the understandings of the gifts and glories of the Alps, the fancying forth of all the fountains that well from its rocky walls, and strong rivers that are born out of its ice, and of all the pleasant valleys that wind between its cliffs, and all the châlets that gleam among its clouds, and happy farmsteads couched upon its pastures; while together with the thoughts of these, rise strange sympathies with all the unknown of human life, and happiness, and death, signified by that narrow white flame of the everlasting snow, seen so far in the morning sky.

These images, and far more than these, lie at the root of the emotion which you feel at the sight of the Alp. You may not trace them in your heart, for there is a great deal more in your heart, of evil and good, than you ever can trace; but they stir you and quicken you for all that. Assuredly, so far as you feel more at beholding the snowy mountain than any other object of the same sweet silvery grey, these are the kind of images which cause you to do so; and, observe, these are nothing more than a greater apprehension of the *facts* of the thing. We call the power 'Imagination', because it imagines or conceives; but it is only noble imagination if it imagines or conceives *the truth*. And, according to the degree of knowledge possessed, and of sensibility to the pathetic or impressive character of the things known, will be the degree of this imaginative delight.

But the main point to be noted at present is, that if the imagination can be excited to this its peculiar work, it matters comparatively little what it is excited by. If the smoke had not cleared partially away, the glass roof might have pleased me as well as an Alp, until I had quite lost sight of it; and if, in a picture, the imagination can be once caught, and, without absolute affront from some glaring fallacy, set to work in its own field, the imperfection of the historical details themselves is, to the spectator's enjoyment, of small consequence.

Hence it is, that poets, and men of strong feeling in general, are apt to be among the very worst judges of painting. The slightest hint is enough for them. Tell them that a white stroke means a ship, and a black stain, a thunderstorm, and they will be perfectly satisfied with both, and immediately proceed to remember all that they ever felt about ships and thunderstorms, attributing the whole current and fulness of their own feelings to the painter's work; while probably, if the picture be really good, and full of stern fact, the poet, or man of feeling, will find some of its fact *in his way*, out of the particular course of his own thoughts, – be offended at it, take to criticizing and wondering at it, detect, at last, some imperfection in it, such as must be inherent in all human work, – and so finally quarrel with, and reject the whole thing. Thus, Wordsworth writes many sonnets to Sir George Beaumont and Haydon; none to Sir Joshua [Reynolds] or to Turner.

Hence, also, the error into which many superficial artists fall, in speaking of 'addressing the imagination' as the only end of art. It is quite true that the imagination must be addressed; but it may be very sufficiently addressed by the stain left by an ink-bottle thrown at the wall. The thrower has little credit, though an imaginative observer may find, perhaps, more to amuse him in the erratic nigrescence than in many a laboured picture. And thus, in a slovenly or ill-finished picture, it is no credit to the artist that he has 'addressed the imagination'; nor is the success of such an appeal any criterion whatever of the merit of the work. The duty of an artist is not only to address and awaken, but to *guide* the imagination; and there is no safe guidance but that of simple concurrence with fact. It is no matter that the picture takes the fancy of A. or B., that C. writes sonnets to it, and D. feels it to be divine. This is still the only question for the artist, or for us:– 'Is it a fact? Are things really so?' Is the picture an Alp among pictures, full, firm, eternal; or only a glass house, frail, hollow, contemptible, demolishable; calling, at all honest hands, for detection and demolition?

Hence it is also that so much grievous difficulty stands in the way of obtaining *real opinion* about pictures at all. Tell any man, of the slightest imaginative power, that such and such a picture is good, and means this or that: tell him, for instance, that a Claude is good, and that it means trees, and grass, and water; and forthwith, whatever faith, virtue, humility, and imagination there are in the man, rise up to help Claude, and to declare that indeed it is all 'excellent good, i'faith'; and whatever in the course of his life he has felt of pleasure in trees and grass, he will begin to reflect upon and enjoy anew, supposing all the while it is the picture he is enjoying. Hence, when once a painter's reputation is accredited, it must be a stubborn kind of person indeed whom he will not please, or seem to please; for all the vain and weak people pretend to be pleased with him, for their own credit's sake, and all the humble and imaginative people seriously and honestly fancy they *are* pleased with him, deriving indeed, very certainly, delight from his work, but a delight which, if they were kept in the same temper, they would equally derive (and, indeed, constantly do derive) from the grossest daub that can be manufactured in imitation by the pawnbroker. Is, therefore, the pawnbroker's imitation as good as the original? Not so. There is the certain test of goodness and badness, which I am always striving to get people to use. As long as they are satisfied if they find their feelings pleasantly stirred and their fancy gaily occupied, so long there is for them no good, no bad. Anything may please, or anything displease, them; and their entire manner of thought and talking about art is mockery, and all their judgments are laborious injustices. But let them, in the teeth of their pleasure or displeasure, simply put the calm question, – Is it so? Is that the way a stone is shaped, the way a cloud is wreathed, the way a leaf is veined? and they are safe. They will do no more injustice to themselves nor to other men; they will learn to whose guidance they may trust their imagination, and from whom they must for ever withhold its reins.

'Well, but why have you dragged in this poor spectator's imagination at all, if you have nothing more to say for it than this; if you are merely going to abuse it, and go back to your tiresome facts?'

Nay; I am not going to abuse it. On the contrary, I have to assert, in a temper profoundly venerant of it, that though we must not suppose everything is right when this is aroused, we may be sure that something is wrong when this is *not* aroused. The something wrong may be in the spectator or in the picture; and if the picture be demonstrably in accordance with truth, the odds are, that it is in the spectator; but there is wrong somewhere; for the work of the picture is indeed eminently to get at this imaginative power in the beholder, and all its facts are of no use whatever if it does not. No matter how much truth it tells if the hearer be asleep. Its first work is to wake him, then to teach him.

Now, observe, while, as it penetrates into the nature of things, the imagination is pre-eminently a beholder of things, *as they are*, it is, in its creative function, an eminent beholder of things *when* and *where* they are NOT; a seer, that is, in the prophetic sense, calling the things that are not as though they were', [Corinthians 1:28; Revelations 1.19], and for ever delighting to dwell on that which is not tangibly present. And its great function being the calling forth, or back, that which is not visible to bodily sense, it has of course been made to take delight in the fulfilment of its proper function, and pre-eminently to enjoy, and spend its energy on, things past and future, or out of sight, rather than things present, or in sight. So that if the imagination is to be called to take delight in any object, it will not be always well, if we can help it, to put the *real* object there, before it. The imagination would on the whole rather have it *not* there; – the reality and substance are rather in the imagination's way; it would think a good deal more of the thing if it could not see it. Hence, that strange and sometimes fatal charm, which there is in all things as long as we wait for them, and the moment we have lost them; but which fades while we possess them; – that sweet bloom of all that is far away, which perishes under our touch. Yet the feeling of this is not a weakness; it is one of the most glorious gifts of the human mind, making the whole infinite future, and imperishable past, a richer inheritance, if faithfully inherited, than the changeful, frail, fleeting present: it is also one of the many witnesses in us to the truth that these present and tangible things are not meant to satisfy us. The instinct becomes a weakness only when it is weakly indulged, and when the faculty which was intended by God to give back to us what we have lost, and gild for us what is to come, is so perverted as only to darken what we possess. But, perverted or pure, the instinct itself is everlasting, and the substantial presence even of the things which we love the best, will inevitably and for ever be found wanting in *one* strange and tender charm, which belonged to the dreams of them.

Another character of the imagination is equally constant, and, to our present inquiry, of yet greater importance. It is eminently a *weariable* faculty, eminently delicate, and incapable of bearing fatigue; so that if we give it too many objects at a time to employ itself upon, or very grand ones for a long time together, it fails under the effort, becomes jaded, exactly as the limbs do by bodily fatigue, and incapable of answering any farther appeal till it has had rest. And this is the real nature of the weariness which is so often felt in travelling, from seeing too much. It is not that the monotony and number of the beautiful things seen have made them valueless, but that the imaginative power has been over-taxed; and, instead of letting it rest, the traveller, wondering to find himself dull, and incapable of admiration, seeks for some-thing more admirable, excites and torments, and drags the poor fainting imagination up by the shoulders: 'Look at this, and look at that, and this more wonderful still!' – until the imaginative faculty faints utterly away, beyond all further torment, or pleasure, dead for many a day to come; and the despairing prodigal takes to horse-racing in the Campagna, good now for nothing else than that; whereas, if the imagination had only been laid down on the grass, among simple things, and left quiet for a little while, it would have come to itself gradually, recovered its strength and colour, and soon been fit for work again. So that, whenever the imagination is tired, it is necessary to find for it something, not *more* admirable but *less* admirable; such as in that weak state it can deal with; then give it peace, and it will recover.[f]

---

[f] *On Weariness*:

And if we grow impatient under it, and seek to recover the mental energy by more quickly repeated and brighter novelty, it is all over with our enjoyment. There is no cure for this evil, any more than for the weariness of the imagination already described, but in patience and rest: if we try to obtain perpetual change, change itself will become monotonous; and then we are reduced to that old despair, 'If water chokes, what will you drink after it?' And the two points of practical wisdom in this matter are, first, to be content with as little novelty as possible at a time; and, secondly, to preserve, as much as possible in the world, the sources of novelty.

I say, first, to be content with as little change as possible. If the attention is awake, and the feelings in proper train, a turn of a country road, with a cottage beside it, which we have not seen before, is as much as we need for refreshment; if we hurry past it, and take two cottages at a time, it is already too much: hence, to any person who has all his senses about him, a quiet walk along not more than ten or twelve miles of road a day, is the most amusing of

I well recollect the walk on which I first found out this; it was on the winding road from Sallenches, sloping up the hills towards St Gervais, one cloudless Sunday afternoon.[10] The road circles softly

all travelling; and all travelling becomes dull in exact proportion to its rapidity. Going by railroad I do not consider as travelling at all; it is merely 'being sent' to a place, and very little different from becoming a parcel . . . If we walk more than ten or twelve miles, it breaks up the day too much; leaving no time for stopping at the stream sides or shady banks, or for any work at the end of the day; besides that the last few miles are apt to be done in a hurry, and may then be considered as lost ground. But if, advancing thus slowly, after some days we approach any more interesting scenery, every yard of the changeful ground becomes precious and piquant; and the continual increase of hope, and of surrounding beauty, affords one of the most exquisite enjoyments possible to the healthy mind; besides that real knowledge is acquired of whatever it is the object of travelling to learn, and a certain sublimity given to all places, so attained, by the true sense of the spaces of earth that separate them. A man who really loves travelling would as soon consent to pack a day of such happiness into an hour of railroad, as one who loved eating would agree, if it were possible, to concentrate his dinner into a pill. . .

For there are two classes of precious things in the world: those that God gives us for nothing – sun, air, and life (both mortal life and immortal); and the secondarily precious things which He gives us for a price: these secondarily precious things, worldly wine and milk, can only be bought for definite money; they never can be cheapened. No cheating nor bargaining will ever get a single thing out of nature's 'establishment' at half-price. Do we want to be strong? – we must work. To be hungry? – we must starve. To be happy? – we must be kind. To be wise? – we must look and think. No changing of place at a hundred miles an hour, nor making of stuffs a thousand yards a minute, will make us one whit stronger, happier, or wiser. There was always more in the world than men could see, walked they ever so slowly; they will see it no better for going fast. And they will at last, and soon too, find out that their grand inventions for conquering (as they think) space and time, do, in reality, conquer nothing; for space and time are, in their own essence, unconquerable, and besides did not want any sort of conquering; they wanted *using*. A fool always wants to shorten space and time: a wise man wants to lengthen both. A fool wants to kill space and kill time: a wise man, first to gain them, then to animate them. Your railroad, when you come to understand it, is only a device for making the world smaller: and as for being able to talk from place to place, that is, indeed, well and convenient; but suppose you have, originally, nothing to say. We shall be obliged at last to confess, what we should long ago have known, that the really precious things are thought and sight, not pace. It does a bullet no good to go fast; and a man, if he be truly a man, no harm to go slow; for his glory is not at all in going, but in being. (MP III, Pt. IV, Ch. XVII, paras. 23–4, 35)

between bits of rocky bank and mounded pasture; little cottages and chapels gleaming out from among the trees at every turn. Behind me, some leagues in length, rose the jagged range of the mountains of the Réposoir; on the other side of the valley, the mass of the Aiguille de Varens, heaving its seven thousand feet of cliff into the air at a single effort, its gentle gift of waterfall, the Nant d'Arpenaz, like a pillar of cloud at its feet; Mont Blanc and all its aiguilles, one silver flame, in front of me; marvellous blocks of mossy granite and dark glades of pine around me; but I could enjoy nothing, and could not for a long while make out what was the matter with me, until at last I discovered that if I confined myself to one thing, – and that a little thing, – a tuft of moss or a single crag at the top of the Varens, or a wreath or two of foam at the bottom of the Nant d'Arpenaz, I began to enjoy it directly, because then I had mind enough to put into the thing, and the enjoyment arose from the quantity of the imaginative energy I could bring to bear upon it; but when I looked at or thought of all together, moss, stones, Varens, Nant d'Arpenaz, and Mont Blanc, I had not mind enough to give to all, and none were of any value. The conclusion which would have been formed, upon this, by a German philosopher, would have been that the Mont Blanc *was* of no value; that he and his imagination only were of value; that the Mont Blanc, in fact, except so far as he was able to look at it, could not be considered as having any existence. But the only conclusion which occurred to me as reasonable under the circumstances (I have seen no ground for altering it since) was, that I was an exceedingly small creature, much tired, and, at the moment, not a little stupid; for whom a blade of grass, or a wreath of foam, was quite food enough and to spare, and that if I tried to take any more, I should make myself ill. Whereupon, associating myself fraternally with some ants, who were deeply interested in the conveyance of some small sticks over the road, and rather, as I think they generally are, in too great a hurry about it, I returned home in a little while with great contentment; thinking how well it was ordered that, as Mont Blanc and his pine forests could not be everywhere, nor all the world come to see them, the human mind, on the whole, should enjoy itself most surely, in an ant-like manner, and be happy and busy with the bits of sticks and grains of crystal that fall in its way to be handled, in daily duty.

It follows evidently from the first of these characters of the imagination, its dislike of substance and presence, that a picture has in some measure even an advantage with us in not being real. The imagination rejoices in having something to do, springs up with all its willing power, flattered and happy;[g] and ready with its

[g] *Compare Ruskin's diary (later incorporated in* Praeterita Vol. II, Ch. III, *paras.* 45–7):

December *30th 1840.* I should write much more here, were it not for my eyes, and perhaps a little indolence. It is a great bore to keep a diary but a great delight to have kept one. I have been walking backwards and forwards on the Pincian, being unable to do anything else since this confounded illness, and trying to find out why every imaginable delight palls so very rapidly on even the keenest feelings. I had all Rome before me – towers, cupolas, cypresses and palaces, mingled in every possible grouping – a light Decemberish mist, mixed with the slightest vestige of wood smoke, hovering between the distances, and between the eye and the sun, giving beautiful grey outlines of every form; the sun itself a little watery, forcing through heavy fleecy fragments of broken cloud covering the whole sky. St. Peter's clear, and the masses of the Vatican running white along the hills beside it; St. Onofrio and its hills very indistinct, but the uppermost line of pines showing their broad tops against a line of silver light; the Colonna palace and its pine coming dark against the sun, and the tower of the Capitol rising conspicuous over the city, the centre of interest if not of form. There was a very perfect piece of tower above, broken and varied in form, with a cypress or two; and the marble balustrades of the hill grouped well with the tops of the churches in the Piazza del Popolo. What was more than all to me, on the other side, seen over the rich evergreen oaks of the Borghese gardens, rose a range of dark blue Apennines, with one principal pyramid of pure snow, central and highest, lighted by unbroken sun: for the veil of clouds overhead stopped suddenly at the horizon, and the white mountain caught the full blaze of the noon, and glowed like a piece of sudden comet light fallen on the earth. It was not like moonlight, nor like sun, but as soft as the one and as powerful as the other. And yet with all this around me, I could not *feel* it. I was perfectly well; had no blueness about me, nor anything to prevent me from enjoyment; and yet was as tired of my walk, and as glad when I thought I had done duty, as I ever was on the Norwood road. I have felt as much, and more, looking over London and the Norwood hills, on a summer's day, as I did to day. There was something in the weather – it was dull and Novemberish – and the objects wanted the true light in which they rejoice, and in which only they can be truly seen. But all was exquisitely beautiful, nevertheless; and I saw this, though I could not feel it, and got into a rage with myself, to no purpose. There was a girl walking up and down with some children, with a light cap prettily set on very well dressed hair; the features – though nothing particular in themselves – lighted by the playful and arch expression which is a great rarity here among the meaningless black eyes and round red cheeks of the Italians. Long before I heard her complain to one of her charges, who was jabbering English as fast as the fountain tinkled on the other

fairest colours and most tender pencilling, to prove itself worthy of the trust, and exalt into sweet supremacy the shadow that has been confided to its fondness. And thus, so far from its being at all an object to the painter to make his work look real, he ought to dread such a consummation as the loss of one of its most precious claims upon the heart. So far from striving to convince the beholder that what he sees is substance, his mind should be to what he paints as the fire to the body on the pile, burning away the ashes, leaving the unconquerable shade – an immortal dream. So certain is this, that the slightest local success in giving the deceptive appearance of reality – the imitation, for instance, of the texture of a bit of wood, with its grain in relief – will instantly destroy the charm of a whole picture; the imagination feels itself

side of the road, qu'elle 'n'en comprenait pas un mot', I had set her down for a French bonne. There is nothing like Frenchwomen for real bright, playful, changing expression; our English faces are all just so much waxwork till they fall in love, and then, if there is any expression at all, it is mere sugar and water. However, this girl, after two or three turns, sat down beside another bonne, with a larger animal to look after, and they began chatting. There they sat, all the while I was sentinelizing, laughing and chattering with the expression of perfect happiness on their faces, thinking no more of the Alpine heights behind, or the sweep of city before – which they never looked at – than of Constantinople; but they were happy, while I, with every faculty cultivated and directed to receive the impression of beauty, with every sensation and feeling raised, I should think, to a great degree above theirs, was in a state of actual severe mental pain, because I could perceive materials of the highest mental pleasure about me, and could not receive it from them. I could see a glory in things, of whose existence *they* were hardly aware; and yet they were happy, to all appearance, and I felt the time heavy upon me. Then I met a couple of mustachioed beasts, apparently without brains or feeling of any kind whatsoever, roaring together at the top of their voices, and switching their boots with their canes – but still *happy*, while I was tormented with vague desires of possessing all the beauty that I saw, of keeping every outline and colour in my mind, and pained at the knowledge that I must forget it all; that in a year or two, I shall have no more of that landscape left about me than a confused impression of cupola and pine. The present glory is of no use to me; it hurts me from my fear of leaving it and losing it, and yet I know that were I to stay here it would soon cease to be beauty to me – that it *has* ceased, already, to produce the impression and the delight. I believe the only part of a journey really enjoyable to be the first six weeks, when every feeling is fresh, and the dread of losing what we love is lost in the delirium of its possession. (*The Diaries of John Ruskin*, ed. by Joan Evans and John Howard Whitehouse, 3 vols (Oxford 1956–9) Vol. I 1835–1847, pp. 129–30.)

insulted and injured, and passes by with cold contempt; nay, however beautiful the whole scene may be, as of late in much of our highly wrought painting for the stage, the mere fact of its being deceptively real is enough to make us tire of it; we may be surprised and pleased for a moment, but the imagination will not on those terms be persuaded to give any of its help, and, in a quarter of an hour we wish the scene would change.

'Well, but then, what becomes of all these long dogmatic chapters of yours about giving nothing but the truth, and as much truth as possible?'

The chapters are all quite right. 'Nothing but the Truth,' I say still. 'As much Truth as possible,' I say still. But truth so presented that it will need the help of the imagination to make it real. Between the painter and the beholder, each doing his proper part, the reality should be sustained; and after the beholding imagination has come forward and done its best, then, with its help and in the full action of it, the beholder should be able to say, I feel as if I were at the real place, or seeing the real incident. But not without that help.

Farther, in consequence of that other character of the imagination, fatiguableness, it is a great advantage to the picture that it need not present too much at once, and that what it does present may be so chosen and ordered as not only to be more easily seized, but to give the imagination rest, and, as it were, places to lie down and stretch its limbs in; kindly vacancies, beguiling it back into action, with pleasant and cautious sequence of incident; all jarring thoughts being excluded, all vain redundance denied, and all just and sweet transition permitted.

And thus it is, that, for the most part, imperfect sketches, engravings, outlines, rude sculptures, and other forms of abstraction, possess a charm which the most finished picture frequently wants. For not only does the finished picture excite the imagination less, but, like nature itself, it *taxes* it more. None of it can be enjoyed till the imagination is brought to bear upon it; and the details of the completed picture are so numerous, that it needs greater strength and willingness in the beholder to follow them all out; the redundance, perhaps, being not too great for the mind of a careful observer, but too great for a casual or careless observer. So that, although the perfection of art will always consist in the utmost *acceptable* completion, yet, as every added idea will increase the difficulty of apprehension, and every added touch advance the dangerous realism which makes the imagination languid, the difference between a noble and ignoble painter is in nothing more sharply defined than in this, – that he first wishes to put into his work as much truth as possible, and yet to keep it looking *un*-real: the second wishes to get through his work lazily, with as little truth as possible, and yet to make it look real; and, so far as they add colour to their abstract sketch, the first realizes for the sake of the colour, and the second colours for the sake of the realization.

And then, lastly, it is another infinite advantage possessed by the picture, that in these various differences from reality it becomes the expression of the power and intelligence of a companionable human soul. In all this choice, arrangement, penetrative sight, and kindly guidance, we recognize a super-natural operation, and perceive, not merely the landscape or incident as in a mirror; but, besides, the presence of what, after all, may perhaps be the most wonderful piece of divine work in the whole matter – the great human spirit through which it is manifested to us. So that, although with respect to many important scenes, it might, as we saw above, be one of the most precious gifts that could be given us to see them with *our own eyes*, yet also in many things it is more desirable to be permitted to see them with the eyes of others; and although, to the small, conceited, and affected painter displaying his narrow knowledge and tiny dexterities, our only word may be, 'Stand aside from between that nature and me': yet to the great imaginative painter – greater a million times in every faculty of soul than we – our word may wisely be, 'Come between this nature and me – this nature which is too great and too wonderful for me; temper it for me, interpret it to me; let me see with your eyes, and hear with your ears, and have help and strength from your great spirit.'

All the noblest pictures have this character. They are true or inspired ideals, seen in a moment to *be* ideal; that is to say, the result of all the highest powers of the imagination, engaged in the discovery and apprehension of the purest truths, and having so arranged them as best to show their preciousness and exalt their clearness. They are always orderly, always one, ruled by one great purpose throughout, in the fulfilment of which every atom of the detail is called to help, and would be missed if removed; this peculiar oneness being the result, not of obedience to any teachable law, but of the magnificence of tone in the perfect mind, which accepts only what is good for its great purposes, rejects whatever is foreign or redundant, and instinctively and instantaneously ranges whatever it accepts, in sublime subordination and helpful brotherhood.

Then, this being the greatest art, the lowest art is the mimicry of it, – the subordination of nothing to nothing; the elaborate arrangement of sightlessness and emptiness: the order which has no object; the unity which has no life, and the law which has no love; the light which has nothing to illumine, and shadow which has nothing to relieve.

And then, between these two, comes the wholesome, happy, and noble – though not noblest – art of simple transcript from nature; into which, so far as our modern Pre-Raphaelitism falls, it will indeed do sacred service in ridding us of the old fallacies and componencies, but cannot itself rise above the level of simple and happy usefulness. So far as it is to be great, it must add, – and so far as it *is* great, has already added, – the great imaginative element to all its faithfulness in transcript. And for this reason. I said in the close of my Edinburgh Lectures,[11] that Pre-Raphaelitism, as long as it confined itself to the simple copying of nature, could not take the character of the highest class of art. But it has already, almost unconsciously, supplied the defect, and taken that character, in all its best results; and, so far as it ought, hereafter, it will assuredly do so, as soon as it is permitted to maintain itself in any other position than that of stern antagonism to the composition-teachers around it. I say 'so far as it ought', because, as already noticed in that same place, we have enough, and to spare, of noble *inventful* pictures: so many have we, that we let them moulder away on the walls and roofs of Italy without one regretful thought about them. But of simple transcripts from nature, till now we have had none; even Van Eyck and Albert Dürer having been strongly filled with the spirit of grotesque idealism; so that the Pre-Raphaelites have, to the letter, fulfilled Steele's description of the author, who 'determined to write in an entirely new manner, and describe things exactly as they took place'.[12]

We have now, I believe, in some sort answered most of the questions which were suggested to us during our statement of the nature of great art. I could recapitulate the answers; but perhaps the reader is already sufficiently wearied of the recurrence of the terms 'Ideal', 'Nature', 'Imagination', 'Invention', and will hardly care to see them again interchanged among each other, in the formalities of a summary. What difficulties may yet occur to him, will, I think, disappear as he either re-reads the passages which suggested them, or follows out the consideration of the subject for himself: — this very simple, but very precious conclusion being continually remembered by him as the sum of all; that greatness in art (as assuredly in all other things, but more distinctly in this than in most of them) is not a teachable nor gainable thing, but *the expression of a mind of a God-made great man*; that teach, or preach, or labour as you will, everlasting difference is set between one man's capacity and another's; and that this God-given supremacy is the priceless thing, always just as rare in the world at one time as another. What you can manufacture or communicate, you can lower the price of, but this mental supremacy is incommunicable; you will never multiply its quantity, nor lower its price; and nearly the best thing that men can generally do is to set themselves, not to the attainment, but the discovery of this; learning to know gold, when we see it, from iron-glance, and diamonds from flint-sand, being for most of us a more profitable employment than trying to make diamonds out of our own charcoal. And for this God-made supremacy, I generally have used, and shall continue to use, the word Inspiration, not carelessly nor lightly, but in all logical calmness and perfect reverence. We English have many false ideas about reverence; we should be shocked, for instance, to see a market-woman come into church with a basket of eggs on her arm: we think it more reverent to lock her out till Sunday; and to surround the church with respectability of iron railings, and defend it with pacing inhabitation of beadles. I believe this to be *ir*reverence; and that it is more truly reverent, when the market-woman, hot and hurried, at six in the morning, her head much confused with calculations of the probable price of eggs, can nevertheless get within church porch, and church aisle, and church chancel, lay the basket down on the very steps of the altar, and receive thereat so much of help and hope as may serve her for the day's work. In like manner we are solemnly, but I think not wisely, shocked at any one who comes hurriedly into church, in any figurative way, with his basket on his arm; and perhaps so long as we feel it so, it is better to keep the basket out. But, as for this one commodity of high mental supremacy, it cannot be kept out, for the very fountain of it is in the church wall, and there is no other right word for it but this of Inspiration; a word, indeed, often ridiculously perverted, and irreverently used of fledgling poets and pompous orators – no one being offended then: and yet cavilled at when quietly used of the spirit that is in a truly great man; cavilled at, chiefly, it seems to me, because we expect to know inspiration by the look of it. Let a man have shaggy hair, dark eyes, a rolling voice, plenty of animal energy, and a facility of rhyming or sentencing, and – improvisatore or sentimentalist – we call him 'inspired' willingly enough; but let him be a rough, quiet worker, not proclaiming himself melodiously in anywise, but familiar with us, unpretending, and letting all his littleness and feebleness be seen, unhindered, – wearing an ill-cut coat withal; and, though he be such a man as is only sent upon the earth once in five hundred years, for some special human teaching, it is irreverent to call him 'inspired'. But, be it irreverent or not, this word I must always use; and the rest of what work I have here before me, is simply to prove the truth of it, with respect to the one among these mighty spirits whom we have just lost [J. M. W. Turner]; who divided his hearers, as many an inspired speaker has done before now, into two great sects – a large and a narrow; these searching the Nature-scripture calmly, 'whether those things were so', and those standing haughtily on their Mars' hill, asking, 'What will this babbler say?' [Acts xvii. 11, 18]   (MP III, Pt. IV, Ch. X, paras. 1–22)

'Of Turnerian Mystery' – as 'essential' to life

Not only is there a *partial* and variable mystery thus caused by clouds and vapours throughout great spaces of landscape; there is a continual mystery caused throughout *all* spaces, caused by the absolute infinity of things. WE NEVER SEE ANYTHING CLEARLY.[13] I stated this fact partly in the chapter on Truth of Space, in the first volume [see p. 8ff.], but not with sufficient illustration, so that the reader might by that chapter have been led to infer that the mystery spoken of belonged to some special distance of the landscape, whereas the fact is, that everything we look at, be it large or small, near or distant, has an equal quantity of mystery in it; and the only question is, not how much mystery there is, but at what part of the object mystification begins. We suppose we see the ground under our feet clearly, but if we try to number its grains of dust, we shall find that it is as full of confusion and doubtful form, as anything else; so that there is literally *no* point of clear sight, and there never can be. What we call seeing a thing clearly, is only seeing enough of it to *make out what it is*; this point of intelligibility varying in distance for different magnitudes and kinds of things, while the appointed quantity of mystery remains nearly the same for all. Thus: throwing an open book and an embroidered handkerchief on a lawn, at a distance of a quarter of a mile we cannot tell which is which; that is the point of mystery for the whole of those things. They are then merely white spots of indistinct shape. We approach them, and perceive that one is a book, the other a handkerchief, but cannot read the one, nor trace the embroidery of the other. The mystery has ceased to be in the whole things, and has gone into their details. We go nearer, and can now read the text and trace the embroidery, but cannot see the fibres of the paper, nor the threads of the stuff. The mystery has gone into a third place. We take both up and look closely at them; we see the watermark and the threads, but not the hills and dales in the paper's surface, nor the fine fibres which shoot off from every thread. The mystery has gone into a fourth place, where it must stay, till we take a microscope, which will send it into a fifth, sixth, hundredth, or thousandth place, according to the power we use. When, therefore, we say, we see the book *clearly*, we mean only that we know it is a book. When we say that we see the letters clearly, we mean that we know what letters they are; and artists feel that they are drawing objects at a convenient distance when they are so near them as to know, and to be able in painting to show that they know, what the objects are, in a tolerably complete manner: but this power does not depend on any definite distance of the object, but on its size, kind, and distance, together; so that a small thing in the foreground may be precisely in the same *phase* or place of mystery as a large thing far away.

The other day,[14] as I was lying down to rest on the side of the hill round which the Rhone sweeps in its main angle, opposite Martigny, and looking carefully across the valley to the ridge of the hill which rises above Martigny itself, then distant about four miles, a plantain seed-vessel about an inch long, and a withered head of a scabious half an inch broad, happened to be seen rising up, out of the grass near me, across the outline of the distant hill, so as seemingly to set themselves closely beside the large pines and chestnuts which fringed that distant ridge. The plantain was eight yards from me, and the scabious seven; and to my sight, at these distances, the plantain and the far-away pines were equally clear (it being a clear day, and the sun stooping to the west). The pines, four miles off, showed their branches, but I could not count them: and two or three young and old Spanish chestnuts beside them showed their broken masses distinctly; but I could not count those masses, only I knew the trees to be chestnuts by their general look. The plaintain and scabious in like manner I knew to be a plantain and scabious by their general look. I saw the plantain seed-vessel to be, somehow, rough, and that there were two little projections at the bottom of the scabious head which I knew to mean the leaves of the calyx; but I could no more count distinctly the seeds of the plantain, or the group of leaves forming the calyx of the scabious, than I could count the branches of the far-away pines.

Under these circumstances, it is quite evident that neither the pine nor plantain could have been rightly represented by a single dot or stroke of colour. Still less could they be represented by a definite drawing, on a small scale, of a pine with all its branches clear, or of a plantain with all its seeds clear. The round dot or long stroke would represent nothing, and the clear delineation too much. They were not mere dots of colour which I saw on the hill, but something full of essence of pine; out of which I could gather which were young and which were old, and discern the distorted and crabbed pines from the symmetrical and healthy pines; and feel how the evening sun was sending its searching threads among their dark leaves;— assuredly they were more than dots of colour. And yet not one of their boughs or outlines could be distinctly made out, or distinctly drawn. Therefore, if I had drawn either a definite pine, or a dot, I should have been equally wrong, the right lying in an inexplicable, almost inimitable, confusion between the two.

'But is not this only the case with pines four miles away, and with plantains eight yards?'

Not so. Everything in the field of sight is equally puzzling, and can only be drawn rightly on the same difficult conditions. Try it fairly. Take the commonest, closest, most familiar thing, and strive to draw it verily as you see it. Be sure of this last fact, for otherwise you will find yourself continually drawing, not what you *see*, but what you *know*. The best practice to begin with is, sitting about three yards from a bookcase (not your own, so that you may *know* none of the titles of the books), to try to draw the books accurately, with the titles on the backs, and patterns on the bindings, as you see them. You are not to stir from your place to look what they are, but to draw them simply as they appear, giving the perfect look of neat lettering; which, nevertheless, must be (as you will find it on most of the books) absolutely illegible. Next try to draw a piece of patterned muslin or lace (of which you do not know the pattern), a little way off, and rather in the shade; and be sure you get all the grace and *look* of the pattern without going a step nearer to see what it is. Then try to draw a bank of grass, with all its blades; or a bush, with all its leaves; and you will soon begin to understand under what a universal law of obscurity we live, and perceive that all *distinct* drawing must be *bad* drawing, and that nothing can be right, till it is unintelligible.

'How! and Pre-Raphaelitism and Dürerism, and all that you have been talking to us about for these five hundred pages!'

Well, it is all right; Pre-Raphaelitism is quite as unintelligible as need be (I will answer for Dürerism farther on). Examine your Pre-Raphaelite painting well, and you will find it is the precise fulfilment of these laws. You can make out your plantain head and your pine, and see entirely what they are; but yet they are full of mystery, and suggest more than you can see. So also with Turner, the true head of Pre-Raphaelitism. You shall see the spots of the trout lying dead on the rock in his foreground, but not count them. It is only the Germans and the so-called masters of drawing and defining that are wrong, not the Pre-Raphaelites.

Not, that is to say, so far as it is *possible* to be right. No human skill can get the absolute truth in this matter; but a drawing by Turner of a large scene, and by Holman Hunt of a small one, are as close to truth as human eyes and hands can reach.

'Well, but how of Veronese and all the firm, fearless draughts-men of days gone by?'

They are indeed firm and fearless, but they are all mysterious. Not one great man of them, but he will puzzle you, if you look close, to know what he means. Distinct enough, as to his general intent, indeed, just as Nature is distinct in her general intent, but examine his touches, and you will find in Veronese, in Titian, in Tintoret, in Correggio, and in all the great *painters*, properly so called, a peculiar melting and mystery about the pencilling, sometimes called softness, sometimes freedom, sometimes breadth; but in reality a most subtle confusion of colours and forms, obtained either by the apparently careless stroke of the brush, or by careful retouching with tenderest labour; but always obtained in one way or another; so that though, when compared with work that has no meaning, all great work is *distinct*, — compared with work that has narrow and stubborn meaning, all great work is *in*distinct; and if we find, on examining any picture closely, that it is all clearly to be made out, it cannot be, as painting, first-rate. There is no exception to this rule. EXCELLENCE OF THE HIGHEST KIND, WITHOUT OBSCURITY, CANNOT EXIST.[h]

[h] In all extensive hill ranges, there are five or six lateral chains separated by deep valleys, which rise between the spectator and the central ridge, showing their tops one over another, wave beyond wave, until the eye is carried back to the faintest and highest forms of the principal chain. These successive ridges, and I speak now not merely of the Alps, but of mountains generally, even as low as 3000 feet above the sea, show themselves, in extreme distance, merely as vertical shades, with very sharp outlines, detached from one another by greater intensity, according to their nearness. It is with the utmost difficulty that the eye can discern any solidity or roundness in them; the lights and shades of solid form are both equally lost in the blue of the atmosphere, and the mountain tells only as a flat sharp-edged film, of which multitudes intersect and overtop each other, separated by the greater faintness of the retiring masses. This is the most simple and easily imitated arrangement possible, and yet, both in nature and art, it expresses distance and size in a way otherwise quite unattainable. For thus, the whole mass of one mountain being of one shade only, the smallest possible difference in shade will serve completely to detach it from another, and thus ten or twelve distances may be made evident, when the darkest and nearest is an aërial grey as faint as the sky; and the beauty of such arrangements carried out as nature carries them, to their highest degree, is, perhaps, the most striking feature connected with hill scenery. You will never, by any chance, perceive in extreme distance anything like solid form or projection of the hills. Each is a dead, flat, perpendicular film or shade, with a sharp edge darkest at the summit, and lost as it descends, and about equally dark whether turned towards the light or from it. And of these successive films of mountain you will probably have half a dozen, one behind another, all showing with perfect clearness their every chasm and peak in the outline, and not one of them showing the slightest vestige of solidity; but, on the contrary, looking so thoroughly transparent, that if it so happens, as I have seen frequently, that a conical near hill meets with its summit the separation of two distant ones, so that the right-hand slope of the nearer hill forms an apparent continuation of the right-hand slope of the left-hand farther hill, and *vice versâ*, it is impossible to get rid of the impression that one of the more distant peaks is seen *through* the other.

I may point out, in illustration of these facts, the engravings of two drawings of precisely the same chain of distant hills; Stanfield's Borromean Islands, with the St Gothard in the distance; and Turner's Arona, also with the St. Gothard in the distance.[15] Far be it from me to indicate the former of these plates as in any way exemplifying the power of Stanfield, or affecting his reputation; it is an unlucky drawing, murdered by the engraver, and as far from being characteristic of Stanfield as it is from being like nature; but it is just what I want, to illustrate the particular error of which I speak; and I prefer showing this error where it accidentally exists in the works of a really great artist, standing there alone, to pointing it out where it is confused with other faults and falsehoods in the works of inferior hands. The former of these plates is an example of everything which a hill distance is not, and the latter of everything which it is. In the former, we have the mountains covered with patchy lights, which being of equal intensity, whether near or distant, confuse all the distances together; while the eye, perceiving that the light falls so as to give details of solid form, yet finding nothing but insipid and formless spaces displayed by it, is compelled to suppose that the whole body of the hills is equally monotonous and devoid of character; and the effect upon it is not one whit more impressive and agreeable than might be received from a group of sand-heaps, washed into uniformity by recent rain.

Compare with this the distance of Turner in Arona [Plate 15]. It is totally impossible here to say which way the light falls on the distant hills, except by the slightly increased decision of their edges turned towards it, but the greatest attention is paid to get these edges decisive, yet full of gradation, and perfectly true in character of form. All the rest of the mountain is then undistinguishable haze; and by the bringing of these edges more and more decisively over one another, Turner has given us, between the righthand side of the picture and the snow, fifteen distinct distances, yet every one of these distances in itself palpitating, changeful, and suggesting subdivision into countless multitude. Something of this is traceable even in the engraving, and all the essential characters are perfectly well marked. I think even the least experienced eye can scarcely but feel the truth of this distance as compared with Stanfield's. In the latter, the eye gets something of the form, and so wonders it sees no more; the impression on it, therefore, is of hills within distinctly visible distance, indiscernible through want of light or dim atmosphere, and the effect is, of course, smallness of space, with obscurity of light and thickness of air. In Turner's, the eye gets nothing of the substance, and wonders it sees so much of the outline; the impression is, therefore, of mountains too far off to be ever distinctly seen, rendered clear by brilliancy of light and purity of atmosphere; and the effect, consequently, vastness of space, with intensity of light and crystalline transparency of air.

These truths are invariably given in every one of Turner's distances, that is to say, we have always in them two principal facts forced on our notice: transparency, or filminess of mass, and excessive sharpness of edge. And I wish particularly to insist upon this sharpness of edge, because it is not a casual or changeful habit of nature; it is the unfailing characteristic of all very great distances. . .

If a thing has character upon its outline, as a tree, for instance, or a mossy stone, the farther it is removed from us, the sharper the outline of the whole mass will become, though in doing so the particular details which make up the character will become confused . . . A tree fifty yards from us, taken as

Plate 15 *Arona, Lago Maggiore*

As all subjects have a mystery in *them*, so all drawing must have a mystery in *it*; and from the nearest object to the most distant, if we can quite make out what the artist would be at, there is something wrong. The strokes of paint, examined closely, must be confused, odd, incomprehensible; having neither beginning nor end, – melting into each other, or straggling over each other, or going wrong and coming right again, or fading away altogether; and if we can make anything of them quite out, that part of the drawing is wrong, or incomplete.

Only, observe, the method by which the confusion is obtained may vary considerably according to the distance and scale of the picture itself; for very curious effects are produced upon all paintings by the distance of the eye from them. One of these is the giving a certain softness to all colours, so that hues which would look coarse or bald if seen near, may sometimes safely be left, and are left, by the great workmen in their large works, to be corrected by the kind of *bloom* which the distance of thirty or forty feet sheds over them. I say, 'sometimes', because this optical effect is a very subtle one, and seems to take place chiefly on certain colours, dead fresco colours especially; also the practice of the great workmen is very different, and seems much to be regulated by the time at their disposal. Tintoret's picture of Paradise, with 500 figures in it, adapted to a supposed distance of from fifty to a hundred feet, is yet coloured so tenderly that the nearer it is approached the better it looks; nor is it at all certain that the colour which is wrong near, will look right a little way off, or even a great way off: I have never seen any of our Academy portraits made to look like Titians by being hung above the line: still, distance *does* produce a definite effect on pictorial colour, and in general an improving one. It also deepens the relative power of all strokes and shadows. A touch of shade which, seen near, is all but invisible, and, as far as effect on the picture is concerned, quite powerless, will be found a little way off, to tell as a definite shadow, and to have a notable result on all that is near it; and so markedly is this the case, that in all fine and first-rate drawing there are many passages in which if we *see* the touches we are putting on, we are doing too much; they must be put on by the

---

a mass, has a soft outline, because the leaves and interstices have some effect on the eye; but put it ten miles off against the sky, and its outline will be so sharp that you cannot tell it from a rock. (MP I, Pt. II, Sec. IV, Ch. II, paras. 12–16)

feeling of the hand only, and have their effect on the eye when seen in unison, a little way off. This seems strange; but I believe the reason of it is, that, seen at some distance, the parts of the touch or touches are gathered together, and their relations truly shown; while, seen near, they are scattered and confused . . .

Not only, however, does this take place in a picture very notably, so that a group of touches will tell as a compact and intelligible mass, a little way off, though confused when seen near; but also a dark touch gains at a little distance in apparent *darkness*, a light touch in apparent *light*, and a coloured touch in apparent colour, to a degree inconceivable by an unpractised person; so that literally, a good painter is obliged, working near his picture, to do in everything only about half of what he wants, the rest being done by the distance. And if the effect, at such distance, is to be of confusion, then sometimes, seen near, the work must be a confusion worse confounded, almost utterly unintelligible: hence the amazement and blank wonder of the public at some of the finest passages of Turner, which look like a mere meaningless and disorderly work of chance: but, rightly understood, are preparations for a given result, like the most subtle moves of a game of chess, of which no bystander can for a long time see the intention, but which are, in dim, underhand, wonderful way, bringing out their foreseen and inevitable result.

And, be it observed, no other means would have brought out that result. Every distance and size of picture has its own proper method of work; the artist will necessarily vary that method somewhat according to circumstances and expectations: he may sometimes finish in a way fitted for close observation, to please his patron, or catch the public eye; and sometimes be tempted into such finish by his zeal, or betrayed into it by forgetfulness, as I think Tintoret has been, slightly, in his Paradise, above mentioned. But there never yet was a picture thoroughly effective at a distance, which did not look more or less unintelligible near. Things which in distant effect are folds of dress, seen near are only two or three grains of golden colour set there apparently by chance; what far off is a solid limb, near, is a grey shade with a misty outline, so broken that it is not easy to find its boundary; and what far off may perhaps be a man's face, near, is only a piece of thin brown colour, enclosed by a single flowing wave of a brush loaded with white, while three brown touches across one edge of it, ten feet away, become a mouth and eyes. The more subtle the power of the artist, the more curious the difference will be between the apparent means and the effect produced: and one of the most sublime feelings connected with art consists in the perception of this very strangeness, and in a sympathy with the foreseeing and foreordaining power of the artist. In Turner, Tintoret, and Paul Veronese, the intenseness of perception, first, as to what is to be done, and then, of the means of doing it, is so colossal, that I always feel in the presence of their pictures just as other people would in that of a supernatural being. Common talkers use the word 'magic' of a great painter's power without knowing what they mean by it. They mean a great truth. That power *is* magical; so magical, that, well understood, no enchanter's work could be more miraculous or more *appalling*; and though I am not often kept from saying things by timidity, I should be afraid of offending the reader, if I were to define to him accurately the kind and the degree of awe, with which I have stood before Tintoret's Adoration of the Magi, at Venice, and Veronese's Marriage in Cana, in the Louvre.

It will now, I hope, be understood how easy it is for dull artists to mistake the mystery of great masters for carelessness, and their subtle concealment of intention for want of intention. For one person who can perceive the delicacy, invention, and veracity of Tintoret, or Reynolds, there are thousands who can perceive the dash of the brush and the confusion of the colour. They suppose that the merit consists in dash and confusion, and that they may easily rival Reynolds by being unintelligible, and Tintoret by being impetuous. But I assure them, very seriously, that obscurity is *not* always admirable, nor impetuosity always right; that disorder does not necessarily imply discretion, nor haste, security. It is sometimes difficult to understand the words of a deep thinker; but it is equally difficult to understand an idiot: and young students will find it, on the whole, the best thing they can do, to strive to be *clear*; not affectedly clear, but manfully and firmly. Mean something, and say something, whenever you touch canvas; yield neither to the affectation of precision nor of speed, and trust to time, and your honest labour, to invest your work gradually, in such measure and kind as your genius can reach, with the tenderness that comes of love, and the mystery that comes of power. (MP IV, Pt. V, Ch. IV, paras. 4–9, 12–16)

'Of Turnerian Mystery' — as 'wilful' or particular to Turner

In former parts of this work we were able to trace a certain delightfulness in every visible feature of natural things which was typical of any great spiritual truth; surely, therefore, we need not wonder now, that mist and all its phenomena have been made delightful to us, since our happiness as thinking beings must depend on our being content to accept our partial knowledge, even in those matters which chiefly concern us. If we insist upon perfect intelligibility and complete declaration in every moral subject, we shall instantly fall into misery of unbelief. Our whole happiness and power of energetic action depend upon our being able to breathe and live in the cloud; content to see it opening here and closing there; rejoicing to catch, through the thinnest films of it, glimpses of stable and substantial things; but yet perceiving a nobleness even in the concealment, and rejoicing that the kindly veil is spread where the untempered light might have scorched us, or the infinite clearness wearied.

And I believe that the resentment of this interference of the mist is one of the forms of proud error which are too easily mistaken for virtues. To be content in utter darkness and ignorance is indeed unmanly, and therefore we think that to love light and seek knowledge must always be right. Yet (as in all matters before observed), wherever *pride* has any share in the work, even knowledge and light may be ill pursued. Knowledge is good, and light is good, yet man perished in seeking knowledge, and moths perish in seeking light; and if we, who are crushed before the moth, will not accept such mystery as is needful for us, we shall perish in like manner. But accepted in humbleness, it instantly becomes an element of pleasure; and I think that every rightly constituted mind ought to rejoice, not so much in knowing anything clearly, as in feeling that there is infinitely more which it cannot know. None but proud or weak men would mourn over this, for we may always know more if we choose, by working on; but the pleasure is, I think, to humble people, in knowing that the journey is endless, the treasure inexhaustible, — watching the cloud still march before them with its summitless pillar, and being sure that, to the end of time and to the length of eternity, the mysteries of its infinity will still open farther and farther, their dimness being the sign and necessary adjunct of their inexhaustibleness [Exodus. xiii. 21-2]. I know there are an evil mystery and a deathful dimness, – the mystery of the great Babylon – the dimness of the sealed eye and soul; but do not let us confuse these with the glorious mystery of the things which the angels 'desire to look into' [1 Peter i. 12], or with the dimness which, even before the clear eye and open soul, still rests on sealed pages of the eternal volume.

And going down from this great truth to the lower truths which are types of it in smaller matters, we shall find, that as soon as people try honestly to see all they can of anything, they come to a point where a noble dimness begins. They see more than others; but the consequence of their seeing more is, that they feel they cannot see all; and the more intense their perception, the more the crowd of things which they *partly* see will multiply upon them; and their delight may at last principally consist in dwelling on this cloudy part of their prospect, somewhat casting away or aside what to them has become comparatively common, but is perhaps the sum and substance of all that other people see in the thing, for the utmost subtleties and shadows and glancings of it cannot be caught, but by the most practised vision. And as a delicate ear rejoices in the slighter and more modulated passages of sound which to a blunt ear are utterly monotonous in their quietness, or unintelligible in their complication, so, when the eye is exquisitely keen and clear, it is fain to rest on grey films of shade, and wandering rays of light, and intricacies of tender form, passing over hastily, as unworthy or commonplace, what to a less educated sense appears the whole of the subject. In painting, this progress of the eye is marked always by one consistent sign – its sensibility, namely, to effects of *gradation* in light and colour, and habit of looking for them, rather even than for the signs of the essence of the subject. It will, indeed, see more of that essence than is seen by other eyes; and its choice of the points to be seized upon will be always regulated by that special sympathy which we have above examined as the motive of the Turnerian picturesque: but yet, the more it is cultivated, the more of light and colour it will perceive, the less of substance.

Thus, when the eye is quite uncultivated, it sees that a man is a man, and a face is a face, but has no idea what shadows or lights fall upon the form or features. Cultivate it to some degree of artistic power, and it will then see shadows distinctly, but only the more vigorous of them. Cultivate it still farther, and it will see light within light, and shadow within shadow, and will continually refuse to rest in what it had already discovered, that it may pursue what is more removed and more subtle, until at last it comes to give its chief attention and display its chief power on gradations which to an untrained faculty are partly matters of indifference, and partly imperceptible. That these subtle gradations have indeed become matters of primal importance to it, may be ascertained by observing that they are the things it will last part with, as the object retires into distance; and that, though this distance may become so great as to render the real nature of the object quite undiscernible, the gradations of light upon it will not be lost.

For instance, Fig. 1, Plate 16, is a tolerably faithful rendering of the look of a wall tower of a Swiss town as it would be seen within some hundred yards of it. Fig. 2 is (as nearly as I can render it) a facsimile of Turner's actual drawing of this tower, at a presumed distance of about half a mile. It has far less of intelligible delineation, either of windows, cornices, or tiles; but intense care has still been given to get the pearly roundness of the side, and the exact relations of all the tones of shade. And now, if Turner wants to remove the tower still farther back, he will gradually let the windows and stones all disappear together, before he will quit his shadows and delicately centralized rays. At Fig. 3 the tower is nearly gone, but the pearly roundness of it and principal lights of it are there still. At Fig. 4 (Turner's ultimate condition in distance) the essence of the thing is quite unintelligible; we cannot answer for its being a tower at all. But the gradations of light are still there, and as much pains have been taken to get them as in any of the other instances. A vulgar artist would have kept something of the form of the tower, expressing it by a few touches; and people would call it clever drawing. Turner lets the tower melt into air, but still he works half an hour or so over those delicate last gradations, which perhaps not many people in England besides himself can fully see, as not many people can understand the final work of a great mathematician. I assume, of course, in this example, that the tower, as it grows less and less distinct, becomes part of the subject of a *larger* picture. Fig. 1 represents nearly what Turner's treatment of it would be if it were the principal subject of a vignette; and Fig. 4 his treatment of it as an object in the extreme distance of a large oil picture. If at the same supposed distance it entered into a smaller drawing, so as to be much smaller in size, he

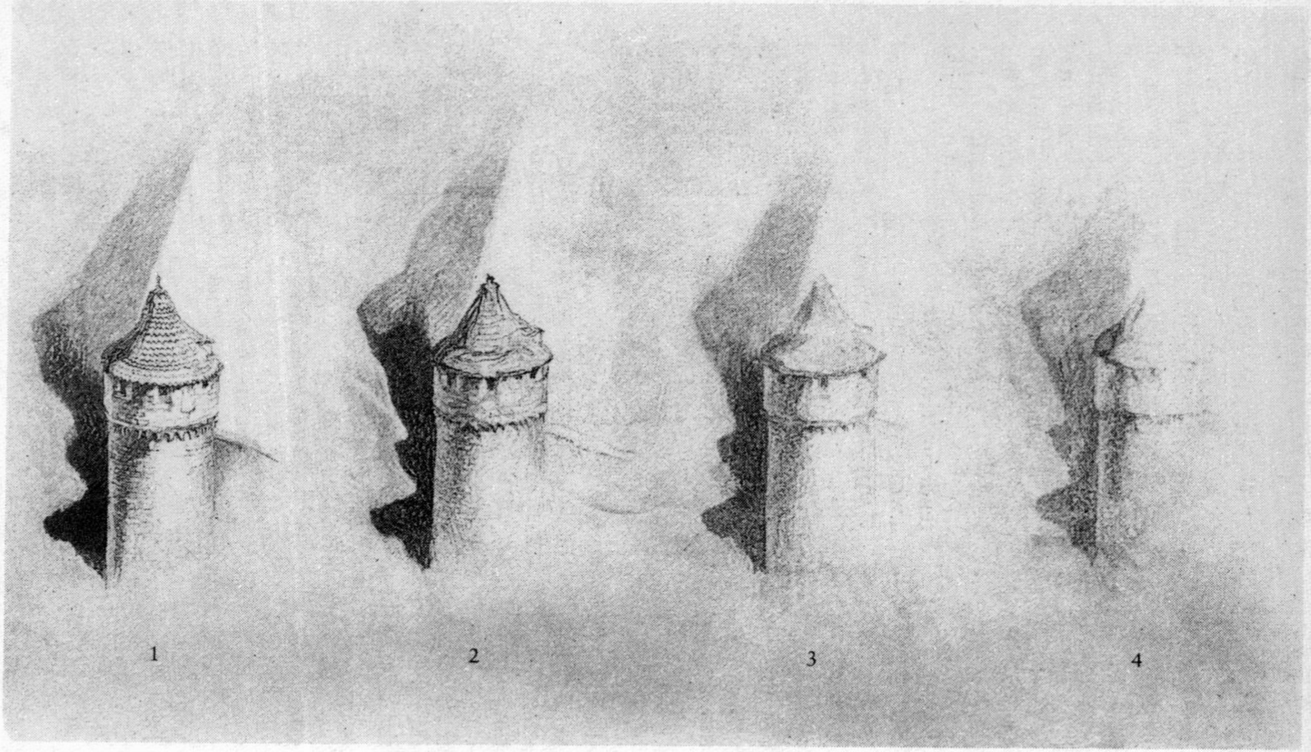

Plate 16 *Tower of a Swiss Town/The Law of Evanescence*

might get the gradations with less trouble, sometimes even by a single sweep of the brush; but *some* gradation would assuredly be retained, though the tower were diminished to the height of one of the long letters of this type.

'But is Turner right in doing this?'

Yes. The truth is indeed so. If you watch any object as it fades in distance, it will lose gradually its force, its intelligibility, its anatomy, its whole comprehensible being; but it will *never* lose its gradation of light. Up to the last moment, what light is seen on it, feebly glimmering and narrowed almost to a point or a line, is still full of change. One part is brighter than another, and brighter with as lovely and tender increase as it was when nearest to us; and at last, though a white house ten miles away will be seen only as a small square spot of light, its windows, doors, or roof being as utterly invisible as if they were not in existence, the gradation of its light will not be lost; one part of the spot will be seen to be brighter than another.

Is there not a deep meaning in this? We, in our daily looking at the thing, think that its own make is the most important part of it. Windows and porticoes, eaves and cornices, how interesting or how useful are they! Surely, the chief importance of the thing is in these. No; not in these, but in the play of the light of heaven upon it. There is a place and time when all those windows and porticoes will be lost sight of; when the only question becomes, 'What light had it?' How much of heaven was looking upon it? What were the broad relations of it, in light and darkness, to the sky and earth, and all things around it? It might have strange humours and ways of its own – many a rent in its wall, and many a roughness on its roof; or it might have many attractivenesses and noblenesses of its own – fair mouldings and gay ornaments; but the time comes when all these are vain, and when the slight, wandering warmth of heaven's sunshine which the building itself felt not, and not one eye in a thousand saw, becomes all in all. I leave the reader to follow out the analogies of this.

'Well, but,' it is still objected, 'if this be so, why is it necessary to insist, as you do always, upon the most minute and careful renderings of form?'

Because, though these gradations of light are indeed, as an object dies in distance, the only things it can retain, yet as it lives its active life near us, those very gradations can only be seen properly by the effect they have on its character. You can only show how the light affects the object, by knowing thoroughly what the object is; and noble mystery differs from ignoble, in being a veil thrown between us and something definite, known, and substantial; but the ignoble mystery is a veil cast before chaos, the studious concealment of Nothing.

There is even a way in which the very definiteness of Turner's knowledge adds to the mystery of his pictures . . .

I believe the reader must now sufficiently perceive that the right of being obscure is not one to be lightly claimed; it can only be founded on long effort to be intelligible, and on the present power of *being* intelligible to the exact degree which the nature of the thing admits. (MP IV, Pt. V, Ch. V, paras. 3–12)

CHAPTER 5

The Stones of Venice

The three volumes of The Stones of Venice *appeared in 1851 and 1853 and, with* The Seven Lamps of Architecture *(1849), account for much of the ten-year gap between* Modern Painters Vol. II *(1846) and* Modern Painters Vol. III *(1856).*

This collection seeks to combine a sense of the sudden new moves of Ruskin's career with his own recognition of the unity unfolding within his development. The architectural writings serve as a bridge or hinge between the first half of Modern Painters Vol. III, *which is the culmination of the work of the first two volumes, and the second half, which leads towards the investigation of the modern problems of knowing and being and believing in the last two volumes. It is the central distinction in* The Stones of Venice *between the old Gothic way and the modern inheritance of the Renaissance attitude that provides the background to* Modern Painters Vol. III *onwards.*

Even so, as Ruskin explains in Praeterita, *his father began to fear after 1846 that the architectural work was no more and no less than a grave interruption of* Modern Painters, *a fragmentary distraction from the achievement of a grand design. His son was staring at, and drawing bits of, mere walls:*

After our usual rest at Champagnole, we went on over the Cenis to Turin, Verona, and Venice; whereat I began showing my father all my new discoveries in architecture and painting. But there began now to assert itself a difference between us I had not calculated on. For the first time I verily perceived that my father was older than I, and not immediately nor easily to be put out of his way of thinking in anything. We had been entirely of one mind about the carved porches of Abbeville, and living pictures of Vandyck; but when my father now found himself required to admire also flat walls, striped like the striped calico of an American flag, and oval-eyed saints like the figures on a Chinese teacup, he grew restive. Farther, all the fine writing and polite éclat of 'Modern Painters' had never reconciled him to my total resignation of the art of poetry; and beyond this, he

entirely, and with acute sense of loss to himself, doubted and
deplored my now constant habit of making little patches and
scratches of the sections and fractions of things in my waistcoat
pocket.

Praeterita, Vol. II, Ch. X, para. 188

*Ruskin too had his own initial doubts. At times in 1845 he felt it 'a
woeful thing to take an interest in anything that man has done' —
so much of man-made architecture fell into decay as the great
natural mountains of the world did not. But he became convinced
that architecture was almost literally and substantially bringing
art out into the world — into the midst of the ordinary life of cities.*

*Ruskin's partial shift of emphasis from painting to architecture
involved his not only seeing buildings in merely picturesque
relation to nature — as decaying features in a landscape — but also
in relation to man, as expressions of the urge to re-create within
the world itself the forms of nature by human means. As human
artefact, the earliest architecture was — despite its mortal
limitations — spiritually analogous to the divine architecture of
clouds and mountains and trees. Architecture formed another
connection in that Wordsworth-like story of 'love of nature
leading to love of mankind'.*

*The first part of this chapter offers an introduction to Ruskin's
architectural principles — with excerpts on the power of walls and
surfaces, the sense of weight and mass and lift, and the use of
shadow. It serves as a replacement for the more lengthy and
minute depiction of the fundamental details of architecture given
in the first volume of* The Stones of Venice.

*The raising of stone into the air is at its most miraculous in
Venice. The central section of this chapter is devoted to Ruskin's
important description of 'The Nature of Gothic' in the second
volume of* The Stones of Venice. *Venetian examples are offered in
illustration of that rich variety and free creativity that Ruskin
found were celebrated in Gothic art.*

The third volume of The Stones of Venice *follows the rise of
Venice and Gothic with what Ruskin describes as 'the Fall' into
the Renaissance. The final part of this chapter is concerned with
the Nature of the Renaissance — first in its early days, but most of
all in its Roman prime when, to Ruskin, the world was all too in
love with the idea of human perfection and mathematical
symmetry. A contrast between the Gothic treatment of the
Grotesque and its Renaissance equivalent gives way to a final*

conclusive comparison between Gothic and Renaissance as rival ways of human being, the choice between which bearing serious consequences for the Modern Age.

Foundations: Ruskin's architectural principles. The Power of Walls

Of the many broad divisions under which architecture may be considered, none appear to me more significant than that into buildings, whose interest is in their walls, and those whose interest is in the lines dividing their walls. In the Greek temple the wall is as nothing; the entire interest is in the detached columns and the frieze they bear; in French Flamboyant, and in our detestable Perpendicular, the object is to get rid of the wall surface, and keep the eye altogether on tracery of line: in Romanesque work and Egyptian, the wall is a confessed and honoured member, and the light is often allowed to fall on large areas of it, variously decorated. Now, both these principles are admitted by Nature, the one in her woods and thickets, the other in her plains, and cliffs, and waters; but the latter is pre-eminently the principle of power, and, in some sense, of beauty also. For, whatever infinity of fair form there may be in the maze of the forest, there is a fairer, as I think, in the surface of the quiet lake; and I hardly know that association of shaft or tracery, for which I would exchange the warm sleep of sunshine on some smooth, broad, human-like front of marble. Nevertheless, if breadth is to be beautiful, its substance must in some sort be beautiful; and we must not hastily condemn the exclusive resting of the northern architects in divided lines, until at least we have remembered the difference between a blank surface of Caen stone, and one mixed from Genoa and Carrara, of serpentine with snow: but as regards abstract power and awfulness, there is no question; without breadth of surface it is in vain to seek them, and it matters little, so that the surface be wide, bold, and unbroken, whether it be of brick or of jasper; the light of heaven upon it, and the weight of earth in it, are all we need: for it is singular how forgetful the mind may become both of material and workmanship, if only it have space enough over which to range, and to remind it, however feebly, of the joy that it has in contemplating the flatness and sweep of great plains and broad seas. And it is a noble thing for men to do this with their cut stone or moulded clay, and to make the face of a wall look infinite, and its edge against the sky like an horizon: or even if less than this be reached, it is still delightful to mark the play of passing light on its broad surface, and to see by how many artifices and gradations of tinting and shadow, time and storm will set their wild signatures upon it; and how in the rising or declining of the day the unbroken twilight rests long and luridly on its high lineless forehead, and fades away untraceably down its tiers of confused and countless stone. (SL, Ch. III ['The Lamp of Power'], para. 8)

The Power of Surfaces:
Linear Gothic, illustrated by the head of a lateral niche from the south door of St Wulfran, Abbeville, in contrast to the Surface Gothic of a corresponding niche from the tomb of the Ca' Grande at Verona

The one from Abbeville (1), though it contains much floralwork of the crisp Northern kind in its finial and crockets, yet depends for all its effect on the various patterns of foliation with which its spaces are filled; and it is so cut through and through that it is hardly stronger than a piece of lace: whereas the pinnacle from Verona (2) depends for its effect on one broad mass of shadow, boldly shaped into the trefoil in its bearing arch; and there is no other trefoil on that side of the niche. All the rest of its decoration is floral, or by almonds and bosses; and its surface of stone is unpierced, and kept in broad light, and the mass of it thick and strong enough to stand for as many centuries as it has already stood, scatheless, in the open street of Verona. The figures 3 and 4, above each niche, show how the same principles are carried out into the smallest details of the two edifices, 3 being the moulding which borders the gable at Abbeville, and 4 that in the same position at Verona; and as thus in all cases the distinction in their treatment remains the same, the one attracting the eye to broad sculptured *surfaces*, the other to involutions of intricate *lines*, I shall hereafter characterize the two schools, the one as Surface Gothic, the other as Linear Gothic ... The Veronese Gothic is strong in its masonry, simple in its masses, but perpetual in its variety. The late French Gothic is weak in masonry, broken in mass, and repeats the same idea continually. It is very beautiful but the Italian Gothic is the nobler style. (SV II, Ch. VI, paras. 102–3).

Plate 17 *Linear and Surface Gothic*
(*1 Abbeville, 2 Verona, 3 and 4 as indicated*)

The Power of Weight

For there is a crust about the impressible part of men's minds, which must be pierced through before they can be touched to the quick; and though we may prick at it and scratch it in a thousand separate places, we might as well have let it alone if we do not come through somewhere with a deep thrust: and if we can give such a thrust anywhere, there is no need of another; it need not be even so 'wide as a church door', [*Romeo and Juliet*, III i 100] so that it be *enough*. And mere weight will do this; it is a clumsy way of doing it, but an effectual one, too; and the apathy which cannot be pierced through by a small steeple, nor shone through by a small window, can be broken through in a moment by the mere weight of a great wall. Let, therefore, the architect who has not large resources, choose his point of attack first, and, if he chooses size, let him abandon decoration; for, unless they are concentrated, and numerous enough to make their concentration conspicuous, all his ornaments together will not be worth one huge stone. (SL, Ch. III, para. 5).

Superimposition, wisely practised, is of two kinds, directly contrary to each other, of weight on lightness, and of lightness on weight; while the superimposition of weight on weight, or lightness on lightness, is nearly always wrong.

(1) Weight on lightness; I do not say weight on *weakness*. The superimposition of the human body on its limbs I call weight on lightness; the superimposition of the branches on a tree trunk I call lightness on weight: in both cases the support is fully adequate to the work, the form of support being regulated by the differences of requirement. Nothing in architecture is half so painful as the apparent want of sufficient support when the weight above is visibly passive; for all buildings are not passive; some seem to rise by their own strength, or float by their own buoyancy; a dome requires no visibility of support, one fancies it supported by the air. But passive architecture without help for its passiveness is unendurable. In a lately built house, No. 86, in Oxford Street, three huge stone pillars in the second story are carried apparently by the edges of three sheets of plate glass in the first. I hardly know anything to match the painfulness of this and some other of our shop structures, in which the ironwork is concealed; nor even when it is apparent, can the eye ever feel satisfied of their security, when built, as at present, with fifty or sixty feet of wall above a rod of iron not the width of this page.

The proper forms of this superimposition of weight on lightness have arisen, for the most part, from the necessity or desirableness, in many situations, of elevating the inhabited portions of buildings considerably above the ground level, especially those exposed to damp or inundation, and the consequent abandonment of the ground story as unserviceable, or else the surrender of it to public purposes . . .

(2) The second kind of superimposition, lightness on weight, is . . . the system of many buildings of the kind which I have above called Architecture of Position, that is to say, architecture of which the greater part is intended merely to keep something in a peculiar position; as in lighthouses, and many towers and belfries . . . [in] the elevation of gradually diminishing weight on massy or even solid foundation. Nevertheless since the tower is in its origin a building for strength of defence, and faithfulness of watch, rather than splendour of aspect, its true expression is of just so much diminution of weight upwards as may be necessary to its fully balanced strength, not a jot more. There must be no light-headedness in your noble tower: impregnable foundation, wrathful crest, with the vizor down, and the dark vigilance seen through the clefts of it; not the filigree crown or embroidered cap. No towers are so grand as the square browed ones, with massy cornices and rent battlements: next to these come the fantastic towers with their various forms of steep roof; the best, not the cone, but the plain gable thrown very high; last of all in my mind (of good towers), those with spires or crowns, though these, of course, are fittest for ecclesiastical purposes, and capable of the richest ornament. The paltry four or eight pinnacled things we call towers in England (as in York Minster), are mere confectioner's Gothic, and not worth classing.

But, in all of them, this I believe to be a point of chief necessity, — that they shall seem to stand, and shall verily stand, in their own strength; not by help of buttresses, nor artful balancings on this side and on that. Your noble tower must need no help, must be sustained by no crutches, must give place to no suspicion of decrepitude. Its office may be to withstand war, look forth for tidings, or to point to heaven: but it must have in its own walls the strength to do this; it is to be itself a bulwark, not to be sustained by other bulwarks; to rise and look forth, 'the tower of Lebanon that looketh toward Damascus', [Song of Solomon vii. 4] like a stern sentinel, not like a child held up in its nurse's arms . . . And

here I may not unfitly note the important distinction . . . between
the marvellous and the perilous in apparent construction. There
are many edifices which are awful or admirable in their height,
and lightness, and boldness of form, respecting which, nevertheless, we have no fear that they should fall. Many a mighty dome
and aërial aisle and arch may seem to stand, as I said, by miracle,
but by steadfast miracle notwithstanding; there is no fear that the
miracle should cease. We have a sense of inherent power in them,
or, at all events, of concealed and mysterious provision for their
safety. (SL, Ch. XIX, paras. 5–6, 9, 11–12, 16)

The Power of Energetic Shadow

Penetrations which, seen from within, are forms of light, and,
from without, are forms of shade. In Italian traceries the eye is
exclusively fixed upon the dark forms of the penetrations, and the
whole proportion and power of the design are caused to
depend upon them. The intermediate spaces are, indeed, in the
most perfect early examples, filled with elaborate ornament; but
this ornament was so subdued as never to disturb the simplicity
and force of the dark masses; and in many instances is entirely
wanting. The composition of the whole depends on the proportioning and shaping of the darks; and it is impossible that any
thing can be more exquisite than their placing in the head window
of the Giotto campanile [Plates 19, 20] or the Church of Or San
Michele [Plate 18]. So entirely does the effect depend upon them,
that it is quite useless to draw Italian tracery in outline; if with any
intention of rendering its effect, it is better to mark the black
spots, and let the rest alone. Of course, when it is desired to obtain
an accurate rendering of the design, its lines and mouldings are
enough; but it often happens that works on architecture are of
little use, because they afford the reader no means of judging of
the effective intention of the arrangements which they state. No
person, looking at an architectural drawing of the richly foliated
cusps and intervals of Or San Michele, would understand that all
this sculpture was extraneous, was a mere added grace, and had
nothing to do with the real anatomy of the work, and that by a few
bold cuttings through a slab of stone he might reach the main
effect of it all, at once. I have, therefore, in the plate of the design
of Giotto, endeavoured especially to mark these points of
purpose; there, as in every other instance, black shadows of a

Plate 18 *Arch from San Michele, Lucca*

graceful form lying on the white surface of the stone, like dark leaves laid upon snow. Hence, as before observed, the universal name of foil applied to such ornaments. (SL, Ch. III, para. 18)

Positive shade is a more necessary and more sublime thing in an architect's hands than in a painter's. For the latter being able to temper his light with an undertone throughout, and to make it delightful with sweet colour, or awful with lurid colour, and to represent distance, and air, and sun, by the depth of it, and fill its whole space with expression, can deal with an enormous, nay, almost with an universal, extent of it, and the best painters most delight in such extent; but as light, with the architect, is nearly always liable to become full and untempered sunshine seen upon solid surface, his only rests, and his chief means of sublimity, are definite shades. So that, after size and weight, the Power of architecture may be said to depend on the quantity (whether measured in space or intenseness) of its shadow; and it seems to me, that the reality of its works, and the use and influence they have in the daily life of men, (as opposed to those works of art with which we have nothing to do but in times of rest or of pleasure,) require of it that it should express a kind of human sympathy, by a measure of darkness as great as there is in human life: and that as the great poem and great fiction generally affect us most by the majesty of their masses of shade, and cannot take hold upon us if they affect a continuance of lyric sprightliness, but must be often serious, and sometimes melancholy, else they do not express the truth of this wild world of ours; so there must be, in this magnificently human art of architecture, some equivalent expression for the trouble and wrath of life, for its sorrow and its mystery: and this it can only give by depth or diffusion of gloom, by the frown upon its front, and the shadow of its recess. So that Rembrandtism is a noble manner in architecture, though a false one in painting; and I do not believe that ever any building was truly great, unless it had mighty masses, vigorous and deep, of shadow mingled with its surface. And among the first habits that a young architect should learn, is that of thinking in shadow, not looking at a design in its miserable liny skeleton; but conceiving it as it will be when the dawn lights it, and the dusk leaves it; when its stones will be hot, and its crannies cool; when the lizards will bask on the one, and the birds build in the other. Let him design with the sense of cold and heat upon him; let him cut out the shadows, as men dig wells in unwatered plains; and lead along the

Plate 19 *Campanile at Florence*

Plate 20 *Campanile at Florence*

lights, as a founder does his hot metal; let him keep the full command of both, and see that he knows how they fall, and where they fade. His paper lines and proportions are of no value: all that he has to do must be done by spaces of light and darkness; and his business is to see that the one is broad and bold enough not to be swallowed up by twilight, and the other deep enough not to be dried like a shallow pool by a noon-day sun. (SL, Ch. III, para. 13)

The Primal Power of Architecture

For every distance from the eye there is a peculiar kind of beauty, or a different system of lines of form; the sight of that beauty is reserved for that distance, and for that alone. If you approach nearer, that kind of beauty is lost, and another succeeds, to be disorganised and reduced to strange and incomprehensible means and appliances in its turn. If you desire to perceive the great harmonies of the form of a rocky mountain, you must not ascend upon its sides. All is there disorder and accident, or seems so; sudden starts of its shattered beds hither and thither; ugly struggles of unexpected strength from under the ground; fallen fragments, toppling one over another into more helpless fall. Retire from it, and, as your eye commands it more and more, as you see the ruined mountain world with a wider glance, behold! dim sympathies begin to busy themselves in the disjointed mass; line binds itself into stealthy fellowship with line; group by group, the helpless fragments gather themselves into ordered companies; new captains of hosts and masses of battalions become visible, one by one, and far away answers of foot to foot, and of bone to bone, until the powerless chaos is seen risen up with girded loins, and not one piece of all the unregarded heap could now be spared from the mystic whole.

Now it is indeed true that where nature loses one kind of beauty, as you approach it, she substitutes another; this is worthy of her infinite power: and, as we shall see, art can sometimes follow her even in doing this. (SV I, Ch. XXI, paras. 17–18)

The rolling heap of the thunder-cloud, divided by rents, and multiplied by wreaths, yet gathering them all into its broad, torrid, and towering zone, and its midnight darkness opposite; the scarcely less majestic heave of the mountain side, all torn and traversed by depth of defile and ridge of rock, yet never losing the unity of its illumined swell and shadowy decline; and the head of every mighty tree, rich with tracery of leaf and bough, yet terminated against the sky by a true line, and rounded by a green horizon, which, multiplied in the distant forest, makes it look bossy from above; all these mark, for a great and honoured law, that diffusion of light for which the Byzantine ornaments were designed; and show us that those builders had truer sympathy with what God made majestic, than the self-contemplating and self-contented Greek. I know that they are barbaric in comparison; but there is a power in their barbarism of sterner tone, a power not sophistic nor penetrative, but embracing and mysterious; a power faithful more than thoughtful, which conceived and felt more than it created; a power that neither comprehended nor ruled itself, but worked and wandered as it listed, like mountain streams and winds; and which could not rest in the expression or seizure of finite form. It could not bury itself in acanthus leaves. Its imagery was taken from the shadows of the storms and hills, and had fellowship with the night and day of the earth itself. (SL, Ch. III, para. 15)

The Discovery of Venice:
the church of Tortello, imagined first landing place of the exiles who were to found Venice seven miles further south –

It has evidently been built by men in flight and distress, who sought in the hurried erection of their island church such a shelter for their earnest and sorrowful worship as, on the one hand, could not attract the eyes of their enemies by its splendour, and yet, on the other, might not awaken too bitter feelings by its contrast with the churches which they had seen destroyed. There is visible everywhere a simple and tender effort to recover some of the form of the temples which they had loved, and to do honour to God by that which they were erecting, while distress and humiliation prevented the desire, and prudence precluded the admission, either of luxury of ornament or magnificence of plan. The exterior is absolutely devoid of decoration, with the exception only of the western entrance and the lateral door, of which the former has carved sideposts and architrave, and the latter, crosses of rich sculpture; while the massy stone shutters of the windows, turning on huge rings of stone, which answer the double purpose of stanchions and brackets, cause the whole building rather to

Plate 21 *West Porch of Rouen Cathedral – architectural power*

resemble a refuge from Alpine storm than the cathedral of a populous city; and, internally, the two solemn mosaics of the eastern and western extremities, – one representing the Last Judgment, the other the Madonna, her tears falling as her hands are raised to bless, – and the noble range of pillars which enclose the space between, terminated by the high throne for the pastor and the semicircular raised seats for the superior clergy, are expressive at once of the deep sorrow and the sacred courage of men who had no home left them upon earth, but who looked for one to come [Isaiah xli. 25], of men 'persecuted but not forsaken, cast down but not destroyed' [2 Corinthians iv. 9].

I am not aware of any other early church in Italy which has this peculiar expression in so marked a degree; and it is so consistent with all that Christian architecture ought to express in every age (for the actual condition of the exiles who built the cathedral of Torcello is exactly typical of the spiritual condition which every Christian ought to recognise in himself, a state of homelessness on earth, except so far as he can make the Most High his habitation), that I would rather fix the mind of the reader on this general character than on the separate details, however interesting, of the architecture itself . . .

What is very peculiar to this church [is] its luminousness. This perhaps strikes the traveller more from its contrast with the excessive gloom of the Church of St Mark's; but it is remarkable when we compare the Cathedral of Torcello with any of the contemporary basilicas in South Italy or Lombardic churches in the North. St Ambrogio at Milan, St Michele at Pavia, St. Zeno at Verona, St Frediano at Lucca, St Miniato at Florence, are all like sepulchral caverns compared with Torcello, where the slightest details of the sculptures and mosaics are visible, even when twilight is deepening. And there is something especially touching in our finding the sunshine thus freely admitted into a church built by men in sorrow. They did not need the darkness; they could not perhaps bear it. There was fear and depression upon them enough, without a material gloom. They sought for comfort in their religion, for tangible hopes and promises, not for threatenings or mysteries; and though the subjects chosen for the mosaics on the walls are of the most solemn character, there are no artificial shadows cast upon them, nor dark colours used in them: all is fair and bright, and intended evidently to be regarded in hopefulness, and not with terror.[1] (SV II, Ch. II, paras. 3–4, 8)

The Rise of Venice itself

The strange rising of its walls and towers out of the midst, as it seemed, of the deep sea . . . Well might it seem that such a city had owed her existence rather to the rod of the enchanter, than the fear of the fugitive; that the waters which encircled her had been chosen for the mirror of her state, rather than the shelter of her nakedness; and that all which in nature was wild or merciless, – Time and Decay, as well as the waves and tempests, – had been won to adorn her instead of to destroy, and might still spare, for ages to come, that beauty which seemed to have fixed for its throne the sands of the hour-glass as well as of the sea. (SV II, Ch. I, para. 1)

So precious, indeed, and so full of majesty, that sometimes when walking at evening on the Lido, whence the great chain of the Alps, crested with silver clouds, might be seen rising above the front of the Ducal Palace, I used to feel as much awe in gazing on the building as on the hills, and could believe that God had done a greater work in breathing into the narrowness of dust the mighty spirits by which its haughty walls had been raised, and its burning legends written, than in lifting the rocks of granite higher than the clouds of heaven, and veiling them with their various mantle of purple flower and shadowy pine. (SV II, Ch. VIII, para. 140)

The Ducal Palace:
the balance of linear and surface Gothic

In whatever direction the building is contracted, in that direction the eye will be drawn to its terminal lines; and the sense of surface will only be at its fullest when those lines are removed, in every direction, as far as possible. Thus the square and circle are pre-eminently the areas of power among those bounded by purely straight or curved lines; and these, with their relative solids, the cube and sphere, and relative solids of progression, (as in the investigation of the laws of proportion I shall call those masses which are generated by the progression of an area of given form along a line in a given direction,) the square and cylindrical column, are the elements of utmost power in all architectural arrangements. On the other hand, grace and perfect proportion require an elongation in some one direction: and a sense of power may be communicated to this form of magnitude by a continuous series of any marked features, such as the eye may be unable to number; while yet we feel, from their boldness, decision, and simplicity, that it is indeed their multitude which has embarrassed us, not any confusion or indistinctness of form. This expedient of continued series forms the sublimity of arcades and aisles, of all ranges of columns, and, on a smaller scale, of those Greek mouldings, of which, repeated as they now are in all the meanest and most familiar forms of our furniture, it is impossible altogether to weary. Now, it is evident that the architect has choice of two types of form, each properly associated with its own kind of interest or decoration: the square, or greatest area, to be chosen especially when the *surface* is to be the subject of thought; and the elongated area, when the *divisions* of the surface are to be subjects of thought. Both these orders of form, as I think nearly every other source of power and beauty, are marvellously united in that building which I fear to weary the reader by bringing forward too frequently, as a model of all perfection – the Doge's palace at Venice: its general arrangement, a hollow square; its principal façade, an oblong, elongated to the eye by a range of thirty-four small arches, and thirty-five columns, while it is separated by a richly canopied window in the centre, into two massive divisions, whose height and length are nearly as four to five; the arcades which give it length being confined to the lower storeys, and the upper, between its broad windows, left a mighty surface of smooth marble, chequered with blocks of alternate rose-colour and white. It would be impossible, I believe, to invent a more magnificent arrangement of all that is in building most dignified and most fair. (SL, Ch. III, para. 9)

'The Nature of Gothic'

I believe, then, that the characteristic or moral elements of Gothic are the following, placed in the order of their importance:

1. Savageness
2. Changefulness
3. Naturalism
4. Grotesqueness
5. Rigidity
6. Redundance

These characters are here expressed as belonging to the

Plate 22 *The Ducal Palace, Venice*

building; as belonging to the builder, they would be expressed thus:— 1. Savageness or Rudeness. 2. Love of Change. 3. Love of Nature. 4. Disturbed Imagination. 5. Obstinacy. 6. Generosity. And I repeat, that the withdrawal of any one, or any two, will not at once destroy the Gothic character of a building, but the removal of a majority of them will. I shall proceed to examine them in their order.

(1) SAVAGENESS. I am not sure when the word 'Gothic' was first generically applied to the architecture of the North; but I presume that, whatever the date of its original usage, it was intended to imply reproach, and express the barbaric character of the nations among whom that architecture arose. It never implied that they were literally of Gothic lineage, far less that their architecture had been originally invented by the Goths themselves; but it did imply that they and their buildings together exhibited a degree of sternness and rudeness, which, in contradistinction to the character of Southern and Eastern nations, appeared like a perpetual reflection of the contrast between the Goth and the Roman in their first encounter. And when that fallen Roman, in the utmost impotence of his luxury, and insolence of his guilt, became the model for the imitation of civilized Europe, at the close of the so-called Dark ages, the word Gothic became a term of unmitigated contempt, not unmixed with aversion. From that contempt, by the exertion of the antiquaries and architects of this century, Gothic architecture has been sufficiently vindicated; and perhaps some among us, in our admiration of the magnificent science of its structure, and sacredness of its expression, might desire that the term of ancient reproach should be withdrawn, and some other, of more apparent honourableness, adopted in its place. There is no chance, as there is no need, of such a substitution. As far as the epithet was used scornfully, it was used falsely; but there is no reproach in the word, rightly understood; on the contrary, there is a profound truth, which the instinct of mankind almost unconsciously recognizes. It is true, greatly and deeply true, that the architecture of the North is rude and wild; but it is not true, that, for this reason, we are to condemn it, or despise. Far otherwise: I believe it is in this very character that it deserves our profoundest reverence.

The charts of the world which have been drawn up by modern science have thrown into a narrow space the expression of a vast amount of knowledge, but I have never yet seen any one pictorial enough to enable the spectator to imagine the kind of contrast in physical character which exists between Northern and Southern countries. We know the differences in detail, but we have not that broad glance and grasp which would enable us to feel them in their fulness. We know that gentians grow on the Alps, and olives on the Apennines; but we do not enough conceive for ourselves that variegated mosaic of the world's surface which a bird sees in its migration, that difference between the district of the gentian and of the olive which the stork and the swallow see far off, as they lean upon the sirocco wind. Let us, for a moment, try to raise ourselves even above the level of their flight, and imagine the Mediterranean lying beneath us like an irregular lake, and all its ancient promontories sleeping in the sun: here and there an angry spot of thunder, a grey stain of storm, moving upon the burning field; and here and there a fixed wreath of white volcano smoke, surrounded by its circle of ashes; but for the most part a great peacefulness of light, Syria and Greece, Italy and Spain, laid like pieces of a golden pavement into the sea-blue, chased, as we stoop nearer to them, with bossy beaten work of mountain chains, and glowing softly with terraced gardens, and flowers heavy with frankincense, mixed among masses of laurel, and orange, and plumy palm, that abate with their grey-green shadows the burning of the marble rocks, and of the ledges of porphyry sloping under lucent sand. Then let us pass farther towards the north, until we see the orient colours change gradually into a vast belt of rainy green, where the pastures of Switzerland, and poplar valleys of France, and dark forests of the Danube and Carpathians stretch from the mouths of the Loire to those of the Volga, seen through clefts in grey swirls of rain-cloud and flaky veils of the mist of the brooks, spreading low along the pasture lands: and then, farther north still, to see the earth heave into mighty masses of leaden rock and healthy moor, bordering with a broad waste of gloomy purple that belt of field and wood, and splintering into irregular and grisly islands amidst the northern seas, beaten by storm, and chilled by ice-drift, and tormented by furious pulses of contending tide, until the roots of the last forests fail from among the hill ravines, and the hunger of the north wind bites their peaks into barrenness; and, at last, the wall of ice, durable like iron, sets, deathlike, its white teeth against us out of the polar twilight. And, having once traversed in thought this gradation of the zoned iris of the earth in all its material vastness, let us go down nearer to it, and watch the parallel change in the belt of animal life; the multitudes of swift and brilliant creatures that glance in the air and sea, or tread the sands of the southern zone; striped zebras and spotted leopards, glistening serpents, and birds arrayed in purple and scarlet. Let us contrast their delicacy and brilliancy of colour, and swiftness of motion, with the frost-cramped strength, and shaggy covering, and dusky plumage of the northern tribes; contrast the Arabian horse with the Shetland, the tiger and leopard with the wolf and bear, the antelope with the elk, the bird of paradise with the osprey; and then, submissively acknowledging the great laws by which the earth and all that it bears are ruled throughout their being, let us not condemn, but rejoice in the expression by man of his own rest in the statutes of the lands that gave him birth. Let us watch him with reverence as he sets side by side the burning gems, and smooths with soft sculpture the jasper pillars, that are to reflect a ceaseless sunshine, and rise into a cloudless sky: but not with less reverence let us stand by him, when, with rough strength and hurried stroke, he smites an uncouth animation out of the rocks which he has torn from among the moss of the moorland, and heaves into the darkened air the pile of iron buttress and rugged wall, instinct with work of an imagination as wild and wayward as the northern sea; creatures of ungainly shape and rigid limb, but full of wolfish life; fierce as the winds that beat, and changeful as the clouds that shade them.

There is, I repeat, no degradation, no reproach in this, but all dignity and honourableness: and we should err grievously in refusing either to recognize as an essential character of the existing architecture of the North, or to admit as a desirable character in that which it yet may be, this wildness of thought, and roughness of work; this look of mountain brotherhood between the cathedral and the Alp; this magnificence of sturdy power, put forth only the more energetically because the fine finger-touch was chilled away by the frosty wind, and the eye dimmed by the moor-mist, or blinded by the hail; this out-speaking of the strong spirit of men who may not gather redundant fruitage from the earth, nor bask in dreamy benignity of sunshine, but must break the rock for bread, and cleave the forest for fire, and show, even in what they did for their delight, some of the hard habits of the arm and heart that grew on them as they swung the axe or pressed the plough.

If, however, the savageness of Gothic architecture, merely as an expression of its origin among Northern nations, may be considered, in some sort, a noble character, it possesses a higher nobility still, when considered as an index, not of climate, but of religious principle.

In the 13th and 14th paragraphs of Chapter XXI of the first volume of this work, it was noticed that the systems of architectural ornament, properly so called, might be divided into three:— 1. Servile ornament, in which the execution or power of the inferior workman is entirely subjected to the intellect of the higher;— 2. Constitutional ornament, in which the executive inferior power is, to a certain point, emancipated and independent, having a will of its own, yet confessing its inferiority and rendering obedience to higher powers;— and 3. Revolutionary ornament, in which no executive inferiority is admitted at all. I must here explain the nature of these divisions at somewhat greater length.

Of Servile ornament, the principal schools are the Greek, Ninevite, and Egyptian; but their servility is of different kinds. The Greek master-workman was far advanced in knowledge and power above the Assyrian or Egyptian. Neither he nor those for whom he worked could endure the appearance of imperfection in anything; and, therefore, what ornament he appointed to be done by those beneath him was composed of mere geometrical forms, – balls, ridges, and perfectly symmetrical foliage, – which could be executed with absolute precision by line and rule, and were as perfect in their way, when completed, as his own figure sculpture. The Assyrian and Egyptian, on the contrary, less cognisant of accurate form in anything, were content to allow their figure sculpture to be executed by inferior workmen, but lowered the method of its treatment to a standard which every workman could reach, and then trained him by discipline so rigid, that there was no chance of his falling beneath the standard appointed. The Greek gave to the lower workman no subject which he could not perfectly execute. The Assyrian gave him subjects which he could only execute imperfectly, but fixed a legal standard for his imperfection. The workman was, in both systems, a slave.[a]

---

[a] *Ruskin adds a footnote:*
The third kind of ornament, the Renaissance, is that in which the inferior detail becomes principal, the executor of every minor portion being required to

But in the mediæval, or especially Christian, system of ornament, this slavery is done away with altogether; Christianity
having recognized, in small things as well as great, the individual
value of every soul. But it not only recognizes its value; it confesses
its imperfection, in only bestowing dignity upon the acknowledgment of unworthiness. That admission of lost power and
fallen nature, which the Greek or Ninevite felt to be intensely
painful, and, as far as might be, altogether refused, the Christian
makes daily and hourly, contemplating the fact of it without fear,
as tending, in the end, to God's greater glory. Therefore, to every
spirit which Christianity summons to her service, her exhortation
is: Do what you can, and confess frankly what you are unable to
do; neither let your effort be shortened for fear of failure, nor your
confession silenced for fear of shame. And it is, perhaps, the
principal admirableness of the Gothic schools of architecture,
that they thus receive the results of the labour of inferior minds;
and out of fragments full of imperfection, and betraying that
imperfection in every touch, indulgently raise up a stately and
unaccusable whole.

But the modern English mind has this much in common with
that of the Greek, that it intensely desires, in all things, the utmost
completion or perfection compatible with their nature. This is a
noble character in the abstract, but becomes ignoble when it
causes us to forget the relative dignities of that nature itself, and to
prefer the perfectness of the lower nature to the imprefection of
the higher; not considering that as, judged by such a rule, all the

exhibit skill and possess knowledge as great as that which is possessed by the
master of the design; and in the endeavour to endow him with this skill and
knowledge, his own original power is overwhelmed, and the whole building
becomes a wearisome exhibition of well-educated imbecility. We must fully
inquire into the nature of this form of error, when we arrive at the examination
of the Renaissance schools.

Ruskin's rule on true ornament was:
That it be beautiful in its place, and nowhere else, and that it aid the effect of
every portion of the building over which it has influence; that it does not, by its
richness, make other parts bald, or by its delicacy, make other parts coarse.
Every one of its qualities has reference to its place and use: *and it is fitted for its
service by what would be faults and deficiencies if it had no especial duty.*
Ornament, the servant, is often formal, where sculpture, the master, would
have been free; the servant is often silent where the master would have been
eloquent; or hurried, where the master would have been serene. (SV I, Ch. XXI,
para. 4)

brute animals would be preferable to man, because more perfect in their functions and kind, and yet are always held inferior to him, so also in the works of man, those which are more perfect in their kind are always inferior to those which are, in their nature, liable to more faults and shortcomings. For the finer the nature, the more flaws it will show through the clearness of it; and it is a law of this universe, that the best things shall be seldomest seen in their best form. The wild grass grows well and strongly, one year with another; but the wheat is, according to the greater nobleness of its nature, liable to the bitterer blight. And therefore, while in all things that we see or do, we are to desire perfection, and strive for it, we are nevertheless not to set the meaner thing, in its narrow accomplishment, above the nobler thing, in its mighty progress; not to esteem smooth minuteness above shattered majesty; not to prefer mean victory to honourable defeat; not to lower the level of our aim, that we may the more surely enjoy the complacency of success.[2] But, above all, in our dealings with the souls of other men, we are to take care how we check, by severe requirement or narrow caution, efforts which might otherwise lead to a noble issue; and, still more, how we withhold our admiration from great excellencies, because they are mingled with rough faults. Now, in the make and nature of every man, however rude or simple, whom we employ in manual labour, there are some powers for better things; some tardy imagination, torpid capacity of emotion, tottering steps of thought, there are, even at the worst; and in most cases it is all our own fault that they *are* tardy or torpid. But they cannot be strengthened, unless we are content to take them in their feebleness, and unless we prize and honour them in their imperfection above the best and most perfect manual skill. And this is what we have to do with all our labourers; to look for the *thoughtful* part of them, and get that out of them, whatever we lose for it, whatever faults and errors we are obliged to take with it. For the best that is in them cannot manifest itself, but in company with much error. Understand this clearly: You can teach a man to draw a straight line, and to cut one; to strike a curved line, and to carve it; and to copy and carve any number of given lines or forms, with admirable speed and perfect precision; and you find his work perfect of its kind: but if you ask him to think about any of those forms, to consider if he cannot find any better in his own head, he stops; his execution becomes hesitating; he thinks, and ten to one he thinks wrong; ten to one he makes a mistake in the first touch he gives to his work as a thinking being. But you have made a man of him for all that. He was only a machine before, an animated tool.

And observe, you are put to stern choice in this matter. You must either make a tool of the creature, or a man of him. You cannot make both. Men were not intended to work with the accuracy of tools, to be precise and perfect in all their actions. If you will have that precision out of them, and make their fingers measure degrees like cog-wheels, and their arms strike curves like compasses, you must unhumanize them. All the energy of their spirits must be given to make cogs and compasses of themselves. All their attention and strength must go to the accomplishment of the mean act. The eye of the soul must be bent upon the finger-point, and the soul's force must fill all the invisible nerves that guide it, ten hours a day, that it may not err from its steely precision, and so soul and sight be worn away, and the whole human being be lost at last — a heap of sawdust, so far as its intellectual work in this world is concerned: saved only by its Heart, which cannot go into the form of cogs and compasses, but expands, after the ten hours are over, into fireside humanity. On the other hand, if you will make a man of the working creature, you cannot make a tool. Let him but begin to imagine, to think, to try to do anything worth doing; and the engine-turned precision is lost at once. Out come all his roughness, all his dulness, all his incapability; shame upon shame, failure upon failure, pause after pause: but out comes the whole majesty of him also; and we know the height of it only when we see the clouds settling upon him. And, whether the clouds be bright or dark, there will be transfiguration behind and within them.

And now, reader, look round this English room of yours, about which you have been proud so often, because the work of it was so good and strong, and the ornaments of it so finished. Examine again all those accurate mouldings, and perfect polishings, and unerring adjustments of the seasoned wood and tempered steel. Many a time you have exulted over them, and thought how great England was, because her slightest work was done so thoroughly. Alas! if read rightly, these perfectnesses are signs of a slavery in our England a thousand times more bitter and more degrading than that of the scourged African, or helot Greek. Men may be beaten, chained, tormented, yoked like cattle, slaughtered like summer flies, and yet remain in one sense, and the best sense, free.

But to smother their souls with them, to blight and hew into rotting pollards the suckling branches of their human intelligence, to make the flesh and skin which, after the worm's work on it, is to see God [Job xix. 26], into leathern thongs to yoke machinery with, – this is to be slave-masters indeed; and there might be more freedom in England, though her feudal lords' lightest words were worth men's lives, and though the blood of the vexed husband-man dropped in the furrows of her fields, than there is while the animation of her multitudes is sent like fuel to feed the factory smoke, and the strength of them is given daily to be wasted into the fineness of a web, or racked into the exactness of a line.

And, on the other hand, go forth again to gaze upon the old cathedral front, where you have smiled so often at the fantastic ignorance of the old sculptors: examine once more those ugly goblins, and formless monsters, and stern statues, anatomiless and rigid; but do not mock at them, for they are signs of the life and liberty of every workman who struck the stone; a freedom of thought, and rank in scale of being, such as no laws, no charters, no charities can secure; but which it must be the first aim of all Europe at this day to regain for her children.

Let me not be thought to speak wildly or extravagantly. It is verily this degradation of the operative into a machine, which, more than any other evil of the times, is leading the mass of the nations everywhere into vain, incoherent, destructive struggling for a freedom of which they cannot explain the nature to themselves. Their universal outcry against wealth, and against nobility, is not forced from them either by the pressure of famine, or the sting of mortified pride. These do much, and have done much in all ages; but the foundations of society were never yet shaken as they are at this day. It is not that men are ill fed, but that they have no pleasure in the work by which they make their bread, and therefore look to wealth as the only means of pleasure. It is not that men are pained by the scorn of the upper classes, but they cannot endure their own; for they feel that the kind of labour to which they are condemned is verily a degrading one, and makes them less than men. Never had the upper classes so much sympathy with the lower, or charity for them, as they have at this day, and yet never were they so much hated by them: for, of old, the separation between the noble and the poor was merely a wall built by law; now it is a veritable difference in level of standing, a precipice between upper and lower grounds in the field of humanity, and there is pestilential air at the bottom of it. I know not if a day is ever to come when the nature of right freedom will be understood, and when men will see that to obey another man, to labour for him, yield reverence to him or to his place, is not slavery. It is often the best kind of liberty, – liberty from care. The man who says to one, Go, and he goeth, and to another, Come, and he cometh [Matthew viii. 9], has, in most cases, more sense of restraint and difficulty than the man who obeys him. The movements of the one are hindered by the burden on his shoulder; of the other by the bridle on his lips: there is no way by which the burden may be lightened; but we need not suffer from the bridle if we do not champ at it. To yield reverence to another, to hold ourselves and our likes at his disposal, is not slavery; often it is the noblest state in which a man can live in this world. There is, indeed, a reverence which is servile, that is to say, irrational or selfish: but there is also noble reverence, that is to say, reasonable and loving; and a man is never so noble as when he is reverent in this kind; nay, even if the feeling pass the bounds of mere reason, so that it be loving, a man is raised by it. Which had, in reality, most of the serf nature in him, – the Irish peasant who was lying in wait yesterday for his landlord, with his musket muzzle thrust through the ragged hedge,[3] or that old mountain servant, who 200 years ago, at Inverkeithing, gave up his own life and the lives of his seven sons for his chief? – as each fell, calling forth his brother to the death, 'Another for Hector!'[4] And therefore, in all ages and all countries, reverence has been paid and sacrifice made by men to each other, not only without complaint, but rejoicingly; and famine, and peril, and sword, and all evil, and all shame, have been borne willingly in the causes of masters and kings; for all these gifts of the heart ennobled the men who gave, not less than the men who received them, and nature prompted, and God rewarded the sacrifice. But to feel their souls withering within them, unthanked, to find their whole being sunk into an unrecognized abyss, to be counted off into a heap of mechanism numbered with its wheels, and weighed with its hammer strokes – this, nature bade not, – this, God blesses not, – this, humanity for no long time is able to endure.

We have much studied and much perfected, of late, the great civilized invention of the division of labour;[5] only we give it a false name. It is not, truly speaking, the labour that is divided; but the men: – Divided into mere segments of men – broken into small fragments and crumbs of life; so that all the little piece of intelligence that is left in a man is not enough to make a pin, or a nail, but exhausts itself in making the point of a pin or the head of a nail. Now it is a good and desirable thing, truly, to make many pins in a day; but if we could only see with what crystal sand their points were polished, – sand of human soul, much to be magnified before it can be discerned for what it is – we should think there might be some loss in it also. And the great cry that rises from all our manufacturing cities, louder than their furnace blast, is all in very deed for this, – that we manufacture everything there except men; we blanch cotton, and strengthen steel, and refine sugar, and shape pottery; but to brighten, to strengthen, to refine, or to form a single living spirit, never enters into our estimate of advantages. And all the evil to which that cry is urging our myriads can be met only in one way: not by teaching nor preaching, for to teach them is but to show them their misery, and to preach to them, if we do nothing more than preach, is to mock at it. It can be met only by a right understanding, on the part of all classes, of what kinds of labour are good for men, raising them, and making them happy; by a determined sacrifice of such convenience, or beauty, or cheapness as is to be got only by the degradation of the workman; and by equally determined demand for the products and results of healthy and ennobling labour.

And how, it will be asked, are these products to be recognized, and this demand to be regulated? Easily: by the observance of three broad and simple rules:

1. Never encourage the manufacture of any article not absolutely necessary, in the production of which *Invention* has no share.

2. Never demand an exact finish for its own sake, but only for some practical or noble end.

3. Never encourage imitation or copying of any kind, except for the sake of preserving records of great works.

The second of these principles is the only one which directly rises out of the consideration of our immediate subject; but I shall briefly explain the meaning and extent of the first also, reserving the enforcement of the third for another place.

1. Never encourage the manufacture of anything not necessary, in the production of which invention has no share.

For instance. Glass beads are utterly unnecessary, and there is no design or thought employed in their manufacture. They are formed by first drawing out the glass into rods; these rods are chopped up into fragments of the size of beads by the human hand, and the fragments are then rounded in the furnace. The men who chop up the rods sit at their work all day, their hands vibrating with a perpetual and exquisitely timed palsy, and the beads dropping beneath their vibration like hail. Neither they, nor the men who draw out the rods or fuse the fragments, have the smallest occasion for the use of any single human faculty; and every young lady, therefore, who buys glass beads is engaged in the slave-trade, and in a much more cruel one than that which we have so long been endeavouring to put down.[6]

But glass cups and vessels may become the subjects of exquisite invention; and if in buying these we pay for the invention, that is to say, for the beautiful form, or colour, or engraving, and not for mere finish of execution, we are doing good to humanity.

So, again, the cutting of precious stones, in all ordinary cases, requires little exertion of any mental faculty; some tact and judgment in avoiding flaws, and so on, but nothing to bring out the whole mind. Every person who wears cut jewels merely for the sake of their value is, therefore, a slave-driver.

But the working of the goldsmith, and the various designing of grouped jewellery and enamel-work, may become the subject of the most noble human intelligence. Therefore, money spent in the purchase of well-designed plate, of precious engraved vases, cameos, or enamels, does good to humanity; and in work of this kind, jewels may be employed to heighten its splendour; and their cutting is then a price paid for the attainment of a noble end, and thus perfectly allowable.

I shall perhaps press this law farther elsewhere, but our immediate concern is chiefly with the second, namely, never to demand an exact finish, when it does not lead to a noble end. For observe, I have only dwelt upon the rudeness of Gothic, or any other kind of imperfectness, as admirable, where it was impossible to get design or thought without it. If you are to have the thought of a rough and untaught man, you must have it in a rough and untaught way; but from an educated man, who can without effort express his thoughts in an educated way, take the graceful expression, and be thankful. Only *get* the thought, and do not silence the peasant because he cannot speak good grammar, or until you have taught him his grammar. Grammar and refinement are good things, both, only be sure of the better thing first. And thus in art, delicate finish is desirable from the greatest masters, and is always given by them. In some places Michael Angelo, Leonardo, Phidias, Perugino, Turner, all finished with the most exquisite care; and the finish they give always leads to the fuller accomplishment of their noble purposes. But lower men than these cannot finish, for it requires consummate knowledge to finish consummately, and then we must take their thoughts as they are able to give them. So the rule is simple: Always look for invention first, and after that, for such execution as will help the invention, and as the inventor is capable of without painful effort, and *no more*. Above all, demand no refinement of execution where there is no thought, for that is slaves' work, unredeemed. Rather choose rough work than smooth work, so only that the practical purpose be answered, and never imagine there is reason to be proud of anything that may be accomplished by patience and sand-paper.

I shall only give one example, which however will show the reader what I mean, from the manufacture already alluded to, that of glass. Our modern glass is exquisitely clear in its substance, true in its form, accurate in its cutting. We are proud of this. We ought to be ashamed of it. The old Venice glass was muddy, inaccurate in all its forms, and clumsily cut, if at all. And the old Venetian was justly proud of it. For there is this difference between the English and Venetian workman, that the former thinks only of accurately matching his patterns, and getting his curves perfectly true and his edges perfectly sharp, and becomes a mere machine for rounding curves and sharpening edges; while the old Venetian cared not a whit whether his edges were sharp or not, but he invented a new design for every glass that he made, and never moulded a handle or a lip without a new fancy in it. And therefore, though some Venetian glass is ugly and clumsy enough when made by clumsy and uninventive workmen, other Venetian glass is so lovely in its forms that no price is too great for it; and we never see the same form in it twice. Now you cannot have the finish and the varied form too. If the workman is thinking about his edges, he cannot be thinking of his design; if of his design, he cannot think of his edges. Choose whether you will pay for the lovely form or the perfect finish, and choose at the same moment whether you will make the worker a man or a grindstone.

Nay, but the reader interrupts me, – 'If the workman can design beautifully, I would not have him kept at the furnace. Let him be taken away and made a gentleman, and have a studio, and design his glass there, and I will have it blown and cut for him by common workmen, and so I will have my design and my finish too.'

All ideas of this kind are founded upon two mistaken suppositions: the first, that one man's thoughts can be, or ought to be, executed by another man's hands; the second, that manual labour is a degradation, when it is governed by intellect.

On a large scale, and in work determinable by line and rule, it is indeed both possible and necessary that the thoughts of one man should be carried out by the labour of others; in this sense I have already defined the best architecture to be the expression of the mind of manhood by the hands of childhood.[7] But on a smaller scale, and in a design which cannot be mathematically defined, one man's thoughts can never be expressed by another: and the difference between the spirit of touch of the man who is inventing, and of the man who is obeying directions, is often all the difference between a great and a common work of art. How wide the separation is between original and second-hand execution, I shall endeavour to show elsewhere;[8] it is not so much to our purpose here as to mark the other and more fatal error of despising manual labour when governed by intellect; for it is no less fatal an error to despise it when thus regulated by intellect, than to value it for its own sake. We are always in these days endeavouring to separate the two; we want one man to be always thinking, and another to be always working, and we call one a gentleman, and the other an operative; whereas the workman ought often to be thinking, and the thinker often to be working, and both should be gentlemen, in the best sense. As it is, we make both ungentle, the one envying, the other despising, his brother; and the mass of society is made up of morbid thinkers, and miserable workers. Now it is only by labour that thought can be made healthy, and only by thought that labour can be made happy, and the two cannot be separated with impunity. It would be well if all of us were good handicraftsmen in some kind, and the dishonour of manual labour done away with altogether; so that though there should still be a trenchant distinction of race between nobles and commoners, there should not, among the latter, be a trenchant distinction of employment, as between idle and working men, or between men of liberal and illiberal professions. All professions should be liberal, and there should be less pride felt in peculiarity of employment, and more in excellence of achievement. And yet more, in each several profession, no master should be too proud to do its hardest work. The painter should grind his own colours; the architect work in the mason's yard with his men; the master-manufacturer be himself a more skilful operative than any man in his mills; and the distinction between one man and another be only in experience and skill, and the authority and wealth which these must naturally and justly obtain.

I should be led far from the matter in hand, if I were to pursue this interesting subject. Enough, I trust, has been said to show the reader that the rudeness or imperfection which at first rendered the term 'Gothic' one of reproach is indeed, when rightly understood, one of the most noble characters of Christian architecture, and not only a noble but an *essential* one. It seems a fantastic paradox, but it is nevertheless a most important truth, that no architecture can be truly noble which is *not* imperfect. And this is easily demonstrable. For since the architect, whom we will suppose capable of doing all in perfection, cannot execute the whole with his own hands, he must either make slaves of his workmen in the old Greek, and present English fashion, and level his work to a slave's capacities, which is to degrade it; or else he must take his workmen as he finds them, and let them show their weaknesses together with their strength, which will involve the Gothic imperfection, but render the whole work as noble as the intellect of the age can make it.

But the principle may be stated more broadly still. I have confined the illustration of it to architecture, but I must not leave it as if true of architecture only. Hitherto I have used the words imperfect and perfect merely to distinguish between work grossly unskilful, and work executed with average precision and science; and I have been pleading that any degree of unskilfulness should be admitted, so only that the labourer's mind had room for expression. But, accurately speaking, no good work whatever can be perfect, and *the demand for perfection is always a sign of a misunderstanding of the ends of art*.

This for two reasons, both based on everlasting laws. The first, that no great man ever stops working till he has reached his point of failure: that is to say, his mind is always far in advance of his powers of execution, and the latter will now and then give way in trying to follow it; besides that he will always give to the inferior portions of his work only such inferior attention as they require; and according to his greatness he becomes so accustomed to the feeling of dissatisfaction with the best he can do, that in moments of lassitude or anger with himself he will not care though the beholder be dissatisfied also. I believe there has only been one man who would not acknowledge this necessity, and strove always to reach perfection, Leonardo; the end of his vain effort being merely that he would take ten years to a picture and leave it unfinished. And therefore, if we are to have great men working at all, or less men doing their best, the work will be imperfect, however beautiful. Of human work none but what is bad can be perfect, in its own bad way.

The second reason is, that imperfection is in some sort essential to all that we know of life. It is the sign of life in a mortal body, that is to say, of a state of progress and change. Nothing that lives is, or can be, rigidly perfect; part of it is decaying, part nascent. The foxglove blossom, – a third part bud, a third part past, a third part in full bloom, – is a type of the life of this world. And in all things that live there are certain irregularities and deficiencies which are not only signs of life, but sources of beauty. No human face is exactly the same in its lines on each side, no leaf perfect in its lobes, no branch in its symmetry. All admit irregularity as they imply change; and to banish imperfection is to destroy expression, to check exertion, to paralyze vitality. All things are literally better, lovelier, and more beloved for the imperfections which have been divinely appointed, that the law of human life may be Effort, and the law of human judgment, Mercy.

Accept this then for a universal law, that neither architecture nor any other noble work of man can be good unless it be imperfect; and let us be prepared for the otherwise strange fact, which we shall discern clearly as we approach the period of the Renaissance, that the first cause of the fall of the arts of Europe was a relentless requirement of perfection, incapable alike either of being silenced by veneration for greatness, or softened into forgiveness of simplicity.

Thus far then of the Rudeness or Savageness, which is the first mental element of Gothic architecture. It is an element in many other healthy architectures also, as the Byzantine and Romanesque; but true Gothic cannot exist without it.

The second mental element above named was CHANGEFULNESS, or Variety.

I have already enforced the allowing independent operation to the inferior workman, simply as a duty to *him*, and as ennobling the architecture by rendering it more Christian. We have now to consider what reward we obtain for the performance of this duty, namely, the perpetual variety of every feature of the building.

Wherever the workman is utterly enslaved, the parts of the building must of course be absolutely like each other; for the perfection of his execution can only be reached by exercising him in doing one thing, and giving him nothing else to do. The degree in which the workman is degraded may be thus known at a glance, by observing whether the several parts of the building are similar or not; and if, as in Greek work, all the capitals are alike, and all the mouldings unvaried, then the degradation is complete; if, as in Egyptian or Ninevite work, though the manner of executing certain figures is always the same, the order of design is perpetually varied, the degradation is less total; if, as in Gothic work, there is perpetual change both in design and execution, the workman must have been altogether set free.

How much the beholder gains from the liberty of the labourer may perhaps be questioned in England, where one of the strongest instincts in nearly every mind is that Love of Order which makes us desire that our house windows should pair like our carriage horses, and allows us to yield our faith unhesitatingly to architectural theories which fix a form for everything, and forbid variation from it. I would not impeach love of order: it is one of the most useful elements of the English mind; it helps us in our commerce and in all purely practical matters; and it is in many cases one of the foundation stones of morality. Only do not let us suppose that love of order is love of art. It is true that order, in its highest sense, is one of the necessities of art, just as time is a necessity of music; but love of order has no more to do with our right enjoyment of architecture or painting, than love of punctuality with the appreciation of an opera. Experience, I fear, teaches us that accurate and methodical habits in daily life are seldom characteristic of those who either quickly perceive, or richly possess, the creative powers of art; there is, however, nothing inconsistent between the two instincts, and nothing to hinder us from retaining our business habits, and yet fully allowing and enjoying the noblest gifts of Invention. We already do so, in every other branch of art except architecture, and we only do *not* so there because we have been taught that it would be wrong. Our architects gravely inform us that, as there are four rules of arithmetic, there are five orders of architecture; we, in our simplicity, think that this sounds consistent, and believe them. They inform us also that there is one proper form for Corinthian capitals, another for Doric, and another for Ionic. We, considering that there is also a proper form for the letters A, B, and C, think that this also sounds consistent, and accept the proposition. Understanding, therefore, that one form of the said capitals is proper, and no other, and having a conscientious horror of all impropriety, we allow the architect to provide us with the said capitals, of the proper form, in such and such a quantity, and in all other points to take care that the legal forms are observed; which having done, we rest in forced confidence that we are well housed.

But our higher instincts are not deceived. We take no pleasure in the building provided for us, resembling that which we take in a new book or a new picture. We may be proud of its size, complacent in its correctness, and happy in its convenience. We may take the same pleasure in its symmetry and workmanship as in a well-ordered room, or a skilful piece of manufacture. And this we suppose to be all the pleasure that architecture was ever intended to give us. The idea of reading a building as we would read Milton or Dante, and getting the same kind of delight out of the stones as out of the stanzas, never enters our mind for a moment. And for good reason; – There is indeed rhythm in the verses, quite as strict as the symmetries or rhythm of the architecture, and a thousand times more beautiful, but there is something else than rhythm. The verses were neither made to order, nor to match, as the capitals were; and we have therefore a kind of pleasure in them other than a sense of propriety. But it requires a strong effort of common sense to shake ourselves quit of all that we have been taught for the last two centuries, and wake to the perception of a truth just as simple and certain as it is new: that great art, whether expressing itself in words, colours, or stones, does *not* say the same thing over and over again; that the merit of architectural, as of every other art, consists in its saying new and different things; that to repeat itself is no more a characteristic of genius in marble than it is of genius in print; and that we may, without offending any laws of good taste, require of an architect, as we do of a novelist, that he should be not only correct, but entertaining.

Yet all this is true, and self-evident; only hidden from us, as many other self-evident things are, by false teaching. Nothing is a great work of art, for the production of which either rules or models can be given. Exactly so far as architecture works on known rules, and from given models, it is not an art, but a manufacture; and it is, of the two procedures, rather less rational (because more easy) to copy capitals or mouldings from Phidias, and call ourselves architects, than to copy heads and hands from Titian, and call ourselves painters.

Let us then understand at once that change or variety is as much a necessity to the human heart and brain in buildings as in books; that there is no merit, though there is some occasional use, in monotony; and that we must no more expect to derive either pleasure or profit from an architecture whose ornaments are of one pattern, and whose pillars are of one proportion, than we should out of a universe in which the clouds were all of one shape, and the trees all of one size.

And this we confess in deeds, though not in words. All the pleasure which the people of the nineteenth century take in art, is in pictures, sculpture, minor objects of virtù, or mediæval architecture, which we enjoy under the term picturesque: no pleasure is taken anywhere in modern buildings, and we find all men of true feeling delighting to escape out of modern cities into natural scenery; hence, as I shall hereafter show, that peculiar love of landscape, which is characteristic of the age.[b] It would be well, if in all other matters, we were as ready to put up with what we dislike, for the sake of compliance with established law, as we are in architecture.

How so debased a law ever came to be established, we shall see when we come to describe the Renaissance schools; here we have only to note, as a second most essential element of the Gothic

[b] *Here Ruskin suddenly saw the link between his architectural work in Venice and his suspended work on* Modern Painters, *for as he wrote to his father, 22 February 1852:* 'I see a very interesting connexion . . . For, so long as the Gothic and other fine architecture existed, the love of Nature, which was an essential and a peculiar feature of Christianity, found expression and food in them . . . But when the Heathen architecture came back [in the Renaissance], this love of Nature, still happily existing in some minds, could find no more food there – it turned to landscape painting and has gradually worked up into Turner. The last part of this book, therefore, will be an introduction to the last of *Modern Painters.' Thus to Ruskin, Turner, in continuing the Gothic tradition, was a religious descendant of the medieval sculptors.*

spirit, that it broke through that law wherever it found it in existence; it not only dared, but delighted in, the infringement of every servile principle; and invented a series of forms of which the merit was, not merely that they were new, but that they were *capable of perpetual novelty*. The pointed arch was not merely a bold variation from the round, but it admitted of millions of variations in itself; for the proportions of a pointed arch are changeable to infinity, while a circular arch is always the same. The grouped shaft was not merely a bold variation from the single one, but it admitted of millions of variations in its grouping, and in the proportions resultant from its grouping. The introduction of tracery was not only a startling change in the treatment of window lights, but admitted endless changes in the interlacement of the tracery bars themselves. So that, while in all living Christian architecture the love of variety exists, the Gothic schools exhibited that love in culminating energy; and their influence, wherever it extended itself, may be sooner and farther traced by this character than by any other; the tendency to the adoption of Gothic types being always first shown by greater irregularity, and richer variation in the forms of architecture it is about to supersede, long before the appearance of the pointed arch or of any other recognizable *outward* sign of the Gothic mind.

We must, however, herein note carefully what distinction there is between a healthy and a diseased love of change; for as it was in healthy love of change that the Gothic architecture rose, it was partly in consequence of diseased love of change that it was destroyed. In order to understand this clearly, it will be necessary to consider the different ways in which change and monotony are presented to us in nature; both having their use, like darkness and light, and the one incapable of being enjoyed without the other: change being most delightful after some prolongation of monotony, as light appears most brilliant after the eyes have been for some time closed.

I believe that the true relations of monotony and change may be most simply understood by observing them in music. We may therein notice first, that there is a sublimity and majesty in monotony, which there is not in rapid or frequent variation. This is true throughout all nature. The greater part of the sublimity of the sea depends on its monotony; so also that of desolate moor and mountain scenery; and especially the sublimity of motion, as in the quiet, unchanged fall and rise of an engine beam. So also there is sublimity in darkness which there is not in light.

Again, monotony after a certain time, or beyond a certain degree, becomes either uninteresting or intolerable, and the musician is obliged to break it in one of two ways: either while the air or passage is perpetually repeated, its notes are variously enriched and harmonized; or else, after a certain number of repeated passages, an entirely new passage is introduced, which is more or less delightful according to the length of the previous monotony. Nature, of course, uses both these kinds of variation perpetually. The sea-waves, resembling each other in general mass, but none like its brother in minor divisions and curves, are a monotony of the first kind; the great plain, broken by an emergent rock or clump of trees, is a monotony of the second.

Farther: in order to the enjoyment of the change in either case, a certain degree of patience is required from the hearer or observer. In the first case, he must be satisfied to endure with patience the recurrence of the great masses of sound or form, and to seek for entertainment in a careful watchfulness of the minor details. In the second case, he must bear patiently the infliction of the monotony for some moments, in order to feel the full refreshment of the change. This is true even of the shortest musical passage in which the element of monotony is employed. In cases of more majestic monotony, the patience required is so considerable that it becomes a kind of pain, – a price paid for the future pleasure.

Again: the talent of the composer is not in the monotony, but in the changes: he may show feeling and taste by his use of monotony in certain places or degrees; that is to say, by his *various* employment of it; but it is always in the new arrangement or invention that his intellect is shown, and not in the monotony which relieves it.

Lastly: if the pleasure of change be too often repeated, it ceases to be delightful, for then change itself becomes monotonous, and we are driven to seek delight in extreme and fantastic degrees of it. This is the diseased love of change of which we have above spoken.

From these facts we may gather generally that monotony is, and ought to be, in itself painful to us, just as darkness is; that an architecture which is altogether monotonous is a dark or dead architecture; and of those who love it, it may be truly said, 'they love darkness rather than light' [John iii. 19]. But monotony in certain measure, used in order to give value to change, and above all, that *transparent* monotony, which, like the shadows of a great painter, suffers all manner of dimly suggested form to be seen through the body of it, is an essential in architectural as in all other composition; and the endurance of monotony has about the same place in a healthy mind that the endurance of darkness has: that is to say, as a strong intellect will have pleasure in the solemnities of storm and twilight, and in the broken and mysterious lights that gleam among them, rather than in mere brilliancy and glare, while a frivolous mind will dread the shadow and the storm; and as a great man will be ready to endure much darkness of fortune in order to reach greater eminence of power or felicity, while an inferior man will not pay the price; exactly in like manner a great mind will accept, or even delight in, monotony which would be wearisome to an inferior intellect, because it has more patience and power of expectation, and is ready to pay the full price for the great future pleasure of change. But in all cases it is not that the noble nature loves monotony, any more than it loves darkness or pain. But it can bear with it, and receive a high pleasure in the endurance or patience, a pleasure necessary to the well-being of this world; while those who will not submit to the temporary sameness, but rush from one change to another, gradually dull the edge of change itself, and bring a shadow and weariness over the whole world from which there is no more escape.

From these general uses of variety in the economy of the world, we may at once understand its use and abuse in architecture. The variety of the Gothic schools is the more healthy and beautiful, because in many cases it is entirely unstudied, and results, not from mere love of change, but from practical necessities. For in one point of view Gothic is not only the best, but the *only rational* architecture, as being that which can fit itself more easily to all services, vulgar or noble. Undefined in its slope of roof, height of shaft, breadth of arch, or disposition of ground plan, it can shrink into a turret, expand into a hall, coil into a staircase, or spring into a spire, with undegraded grace and unexhausted energy; and whenever it finds occasion for change in its form or purpose, it submits to it without the slightest sense of loss either to its unity or majesty, – subtle and flexible like a fiery serpent, but ever attentive to the voice of the charmer. And it is one of the chief virtues of the Gothic builders, that they never suffered ideas of outside sym- metries and consistencies to interfere with the real use and value of what they did. If they wanted a window, they opened one; a room, they added one; a buttress, they built one; utterly regardless of any established conventionalities of external appearance, knowing (as indeed it always happened) that such daring interruptions of the formal plan would rather give additional interest to its symmetry than injure it. So that, in the best times of Gothic, a useless window would rather have been opened in an unexpected place for the sake of the surprise, than a useful one forbidden for the sake of symmetry. Every successive architect, employed upon a great work, built the pieces he added in his own way, utterly regardless of the style adopted by his predecessors; and if two towers were raised in nominal correspondence at the sides of a cathedral front, one was nearly sure to be different from the other, and in each the style at the top to be different from the style at the bottom.

These marked variations were, however, only permitted as part of the great system of perpetual change which ran through every member of Gothic design, and rendered it as endless a field for the beholder's inquiry as for the builder's imagination: change, which in the best schools is subtle and delicate, and rendered more delightful by intermingling of a noble monotony; in the more barbaric schools is somewhat fantastic and redundant; but, in all, a necessary and constant condition of the life of the school. Sometimes the variety is in one feature, sometimes in another; it may be in the capitals or crockets, in the niches or the traceries, or in all together, but in some one or other of the features it will be found always. If the mouldings are constant, the surface sculpture will change; if the capitals are of a fixed design, the traceries will change; if the traceries are monotonous, the capitals will change; and if even, as in some fine schools, the early English for example, there is the slightest approximation to an unvarying type of mouldings, capitals, and floral decoration, the variety is found in the disposition of the masses, and in the figure sculpture.

I must now refer for a moment, before we quit the consideration of this, the second mental element of Gothic, to the opening of the third chapter of the *Seven Lamps of Architecture*,[c] in which

---

[c] *On architecture as 'the primal art of man'*:
'Whatever is in architecture fair or beautiful, is imitated from natural forms; and what is not so derived, but depends for its dignity upon arrangement and government received from human mind, becomes the expression of the power of that mind, and receives a sublimity high in proportion to the power

the distinction was drawn between man gathering and man governing; between his acceptance of the sources of delight from nature, and his development of authoritative or imaginative power in their arrangment: for the two mental elements, not only of Gothic, but of all good architecture, which we have just been examining, belong to it, and are admirable in it, chiefly as it is, more than any other subject of art, the work of man, and the expression of the average power of man. A picture or poem is often little more than a feeble utterance of man's admiration of something out of himself; but architecture approaches more to a creation of his own, born of his necessities, and expressive of his nature. It is also, in some sort, the work of the whole race, while the picture or statue is the work of one only, in most cases more highly gifted than his fellows. And therefore we may expect that the first two elements of good architecture should be expressive of some great truths commonly belonging to the whole race, and necessary to be understood or felt by them in all their work that they do under the sun. And observe what they are: the confession of Imperfection, and the confession of Desire of Change. The building of the bird and the bee needs not express anything like this. It is perfect and unchanging. But just because we are something better than birds or bees, our building must confess that we have not reached the perfection we can imagine, and cannot rest in the condition we have attained. If we pretend to have reached either perfection or satisfaction, we have degraded ourselves and our work. God's work only may express that; but ours may never have that sentence written upon it, – 'And behold, it was very good' [Genesis i. 31]. And, observe again, it is not merely as it renders the edifice a book of various knowledge, or a mine of precious thought, that variety is essential to its nobleness. The vital principle is not the love of *Knowledge*, but the love of *Change*.[d] It is that strange *disquietude* of the Gothic spirit that is

expressed. All building, therefore, shows man either as gathering or governing; and the secrets of his success are his knowing what to gather, and how to rule. There are the two great intellectual Lamps of Architecture: the one consisting in a just and humble veneration for the works of God upon the earth, and the other in an understanding of the dominion over those works which has been vested in man.' (SL, Ch. III, para. 2)

[d] *Examples of changefulness*:
We must remember that the correspondence of workmanship with thought is, in existent examples, interfered with by the adoption of the designs of an

its greatness; that restlessness of the dreaming mind, that wanders hither and thither among the niches, and flickers feverishly around the pinnacles, and frets and fades in labyrinthine knots and shadows along wall and roof, and yet is not satisfied, nor shall be satisfied. The Greek could stay in his triglyph furrow, and be at

advanced period by the workmen of a rude one. All the beginnings of Christian architecture are of this kind, and the necessary consequence is of course an increase of the visible interval between the power of realization and the beauty of the idea. We have at first an intimation, almost savage in its rudeness, of a classical design; as the art advances, the design is modified by a mixture of Gothic grotesqueness, and the execution more complete, until a harmony is established between the two, in which balance they advance to new perfection. Now during the whole period in which the ground is being recovered, there will be found in the living architecture marks, not to be mistaken, of intense impatience; a struggle towards something unattained, which causes all minor points of handling to be neglected; and a restless disdain of all qualities which appear either to confess contentment, or to require a time and care which might be better spent. And, exactly as a good and earnest student of drawing will not lose time in ruling lines or finishing backgrounds about studies which, while they have answered his immediate purpose, he knows to be imperfect and inferior to what he will do hereafter, – so the vigour of a true school of early architecture, which is either working under the influence of high example or which is itself in a state of rapid development, is very curiously traceable, among other signs, in the contempt of exact symmetry and measurement, which in dead architecture are the most painful necessities . . .

There is something very delightful in this bold expression of the mind of the great master. I do not say that it is the 'perfect work' of patience [James, i. 4], but I think that impatience is a glorious character in an advancing school: and I love the Romanesque and early Gothic especially, because they afford so much room for it; accidental carelessness of measurement or of execution being mingled undistinguishably with the purposed departures from symmetrical regularity, and the luxuriousness of perpetually variable fancy, which are eminently characteristic of both styles. How great, how frequent they are, and how brightly the severity of architectural law is relieved by their grace and suddenness, has not, I think, been enough observed; still less, the unequal measurements of even important features professing to be absolutely symmetrical. I am not so familiar with modern practice as to speak with confidence respecting its ordinary precision; but I imagine that the following measures of the western front of the cathedral of Pisa [Plate 23], would be looked upon by present architects as very blundering approximations. That front is divided into seven arched compartments, of which the second, fourth or central, and sixth contain doors; the seven are in a most subtle alternating proportion; the central being the largest, next to it the second and sixth, then the first and seventh, lastly the third and fifth. By this arrangement, of course,

peace; but the work of the Gothic heart is fretwork still, and it can neither rest in, nor from, its labour, but must pass on, sleeplessly, until its love of change shall be pacified for ever in the change that must come alike on them that wake and them that sleep.[9]

these three pairs should be equal; and they are so to the eye, but I found their actual measures to be the following, taken from pillar to pillar, in Italian braccia, palmi (four inches each), and inches:—

		Braccia	Palmi	Inches	Total in Inches
1	Central door	8	0	0	= 192
2	Northern door ⎱	6	3	1½	= 157½
3	Southern door ⎰	6	4	3	= 163
4	Extreme northern space ⎱	5	5	3½	= 143½
5	Extreme southern space ⎰	6	1	0½	= 148½
6	Northern intervals between the doors ⎱	5	2	1	= 129
7	Southern intervals between the doors ⎰	5	2	1½	= 129½

There is thus a difference, severally, between 2, 3 and 4, 5, of five inches and a half in the one case, and five inches in the other.

This, however, may perhaps be partly attributable to some accommodation of the accidental distortions which evidently took place in the walls of the cathedral during their building, as much as in those of the campanile. To my mind, those of the Duomo are far the more wonderful of the two; I do not believe that a single pillar of its walls is absolutely vertical: the pavement rises and falls to different heights, or rather the plinth of the walls sinks into it continually to different depths, the whole west front literally overhangs, (I have not plumbed it; but the inclination may be seen by the eye, by bringing it into visual contact with the upright pilasters of the Campo Santo:) and a most extraordinary distortion in the masonry of the southern wall shows that this inclination had begun when the first storey was built. The cornice above the first arcade of that wall touches the tops of eleven out of its fifteen arches; but it suddenly leaves the tops of the four westernmost; the arches nodding westward and sinking into the ground, while the cornice rises (or seems to rise), leaving at any rate, whether by the rise of the one or the fall of the other, an interval of more than two feet between it and the top of the western arch, filled by added courses of masonry. There is another very curious evidence of this struggle of the architect with his yielding wall in the columns of the main entrance. (These notices are perhaps somewhat irrelevant to our immediate subject, but they appear to me highly interesting; and they at all events, prove one of the points on which I would insist, – how much of imperfection and variety in things professing to be symmetrical the eyes of those eager builders could endure; they looked to loveliness in detail, to nobility in the whole, never to petty measurements.) Those columns of the principal entrance are among the loveliest in Italy; cylindrical, and decorated with a rich arabesque of sculptured

Plate 23 *West Front, Pisa Cathedral*

'In the Lombard Romanesque, the two principles [of surface and
division] are more fused into each other, as most characteristically in the
cathedral of Pisa: length of proportion, exhibited by an arcade of
twenty-one arches above, and fifteen below, at the side of the nave; bold
square proportion in the front; that front divided into arcades, placed one
above the other, the lowest with its pillars engaged, of seven arches, the
four uppermost thrown out boldly from the receding wall, and casting
deep shadows; the first, above the basement, of nineteen arches; the
second, of twenty-one; the third and fourth of eight each; sixty-three
arches in all; all circular headed, all with cylindrical shafts, and the lowest
with square panellings, set diagonally under their semicircles, an
universal ornament in this style; the apse a semicircle, with a
semidome for its roof, and three ranges of circular arches for its exterior
ornament; in the interior of the nave, a range of circular arches below a
circular-arched triforium, and a vast flat surface, observe, of wall
decorated with striped marble above; the whole arrangement (not a
peculiar one, but characteristic of every church of the period; and, to my
feeling, the most majestic; not perhaps the fairest, but the mightiest type
of form which the mind of man has ever conceived) based exclusively on
associations of the circle and the square.' (SL, Ch. III, para. 10)

The third constituent element of the Gothic mind was stated to be NATURALISM; that is to say, the love of natural objects for their own sake, and the effort to represent them frankly, unconstrained by artistical laws.

foliage, which at the base extends nearly all round them, up to the black pilaster in which they are lightly engaged: but the shield of foliage, bounded by a severe line, narrows to their tops, where it covers their frontal segment only; thus giving, when laterally seen, a terminal line sloping boldly outwards, which, as I think, was meant to conceal the accidental leaning of the western walls, and, by its exaggerated inclination in the same direction, to throw them by comparison into a seeming vertical.

There is another very curious instance of distortion above the central door of the west front. All the intervals between the seven arches are filled with black marble, each containing in its centre a white parallelogram filled with animal mosaics, and the whole surmounted by a broad white band, which, generally, does not touch the parallelogram below. But the parallelogram on the north of the central arch has been forced into an oblique position, and touches the white band; and, as if the architect was determined to show that he did not care whether it did or not, the white band suddenly gets thicker at that place, and remains so over the next two arches. And these differences are the more curious because the workmanship of them all is most finished and masterly, and the distorted stones are fitted with as much neatness as if they tallied to a hair's breadth. There is no look of slurring or blundering about it; it is all coolly filled in, as if the builder had no sense of anything being wrong or extraordinary; I only wish we had a little of his impudence.

Still, the reader will say that all these variations are probably dependent more on the bad foundation than on the architect's feelings. Not so the exquisite delicacies of change in the proportions and dimensions of the apparently symmetrical arcades of the west front. It will be remembered that I said the tower of Pisa was the only ugly tower in Italy, because its tiers were equal, or nearly so, in height, a fault this, so contrary to the spirit of the builders of the time, that it can be considered only as an unlucky caprice. Perhaps the general aspect of the west front of the cathedral may then have occurred to the reader's mind, as seemingly another contradiction of the rule I had advanced. It would not have been so, however, even had its four upper arcades been actually equal; as they are subordinated to the great seven-arched lower storey, in the manner before noticed respecting the spire of Salisbury, and as is actually the case in the Duomo of Lucca and Tower of Pistoja. But the Pisan front is far more subtly proportioned. Not one of its four arcades is of like height with another. The highest is the third, counting upwards; and they diminish in nearly arithmetical proportion alternately; in the order 3rd, 1st, 2nd, 4th. The inequalities in their arches are not less remarkable: they at first strike the eye as all equal; but there is a grace about them which equality never obtained: on closer observation, it is perceived that in the first row of nineteen arches, eighteen are equal, and the

This characteristic of the style partly follows in necessary connection with those named above. For, so soon as the workman is left free to represent what subjects he chooses, he must look to the nature that is round him for material, and will endeavour to represent it as he sees it, with more or less accuracy according to the skill he possesses, and with much play of fancy, but with small respect for law. There is, however, a marked distinction between

central one larger than the rest; in the second arcade, the nine central arches stand over the nine below, having, like them, the ninth central one largest. But on their flanks, where is the slope of the shoulder-like pediment, the arches vanish, and a wedge-shaped frieze takes their place, tapering outwards, in order to allow the columns to be carried to the extremity of the pediment; and here, where the heights of the shafts are so fast shortened, they are set thicker; five shafts, or rather four and a capital, above, to four of the arcade below, giving twenty-one intervals instead of nineteen. In the next or third arcade, – which, remember, is the highest, eight arches, all equal, are given in the space of the nine below, so that there is now a central shaft instead of a central arch, and the span of the arches is increased in proportion to their increased height. Finally, in the uppermost arcade, which is the lowest of all, the arches, the same in number as those below, are narrower than any of the façade; the whole eight going very nearly above the six below them, while the terminal arches of the lower arcade are surmounted by flanking masses of decorated wall with projecting figures.

Now I call *that* Living Architecture. There is sensation in every inch of it, and an accommodation to every architectural necessity, with a determined variation in arrangement, which is exactly like the related proportions and provisions in the structure of organic form. I have not space to examine the still lovelier proportioning of the external shafts of the apse of this marvellous building. I prefer, lest the reader should think it a peculiar example, to state the structure of another church, the most graceful and grand piece of Romanesque work, as a fragment, in north Italy, that of San Giovanni Evangelista, at Pistoja [Plate 24].

The side of that church has three storeys of arcade, diminishing in height in bold geometrical proportion, while the arches, for the most part, increase in number in arithmetical, *i.e.* two in the second arcade, and three in the third, to one in the first. Lest, however, this arrangement should be too formal, of the fourteen arches in the lowest series, that which contains the door is made larger than the rest, and is not in the middle, but the sixth from the West, leaving five on one side and eight on the other. Farther: this lowest arcade is terminated by broad flat pilasters, about half the width of its arches; but the arcade above is continuous; only the two extreme arches at the west end are made larger than all the rest, and instead of coming, as they should, into the space of the lower extreme arch, take in both it and its broad pilaster. Even this, however, was not out of order enough to satisfy the architect's eye; for there were still two arches

Plate 24 *San Giovanni Fuorcivitas, Pistoia*

the imaginations of the Western and Eastern races, even when both are left free; the Western, or Gothic, delighting most in the representation of facts, and the Eastern (Arabian, Persian, and Chinese) in the harmony of colours and forms. Each of these intellectual dispositions has its particular forms of error and abuse, which, though I have often before stated, I must here again briefly explain; and this the rather, because the word Naturalism is, in one of its senses, justly used as a term of reproach, and the questions respecting the real relations of art and nature are so many and so confused throughout all the schools of Europe at this day, that I cannot clearly enunciate any single truth without appearing to admit, in fellowship with it, some kind of error, unless the reader will bear with me in entering into such an analysis of the subject as will serve us for general guidance.

We are to remember, in the first place, that the arrangement of

above to each single one below: so, at the east end, where there were more arches, and the eye might be more easily cheated, what does he do but *narrow* the two extreme *lower* arches by half a braccio; while he at the same time slightly enlarged the upper ones, so as to get only seventeen upper to nine lower, instead of eighteen to nine. The eye is thus thoroughly confused, and the whole building thrown into one mass, by the curious variations in the adjustments of the superimposed shafts, not one of which is either exactly in, or positively out of, its place; and to get this managed the more cunningly, there is from an inch to an inch and a half of gradual gain in the space of the four eastern arches, besides the confessed half braccio. Their measures, counting from the east, I found as follows:—

	Braccia	Palmi	Inches
1st	3	0	1
2nd	3	0	2
3rd	3	3	2
4th	3	3	$3\frac{1}{2}$

The upper arcade is managed on the same principle: it looks at first as if there were three arches to each under pair; but there are, in reality, only thirty-eight (or thirty-seven, I am not quite certain of this number) to the twenty-seven below; and the columns get into all manner of relative positions. Even then, the builder was not satisfied, but must needs carry the irregularity into the spring of the arches, and actually, while the general effect is of a symmetrical arcade, there is not one of the arches the same in height as another; their tops undulate all along the wall like waves along a harbour quay, some nearly touching the string course above, and others falling from it as much as five or six inches. (SL, Ch. V, paras. 7, 9–13)

colours and lines is an art analogous to the composition of music, and entirely independent of the representation of facts. Good colouring does not necessarily convey the image of anything but itself. It consists in certain proportions and arrangements of rays of light, but not in likenesses to anything. A few touches of certain greys and purples laid by a master's hand on white paper will be good colouring; as more touches are added beside them, we may find out that they were intended to represent a dove's neck, and we may praise, as the drawing advances, the perfect imitation of the dove's neck. But the good colouring does not consist in that imitation, but in the abstract qualities and relations of the grey and purple.

In like manner, as soon as a great sculptor begins to shape his work out of the block, we shall see that its lines are nobly arranged, and of noble character. We may not have the slightest idea for what the forms are intended, whether they are of man or beast, of vegetation or drapery. Their likeness to anything does not affect their nobleness. They are magnificent forms, and that is all we need care to know of them, in order to say whether the workman is a good or bad sculptor.

Now the noblest art is an exact unison of the abstract value, with the imitative power, of forms and colours. It is the noblest composition, used to express the noblest facts. But the human mind cannot in general unite the two perfections: it either pursues the fact to the neglect of the composition, or pursues the composition to the neglect of the fact.

And it is intended by the Deity that it *should* do this: the best art is not always wanted. Facts are often wanted without art, as in a geological diagram; and art often without facts, as in a Turkey carpet. And most men have been made capable of giving either one or the other, but not both; only one or two, the very highest, can give both.

Observe then. Men are universally divided, as respects their artistical qualifications, into three great classes; a right, a left, and a centre. On the right side are the men of facts, on the left the men of design, in the centre the men of both.[10]

The three classes of course pass into each other by imperceptible gradations. The men of facts are hardly ever altogether without powers of design; the men of design are always in some measure cognizant of facts; and as each class possesses more or less of the powers of the opposite one, it approaches to the character of the central class. Few men, even in that central rank, are so exactly throned on the summit of the crest that they cannot be perceived to incline in the least one way or the other, embracing both horizons with their glance. Now each of these classes has, as I above said, a healthy function in the world, and correlative diseases or unhealthy functions; and, when the work of either of them is seen in its morbid condition, we are apt to find fault with the class of workmen, instead of finding fault only with the particular abuse which has perverted their action . . .

But there is another order of diseases which affect all the three classes, considered with respect to their pursuit of facts. For observe, all the three classes are in some degree pursuers of facts; even the men of design not being in any case altogether independent of external truth. Now, considering them *all* as more or less searchers after truth, there is another triple division to be made of them. Everything presented to them in nature has good and evil mingled in it: and artists, considered as searchers after truth, are again to be divided into three great classes, a right, a left, and a centre. Those on the right perceive, and pursue, the good, and leave the evil: those in the centre, the greatest, perceive and pursue the good and evil together, the whole thing as it verily is: those on the left perceive and pursue the evil, and leave the good.

Let us, then, endeavour briefly to mark the real relations of these three vast ranks of men, whom I shall call for convenience in speaking of them, Purists, Naturalists, and Sensualists . . . There is a tendency in the Naturalists to despise the Purists, and in the Purists to be offended with the Naturalists (not understanding them, and confounding them with the Sensualists); and this is grievously harmful to both.

Of the various forms of resultant mischief it is not here the place to speak; the reader may already be somewhat wearied with a statement which has led us apparently so far from our immediate subject. But the digression was necessary, in order that I might clearly define the sense in which I use the word Naturalism when I state it to be the third most essential characteristic of Gothic architecture. I mean that the Gothic builders belong to the central or greatest rank in *both* the classifications of artists which we have just made; that considering all artists as either men of design, men of facts, or men of both, the Gothic builders were men of both; and that again, considering all artists as either Purists, Naturalists, or Sensualists, the Gothic builders were Naturalists.

I say first, that the Gothic builders were of that central class which unites fact with design; but that the part of the work which was more especially their own was the truthfulness. Their power of artistical invention or arrangement was not greater than that of Romanesque and Byzantine workmen: by those workmen they were taught the principles, and from them received their models, of design; but to the ornamental feeling and rich fancy of the Byzantine the Gothic builder added a love of *fact* which is never found in the South. Both Greek and Roman used conventional foliage in their ornament, passing into something that was not foliage at all, knotting itself into strange cup-like buds or clusters, and growing out of lifeless rods instead of stems; the Gothic sculptor received these types, at first, as things that ought to be, just as we have a second time received them; but he could not rest in them. He saw there was no veracity in them, no knowledge, no vitality. Do what he would, he could not help liking the true leaves better; and cautiously, a little at a time, he put more of nature into his work, until at last it was all true, retaining, nevertheless, every valuable character of the original well-disciplined and designed arrangement . . .

I said . . . that Gothic work, when referred to the arrangement of all art, as purist, naturalist, or sensualist, was naturalist. This character follows necessarily on its extreme love of truth, prevailing over the sense of beauty, and causing it to take delight in portraiture of every kind, and to express the various characters of the human countenance and form, as it did the varieties of leaves and ruggedness of branches. And this tendency is both increased and ennobled by the same Christian humility which we saw expressed in the first character of Gothic work, its rudeness. For as that resulted from a humility which confessed the imperfection of the *workman*, so this naturalist portraiture is rendered more faithful by the humility which confesses the imperfection of the *subject*. The Greek sculptor could neither bear to confess his own feebleness, nor to tell the faults of the forms that he portrayed. But the Christian workman, believing that all is finally to work together for good [Romans viii. 28], freely confesses both, and neither seeks to disguise his own roughness of work, nor his subject's roughness of make. Yet this frankness being joined, for the most part, with depth of religious feeling in other directions, and especially with charity, there is sometimes a tendency to Purism in the best Gothic sculpture; so that it frequently reaches great dignity of form and tenderness of expression, yet never so as to lose the veracity of portraiture wherever portraiture is possible: not exalting its kings into demi-gods, nor its saints into archangels, but giving what kingliness and sanctity was in them, to the full, mixed with due record of their faults; and this in the most part with a great indifference like that of Scripture history, which sets down, with unmoved and unexcusing resoluteness, the virtues and errors of all men of whom it speaks, often leaving the reader to form his own estimate of them, without an indication of the judgment of the historian. And this veracity is carried out by the Gothic sculptors in the minuteness and generality, as well as the equity, of their delineation: for they do not limit their art to the portraiture of saints and kings, but introduce the most familiar scenes and most simple subjects: filling up the backgrounds of Scripture histories with vivid and curious representations of the commonest incidents of daily life, and availing themselves of every occasion in which, either as a symbol, or an explanation of a scene or time, the things familiar to the eye of the workman could be introduced and made of account. Hence Gothic sculpture and painting are not only full of valuable portraiture of the greatest men, but copious records of all the domestic customs and inferior arts of the ages in which it flourished.

There is, however, one direction in which the Naturalism of the Gothic workmen is peculiarly manifested; and this direction is even more characteristic of the school than the Naturalism itself; I mean their peculiar fondness for the forms of Vegetation. In rendering the various circumstances of daily life, Egyptian and Ninevite sculpture is as frank and as diffuse as the Gothic. From the highest pomps of state or triumphs of battle, to the most trivial domestic arts and amusements, all is taken advantage of to fill the field of granite with the perpetual interest of a crowded drama; and the early Lombardic and Romanesque sculpture is equally copious in its description of the familiar circumstances of war and the chase. But in all the scenes portrayed by the workmen of these nations, vegetation occurs only as an explanatory accessary; the reed is introduced to mark the course of the river, or the tree to mark the covert of the wild beast, or the ambush of the enemy, but there is no especial interest in the forms of the vegetation strong enough to induce them to make it a subject of separate and accurate study. Again, among the nations who followed the arts of design exclusively, the forms of foliage introduced were meagre and general, and their real intricacy and life were neither admired nor expressed. But to the Gothic workman the living foliage became a subject of intense affection, and he struggled to render all its characters with as much accuracy as was compatible with the laws of his design and the nature of his material, not unfrequently tempted in his enthusiasm to transgress the one and disguise the other.

There is a peculiar significance in this, indicative both of higher civilization and gentler temperament, than had before been manifested in architecture. Rudeness, and the love of change, which we have insisted upon as the first elements of Gothic, are also elements common to all healthy schools. But here is a softer element mingled with them, peculiar to the Gothic itself. The rudeness or ignorance which would have been painfully exposed in the treatment of the human form, are still not so great as to prevent the successful rendering of the wayside herbage; and the love of change, which becomes morbid and feverish in following the haste of the hunter and the rage of the combatant, is at once soothed and satisfied as it watches the wandering of the tendril, and the budding of the flower. Nor is this all: the new direction of mental interest marks an infinite change in the means and the habits of life. The nations whose chief support was in the chase, whose chief interest was in the battle, whose chief pleasure was in the banquet, would take small care respecting the shapes of leaves and flowers; and notice little in the forms of the forest trees which sheltered them, except the signs indicative of the wood which would make the toughest lance, the closest roof, or the clearest fire. The affectionate observation of the grace and outward character of vegetation is the sure sign of a more tranquil and gentle existence, sustained by the gifts, and gladdened by the splendour, of the earth. In that careful distinction of species, and richness of delicate and undisturbed organization, which characterize the Gothic design, there is the history of rural and thoughtful life, influenced by habitual tenderness, and devoted to subtle inquiry; and every discriminating and delicate touch of the chisel, as it rounds the petal or guides the branch, is a prophecy of the development of the entire body of the natural sciences, beginning with that of medicine, of the recovery of literature, and the establishment of the most necessary principles of domestic wisdom and national peace.

I have before alluded to the strange and vain supposition, that the original conception of Gothic architecture had been derived from vegetation, – from the symmetry of avenues, and the interlacing of branches.[11] It is a supposition which never could have existed for a moment in the mind of any person acquainted with early Gothic; but, however idle as a theory, it is most valuable as a testimony to the character of the perfected style. It is precisely because the reverse of this theory is the fact, because the Gothic did not arise out of, but develop itself into, a resemblance to vegetation, that this resemblance is so instructive as an indication of the temper of the builders. It was no chance suggestion of the form of an arch from the bending of a bough, but a gradual and continual discovery of a beauty in natural forms which could be more and more perfectly transferred into those of stone, that influenced at once the heart of the people, and the form of the edifice. The Gothic architecture arose in massy and mountainous strength, axe-hewn, and iron-bound, block heaved upon block by the monk's enthusiasm and the soldier's force; and cramped and stanchioned into such weight of grisly wall, as might bury the anchoret in darkness, and beat back the utmost storm of battle, suffering but by the same narrow crosslet the passing of the sunbeam, or of the arrow. Gradually, as that monkish enthusiasm became more thoughtful, and as the sound of war became more and more intermittent beyond the gates of the convent or the keep, the stony pillar grew slender and the vaulted roof grew light, till they had wreathed themselves into the semblance of the summer woods at their fairest, and of the dead field-flowers, long trodden down in blood, sweet monumental statues were set to bloom for ever, beneath the porch of the temple, or the canopy of the tomb.

Nor is it only a sign of greater gentleness or refinement of mind, but as a proof of the best possible direction of this refinement, that the tendency of the Gothic to the expression of vegetative life is to be admired. That sentence of Genesis, 'I have given thee every green herb for meat,' [i. 30], like all the rest of the book, has a profound symbolical as well as a literal meaning. It is not merely the nourishment of the body, but the food of the soul, that is intended. The green herb is, of all nature, that which is most essential to the healthy spiritual life of man. Most of us do not need fine scenery; the precipice and the mountain peak are not intended to be seen by all men, – perhaps their power is greatest

over those who are unaccustomed to them. But trees and fields
and flowers were made for all, and are necessary for all. God has
connected the labour which is essential to the bodily sustenance
with the pleasures which are healthiest for the heart; and while He
made the ground stubborn, He made its herbage fragrant, and its
blossoms fair. The proudest architecture that man can build has
no higher honour than to bear the image and recall the memory of
that grass of the field which is, at once, the type and the support of
his existence; the goodly building is then most glorious when it is
sculptured into the likeness of the leaves of Paradise; and the great
Gothic spirit, as we showed it to be noble in its disquietude, is also
noble in its hold of nature; it is, indeed, like the dove of Noah, in
that she found no rest upon the face of the waters, – but like her in
this also, 'Lo, IN HER MOUTH WAS AN OLIVE BRANCH,
PLUCKED OFF' [Genesis viii. 9–11].

The fourth essential element of the Gothic mind was above
stated to be the sense of the GROTESQUE; but I shall defer the
endeavour to define this most curious and subtle character until
we have occasion to examine one of the divisions of the
Renaissance schools, which was morbidly influenced by it. It is the
less necessary to insist upon it here, because every reader familiar
with Gothic architecture must understand what I mean, and will, I
believe, have no hesitation in admitting, that the tendency to
delight in fantastic and ludicrous, as well as in sublime, images, is
a universal instinct of the Gothic imagination.

The fifth element above named was RIGIDITY; and this
character I must endeavour carefully to define, for neither the
word I have used, nor any other that I can think of, will express it
accurately. For I mean, not merely stable, but *active* rigidity; the
peculiar energy which gives tension to movement, and stiffness to
resistance, which makes the fiercest lightning forked rather than
curved, and the stoutest oak-branch angular rather than bending,
and is as much seen in the quivering of the lance as in the glittering
of the icicle.

I have before had occasion to note some manifestations of this
energy or fixedness; but it must be still more attentively considered here, as it shows itself throughout the whole structure and
decoration of Gothic work. Egyptian and Greek buildings stand,
for the most part, by their own weight and mass, one stone
passively incumbent on another; but in the Gothic vaults and
traceries there is a stiffness analogous to that of the bones of a

limb, or fibres of a tree; an elastic tension and communication of force from part to part, and also a studious expression of this throughout every visible line of the building. And, in like manner, the Greek and Egyptian ornament is either mere surface engraving, as if the face of the wall had been stamped with a seal, or its lines are flowing, lithe, and luxuriant; in either case, there is no expression of energy in the framework of the ornament itself. But the Gothic ornament stands out in prickly independence, and frosty fortitude, jutting into crockets, and freezing into pinnacles; here starting up into a monster, there germinating into a blossom, anon knitting itself into a branch, alternately thorny, bossy, and bristly, or writhed into every form of nervous entanglement; but, even when most graceful, never for an instant languid, always quickset: erring, if at all, ever on the side of brusquerie.

The feelings or habits in the workman which give rise to this character in the work, are more complicated and various than those indicated by any other sculptural expression hitherto named. There is, first, the habit of hard and rapid working; the industry of the tribes of the North, quickened by the coldness of the climate, and giving an expression of sharp energy to all they do, as opposed to the languor of the Southern tribes, however much of fire there may be in the heart of that languor, for lava itself may flow languidly. There is also the habit of finding enjoyment in the signs of cold, which is never found, I believe, in the inhabitants of countries south of the Alps. Cold is to them an unredeemed evil, to be suffered and forgotten as soon as may be; but the long winter of the North forces the Goth (I mean the Englishman, Frenchman, Dane, or German), if he would lead a happy life at all, to find sources of happiness in foul weather as well as fair, and to rejoice in the leafless as well as in the shady forest. And this we do with all our hearts; finding perhaps nearly as much contentment by the Christmas fire as in the summer sunshine, and gaining health and strength on the ice-fields of winter, as well as among the meadows of spring. So that there is nothing adverse or painful to our feelings in the cramped and stiffened structure of vegetation checked by cold; and instead of seeking, like the Southern sculpture, to express only the softness of leafage nourished in all tenderness, and tempted into all luxuriance by warm winds and glowing rays, we find pleasure in dwelling upon the crabbed, perverse, and morose animation of plants that have known little kindness from earth or heaven, but, season after season, have had their best efforts palsied by frost, their brightest buds buried under snow, and their goodliest limbs lopped by tempest.

There are many subtle sympathies and affections which join to confirm the Gothic mind in this peculiar choice of subject; and when we add to the influence of these, the necessities consequent upon the employment of a rougher material, compelling the workman to seek for vigour of effect, rather than refinement of texture or accuracy of form, we have direct and manifest causes for much of the difference between the Northern and Southern cast of conception: but there are indirect causes holding a far more important place in the Gothic heart, though less immediate in their influence on design. Strength of will, independence of character, resoluteness of purpose, impatience of undue control, and that general tendency to set the individual reason against authority, and the individual deed against destiny, which, in the Northern tribes, has opposed itself throughout all ages, to the languid submission, in the Southern, of thought to tradition, and purpose to fatality, are all more or less traceable in the rigid lines, vigorous and various masses, and daringly projecting and independent structure of the Northern Gothic ornament: while the opposite feelings are in like manner legible in the graceful and softly guided waves and wreathed bands, in which Southern decoration is constantly disposed; in its tendency to lose its independence, and fuse itself into the surface of the masses upon which it is traced; and in the expression seen so often, in the arrangement of those masses themselves, of an abandonment of their strength to an inevitable necessity, or a listless repose.

There is virtue in the measure, and error in the excess, of both these characters of mind, and in both of the styles which they have created; the best architecture, and the best temper, are those which unite them both; and this fifth impulse of the Gothic heart is therefore that which needs most caution in its indulgence. It is more definitely Gothic than any other, but the best Gothic building is not that which is *most* Gothic: it can hardly be too frank in its confession of rudeness, hardly too rich in its changefulness, hardly too faithful in its naturalism; but it may go too far in its rigidity, and, like the great Puritan spirit in its extreme, lose itself either in frivolity of division, or perversity of purpose. It actually did so in its later times; but it is gladdening to remember that in its utmost nobleness, the very temper which has been thought most adverse to it, the Protestant spirit of self-dependence and inquiry, was expressed in its every line. Faith and aspiration there were, in every Christian ecclesiastical building, from the first century to the fifteenth; but the moral habits to which England in this age owes the kind of greatness that she has, – the habits of philosophical investigation, of accurate thought, of domestic seclusion and independence, of stern self-reliance and sincere upright searching into religious truth, – were only traceable in the features which were the distinctive creation of the Gothic schools, in the veined foliage, and thorny fretwork, and shadowy niche, and buttressed pier, and fearless height of subtle pinnacle and crested tower, sent like an 'unperplexed question up to Heaven'.[12]

Last, because the least essential, of the constituent elements of this noble school, was placed that of REDUNDANCE, – the uncalculating bestowal of the wealth of its labour. There is, indeed, much Gothic, and that of the best period, in which this element is hardly traceable, and which depends for its effect almost exclusively on loveliness of simple design and grace of uninvolved proportion; still, in the most characteristic buildings, a certain portion of their effect depends upon accumulation of ornament; and many of those which have most influence on the minds of men, have attained it by means of this attribute alone. And although, by careful study of the school, it is possible to arrive at a condition of taste which shall be better contented by a few perfect lines than by a whole façade covered with fretwork, the building which only satisfies such a taste is not to be considered the best. For the very first requirement of Gothic architecture being, as we saw above, that it shall both admit the aid, and appeal to the admiration, of the rudest as well as the most refined minds, the richness of the work is, paradoxical as the statement may appear, a part of its humility. No architecture is so haughty as that which is simple; which refuses to address the eye, except in a few clear and forceful lines; which implies, in offering so little to our regards, that all it has offered is perfect; and disdains, either by the complexity or the attractiveness of its features, to embarrass our investigation, or betray us into delight. That humility, which is the very life of the Gothic school, is shown not only in the imperfection, but in the accumulation, of ornament. The inferior rank of the workman is often shown as much in the richness, as the roughness, of his work; and if the co-operation of every hand, and the sympathy of every heart, are to be received, we must be content to allow the redundance which disguises the failure of the feeble, and wins the regard of the inattentive. There are, however, far nobler interests mingling, in the Gothic heart, with the rude love of decorative accumulation: a magnificent enthusiasm, which feels as if it never could do enough to reach the fulness of its ideal; an unselfishness of sacrifice, which would rather cast fruitless labour before the altar than stand idle in the market [Matthew xx. 3]; and, finally, a profound sympathy with the fulness and wealth of the material universe, rising out of that Naturalism whose operation we have already endeavoured to define. The sculptor who sought for his models among the forest leaves, could not but quickly and deeply feel that complexity need not involve the loss of grace, nor richness that of repose; and every hour which he spent in the study of the minute and various work of Nature, made him feel more forcibly the barrenness of what was best in that of man: nor is it to be wondered at, that, seeing her perfect and exquisite creations poured forth in a profusion which conception could not grasp nor calculation sum, he should think that it ill became him to be niggardly of his own rude craftsmanship; and where he saw throughout the universe a faultless beauty lavished on measureless spaces of broidered field and blooming mountain, to grudge his poor and imperfect labour to the few stones that he had raised one upon another, for habitation or memorial. The years of his life passed away before his task was accomplished; but generation succeeded generation with unwearied enthusiasm, and the cathedral front was at last lost in the tapestry of its traceries, like a rock among the thickets and herbage of spring.

We have now, I believe, obtained a view approaching to completeness of the various moral or imaginative elements which composed the inner spirit of Gothic architecture. (SV II, Ch. VI, paras. 6–44, 51, 56, 62–4, 67–79)

An illustration of Gothic unity – in tracery uniting fantasy and law

The more frequent and typical form is that of the double sub-arch, decorated with various piercings of the space between it and the superior arch; with a simple trefoil under a round arch, in the Abbaye aux Hommes, Caen (Plate 25, fig. 1); with a very beautifully proportioned quatrefoil, in the triforium of Eu, and that of the choir of Lisieux; with quatrefoils, sixfoils, and septfoils, in the transept towers of Rouen (Plate 25, fig. 2); with a trefoil awkwardly, and very small quatrefoil above, at Coutances (Plate 25, fig. 3); then, with multiplications of the same figures, pointed or round, giving very clumsy shapes of the intermediate stone, (fig. 4, from one of the nave chapels of Rouen, fig. 5, from one of the nave chapels of Bayeux,) and finally, by thinning out the stony ribs, reaching conditions like that of the glorious typical form of the clerestory of the apse of Beauvais (fig. 6).

Now, it will be noticed that, during the whole of this process, the attention is kept fixed on the forms of the penetrations, that is to say, of the lights as seen from the interior, not of the intermediate stone. All the grace of the window is in the outline of its light; and I have drawn all these traceries as seen from within, in order to show the effect of the light thus treated, at first in far off and separate stars, and then gradually enlarging, approaching, until they come and stand over us, as it were, filling the whole space with their effulgence. And it is in this pause of the star, that we have the great, pure, and perfect form of French Gothic; it was at the instant when the rudeness of the intermediate space had been finally conquered, when the light had expanded to its fullest, and yet had not lost its radiant unity, principality, and visible first causing of the whole, that we have the most exquisite feeling and most faultless judgments in the management alike of the tracery and decorations . . . It was the great watershed of Gothic art. Before it, all had been ascent; after it, all was decline; both, indeed, by winding paths and varied slopes; both interrupted, like the gradual rise and fall of the passes of the Alps, by great mountain outliers, isolated or branching from the central chain, and by retrograde or parallel directions of the valley of access. But the track of the human mind is traceable up to that glorious ridge, in a continuous line, and thence downwards . . .

And at that point, and that instant, reaching the place that was nearest heaven, the builders looked back, for the last time, to the way by which they had come, and the scenes through which their early course had passed. They turned away from them and their morning light, and descended towards a new horizon, for a time in the warmth of western sun, but plunging with every forward step into more cold and melancholy shade.

The change of which I speak, is expressible in few words; but one more important, more radically influential, could not be. It was the substitution of the *line* for the *mass*, as the element of decoration.

We have seen the mode in which the openings or penetration of the window expanded, until what were, at first, awkward forms of intermediate stone, became delicate lines of tracery . . . [For then] the traceries had *caught the eye* of the architect. Up to that time, up to the very last instant in which the reduction and thinning of the intervening stone was consummated, his eye had been on the openings only, on the stars of light. He did not care about the stone; a rude border of moulding was all he needed, it was the penetrating shape which he was watching. But when that shape had received its last possible expansion, and when the stone-work became an arrangement of graceful and parallel lines, that arrangement, like some form in a picture, unseen and accidentally developed, struck suddenly, inevitably, on the sight. It had literally not been seen before. It flashed out in an instant, as an independent form. It became a feature of the work. The architect took it under his care, thought over it, and distributed its members as we see.

Now, the great pause was at the moment when the space and the dividing stone-work were both equally considered.[e] It did not last fifty years. The forms of the tracery were seized with a childish delight in the novel source of beauty; and the intervening space was cast aside, as an element of decoration, for ever. I have confined myself, in following this change, to the window, as the feature in which it is clearest. But the transition is the same in every member of architecture . . .

[e] *Gothic unity – of ornament:*
Observe, however, and this is of the utmost possible importance, that the value of this type does not consist in the mere shutting of the ornament into a certain space, but in the acknowledgment *by* the ornament of the fitness of the limitation; – of its own perfect willingness to submit to it; nay, of a predisposition in itself to fall into the ordained form, without any direct expression of the command to do so; an anticipation of the authority, and an instant and willing submission to it, in every fibre and spray; not merely *willing*, but *happy* submission, as being pleased rather than vexed to have so beautiful a law suggested to it, and one which to follow is so justly in accordance with its own nature. You must not cut out a branch of hawthorn as it grows, and rule a triangle round it, and suppose that it is then submitted to law. Not a bit of it. It is only put in a cage, and will look as if it must get out,

Plate 25 *Traceries from Caen, Bayeux, Rouen, and Beauvais*

The reader will observe that, up to the last expansion of the penetrations, the stone-work was necessarily considered, as it actually is, *stiff*, and unyielding. It was so, also, during the pause of which I have spoken, when the forms of the tracery were still severe and pure; delicate indeed, but perfectly firm.

At the close of the period of pause, the first sign of serious change was like a low breeze, passing through the emaciated tracery, and making it tremble. It began to undulate like the threads of a cobweb lifted by the wind. It lost its essence as a structure of stone. Reduced to the slenderness of threads, it began to be considered as possessing also their flexibility. The architect was pleased with this his new fancy, and set himself to carry it out; and in a little time, the bars of tracery were caused to appear to the eye as if they had been woven together like a net. This was a change which sacrificed a great principle of truth; it sacrificed the expression of the qualities of the material; and, however delightful its results in their first developments, it was ultimately ruinous.

For, observe the difference between the supposition of ductility, and that of elastic structure noticed above in the resemblance to tree form. That resemblance was not sought, but necessary; it resulted from the natural conditions of strength in the pier or trunk, and slenderness in the ribs or branches, while many of the other suggested conditions of resemblance were perfectly true. A tree branch, though in a certain sense flexible, is not ductile; it is as firm in it own form as the rib of stone; both of them will yield up to certain limits, both of them breaking when those limits are exceeded; while the tree trunk will bend no more than the stone pillar. But when the tracery is assumed to be as yielding as a silken

---

for its life, or wither in the confinement. But the spirit of triangle must be put into the hawthorn. It must suck in isoscelesism with its sap. Thorn and blossom, leaf and spray, must grow with an awful sense of triangular necessity upon them, for the guidance of which they are to be thankful, and to grow all the stronger and more gloriously. And though there may be a transgression here and there, and an adaptation to some other need, or a reaching forth to some other end, greater even than the triangle, yet this liberty is to be always accepted under a solemn sense of special permission; and when the full form is reached and the entire submission expressed, and every blossom has a thrilling sense of its responsibility down into its tiniest stamen, you may take your terminal line away if you will. No need for it any more. The commandment is written on the heart of the thing. (SV I, Ch. XXI, para. 32)

cord; when the whole fragility, elasticity, and weight of the material are to the eye, if not in terms, denied; when all the art of the architect is applied to disprove the first conditions of his working, and the first attributes of his materials; *this* is a deliberate treachery, only redeemed from the charge of direct falsehood by the visibility of the stone surface, and degrading all the traceries it affects exactly in the degree of its presence. (SL, Ch. II, paras. 21–4)

*   *   *

The Nature of the Renaissance
Early Renaissance

The first thing that it demanded in all work was, that it should be done in a consummate and learned way; and men altogether forgot that it was possible to consummate what was contemptible, and to know what was useless. Imperatively requiring dexterity of touch, they gradually forgot to look for tenderness of feeling; imperatively requiring accuracy of knowledge, they gradually forgot to ask for originality of thought. The thought and the feeling which they despised departed from them, and they were left to felicitate themselves on their small science and their neat fingering. This is the history of the first attack of the Renaissance upon the Gothic schools, and of its rapid results; more fatal and immediate in architecture than in any other art, because there the demand for perfection was less reasonable, and less consistent with the capabilities of the workman; being utterly opposed to that rudeness or savageness on which, as we saw above, the nobility of the elder schools in great part depends. But, inasmuch as the innovations were founded on some of the most beautiful examples of art, and headed by some of the greatest men that the world ever saw, and as the Gothic with which they interfered was corrupt and valueless, the first appearance of the Renaissance feeling had the appearance of a healthy movement. A new energy replaced whatever weariness or dulness had affected the Gothic mind; an exquisite taste and refinement, aided by extended knowledge, furnished the first models of the new school; and over the whole of Italy a style arose, generally now known as cinquecento, which in sculpture and painting, as I just stated, produced the noblest masters whom the world ever saw, headed by Michael Angelo, Raphael, and Leonardo; but which failed of doing the same in architecture, because, as we have seen above,

perfection is therein not possible, and failed more totally than it
would otherwise have done, because the classical enthusiasm had
destroyed the best types of architectural form . . .

The changes effected in form, however, were the least part of
the evil principles of the Renaissance. As I have just said, its main
mistake, in its early stages, was the unwholesome demand for
perfection, at any cost . . . Men like Verrocchio and Ghiberti were
not to be had every day, nor in every place; and to require from the
common workman execution or knowledge like theirs, was to
require him to become their copyist. Their strength was great
enough to enable them to join science with invention, method
with emotion, finish with fire; but in them the invention and the
fire were first, while Europe saw in them only the method and the
finish. This was new to the minds of men, and they pursued it to
the neglect of everything else. 'This,' they cried, 'we must have in
all our work henceforward': and they were obeyed. The lower
workman secured method and finish, and lost, in exchange for
them, his soul.

Now, therefore, do not let me be misunderstood when I speak
generally of the evil spirit of the Renaissance. The reader may look
through all I have written, from first to last, and he will not find
one word but of the most profound reverence for those mighty
men who could wear the Renaissance armour of proof, and yet
not feel it encumber their living limbs, – Leonardo and Michael
Angelo, Ghirlandajo and Masaccio, Titian and Tintoret. But I
speak of the Renaissance as an evil time, because, when it saw
those men go burning forth into the battle, it mistook their
armour for their strength; and forthwith encumbered with the
painful panoply every stripling who ought to have gone forth only
with his own choice of three smooth stones out of the brook
[Samuel xvii. 40]. (SV III, Ch. I, paras. 16, 20–1)

Roman Renaissance and the Pride in Knowledge

The first notable characteristic of the Renaissance central school
is its introduction of accurate knowledge into all its work, so far
as it possesses such knowledge; and its evident conviction that
such science is necessary to the excellence of the work, and is the
first thing to be expressed therein. So that all the forms introduced, even in its minor ornament, are studied with the utmost
care; the anatomy of all animal structure is thoroughly

understood and elaborately expressed, and the whole of the execution skilful and practised in the highest degree. Perspective, linear and aerial, perfect drawing and accurate light and shade in painting, and true anatomy in all representations of the human form, drawn or sculptured, are the first requirements in all the work of this school.

Now, first considering all this in the most charitable light, as pursued from a real love of truth, and not from vanity, it would, of course, have been all excellent and admirable, had it been regarded as the aid of art, and not as its essence. But the grand mistake of the Renaissance schools lay in supposing that science and art were the same things, and that to advance in the one was necessarily to perfect the other. Whereas they are, in reality, things not only different, but so opposed that to advance in the one is, in ninety-nine cases out of the hundred, to retrograde in the other. This is the point to which I would at present especially bespeak the reader's attention.

Science and art are commonly distinguished by the nature of their actions; the one as knowing, the other as changing, producing, or creating. But there is a still more important distinction in the nature of the things they deal with. Science deals exclusively with things as they are in themselves; and art exclusively with things as they affect the human sense and human soul. Her work is to portray the appearances of things, and to deepen the natural impressions which they produce upon living creatures. The work of science is to substitute facts for appearances, and demonstrations for impressions. Both, observe, are equally concerned with truth; the one with truth of aspect, the other with truth of essence. Art does not represent things falsely, but truly as they appear to mankind. Science studies the relations of things to each other: but art studies only their relations to man: and it requires of everything which is submitted to it imperatively this, and only this, — what that thing is to the human eyes and human heart, what it has to say to men, and what it can become to them: a field of question just as much vaster than that of science, as the soul is larger than the material creation.

Take a single instance. Science informs us that the sun is ninety-five millions of miles distant from, and 111 times broader than, the earth: that we and all the planets revolve round it; and that it revolves on its own axis in 25 days, 14 hours, and 4 minutes. With all this, art has nothing whatsoever to do. It has no care to know anything of this kind. But the things which it does care to know are these: that in the heavens God hath set a tabernacle for the sun, 'which is as a bridegroom coming out of his chamber, and rejoiceth as a strong man to run a race. His going forth is from the end of the heaven, and his circuit unto the ends of it, and there is nothing hid from the heat thereof' [Psalm xix. 5–6].

This, then, being the kind of truth with which art is exclusively concerned, how is such truth as this to be ascertained and accumulated? Evidently, and only, by perception and feeling. Never either by reasoning or report. Nothing must come between Nature and the artist's sight; nothing between God and the artist's soul. Neither calculation nor hearsay, – be it the most subtle of calculations, or the wisest of sayings, – may be allowed to come between the universe, and the witness which art bears to its visible nature. The whole value of that witness depends on its being *eye*-witness; the whole genuineness, acceptableness, and dominion of it depend on the personal assurance of the man who utters it. All its victory depends on the veracity of the one preceding word, 'Vidi'.

The whole function of the artist in the world is to be a seeing and feeling creature; to be an instrument of such tenderness and sensitiveness, that no shadow, no hue, no line, no instantaneous and evanescent expression of the visible things around him, nor any of the emotions which they are capable of conveying to the spirit which has been given him, shall either be left unrecorded, or fade from the book of record. It is not his business either to think, to judge, to argue, or to know. His place is neither in the closet, nor on the bench, nor at the bar, nor in the library. They are for other men, and other work. He may think, in a by-way; reason, now and then, when he has nothing better to do; know, such fragments of knowledge as he can gather without stooping, or reach without pains; but none of these things are to be his care. The work of his life is to be two-fold only; to see, to feel.

Nay, but, the reader perhaps pleads with me, one of the great uses of knowledge is to open the eyes; to make things perceivable which never would have been seen, unless first they had been known.

Not so. This could only be said or believed by those who do not know what the perceptive faculty of a great artist is, in comparison with that of other men. There is no great painter, no great workman in any art, but he sees more with the glance of a moment than he can learn by the labour of a thousand hours.

God has made every man fit for his work; He has given to the man whom He means for a student, the reflective, logical, sequential faculties; and to the man whom He means for an artist, the perceptive, sensitive, retentive faculties. And neither of these men, so far from being able to do the other's work, can even comprehend the way in which it is done. The student has no understanding of the vision, nor the painter of the process; but chiefly, the student has no idea of the colossal grasp of the true painter's vision and sensibility.

The labour of the whole Geological Society, for the last fifty years, has but now arrived at the ascertainment of those truths respecting mountain form which Turner saw and expressed with a few strokes of a camel's hair pencil fifty years ago, when he was a boy. The knowledge of all the laws of the planetary system, and of all the curves of the motion of projectiles, would never enable the man of science to draw a waterfall or a wave; and all the members of Surgeons' Hall helping each other could not at this moment see, or represent, the natural movement of a human body in vigorous action, as a poor dyer's son did two hundred years ago [Tintoret].

But surely, it is still insisted, granting this peculiar faculty to the painter, he will still see more as he knows more, and the more knowledge he obtains, therefore, the better. No; not even so. It is indeed true that, here and there, a piece of knowledge will enable the eye to detect a truth which might otherwise have escaped it; as, for instance, in watching a sunrise, the knowledge of the true nature of the orb may lead the painter to feel more profoundly, and express more fully, the distance between the bars of cloud that cross it, and the sphere of flame that lifts itself slowly beyond them into the infinite heaven. But for one visible truth to which knowledge thus opens the eyes, it seals them to a thousand: that is to say, if the knowledge occur to the mind so as to occupy its powers of contemplation at the moment when the sight-work is to be done, the mind retires inward, fixes itself upon the known fact, and forgets the passing visible ones; and a *moment* of such forgetfulness loses more to the painter than a day's thought can gain. This is no new or strange assertion. Every person accustomed to careful reflection of any kind knows that its natural operation is to close his eyes to the external world. While he is thinking deeply, he neither sees nor feels, even though naturally he may possess strong powers of sight and emotion. He who, having journeyed all day beside the Leman Lake, asked of his companions, at evening, where it was, probably was not wanting in sensibility; but he was generally a thinker, not a perceiver.[13] And this instance is only an extreme one of the effect which, in all cases, knowledge, becoming a subject of reflection, produces upon the sensitive faculties. It must be but poor and lifeless knowledge, if it has no tendency to force itself forward, and become ground for reflection, in despite of the succession of external objects. It will not obey their succession. The first that comes gives it food enough for its day's work; it is its habit, its duty, to cast the rest aside, and fasten upon that. The first thing that a thinking and knowing man sees in the course of the day, he will not easily quit. It is not his way to quit anything without getting to the bottom of it, if possible. But the artist is bound to receive all things on the broad, white, lucid field of his soul, not to grasp at one. For instance, as the knowing and thinking man watches the sunrise, he sees something in the colour of a ray, or the change of a cloud, that is new to him; and this he follows out forthwith into a labyrinth of optical and pneumatical laws, perceiving no more clouds nor rays all the morning. But the painter must catch all the rays, all the colours that come, and see them all truly, all in their real relations and succession; therefore, everything that occupies room in his mind he must cast aside for the time as completely as may be. The thoughtful man is gone far away to seek; but the perceiving man must sit still, and open his heart to receive. The thoughtful man is knitting and sharpening himself into a two-edged sword, wherewith to pierce. The perceiving man is stretching himself into a four-cornered sheet, wherewith to catch. And all the breadth to which he can expand himself, and all the white emptiness into which he can blanch himself, will not be enough to receive what God has to give him.

What then, it will be indignantly asked, is an utterly ignorant and unthinking man likely to make the best artist? No, not so neither. Knowledge is good for him so long as he can keep it utterly, servilely, subordinate to his own divine work, and trample it under his feet, and out of his way, the moment it is likely to entangle him.

And in this respect, observe, there is an enormous difference between knowledge and education. An artist need not be a *learned* man; in all probability it will be a disadvantage to him to become so; but he ought, if possible, always to be an *educated* man: that is, one who has understanding of his own uses and duties in the world, and therefore of the general nature of the things done and existing in the world; and who has so trained himself, or been trained, as to turn to the best and most courteous account whatever faculties or knowledge he has. The mind of an educated man is greater than the knowledge it possesses; it is like the vault of heaven, encompassing the earth which lives and flourishes beneath it; but the mind of an uneducated and learned man is like a caoutchouc band, with an everlasting spirit of contraction in it, fastening together papers which it cannot open, and keeps others from opening.

Half our artists are ruined for want of education, and by the possession of knowledge; the best that I have known have been educated, and illiterate. The ideal of an artist, however, is not that he should be illiterate, but well read in the best books, and thoroughly high bred, both in heart and in bearing. In a word, he should be fit for the best society, *and should keep out of it* . . .

Within its due limits, however, here is one branch of science which the artist may pursue . . . the science of the appearances of things as they have been ascertained and registered by his fellow-men. For no day passes but some visible fact is pointed out to us by others, which, without their help, we should not have noticed; and the accumulation and generalization of visible facts have formed, in the succession of ages, the sciences of light and shade, and perspective, linear and aerial: so that the artist is now at once put in possession of certain truths respecting the appearances of things, which, so pointed out to him, any man may in a few days understand and acknowledge; but which, without aid, he could not probably discover in his lifetime. I say, probably could not, because the time which the history of art shows us to have been actually occupied in the discovery and systematization of such truth is no measure of the time *necessary* for such discovery. The lengthened period which elapsed between the earliest and the perfect development of the science of light (if I may so call it) was not occupied in the actual effort to ascertain its laws, but in *acquiring the disposition to make that effort.* It did not take five centuries to find out the appearance of natural objects; but it took five centuries to make people care about representing them. An artist of the twelfth century did not desire to represent Nature. His work was symbolical and ornamental. So long as it was intelligible and lovely, he had no care to make it like Nature. As, for instance, when an old painter represented the glory round a saint's head by a burnished plate of pure gold, he had no intention of imitating an effect of light. He meant to tell the spectator that the figure so decorated was a saint, and to produce splendour of effect by the golden circle. It was no matter to him what light was like. So soon as it entered into his intention to represent the appearance of light, he was not long in discovering the natural facts necessary for his purpose.

But this being fully allowed, it is still true that the accumulation of facts now known respecting visible phenomena is greater than any man could hope to gather for himself, and that it is well for him to be made acquainted with them; provided always, that he receive them only at their true value, and do not suffer himself to be misled by them. I say, at their true value; that is, an exceedingly small one. All the information which men can receive from the accumulated experience of others is of no use but to enable them more quickly and accurately to see for themselves. It will in nowise take the place of this personal sight. Nothing can be done well in art except by vision. Scientific principles and experiences are helps to the eye, as a microscope is; and they are of exactly as much use *without* the eye. No science of perspective, or of anything else, will enable us to draw the simplest natural line accurately, unless we see it and feel it . . .

Whatever can be measured and handled, dissected and demon-strated, – in a word, whatever is of the body only, – that the schools of knowledge do resolutely and courageously possess themselves of, and portray. But whatever is immeasurable, intangible, indivisible, and of the spirit, that the schools of knowledge do as certainly lose, and blot out of their sight: that is to say, all that is worth art's possessing or recording at all . . .

All our errors in this respect arise from a gross misconception as to the true nature of knowledge itself. We talk of learned and ignorant men, as if there were a certain quantity of knowledge, which to possess was to be learned, and which not to possess was to be ignorant; instead of considering that knowledge is infinite, and that the man most learned in human estimation is just as far from knowing anything as he ought to know it, as the unlettered peasant. Men are merely on a lower or higher stage of an eminence whose summit is God's throne infinitely above all; and there is just as much reason for the wisest as for the simplest man being discontented with his position, as respects the real quantity of knowledge he possesses. And, for both of them, the only true reasons for contentment with the sum of knowledge they possess are these: that it is the kind of knowledge they need for their duty and happiness in life; that all they have is tested and certain, so far as it is in their power; that all they have is well in order, and within reach when they need it; that it has not cost too much time in the getting; that none of it, once got, has been lost; and that there is not too much to be easily taken care of.

Consider these requirements a little, and the evils that result in our education and polity from neglecting them. Knowledge is mental food, and is exactly to the spirit what food is to the body (except that the spirit needs several sorts of food, of which knowledge is only one), and it is liable to the same kind of misuses. It may be mixed and disguised by art, till it becomes unwholesome: it may be refined, sweetened, and made palatable, until it has lost all its power of nourishment; and even of its best kind, it may be eaten to surfeiting, and minister to disease and death.

Therefore, with respect to knowledge, we are to reason and act exactly as with respect to food. We no more live to know, than we live to eat. We live to contemplate, enjoy, act, adore; and we may know all that is to be known in this world, and what Satan knows in the other, without being able to do any of these. We are to ask, therefore, first, is the knowledge we would have fit food for us, good and simple, not artificial and decorated? and secondly, how much of it will enable us best for our work; and will leave our hearts light, and our eyes clear? For no more than that is to be eaten without the old Eve-sin.

Observe, also, the difference between tasting knowledge and hoarding it. In this respect it is also like food; since, in some measure, the knowledge of all men is laid up in granaries, for future use; much of it is at any given moment dormant, not fed upon or enjoyed, but in store. And by all it is to be remembered that knowledge in this form may be kept without air till it rots, or in such unthreshed disorder that it is of no use; and that, however good or orderly, it is still only in being tasted that it becomes of use; and that men may easily starve in their own granaries, men of science, perhaps, most of all, for they are likely to seek accumulation of their store, rather than nourishment from it. Yet let it not be thought that I would undervalue them. The good and great among them are like Joseph, from whom all nations sought to buy corn [Genesis xli. 57]; or like the sower going forth to sow beside all waters, sending forth thither the feet of the ox and the ass [Isaiah xxxii. 20]: only let us remember that this is not all men's work. We are not intended to be all keepers of granaries, nor all to be measured by the filling of the storehouse; but many, nay, most of us, are to receive day by day our daily bread [Luke xi. 3], and shall be as well nourished and as fit for our labour, and often, also, fit for nobler and more divine labour, in feeding from the barrel of meal that does not waste and from the cruse of oil that does not fail [I Kings xvii. 14], than if our barns were filled with plenty, and our presses bursting out with new wine [Proverbs iii. 10].

It is for each man to find his own measure in this matter; in great part, also, for others to find it for him, while he is yet a youth. And the desperate evil of the whole Renaissance system is, that all idea of measure is therein forgotten, that knowledge is thought the one and the only good, and it is never inquired whether men are vivified by it or paralyzed. Let us leave figures. The reader may not believe the analogy I have been pressing so far; but let him consider the subject in itself, let him examine the effect of knowledge in his own heart, and see whether the trees of knowledge and of life are one now, any more than in Paradise. He must feel that the real animating power of knowledge is only in the moment of its being first received, when it fills us with wonder and joy; a joy for which, observe, the previous ignorance is just as necessary as the present knowledge. That man is always happy who is in the presence of something which he cannot know to the full, which he is always going on to know. This is the necessary condition of a finite creature with divinely rooted and divinely directed intelligence; this, therefore, its happy state, — but observe, a state, not of triumph or joy in what it knows, but of joy rather in the continual discovery, of new ignorance, continual self-abasement, continual astonishment. Once thoroughly our own, the knowledge ceases to give us pleasure. It may be practically useful to us, it may be good for others, or good for usury to obtain more; but, in itself, once let it be thoroughly familiar, and it is dead, the wonder is gone from it, and all the fine colour which it had when first we drew it up out of the infinite sea. And what does it matter how much or how little of it we have laid aside, when our only enjoyment is still in the casting of that deep sea line? What does it matter? Nay, in one respect, it matters much, and not to our advantage. For one effect of knowledge is to deaden the force of the imagination and the original energy of the whole man: under the weight of his knowledge he cannot move so lightly as in the days of his simplicity . . .

Here is indeed an expression of aristocracy in its worst characters; coldness, perfectness of training, incapability of emotion, want of sympathy with the weakness of lower men, blank, hopeless, haughty self-sufficiency. All these characters are written in the Renaissance architecture as plainly as if they were graven on it in words. For, observe, all other architectures have something in them that common men can enjoy; some concession to the simplicities of humanity, some daily bread for the hunger of the multitude. Quaint fancy, rich ornament, bright colour, something that shows a sympathy with men of ordinary minds and hearts; and this wrought out, at least in the Gothic, with a rudeness showing that the workman did not mind exposing his own ignorance if he could please others. But the Renaissance is exactly the contrary of all this. It is rigid, cold, inhuman; incapable of glowing, of stooping, of conceding for an instant. Whatever excellence it has is refined, high-trained, and deeply erudite; a kind which the architect well knows no common mind can taste. He proclaims it to us aloud. 'You cannot feel my work unless you study Vitruvius. I will give you no gay colour, no pleasant sculpture, nothing to make you happy; for I am a learned man. All the pleasure you can have in anything I do is in its proud breeding, its rigid formalism, its perfect finish, its cold tranquillity. I do not work for the vulgar, only for the men of the academy and the court.'

And the instinct of the world felt this in a moment. In the new precision and accurate law of the classical forms, they perceived something peculiarly adapted to the setting forth of state in an appalling manner; princes delighted in it, and courtiers. The Gothic was good for God's worship, but this was good for man's worship. The Gothic had fellowship with all hearts, and was universal, like nature: it could frame a temple for the prayer of nations, or shrink into the poor man's winding stair. But here was an architecture that would not shrink, that had in it no submission, no mercy. The proud princes and lords rejoiced in it. It was full of insult to the poor in its every line. It would not be built of the materials at the poor man's hand; it would not roof itself with thatch or shingle and black oak beams: it would not wall itself with rough stone or brick; it would not pierce itself with small windows where they were needed; it would not niche itself,

wherever there was room for it, in the street corners. It would be of hewn stone; it would have its windows and its doors, and its stairs and its pillars, in lordly order and of stately size; it would have its wings and its corridors, and its halls and its gardens, as if all the earth were its own. And the rugged cottages of the mountaineers, and the fantastic streets of the labouring burgher, were to be thrust out of its way, as of a lower species.
(SV III, Ch. II, paras. 6–13, 17–18, 23–8, 38–9)

Gothic versus Renaissance
The Grotesque – in Gothic play of mind

That highest species of playfulness . . . is evidently the condition of a mind, not only highly cultivated, but so habitually trained to intellectual labour that it can bring a considerable force of accurate thought into its moments even of recreation. This is not possible unless so much repose of mind and heart are enjoyed, even at the periods of greatest exertion, that the rest required by the system is diffused over the whole life. To the majority of mankind, such a state is evidently unattainable. They must, perforce, pass a large part of their lives in employments both irksome and toilsome, demanding an expenditure of energy which exhausts the system, and yet consuming that energy upon subjects incapable of interesting the nobler faculties. When such employments are intermitted, those noble instincts, fancy, imagination, and curiosity, are all hungry for the food which the labour of the day has denied to them, while yet the weariness of the body, in a great degree, forbids their application to any serious subject. They therefore exert themselves without any determined purpose, and under no vigorous restraint, but gather, as best they may, such various nourishment, and put themselves to such fantastic exercise, as may soonest indemnify them for their past imprisonment, and prepare them to endure its recurrence. This stretching of the mental limbs as their fetters fall away, – this leaping and dancing of the heart and intellect, when they are restored to the fresh air of heaven, yet half paralyzed by their captivity, and unable to turn themselves to any earnest purpose, – I call necessary play. It is impossible to exaggerate its importance, whether in polity, or in art. (SV III, Ch. III, para. 27)

The Grotesque –
in the Renaissance perversion of creative freedom

The difficulty which . . . exists in distinguishing the playful from the terrible grotesque arises out of this cause: that the mind, under certain phases of excitement, *plays* with *terror*, and summons images which, if it were in another temper, would be awful, but of which, either in weariness or in irony, it refrains for the time to acknowledge the true terribleness. And the mode in which this refusal takes place distinguishes the noble from the ignoble grotesque. For the master of the noble grotesque knows the depth of all at which he seems to mock, and would feel it at another time, or feels it in a certain undercurrent of thought even while he jests with it; but the workman of the ignoble grotesque can feel and understand nothing, and mocks at all things with the laughter of the idiot and the cretin . . . We saw above that the grotesque was produced, chiefly in subordinate or ornamental art, by rude, and in some degree uneducated men, and in their times of rest. At such times, and in such subordinate work, it is impossible that they should represent any solemn or terrible subject with a full and serious entrance into its feeling. It is not in the languor of a leisure hour that a man will set his whole soul to conceive the means of representing some important truth, nor to the projecting angle of a timber bracket that he would trust its representation, if conceived. And yet, in this languor, and in this trivial work, he must find some expression of the serious part of his soul, of what there is within him capable of awe, as well as of love. The more noble the man is, the more impossible it will be for him to confine his thoughts to mere loveliness, and that of a low order. Were his powers and his time unlimited, so that, like Frà Angelico, he could paint the Seraphim, in that order of beauty he could find contentment, bringing down heaven to earth. But by the conditions of his being, by his hard-worked life, by his feeble powers of execution, by the meanness of his employment and the languor of his heart, he is bound down to earth. It is the world's work that he is doing, and world's work is not to be done without fear. And whatever there is of deep and eternal consciousness within him, thrilling his mind with the sense of the presence of sin and death around him, must be expressed in that slight work, and feeble way, come of it what will. He cannot forget it, among all that he sees of beautiful in nature; he may not bury himself among the

leaves of the violet on the rocks, and of the lily in the glen, and
twine out of them garlands of perpetual gladness. He sees more in
the earth than these, – misery and wrath, and discordance and
danger, and all the work of the dragon and his angels; this he sees
with too deep feeling ever to forget. And though, when he returns
to his idle work, – it may be to gild the letters upon the page, or to
carve the timbers of the chamber, or the stones of the pinnacle, –
he cannot give his strength of thought any more to the woe or to
the danger, there is a shadow of them still present with him: and as
the bright colours mingle beneath his touch, and the fair leaves
and flowers grow at his bidding, strange horrors and phantasms
rise by their side; grisly beasts and venomous serpents, and
spectral fiends and nameless inconsistencies of ghastly life, rising
out of things most beautiful, and fading back into them again, as
the harm and the horror of life do out of its happiness. He has seen
these things; he wars with them daily; he cannot but give them
their part in his work, though in a state of comparative apathy to
them at the time. He is but carving and gilding, and must not turn
aside to weep; but he knows that hell is burning on, for all that,
and the smoke of it withers his oak-leaves.

Now, the feelings which give rise to the false or ignoble
grotesque, are exactly the reverse of this. In the true grotesque, a
man of naturally strong feeling is accidentally or resolutely
apathetic; in the false grotesque, a man naturally apathetic is
forcing himself into temporary excitement. The horror which is
expressed by the one comes upon him whether he will or not; that
which is expressed by the other is sought out by him, and
elaborated by his art. And therefore, also, because the fear of the
one is true, and of true things, however fantastic its expression
may be, there will be reality in it, and force. It is not a
manufactured terribleness, whose author, when he had finished it,
knew not if it would terrify any one else or not: but it is a
terribleness taken from the life . . .

The true grotesque being the expression of the *repose* or play of
a *serious* mind, there is a false grotesque opposed to it, which is
the result of the *full exertion* of a *frivolous* one. There is much
grotesque which is wrought out with exquisite care and pains, and
as much labour given to it as if it were of the noblest subject; so
that the workman is evidently no longer apathetic, and has no
excuse for unconnectedness of thought, or sudden unreasonable
fear. If he awakens horror now, it ought to be in some truly

sublime form. His strength is in his work; and he must not give way to sudden humour, and fits of erratic fancy. If he does so, it must be because his mind is naturally frivolous, or is for the time degraded into the deliberate pursuit of frivolity. And herein lies the real distinction between the base grotesque of Raphael and the Renaissance, above alluded to, and the true Gothic grotesque. Those grotesques or arabesques of the Vatican, and other such work, which have become the patterns of ornamentation in modern times, are the fruit of great minds degraded to base objects. (SV III, Ch. III, paras. 45–7, 49)

Gothic versus Renaissance – Conclusion

In examining the nature of Gothic, we concluded that one of the chief elements of power in that, and in *all good* architecture, was the acceptance of uncultivated and rude energy in the workman. In examining the nature of Renaissance, we concluded that its chief element of weakness was that pride of knowledge which not only prevented all rudeness in expression, but gradually quenched all energy which could only be rudely expressed; nor only so, but, for the motive and matter of the work itself, preferred science to emotion, and experience to perception.

The modern mind differs from the Renaissance mind in that its learning is more substantial and extended, and its temper more humble; but its errors, with respect to the cultivation of art, are precisely the same, – nay, as far as regards execution, even more aggravated. We require, at present, from our general workmen, more perfect finish than was demanded in the most skilful Renaissance periods, except in their very finest productions; and our leading principles in teaching, and in the patronage which necessarily gives tone to teaching, are, that the goodness of work consists primarily in firmness of handling and accuracy of science, that is to say, in hand-work and head-work; whereas heart-work, which is the *one* work we want, is not only independent of both, but often, in great degree, inconsistent with either.

Here, therefore, let me finally and firmly enunciate the great principle to which all that has hitherto been stated is subservient: – that art is valuable or otherwise, only as it expresses the personality, activity, and living perception of a good and great human soul; that it may express and contain this with little help from execution, and less from science; and that if it have not this, if it show not the vigour, perception, and invention of a mighty human spirit, it is worthless. Worthless, I mean, as *art*; it may be precious in some other way, but, as art, it is nugatory. Once let this be well understood among us, and magnificent consequences will soon follow. Let me repeat it in other terms, so that I may not be misunderstood. All art is great, and good, and true, only so far as it is distinctively the work of *manhood* in its entire and highest sense; that is to say, not the work of limbs and fingers, but of the soul, aided, according to her necessities, by the inferior powers; and therefore distinguished in essence from all products of those inferior powers unhelped by the soul. For as a photograph is not a work of art, though it requires certain delicate manipulations of paper and acid, and subtle calculations of time, in order to bring out a good result; so, neither would a drawing *like* a photograph, made directly from nature, be a work of art, although it would imply many delicate manipulations of the pencil and subtle calculations of effects of colour and shade . . .

Yet observe, I do not mean to speak of the body and soul as separable. The man is made up of both: they are to be raised and glorified together, and all art is an expression of the one by and through the other. All that I would insist upon is, the necessity of the whole man being in his work; the body *must* be in it. Hands and habits must be in it, whether we will or not: but the nobler part of the man may often not be in it. And that nobler part acts principally in love, reverence, and admiration, together with those conditions of thought which arise out of them. For we usually fall into much error by considering the intellectual powers as having dignity in themselves, and separable from the heart; whereas the truth is, that the intellect becomes noble or ignoble according to the food we give it, and the kind of subjects with which it is conversant. It is not the reasoning power which, of itself, is noble, but the reasoning power occupied with its proper objects. Half of the mistakes of metaphysicians have arisen from their not observing this; namely, that the intellect, going through the same processes, is yet mean or noble according to the matter it deals with, and wastes itself away in mere rotatory motion, if it be set to grind straws and dust. If we reason only respecting words, or lines, or any trifling and finite things, the reason becomes a contemptible faculty; but reason employed on holy and infinite things, becomes herself holy and infinite. So that, by work of the soul, I mean the reader always to understand the work of the entire immortal creature, proceeding from a quick, perceptive, and eager heart, perfected by the intellect, and finally dealt with by the hands, under the direct guidance of these higher powers.

And now observe, the first important consequence of our fully understanding this pre-eminence of the soul, will be the due understanding of that subordination of knowledge respecting which so much has already been said. For it must be felt at once, that the increase of knowledge, merely as such, does not make the soul larger or smaller; that in the sight of God, all the knowledge man can gain is as nothing: but that the soul, for which the great scheme of redemption was laid, be it ignorant or be it wise, is all in all; and in the activity, strength, health, and well-being of this soul, lies the main difference, in His sight, between one man and another. And that which is all in all in God's estimate is also, be assured, all in all in man's labour; and to have the heart open, and the eyes clear, and the emotions and thoughts warm and quick, and not the knowing of this or the other fact, is the state needed for all mighty doing in this world. And therefore, finally, for this, the weightiest of all reasons, let us take no pride in our knowledge. We may, in a certain sense, be proud of being immortal; we may be proud of being God's children; we may be proud of loving, thinking, seeing, and of all that we are by no human teaching: but not of what we have been taught by rote; not of the ballast and freight of the ship of the spirit, but only of its pilotage, without which all the freight will only sink it faster, and strew the sea more richly with its ruin. There is not at this moment a youth of twenty, having received what we moderns ridiculously call education, but he knows more of everything, except the soul, than Plato or St Paul did; but he is not for that reason a greater man, or fitter for his work, or more fit to be heard by others, than Plato or St Paul. There is not at this moment a junior student in our schools of painting, who does not know fifty times as much about the art as Giotto did; but he is not for that reason greater than Giotto; no, nor his work better, nor fitter for our beholding. Let him go on to know all that the human intellect can discover and contain in the term of a long life, and he will not be one inch, one line, nearer to Giotto's feet. But let him leave his academy benches, and, innocently, as one knowing nothing, go out into the highways and hedges, and there rejoice with them that rejoice, and weep with them that weep [Luke xiv. 23, Romans xii. 15]; and in the

next world, among the companies of the great and good, Giotto
will give his hand to him, and lead him into their white circle, and
say, 'This is our brother.'

And the second important consequence of our feeling the soul's
pre-eminence will be our understanding the soul's language,
however broken, or low, or feeble, or obscure in its words; and
chiefly that great symbolic language of past ages, which has now
so long been unspoken.[f] It is strange that the same cold and formal
spirit which the Renaissance teaching has raised amongst us,
should be equally dead to the languages of imitation and of
symbolism; and should at once disdain the faithful rendering of
real nature by the modern school of the Pre-Raphaelites, and the
symbolic rendering of imagined nature in the work of the
thirteenth century . . .

We have just seen that all great art is the work of the whole
living creature, body and soul, and chiefly of the soul. But it is not
only *the work* of the whole creature, it likewise *addresses* the
whole creature. That in which the perfect being speaks must also
have the perfect being to listen. I am not to spend my utmost spirit,
and give all my strength and life to my work, while you, spectator
or hearer, will give me only the attention of half your soul. You
must be all mine, as I am all yours; it is the only condition on
which we can meet each other. All your faculties, all that is in you
of greatest and best, must be awake in you, or I have no reward.
The painter is not to cast the entire treasure of his human nature
into his labour merely to please a part of the beholder: not merely

---

[f] *On the importance of symbolism*:
Even if the symbolic vision itself be not terrible, the scene of what may be veiled
behind it becomes all the more awful in proportion to the insignificance or
strangeness of the sign itself; and, I believe, this thrill of mingled doubt, fear,
and curiosity lies at the very root of the delight which mankind take in
symbolism. It was not an accidental necessity for the conveyance of truth by
pictures instead of words, which led to its universal adoption wherever art was
on the advance; but the Divine fear which necessarily follows on the
understanding that a thing is other and greater than it seems; and which, it
appears probable, has been rendered peculiarly attractive to the human heart,
because God would have us understand that this is true not of invented symbols
merely, but of all things amidst which we live; that there is a deeper meaning
within them than eye hath seen, or ear hath heard (1 Corinthians ii. 9); and
that the whole visible creation is a mere perishable symbol of things eternal and
true. (SV III, Ch. III, para. 63)

to delight his senses, not merely to amuse his fancy, not merely to beguile him into emotion, not merely to lead him into thought; but to do *all* this. Senses, fancy, feeling, reason, the whole of the beholding spirit, must be stilled in attention or stirred with delight; else the labouring spirit has not done its work well. For observe, it is not merely its *right* to be thus met, face to face, heart to heart; but it is its *duty* to evoke this answering of the other soul: its trumpet call must be so clear, that though the challenge may by dulness or indolence be unanswered, there shall be no error as to the meaning of the appeal; there must be a summons in the work, which it shall be our own fault if we do not obey. We require this of it, we beseech this of it. Most men do not know what is in them till they receive this summons from their fellows: their hearts die within them, sleep settles upon them, the lethargy of the world's miasmata; there is nothing for which they are so thankful as that cry, 'Awake, thou that sleepest' [Ephesians v. 14]. And this cry must be most loudly uttered to their noblest faculties; first of all, to the imagination, for that is the most tender, and the soonest struck into numbness by the poisoned air; so that one of the main functions of art, in its service to man, is to rouse the imagination from its palsy, like the angel troubling the Bethesda pool [John v. 4]; and the art which does not do this is false to its duty, and degraded in its nature. It is not enough that it be well imagined, it must task the beholder also to imagine well; and this so imperatively, that if he does not choose to rouse himself to meet the work, he shall not taste it, nor enjoy it in any wise. Once that he is well awake, the guidance which the artist gives him should be full and authoritative: the beholder's imagination should not be suffered to take its own way, or wander hither and thither; but neither must it be left at rest; and the right point of realization, for any given work of art, is that which will enable the spectator to complete it for himself, in the exact way the artist would have him, but not that which will save him the trouble of effecting the completion. So soon as the idea is entirely conveyed, the artist's labour should cease; and every touch which he adds beyond the point when, with the help of the beholder's imagination, the story ought to have been told, is a degradation to his work. So that the art is wrong which either realizes its subject completely, or fails in giving such definite aid as shall enable it to be realized by the beholding imagination.

It follows, therefore, that the quantity of finish or detail which may rightly be bestowed upon any work, depends on the number and kind of ideas which the artist wishes to convey, much more than on the amount of realization necessary to enable the imagination to grasp them. It is true that the differences of judgment formed by one or another observer are in great degree dependent on their unequal imaginative powers, as well as their unequal efforts in following the artist's intention; and it constantly happens that the drawing which appears clear to the painter in whose mind the thought is formed, is slightly inadequate to suggest it to the spectator. These causes of false judgment or imperfect achievement must always exist, but they are of no importance. For, in nearly every mind, the imaginative power, however unable to act independently, is so easily helped and so brightly animated by the most obscure suggestion, that there is no form of artistical language which will not readily be seized by it, if once it set itself intelligently to the task; and even without such effort there are few hieroglyphics of which, once understanding that it is to take them as hieroglyphics, it cannot make itself a pleasant picture.

Thus, in the case of all sketches, etchings, unfinished engravings, etc., no one ever supposes them to be imitations. Black outlines on white paper cannot produce a deceptive resemblance of anything; and the mind, understanding at once that it is to depend on its own powers for great part of its pleasure, sets itself so actively to the task that it can completely enjoy the rudest outline in which meaning exists. Now, when it is once in this temper, the artist is infinitely to be blamed who insults it by putting anything into his work which is not suggestive: having summoned the imaginative power, he must turn it to account and keep it employed, or it will turn against him in indignation. Whatever he does merely to realize and substantiate an idea is impertinent; he is like a dull story-teller, dwelling on points which the hearer anticipates or disregards. The imagination will say to him: 'I knew all that before; I don't want to be told that. Go on; or be silent, and let me go on in my own way. I can tell the story better than you.'

Observe, then, whenever finish is given for the sake of realization, it is wrong; whenever it is given for the sake of adding ideas, it is right. All true finish consists in the addition of ideas, that is to say, in giving the imagination more food; for once well awakened, it is ravenous for food: but the painter who finishes in order to substantiate takes the food out of its mouth, and it will turn and rend him . . .

Now, the truly great artist neither leaves the imagination to itself, like Sir Joshua [Reynolds], nor insults it by realization, like Hobbima, but finds it continual employment of the happiest kind.[14] Having summoned it by his vigorous first touches, he says to it: 'Here is a tree for you, and it is to be an oak. Now I know that you can make it green and intricate for yourself, but that is not enough: an oak is not only green and intricate, but its leaves have most beautiful and fantastic forms, which I am very sure you are not quite able to complete without help; so I will draw a cluster or two perfectly for you, and then you can go on and do all the other clusters. So far so good: but the leaves are not enough; the oak is to be full of acorns, and you may not be quite able to imagine the way they grow, nor the pretty contrast of their glossy almond-shaped nuts with the chasing of their cups; so I will draw a bunch or two of acorns for you, and you can fill up the oak with others like them. Good: but that is not enough; it is to be a bright day in summer, and all the outside leaves are to be glittering in the sunshine as if their edges were of gold: I cannot paint this, but you can; so I will really gild some of the edges nearest you, and you can turn the gold into sunshine, and cover the tree with it. Well done: but still this is not enough; the tree is so full foliaged and so old that the wood birds come in crowds to build there; they are singing, two or three under the shadow of every bough. I cannot show you them all; but here is a large one on the outside spray, and you can fancy the others inside.'

In this way the calls upon the imagination are multiplied as a great painter finishes; and from these larger incidents he may proceed into the most minute particulars, and lead the companion imagination to the veins in the leaves and the mosses on the trunk, and the shadows of the dead leaves upon the grass, but always multiplying thoughts, or subjects of thought, never working for the sake of realization; the amount of realization actually reached depending on his space, his materials, and the nature of the thoughts he wishes to suggest . . .

So then, whatever may be the means, or whatever the more immediate end of any kind of art, all of it that is good agrees in this, that it is the expression of one soul talking to another, and is precious according to the greatness of the soul that utters it. And consider what mighty consequences follow from our acceptance of this truth! what a key we have herein given us for the interpretation of the art of all time! For, as long as we held art to consist in any high manual skill, or successful imitation of natural objects, or any scientific and legalized manner of performance whatever, it was necessary for us to limit our admiration to narrow periods and to few men. According to our own knowledge and sympathies, the period chosen might be different, and our rest might be in Greek statues, or Dutch landscapes, or Italian Madonnas; but, whatever our choice, we were therein captive, barred from all reverence but of our favourite masters, and habitually using the language of contempt towards the whole of the human race to whom it had not pleased Heaven to reveal the arcana of the particular craftsmanship we admired, and who, it might be, had lived their term of seventy years upon the earth, and fitted themselves therein for the eternal world, without any clear understanding, sometimes even with an insolent disregard, of the laws of perspective and chiaroscuro.

But let us once comprehend the holier nature of the art of man, and begin to look for the meaning of the spirit, however syllabled, and the scene is changed; and we are changed also. Those small and dexterous creatures whom once we worshipped, those fur-capped divinities with sceptres of camel's hair, peering and poring in their one-windowed chambers over the minute preciousness of the laboured canvas; how are they swept away and crushed into unnoticeable darkness! And in their stead, as the walls of the dismal rooms that enclosed them, and us, are struck by the four winds of Heaven, and rent away, and as the world opens to our sight, lo! far back into all the depths of time, and forth from all the fields that have been sown with human life, how the harvest of the dragon's teeth is springing! how the companies of the gods are ascending out of the earth! The dark stones that have so long been the sepulchres of the thoughts of nations, and the forgotten ruins wherein their faith lay charnelled, give up the dead that were in them; and beneath the Egyptian ranks of sultry and silent rock, and amidst the dim golden lights of the Byzantine dome, and out of the confused and cold shadows of the Northern cloister, behold, the multitudinous souls come forth with singing, gazing on us with the soft eyes of newly comprehended sympathy, and stretching their white arms to us across the grave, in the solemn gladness of everlasting brotherhood. (SV III, Ch. IV, paras. 4–9, 21–3, 25–6, 28)

After the Renaissance
Turner's restoration, in painting, of what was lost in the
decline of Gothic architecture

It was not possible that one of the strongest instincts of the human race could be deprived altogether of its natural food. Exactly in the degree that the architect withdrew from his buildings the sources of delight which in early days they had so richly possessed, demanding, in accordance with the new principles of taste, the banishment of all happy colour and healthy invention, in that degree the minds of men began to turn to landscape as their only resource. The picturesque school of art rose up to address those capacities of enjoyment for which, in sculpture, architecture, or the higher walks of painting, there was employment no more; and the shadows of Rembrandt, and savageness of Salvator, arrested the admiration which was no longer permitted to be rendered to the gloom or the grotesqueness of the Gothic aisle. And thus the English school of landscape, culminating in Turner, is in reality nothing else than a healthy effort to fill the void which the destruction of Gothic architecture has left.

But the void cannot thus be completely filled; no, nor filled in any considerable degree. The art of landscape-painting will never become thoroughly interesting or sufficing to the minds of men engaged in active life, or concerned principally with practical subjects. The sentiment and imagination necessary to enter fully into the romantic forms of art are chiefly the characteristics of youth; so that nearly all men as they advance in years, and some even from their childhood upwards, must be appealed to, if at all, by the direct and substantial art, brought before their daily observation and connected with their daily interests. No form of art answers these conditions so well as architecture.

(SV III, Ch. IV, paras. 33–4)

CHAPTER 6

The Modern Problem

From Modern Painters III to Modern Painters V

We turn again to Modern Painters, *picking up the story from two different endpoints, one at the close of Chapter Five, the other at the close of Chapter Four.*

In Chapter Five we saw how The Stones of Venice *ended by questioning whether modern landscape painting could fill the religious void left by the demise of Gothic architecture.*

After asking the question *what is the use of* pictures *covered in Chapter Four, Ruskin turns, in what may be thought of as the second half of* Modern Painters Vol. III, *to the even more pointed question of what is the use of painting pictures of* landscapes. The *rise of landscape painting, notes Ruskin in the chapter 'Of the Novelty of Landscape', is a peculiarly modern phenomenon. Related to it is the post-Romantic tendency to employ what Ruskin calls 'The Pathetic Fallacy' – the unwarranted projection of human feelings upon non-human objects, which occurs as mankind, in the cosmic loneliness of the nineteenth century, tries all too literally to find a place for its emotions.*

To *clinch his sense of the modern problem, Ruskin summarizes in* Modern Painters Vol. III *the differing effects of landscape on the human mind in three major periods: classical, medieval and modern. The movement from classical to medieval marks a shift from field to garden, from the necessary uses and pieties of agriculture to a more aristocratic enjoyment of nature as beautiful in itself. There are at once gains and losses in this shift. To the classical Greek, represented by Homer, the flower and the herb were essentially useful – they were honoured as God's gift but as God's gift to him; to medieval man at his finest, as in the person of Dante, the flower was God's work for God's self, irrespective of its being a gift to man. But modern man has the worst of both worlds; he is neither so practical as the men of the classical world nor so devout as those of the Middle Ages. Accordingly, Ruskin goes on to ask at the end of his third volume, in the chapter 'The Moral of Landscape', whether modern love of landscape is merely a form of weakness.*

The fifth and final volume of Modern Painters, *published in 1860, contains four parts. The first two are on leaf beauty and on cloud beauty, and correspond to Ruskin's work on mountains in* Modern Painters Vol. IV *(these very detailed chapters are largely omitted from the present selection); the third part, on invention and composition, we have already seen to have connections with* Modern Painters Vol. II. *But the final part of* Modern Painters Vol. V *returns to the problem of the moral of landscape that was left in the balance at the end of* Modern Painters Vol. III *four years earlier.*

It is necessary to explain how Modern Painters Vol. V *emerges from, relates to, and is the culmination of the previous volumes.*

The first chapter of the final part, 'The Dark Mirror', reaffirms Ruskin's belief in art, even landscape art, as essentially human *expression. The second chapter, 'The Lance of Pallas', then argues that although great art is about humans it is about humans as creatures of God's making.*

Yet Ruskin does not seek to defend a purely Christian art, such as that of Fra Angelico. In 'The Nature of Gothic' in The Stones of Venice *and again in chapters of* Modern Painters Vol. III, *Ruskin had made a distinction between three human types in their dealing with the fact that 'things around us contain mixed good and evil'. There are Purists, who chose the good and left the evil, thus producing a relative childishness of mind and of art, a false ideal 'without shadows, as if the sun were everywhere at once' (MP III, Pt. IV, Ch. VI, para. 3). Such was the art of Fra Angelico, for all its greatness. At the other extreme are the Sensualists, who choose the evil and leave the good. In* Modern Painters Vol. V *Ruskin considers Salvator Rosa as an example of that degraded tendency. Between the two is the Naturalist, who receives both good and evil together and concerns himself simply with things as they* are. *Naturalism accepts 'the weaknesses, faults and wrongnesses in all things that it sees', but, with the aid of imagination associative described in* Modern Painters Vol. II, *'it so places and harmonizes them that they form a noble whole, in which the imperfection of each several part is not only harmless, but absolutely essential' (MP III, Pt. IV, Ch. VII, para. 1).*

Just as earlier in Modern Painters *Vol. III Ruskin had considered Greek, medieval and modern ideas of landscape, so now in Volume V he interrogates the Greek, medieval and modern capacity for sustaining a true vision of life's deep shadows – of suffering, injustice and death. Of the best representatives of what was strongest in the beliefs of each period Ruskin asks: To what extent could they attain the Naturalist ideal? How far could they face and register the whole spectrum of life, without recourse to either over-idealization or grotesque degeneration, to pathetic fallacy or to mere despair?*

In turning to the moderns, Ruskin finally looks again at Turner. At this point in Modern Painters *Vol. V he recalls the opening chapter of* Modern Painters *Vol. IV, 'Of the Turnerian Picturesque' (an excerpt is included in this chapter). 'Of the Turnerian Picturesque' had served partly to bolster Ruskin's earlier demonstration of Turner's superior truthfulness among moderns. But in it Turner is also distinguished from what was alleged in* The Stones of Venice *to be the source of Venetian decline. The Venetian did not desire religion, so much as the delight that resulted from the belief. In 'Of the Turnerian Picturesque', in contrast, Turner is shown not as wanting life merely for the sake of his being able to reproduce it in pictures of delight, but as wanting art only for the sake of the reality it tries faithfully to represent.*

But looking back at 'Of the Turnerian Picturesque' from Modern Painters *Vol. V, Ruskin is then struck not just by Turner's treatment of ruin but that it should be so characteristically a treatment of ruin in the first place. For all his brightness, what was the distinctive effect of light that Turner introduced? What was Turner's favourite light? Ruskin answers: twilight.*

It was clear what in Modern Painters *Vol. III Ruskin had wanted and had expected to receive from Turner: a new religious art developing out of landscape. But by* Modern Painters *Vol. V it was as if Ruskin's vocation and career spent in following Turner on his apparently infinite path might end in ruin, like Venice itself. And why? Because Turner himself had begun amidst ruin and could never shake off the effect of his historical origins. In 'The Two Boyhoods' in* Modern Painters *Vol. V Ruskin begins to turn from continuing reliance on visionary faith to a social and historical explanation for the loss of faith. Here is the source of Ruskin's later political writing: the seeking of historical explanation as a symptom of his own desperation at the modern loss of faith. Ruskin contrasts the propitious circumstances of Giorgione's youth in a Venice still far from decay with Turner's upbringing in a London of dirt and poverty, where religion can hardly seem to believe in itself. Ruskin concludes the volume with a number of contrasts involving not only Turner but other earlier artists of faith who are now recalled in order to give help, in particular, Dürer and Veronese.*

As a postscript to the stoic inconclusiveness at the end of Modern Painters Vol. V, this chapter closes with excerpts from a lecture, 'The Mystery of Life and its Arts', delivered at the Royal College of Science, Dublin, in 1868. Waiving his hosts' general prohibition that no reference be made to religion, Ruskin offers a personal view of his mission on behalf of art and faith in the modern age.

'Of the Novelty of Landscape'

Having now obtained, I trust, clear ideas, up to a certain point, of what is generally right and wrong in all art, both in conception and in workmanship, we have to apply these laws of right to the particular branch of art which is the subject of our present inquiry, namely, landscape-painting. Respecting which, after the various meditations into which we have been led on the high duties and ideals of art, it may not improbably occur to us first to ask, – whether it be worth inquiring about at all.

That question, perhaps the reader thinks, should have been asked and answered before I had written, or he read, two volumes and a half about it. So I *had* answered it in my own mind; but it seems time now to give the grounds for this answer. If, indeed, the reader has never suspected that landscape-painting was anything but good, right, and healthy work, I should be sorry to put any doubt of its being so into his mind; but if, as seems to me more likely, he, living in this busy and perhaps somewhat calamitous age, has some suspicion that landscape-painting is but an idle and empty business, not worth all our long talk about it, then, perhaps, he will be pleased to have such suspicion done away, before troubling himself farther with these disquisitions.

I should rather be glad, than otherwise, that he *had* formed some suspicion on this matter. If he has at all admitted the truth of anything hitherto said respecting great art, and its choices of subject, it seems to me he ought, by this time, to be questioning with himself whether road-side weeds, old cottages, broken stones, and such other materials, be worthy matters for grave men to busy themselves in the imitation of. And I should like him to probe this doubt to the deep of it, and bring all his misgivings out to the broad light, that we may see how we are to deal with them, or ascertain if indeed they are too well-founded to be dealt with.

And to this end I would ask him now to imagine himself entering, for the first time in his life, the room of the Old Water-Colour Society: and to suppose that he has entered it, not for the sake of a quiet examination of the paintings one by one, but in order to seize such ideas as it may generally suggest respecting the state and meaning of modern, as compared with elder, art. I suppose him, of course, that he may be capable of such a comparison, to be in some degree familiar with the different forms in which art has developed itself within the periods historically known to us; but never, till that moment, to have seen any completely modern work. So prepared, and so unprepared, he would, as his ideas began to arrange themselves, be first struck by the number of paintings representing blue mountains, clear lakes, and ruined castles or cathedrals, and he would say to himself: 'There is something strange in the mind of these modern people! Nobody ever cared about blue mountains before, or tried to paint the broken stones of old walls.' And the more he considered the subject, the more he would feel the peculiarity; and, as he thought over the art of Greeks and Romans, he would still repeat, with increasing certainty of conviction: 'Mountains! I remember none. The Greeks did not seem, as artists, to know that such things were in the world. They carved, or variously represented, men, and horses, and beasts, and birds, and all kinds of living creatures, – yes, even down to cuttle-fish; and trees, in a sort of way; but not so much as the outline of a mountain; and as for lakes, they merely showed they knew the difference between salt and fresh water by the fish they put into each.' Then he would pass on to mediæval art; and still he would be obliged to repeat: 'Mountains! I remember none. Some careless and jagged arrangements of blue spires or spikes on the horizon, and, here and there, an attempt at representing an overhanging rock with a hole through it; but merely in order to divide the light behind some human figure. Lakes! No, nothing of the kind, – only blue bays of sea put in to fill up the background when the painter could not think of anything

else. Broken-down buildings! No; for the most part very complete
and well-appointed buildings, if any; and never buildings at all,
but to give place or explanation to some circumstance of human
conduct.' And then he would look up again to the modern
pictures, observing, with an increasing astonishment, that here
the human interest had, in many cases, altogether disappeared.
That mountains, instead of being used only as a blue ground for
the relief of the heads of saints, were themselves the exclusive
subjects of reverent contemplation; that their ravines, and peaks,
and forests, were all painted with an appearance of as much
enthusiasm as had formerly been devoted to the dimples of
beauty, or the frowns of asceticism; and that all the living interest
which was still supposed necessary to the scene, might be supplied
by a traveller in a slouched hat, a beggar in a scarlet cloak, or, in
default of these, even by a heron or a wild duck.

And if he could entirely divest himself of his own modern habits
of thought, and regard the subjects in question with the feelings of
a knight or monk of the Middle Ages, it might be a question
whether those feelings would not rapidly verge towards contempt. 'What!' he might perhaps mutter to himself, 'here are
human beings spending the whole of their lives in making pictures
of bits of stone and runlets of water, withered sticks and flying
fogs, and actually not a picture of the gods or the heroes! none of
the saints or the martyrs! none of the angels and demons! none of
councils or battles, or any other single thing worth the thought of
a man! Trees and clouds indeed! as if I should not see as many
trees as I cared to see, and more, in the first half of my day's
journey tomorrow, or as if it mattered to any man whether the sky
were clear or cloudy, so long as his armour did not get too hot in
the sun!'

There can be no question that this would have been somewhat
the tone of thought with which either a Lacedæmonian, a soldier
of Rome in her strength, or a knight of the thirteenth century,
would have been apt to regard these particular forms of our
present art. Nor can there be any question that, in many respects,
their judgment would have been just. It is true that the indignation
of the Spartan or Roman would have been equally excited against
any appearance of luxurious industry; but the mediæval knight
would, to the full, have admitted the nobleness of art; only he
would have had it employed in decorating his church or his
prayer-book, not in imitating moors and clouds. And the feelings

of all the three would have agreed in this, – that their main ground of offence must have been the want of *seriousness* and *purpose* in what they saw. They would all have admitted the nobleness of whatever conduced to the honour of the gods, or the power of the nation; but they would not have understood how the skill of human life could be wisely spent in that which did no honour either to Jupiter or to the Virgin; and which in no wise tended, apparently, either to the accumulation of wealth, the excitement of patriotism, or the advancement of morality.

And exactly so far forth their judgment would be just, as the landscape-painting could indeed be shown, for others as well as for them, to be art of this nugatory kind; and so far forth unjust, as that painting could be shown to depend upon, or cultivate, certain sensibilities which neither the Greek nor mediæval knight possessed, and which have resulted from some extraordinary change in human nature since their time. We have no right to assume, without very accurate examination of it, that this change has been an ennobling one. The simple fact, that we are, in some strange way, different from all the great races that have existed before us, cannot at once be received as the proof of our own greatness; nor can it be granted, without any question, that we have a legitimate subject of complacency in being under the influence of feelings, with which neither Miltiades nor the Black Prince, neither Homer nor Dante, neither Socrates nor St Francis, could for an instant have sympathized.

Whether, however, this fact be one to excite our pride or not, it is assuredly one to excite our deepest interest. The fact itself is certain. For nearly six thousand years the energies of man have pursued certain beaten paths, manifesting some constancy of feeling throughout all that period, and involving some fellowship at heart, among the various nations who by turns succeeded or surpassed each other in the several aims of art or policy. So that, for these thousands of years, the whole human race might be to some extent described in general terms. Man was a creature separated from all others by his instinctive sense of an Existence superior to his own, invariably manifesting this sense of the being of a God more strongly in proportion to his own perfectness of mind and body; and making enormous and self-denying efforts, in order to obtain some persuasion of the immediate presence or approval of the Divinity. So that, on the whole, the best things he did were done as in the presence, or for the honour, of his gods;

and, whether in statues, to help him to imagine them, or temples raised to their honour, or acts of self-sacrifice done in the hope of their love, he brought whatever was best and skilfullest in him into their service, and lived in a perpetual subjection to their unseen power. Also, he was always anxious to know something definite about them; and his chief books, songs, and pictures were filled with legends about them, or specially devoted to illustration of their lives and nature.

Next to these gods he was always anxious to know something about his human ancestors; fond of exalting the memory, and telling or painting the history of old rulers and benefactors; yet full of an enthusiastic confidence in himself, as having in many ways advanced beyond the best efforts of past time; and eager to record his own doings for future fame. He was a creature eminently warlike, placing his principal pride in dominion; eminently beautiful, and having great delight in his own beauty; setting forth this beauty by every species of invention in dress, and rendering his arms and accoutrements superbly decorative of his form. He took, however, very little interest in anything but what belonged to humanity; caring in no wise for the external world, except as it influenced his own destiny; honouring the lightning because it could strike him, the sea because it could drown him, the fountains because they gave him drink, and the grass because it yielded him seed; but utterly incapable of feeling any special happiness in the love of such things, or any earnest emotion about them, considered as separate from man; therefore giving no time to the study of them; – knowing little of herbs, except only which were hurtful and which healing; of stones, only which would glitter brightest in a crown, or last the longest in a wall: of the wild beasts, which were best for food, and which the stoutest quarry for the hunter; – thus spending only on the lower creatures and inanimate things his waste energy, his dullest thoughts, his most languid emotions, and reserving all his acuter intellect for researches into his own nature and that of the gods; all his strength of will for the acquirement of political or moral power; all his sense of beauty for things immediately connected with his own person and life; and all his deep affections for domestic or divine companionship.

Such, in broad light and brief terms, was man for five thousand years. Such he is no longer. Let us consider what he is now, comparing the descriptions clause by clause.

1 He *was* invariably sensible of the existence of gods, and went about all his speculations or works holding this as an acknowledged fact, making his best efforts in their service. *Now* he is capable of going through life with hardly any positive idea on this subject, – doubting, fearing, suspecting, analyzing, – doing everything, in fact, *but* believing; hardly ever getting quite up to that point which hitherto was wont to be the starting-point for all generations. And human work has accordingly hardly any reference to spiritual beings, but is done either from a patriotic or personal interest, – either to benefit mankind, or reach some selfish end, not (I speak of human work in the broad sense) to please the gods.

2 He *was* a beautiful creature, setting forth this beauty by all means in his power, and depending upon it for much of his authority over his fellows. So that the ruddy cheek of David, and the ivory skin of Atrides, and the towering presence of Saul, and the blue eyes of Cœur de Lion, were among chief reasons why they should be kings; and it was one of the aims of all education, and of all dress, to make the presence of the human form stately and lovely. *Now* it has become the task of grave philosophy partly to depreciate or conceal this bodily beauty; and even by those who esteem it in their hearts, it is not made one of the great ends of education; man has become, upon the whole, an ugly animal, and is not ashamed of his ugliness.

3 He *was* eminently warlike. He is *now* gradually becoming more and more ashamed of all the arts and aims of battle. So that the desire of dominion, which was once frankly confessed or boasted of as a heroic passion, is now sternly reprobated or cunningly disclaimed.

4 He *used* to take no interest in anything but what immediately concerned himself. *Now*, he has deep interest in the abstract nature of things, inquires as eagerly into the laws which regulate the economy of the material world, as into those of his own being, and manifests a passionate admiration of inanimate objects, closely resembling, in its elevation and tenderness, the affection which he bears to those living souls with which he is brought into the nearest fellowship.

It is this last change only which is to be the subject of our present inquiry; but it cannot be doubted that it is closely connected with all the others, and that we can only thoroughly understand its nature by considering it in this connection. For, regarded by itself, we might, perhaps, too rashly assume it to be a natural consequence of the progress of the race. There appears to be a diminution of selfishness in it, and a more extended and heartfelt desire of understanding the manner of God's working; and this the more, because one of the permanent characters of this change is a greater accuracy in the statement of external facts. When the eyes of men were fixed first upon themselves, and upon nature solely and secondarily as bearing upon their interests, it was of less consequence to them what the ultimate laws of nature were, than what their immediate effects were upon human beings. Hence they could rest satisfied with phenomena instead of principles, and accepted without scrutiny every fable which seemed sufficiently or gracefully to account for those phenomena. But so far as the eyes of men are now withdrawn from themselves, and turned upon the inanimate things about them, the results cease to be of importance, and the laws become essential.

In these respects, it might easily appear to us that this change was assuredly one of steady and natural advance. But when we contemplate the others above noted, of which it is clearly one of the branches or consequences, we may suspect ourselves of over-rashness in our self-congratulation, and admit the necessity of a scrupulous analysis both of the feeling itself and of its tendencies.

Of course a complete analysis, or anything like it, would involve a treatise on the whole history of the world. I shall merely endeavour to note some of the leading and more interesting circumstances bearing on the subject, and to show sufficient practical ground for the conclusion, that landscape-painting is indeed a noble and useful art, though one not long known by man. I shall therefore examine, as best I can, the effect of landscape, 1st, on the Classical mind; 2ndly, on the Mediæval mind; and lastly, on the Modern mind. But there is one point of some interest respecting the effect of it on *any* mind, which must be settled first; and this I will endeavour to do in the next chapter [below]. (MP III, Pt. IV, Ch. XI, paras. 1–11)

'The Pathetic Fallacy'

Thus, for instance, in [Charles Kingsley's] *Alton Locke,*—

> They rowed her in across the rolling foam—
> The cruel, crawling foam.

> [Ch. 26]

The foam is not cruel, neither does it crawl. The state of mind which attributes to it these characters of a living creature is one in which the reason is unhinged by grief. All violent feelings have the same effect. They produce in us a falseness in all our impressions of external things, which I would generally characterize as the 'pathetic fallacy'.

Now we are in the habit of considering this fallacy as eminently a character of poetical description, and the temper of mind in which we allow it, as one eminently poetical, because passionate. But I believe, if we look well into the matter, that we shall find the greatest poets do not often admit this kind of falseness, – that it is only the second order of poets who much delight in it.

Thus, when Dante describes the spirits falling from the bank of Acheron 'as dead leaves flutter from a bough', [*Inferno*, 111, 112] he gives the most perfect image possible of their utter lightness, feebleness, passiveness, and scattering agony of despair, without, however, for an instant losing his own clear perception that *these* are souls, and *those* are leaves; he makes no confusion of one with the other. But when Coleridge speaks of

> The one red leaf, the last of its clan,
> That dances as often as dance it can,
> [*Christabel*, I 49–50]

he has a morbid, that is to say, a so far false, idea about the leaf; he fancies a life in it, and will, which there are not; confuses its powerlessness with choice, its fading death with merriment, and the wind that shakes it with music . . .

The temperament which admits the pathetic fallacy, is, as I said above, that of a mind and body in some sort too weak to deal fully with what is before them or upon them; borne away, or over-clouded, or over-dazzled by emotion; and it is a more or less noble state, according to the force of the emotion which has induced it.[a]

---

[a] *Compare Ruskin on the legitimate and unavoidable inclusion of personal associations:*

I believe that the eye cannot rest on a material form, in a moment of depression of exultation, without communicating to that form a spirit and a life, – a life which will make it afterwards in some degree loved or feared, – a charm or a painfulness for which we shall be unable to account even to ourselves, which will not indeed be perceptible, except by its delicate influence on our judgment in cases of complicated beauty. Let the eye but rest on a rough piece of branch

For it is no credit to a man that he is not morbid or inaccurate in his perceptions, when he has no strength of feeling to warp them; and it is in general a sign of higher capacity and stand in the ranks of being, that the emotions should be strong enough to vanquish, partly, the intellect, and make it believe what they choose. But it is still a grander condition when the intellect also rises, till it is strong enough to assert its rule against, or together with, the utmost efforts of the passions; and the whole man stands in an iron glow, white hot, perhaps, but still strong, and in no wise evaporating; even if he melts, losing none of his weight.

So, then, we have the three ranks: the man who perceives rightly, because he does not feel, and to whom the primrose is very accurately the primrose, because he does not love it. Then, secondly, the man who perceives wrongly, because he feels, and to

of curious form during a conversation with a friend, rest however unconsciously, and though the conversation be forgotten, though every circumstance connected with it be as utterly lost to the memory as though it had not been, yet the eye will, through the whole life after, take a certain pleasure in such boughs which it had not before, a pleasure so slight, a trace of feeling so delicate, as to leave us utterly unconscious of its peculiar power; but undestroyable by any reasoning, a part, thenceforward, of our constitution, destroyable only by the same arbitrary process of association by which it was created. Reason has no effect upon it whatsoever. And there is probably no one opinion which is formed by any of us, in matters of taste, which is not in some degree influenced by unconscious association of this kind. In many who have no definite rules of judgment, preference is decided by little else, and thus, unfortunately, its operations are mistaken for, or rather substituted for, those of inherent beauty, and its real position and value in the moral system are in a great measure overlooked . . .

But it is evident that the full exercise of this noble function of the Associative faculty is inconsistent with absolute and incontrovertible conclusions on subjects of theoretic preference. For it is quite impossible for any individual to distinguish in himself the unconscious underworking of indefinite association peculiar to him individually, from those great laws of choice under which he is comprehended with all his race. And it is well for us that it is so, the harmony of God's good work is not in us interrupted by this mingling of universal and peculiar principles: for by these such difference is secured in the feelings as shall make fellowship itself more delightful, by its inter-communicate character; and such variety of feeling also in each of us separately as shall make us capable of enjoying scenes of different kinds and orders, instead of morbidly seeking for some perfect epitome of the Beautiful in one. (MP II, Pt. III, Sec. I, Ch. IV, paras. 9, 11)

whom the primrose is anything else than a primrose: a star, or a sun, or a fairy's shield, or a forsaken maiden. And then, lastly, there is the man who perceives rightly in spite of his feelings, and to whom the primrose is for ever nothing else than itself – a little flower apprehended in the very plain and leafy fact of it, whatever and how many soever the associations and passions may be that crowd around it. And, in general, these three classes may be rated in comparative order, as the men who are not poets at all, and the poets of the second order, and the poets of the first; only however great a man may be, there are always some subjects which *ought* to throw him off his balance; some, by which his poor human capacity of thought should be conquered, and brought into the inaccurate and vague state of perception, so that the language of the highest inspiration becomes broken, obscure, and wild in metaphor, resembling that of the weaker man, overborne by weaker things.

And thus, in full, there are four classes: the men who feel nothing, and therefore see truly; the men who feel strongly, think weakly, and see untruly (second order of poets); the men who feel strongly, think strongly, and see truly (first order of poets); and the men who, strong as human creatures can be, are yet submitted to influences stronger than they, and see in a sort untruly, because what they see is inconceivably above them. This last is the usual condition of prophetic inspiration.

I separate these classes, in order that their character may be clearly understood; but of course they are united each to the other by imperceptible transitions, and the same mind, according to the influences to which it is subjected, passes at different times into the various states. (MP III, Pt. IV, Ch. XII, paras. 5–6, 8–10)

The human relation to landscape
(1) 'Of Classical Landscape'

With us, observe, the idea of the Divinity is apt to get separated from the life of nature; and imagining our God upon a cloudy throne, far above the earth, and not in the flowers or waters, we approach those visible things with a theory that they are dead; governed by physical laws, and so forth. But coming to them, we find the theory fail; that they are not dead; that, say what we choose about them, the instinctive sense of their being alive is too strong for us; and in scorn of all physical law, the wilful fountain sings, and the kindly flowers rejoice. And then, puzzled, and yet happy; pleased, and yet ashamed of being so; accepting sympathy from nature, which we do not believe it gives, and giving sympathy to nature, which we do not believe it receives, – mixing, besides, all manner of purposeful play and conceit with these involuntary fellowships, – we fall necessarily into the curious web of hesitating sentiment, pathetic fallacy, and wandering fancy, which form a great part of our modern view of nature. But the Greek never removed his god out of nature at all; never attempted for a moment to contradict his instinctive sense that God was everywhere. 'The tree *is* glad,' said he, 'I know it is; I can cut it down: no matter, there was a nymph in it. The water *does* sing,' said he; 'I can dry it up; but no matter, there was a naiad in it.' But in thus clearly defining his belief, observe, he threw it entirely into a human form, and gave his faith to nothing but the image of his own humanity. What sympathy and fellowship he had, were always for the spirit *in* the stream, not for the stream; always for the dryad *in* the wood, not for the wood. Content with this human sympathy, he approached the actual waves and woody fibres with no sympathy at all. The spirit that ruled them, he received as a plain fact. Them, also, ruled and material, he received as plain facts; they, without their spirit, were dead enough. A rose was good for scent, and a stream for sound and coolness; for the rest, one was no more than leaves, the other no more than water; he could not make anything else of them; and the divine power, which was involved in their existence, having been all distilled away by him into an independent Flora or Thetis, the poor leaves or waves were left, in mere cold corporealness, to make the most of their being discernibly red and soft, clear and wet, and unacknowledged in any other power whatsoever.

Then, observe farther, the Greeks lived in the midst of the most beautiful nature, and were as familiar with blue sea, clear air, and sweet outlines of mountain, as we are with brick walls, black smoke, and level fields. This perfect familiarity rendered all such scenes of natural beauty unexciting, if not indifferent to them, by lulling and over-wearying the imagination as far as it was concerned with such things; but there was another kind of beauty which they found it required effort to obtain, and which, when thoroughly obtained, seemed more glorious than any of this wild loveliness – the beauty of the human countenance and form. This, they perceived, could only be reached by continual exercise of virtue; and it was in Heaven's sight, and theirs, all the more beautiful because it needed this self-denial to obtain it. So they set themselves to reach this, and having gained it, gave it their principal thoughts, and set it off with beautiful dress as best they might. But making this their object, they were obliged to pass their lives in simple exercise and disciplined employments. Living wholesomely, giving themselves no fever fits, either by fasting or over-eating, constantly in the open air, and full of animal spirit and physical power, they became incapable of every morbid condition of mental emotion. Unhappy love, disappointed ambition, spiritual despondency, or any other disturbing sensation, had little power over the well-braced nerves, and healthy flow of the blood; and what bitterness might yet fasten on them was soon boxed or raced out of a boy, and spun or woven out of a girl, or danced out of both. They had indeed their sorrows, true and deep, but still, more like children's sorrows than ours, whether bursting into open cry of pain, or hid with shuddering under the veil, still passing over the soul as clouds do over heaven, not sullying it, not mingling with it; – darkening it perhaps long or utterly, but still not becoming one with it, and for the most part passing away in dashing rain of tears, and leaving the man unchanged: in nowise affecting, as our sorrow does, the whole tone of his thought and imagination thence-forward.

How far our melancholy may be deeper and wider than theirs in its roots and view, and therefore nobler, we shall consider presently; but at all events, they had the advantage of us in being entirely free from all those dim and feverish sensations which result from unhealthy state of the body. I believe that a large amount of the dreamy and sentimental sadness, tendency to reverie, and general patheticalness of modern life results merely from derangement of stomach; holding to the Greek life the same relation that the feverish night of an adult does to a child's sleep. (MP III, Pt. IV, Ch. XIII, paras. 13–14)

(2) 'Of Medieval Landscape'

The more poetical delight in external nature proceeds just from the fact that it is no longer looked upon with the eye of the farmer; and in proportion as the herbs and flowers cease to be regarded as useful, they are felt to be charming. Leeks are not now the most important objects in the garden, but lilies and roses: the herbage which a Greek would have looked at only with a view to the number of horses it would feed, is regarded by the mediæval knight as a green carpet for fair feet to dance upon, and the beauty of its softness and colour is proportionally felt by him; while the brook, which the Greek rejoiced to dismiss into a reservoir under the palace threshold, would be, by the mediæval, distributed into pleasant pools, or forced into fountains; and regarded alternately as a mirror for fair faces, and a witchery to ensnare the sunbeams and the rainbow.

And this change of feeling involves two others, very important. When the flowers and grass were regarded as means of life, and therefore (as the thoughtful labourer of the soil must always regard them) with the reverence due to those gifts of God which were most necessary to his existence; although their own beauty was less felt, their proceeding from the Divine hand was more seriously acknowledged, and the herb yielding seed, the fruit-tree yielding fruit, though in themselves less admired, were yet solemnly connected in the heart with the reverence of Ceres, Pomona, or Pan. But when the sense of these necessary uses was more or less lost, among the upper classes, by the delegation of the art of husbandry to the hands of the peasant, the flower and fruit, whose bloom or richness thus became a mere source of pleasure, were regarded with less solemn sense of the Divine gift in them; and were converted rather into toys than treasures, chance gifts for gaiety, rather than promised rewards of labour; so that while the Greek could hardly have trodden the formal furrow, or plucked the clusters from the trellised vine, without reverent thoughts of the deities of field and leaf, who gave the seed to fructify, and the bloom to darken, the mediæval knight plucked the violet to wreathe in his lady's hair, or strewed the idle rose on the turf at her feet, with little sense of anything in the nature that gave them, but a frail, accidental, involuntary exuberance; while also the Jewish sacrificial system being now done away, as well as the Pagan mythology, and, with it, the whole conception of meat offering or firstfruits offering, the chiefest seriousness of all the thoughts connected with the gifts of nature faded from the minds of the classes of men concerned with art and literature; while the peasant, reduced to serf-level, was incapable of imaginative thought, owing to his want of general cultivation. But on the other hand, exactly in proportion as the idea of definite spiritual presence in material nature was lost, the mysterious sense of *unaccountable* life in the things themselves would be increased, and the mind would instantly be laid open to all those currents of fallacious, but pensive and pathetic sympathy, which we have seen to be characteristic of modern times.

Farther: a singular difference would necessarily result from the far greater loneliness of baronial life, deprived as it was of all interest in agricultural pursuits. The palace of a Greek leader in early times might have gardens, fields, and farms around it, but was sure to be near some busy city or sea-port: in later times, the city itself became the principal dwelling-place, and the country was visited only to see how the farm went on, or traversed in a line of march. Far other was the life of the mediæval baron, nested on his solitary jut of crag; entering into cities only occasionally for some grave political or warrior's purpose, and, for the most part, passing the years of his life in lion-like isolation; the village inhabited by his retainers straggling indeed about the slopes of the rocks at his feet, but his own dwelling standing gloomily apart, between them and the uncompanionable clouds, commanding, from sunset to sunrise, the flowing flame of some calm unvoyaged river, and the endless undulation of the untraversable hills. How different must the thoughts about nature have been, of the noble who lived among the bright marble porticoes of the Greek groups of temple or palace, – in the midst of a plain covered with corn and olives, and by the shore of a sparkling and freighted sea, – from those of the master of some mountain promontory in the green recesses of Northern Europe, watching night by night, from amongst his heaps of storm-broken stone, rounded into towers, the lightning of the lonely sea flash round the sands of Harlech, or the mists changing their shapes for ever, among the changeless pines that fringe the crests of Jura.

Nor was it without similar effect on the minds of men that their journeyings and pilgrimages became more frequent than those of the Greek, the extent of ground traversed in the course of them larger, and the mode of travel more companionless. To the Greek, a voyage to Egypt, or the Hellespont, was the subject of lasting fame and fable, and the forests of the Danube and the rocks of Sicily closed for him the gates of the intelligible world. What parts of that narrow world he crossed were crossed with fleets or armies; the camp always populous on the plain, and the ships drawn in cautious symmetry around the shore. But to the mediæval knight, from Scottish moor to Syrian sand, the world was one great exercise ground, or field of adventure; the staunch pacing of his charger penetrated the pathlessness of outmost forest, and sustained the sultriness of the most secret desert. Frequently alone, – or, if accompanied, for the most part only by retainers of lower rank, incapable of entering into complete sympathy with any of his thoughts, he must have been compelled often to enter into dim companionship with the silent nature around him, and must assuredly sometimes have talked to the wayside flowers of his love, and to fading clouds of his ambition.

But, on the other hand, the idea of retirement from the world for the sake of self-mortification, of combat with demons, or communion with angels, and with their King, – authoritatively commended as it was to all men by the continual practice of Christ Himself, – gave to all mountain solitude at once a sanctity and a terror, in the mediæval mind, which were altogether different from anything that it had possessed in the un-Christian periods. On the one side, there was an idea of sanctity attached to rocky wilderness, because it had always been among hills that the Deity had manifested Himself most intimately to men, and to the hills that His saints had nearly always retired for meditation, for especial communion with Him, and to prepare for death. Men acquainted with the history of Moses, alone at Horeb, or with Israel at Sinai, – of Elijah by the brook Cherith, and in the Horeb cave; of the deaths of Moses and Aaron on Hor and Nebo; of the preparation of Jephthah's daughter for her death among the Judæa mountains; of the continual retirement of Christ Himself to the mountains for prayer, His temptation in the desert of the Dead Sea, His sermon on the hills of Capernaum, His transfiguration on Mount Hermon, and His evening and morning walks over Olivet for the four or five days preceding His crucifixion[1] were not likely to look with irreverent or unloving eyes upon the blue hills that girded their golden horizon, or drew down upon them the mysterious clouds out of the height of the darker heaven. But with this impression of their greater sanctity was involved also that of a peculiar terror. In all this, – their haunting by the memories of prophets, the presences of angels, and the everlasting thoughts and words of the Redeemer, – the mountain ranges seemed separated from the active world, and only to be fitly approached by hearts which were condemnatory of it. Just in so much as it appeared necessary for the noblest men to retire to the hill-recesses before their missions could be accomplished, or their spirits perfected, in so far did the daily world seem by comparison to be pronounced profane and dangerous; and to those who loved that world, and its work, the mountains were thus voiceful with perpetual rebuke, and necessarily contemplated with a kind of pain and fear, such as a man engrossed by vanity feels at being by some accident forced to hear a startling sermon, or to assist at a funeral service. Every association of this kind was deepened by the practice and the precept of the time; and thousands of hearts, which might otherwise have felt that there was loveliness in the wild landscape, shrank from it in dread, because they knew that the monk retired to it for penance, and the hermit for contemplation. The horror which the Greek had felt for hills only when they were uninhabitable and barren, attached itself now to many of the sweetest spots of earth; the feeling was conquered by political interests, but never by admiration; military ambition seized the frontier rock, or maintained itself in the unassailable pass; but it was only for their punishment, or in their despair, that men consented to tread the crocused slopes of the Chartreuse, or the soft glades and dewy pastures of Vallombrosa. (MP III, Pt. IV, Ch. XIV, paras. 6–10)

(3) 'Of Modern Landscape'

We turn our eyes, therefore, as boldly and as quickly as may be, from these serene fields and skies of mediæval art, to the most characteristic examples of modern landscape. And, I believe, the first thing that will strike us, or that ought to strike us, is their *cloudiness*.

Out of perfect light and motionless air, we find ourselves on a sudden brought under sombre skies, and into drifting wind; and, with fickle sunbeams flashing in our face, or utterly drenched with sweep of rain, we are reduced to track the changes of the shadows on the grass, or watch the rents of twilight through angry cloud. And we find that whereas all the pleasure of the mediæval was in *stability*, *definiteness*, and *luminousness*, we are expected to rejoice in darkness, and triumph in mutability; to lay the foundation of happiness in things which momentarily change or fade; and to expect the utmost satisfaction and instruction from what it is impossible to arrest, and difficult to comprehend.

We find, however, together with this general delight in breeze and darkness, much attention to the real form of clouds, and careful drawing of effects of mist; so that the appearance of objects, as seen through it, becomes a subject of science with us; and the faithful representation of that appearance is made of primal importance, under the name of aerial perspective. The aspects of sunset and sunrise, with all their attendant phenomena of cloud and mist, are watchfully delineated; and in ordinary daylight landscape, the sky is considered of so much importance, that a principal mass of foliage, or a whole foreground, is unhesitatingly thrown into shade merely to bring out the form of a white cloud. So that, if a general and characteristic name were needed for modern landscape art, none better could be invented than 'the service of clouds'.

And this name would, unfortunately, be characteristic of our art in more ways than one. In the last chapter, I said that all the Greeks spoke kindly about the clouds, except Aristophanes; and he, I am sorry to say (since his report is so unfavourable), is the only Greek who had studied them attentively. He tells us, first, that they are 'great goddesses to idle men'; then, that they are 'mistresses of disputings, and logic, and monstrosities, and noisy chattering'; declares that whoso believes in their divinity must first disbelieve in Jupiter, and place supreme power in the hands of an unknown god 'Whirlwind'; and finally, he displays their influence over the mind of one of their disciples, in his sudden desire 'to speak ingeniously concerning smoke' [Aristophanes, *Clouds*, 316–8, 380, 320].

There is, I fear, an infinite truth in this Aristophanic judgment applied to our modern cloud-worship. Assuredly, much of the love of mystery in our romances, our poetry, our art, and, above all, in our metaphysics, must come under that definition so long ago given by the great Greek, 'speaking ingeniously concerning smoke'. And much of the instinct, which, partially developed in painting, may be now seen throughout every mode of exertion of mind, — the easily encouraged doubt, easily excited curiosity, habitual agitation, and delight in the changing and the marvellous, as opposed to the old quiet serenity of social custom and religious faith, — is again deeply defined in those few words, the 'dethroning of Jupiter', the 'coronation of the whirlwind'.

Nor of whirlwind merely, but also of darkness or ignorance respecting all stable facts. That darkening of the foreground to bring out the white cloud is, in one aspect of it, a type of the subjection of all plain and positive fact, to what is uncertain and unintelligible. And, as we examine farther into the matter, we shall be struck by another great difference between the old and modern landscape, namely, that in the old no one ever thought of drawing anything but as well *as he could*. That might not be *well*, as we have seen in the case of rocks; but it was as well as he *could*, and always distinctly. Leaf, or stone, or animal, or man, it was equally drawn with care and clearness, and its essential characters shown. If it was an oak tree, the acorns were drawn; if a flint pebble, its veins were drawn; if an arm of the sea, its fish were drawn; if a group of figures, their faces and dresses were drawn — to the very last subtlety of expression and end of thread that could be got into the space, far off or near. But now our ingenuity is all 'concerning smoke'. Nothing is truly drawn but that; all else is vague, slight, imperfect; got with as little pains as possible. You examine your closest foreground, and find no leaves; your largest oak, and find no acorns; your human figure, and find a spot of red paint instead of a face; and in all this, again and again, the Aristophanic words come true, and the clouds seem to be 'great goddesses to idle men'.

The next thing that will strike us, after this love of clouds, is the love of liberty. Whereas the mediæval was always shutting himself into castles, and behind fosses, and drawing brickwork neatly, and beds of flowers primly, our painters delight in getting to the open fields and moors, abhor all hedges and moats; never paint anything but free-growing trees, and rivers gliding 'at their own sweet will' [Wordsworth, 'Composed upon Westminster Bridge']; eschew formality down to the smallest detail; break and displace the brickwork which the mediæval would have carefully cemented; leave unpruned the thickets he would have delicately trimmed; and, carrying the love of liberty even to license, and the love of wildness even to ruin, take pleasure at last in every aspect of age and desolation which emancipates the objects of nature from the government of men; — on the castle wall displacing its tapestry with ivy, and spreading, through the garden, the bramble for the rose.

Connected with this love of liberty we find a singular manifestation of love of mountains, and see our painters traversing the wildest places of the globe in order to obtain subjects with craggy foregrounds and purple distances. Some few of them remain content with pollards and flat land; but these are always men of third-rate order; and the leading masters, while they do not reject the beauty of the low grounds, reserve their highest powers to paint Alpine peaks or Italian promontories. And it is eminently noticeable, also, that this pleasure in the mountains is never mingled with fear, or tempered by a spirit of meditation, as with the mediæval; but is always free and fearless, brightly exhilarating, and wholly unreflective; so that the painter feels that his mountain foreground may be more consistently animated by a sportsman than a hermit; and our modern society in general goes to the mountains, not to fast, but to feast, and leaves their glaciers covered with chicken-bones and egg-shells.

Connected with this want of any sense of solemnity in mountain scenery, is a general profanity of temper in regarding all the rest of nature; that is to say, a total absence of faith in the presence of any deity therein. Whereas the mediæval never painted a cloud, but with the purpose of placing an angel in it; and a Greek never entered a wood without expecting to meet a god in it; *we* should think the appearance of an angel in the cloud wholly unnatural, and should be seriously surprised by meeting a god anywhere. Our chief ideas about the wood are connected with poaching. We have no belief that the clouds contain more than so many inches of rain or hail, and from our ponds and ditches expect nothing more divine than ducks and watercresses.

Finally: connected with this profanity of temper is a strong tendency to deny the sacred element of colour, and make our boast in blackness. For though occasionally glaring or violent, modern colour is on the whole eminently sombre, tending continually to grey or brown, and by many of our best painters consistently falsified, with a confessed pride in what they call chaste or subdued tints; so that, whereas a mediæval paints his sky bright blue and his foreground bright green, gilds the towers of his castles, and clothes his figures with purple and white, we paint our sky grey, our foreground black, and our foliage brown, and think that enough is sacrificed to the sun in admitting the dangerous brightness of a scarlet cloak or a blue jacket.

These, I believe, are the principal points which would strike us instantly, if we were to be brought suddenly into an exhibition of modern landscapes out of a room filled with mediæval work. It is evident that there are both evil and good in this change; but how much evil, or how much good, we can only estimate by considering, as in the former divisions of our inquiry, what are the real roots of the habits of mind which have caused them.

At first, it is evident that the title 'Dark Ages', given to the mediæval centuries, is, respecting art, wholly inapplicable. They were, on the contrary, the bright ages; ours are the dark ones. I do not mean metaphysically, but literally. They were the ages of gold; ours are the ages of umber.

This is partly mere mistake in us; we build brown brick walls, and wear brown coats, because we have been blunderingly taught to do so, and go on doing so mechanically. There is, however, also some cause for the change in our own tempers. On the whole, these are much *sadder* ages than the early ones; not sadder in a noble and deep way, but in a dim wearied way, – the way of ennui, and jaded intellect, and uncomfortableness of soul and body. The Middle Ages had their wars and agonies, but also intense delights. Their gold was dashed with blood; but ours is sprinkled with dust. Their life was inwoven with white and purple: ours is one seamless stuff of brown. Not that we are without apparent festivity, but festivity more or less forced, mistaken, embittered, incomplete – not of the heart. How wonderfully, since Shakspere's time, have we lost the power of laughing at bad jests! The very finish of our wit belies our gaiety.

The profoundest reason of this darkness of heart is, I believe, our want of faith. There never yet was a generation of men (savage or civilized) who, taken as a body, so wofully fulfilled the words 'having no hope, and without God in the world', [Ephesians ii. 12] as the present civilized European race. A Red Indian or Otaheitan savage has more sense of a divine existence round him, or government over him, than the plurality of refined Londoners and Parisians: and those among us who may in some sense be said to believe, are divided almost without exception into two broad classes, Romanist and Puritan; who, but for the interference of the unbelieving portions of society, would, either of them, reduce the other sect as speedily as possible to ashes; the Romanist having always done so whenever he could, from the beginning of their separation, and the Puritan at this time holding himself in complacent expectation of the destruction of Rome by volcanic fire. Such division as this between persons nominally of one religion, that is to say, believing in the same God, and the same Revelation, cannot but become a stumbling-block of the gravest kind to all thoughtful and far-sighted men, – a stumbling-block which they can only surmount under the most favourable circumstances of early education. Hence, nearly all our powerful men in this age of the world are unbelievers; the best of them in doubt and misery; the worst in reckless defiance: the plurality, in plodding hesitation, doing, as well as they can, what practical work lies ready to their hands. Most of our scientific men are in this last class: our popular authors either set themselves definitely against all religious form, pleading for simple truth and benevolence, (Thackeray, Dickens,) or give themselves up to bitter and fruitless statement of facts, (De Balzac,) or surface-painting, (Scott,) or careless blasphemy, sad or smiling, (Byron, Beranger). Our earnest poets and deepest thinkers are doubtful and indignant, (Tennyson, Carlyle); one or two, anchored, indeed, but anxious or weeping, (Wordsworth, Mrs Browning); and of these two, the first is not so sure of his anchor, but that now and then it drags with him, even to make him cry out,—

> Great God, I had rather be
> A Pagan suckled in some creed outworn;
> So might I, standing on this pleasant lea,
> Have glimpses that would make me less forlorn.
> [Wordsworth, 'The world is too much with us']

In politics, religion is now a name; in art, a hypocrisy or affectation. Over German religious pictures the inscription, 'See how Pious I am', can be read at a glance by any clear-sighted person. Over French and English religious pictures the inscription, 'See how Impious I am', is equally legible. All sincere and modest art is, among us, profane.[2]

This faithlessness operates among us according to our tempers, producing either sadness or levity, and being the ultimate root alike of our discontents and of our wantonnesses. It is marvellous how full of contradiction it makes us: we are first dull, and seek for wild and lonely places because we have no heart for the garden; presently we recover our spirits, and build an assembly-room among the mountains, because we have no reverence for the desert. I do not know if there be game on Sinai, but I am always expecting to hear of some one's shooting over it.

There is, however, another, and a more innocent root of our delight in wild scenery.

All the Renaissance principles of art tended, as I have before often explained, to the setting Beauty above Truth, and seeking for it always at the expense of truth. And the proper punishment of such pursuit — the punishment which all the laws of the universe rendered inevitable – was, that those who thus pursued beauty should wholly lose sight of beauty. All the thinkers of the age, as we saw previously, declared that it did not exist. The age seconded their efforts, and banished beauty, so far as human effort could succeed in doing so, from the face of the earth, and the form of man. To powder the hair, to patch the cheek, to hoop the body, to buckle the foot, were all part and parcel of the same system which reduced streets to brick walls, and pictures to brown stains. One desert of Ugliness was extended before the eyes of mankind; and their pursuit of the beautiful, so recklessly continued, received unexpected consummation in high-heeled shoes and periwigs – Gower Street, and Gaspar Poussin.

Reaction from this state was inevitable, if any true life was left in the races of mankind; and, accordingly, though still forced, by rule and fashion, to the producing and wearing all that is ugly, men steal out, half-ashamed of themselves for doing so, to the fields and mountains; and, finding among these the colour, and liberty, and variety, and power, which are for ever grateful to them, delight in these to an extent never before known; rejoice in all the wildest shattering of the mountain side, as an opposition to Gower Street, gaze in a rapt manner at sunsets and sunrises, to see there the blue, and gold, and purple, which glow for them no longer on knight's armour or temple porch; and gather with care out of the fields, into their blotted herbaria, the flowers which the five orders of architecture have banished from their doors and casements.[3]

The absence of care for personal beauty, which is another great characteristic of the age, adds to this feeling in a twofold way: first, by turning all reverent thoughts away from human nature; and making us think of men as ridiculous or ugly creatures, getting through the world as well as they can, and spoiling it in doing so; not ruling it in a kingly way and crowning all its loveliness. In the Middle Ages hardly anything but vice could be caricatured, because virtue was always visibly and personally noble: now virtue itself is apt to inhabit such poor human bodies, that no aspect of it is invulnerable to jest; and for all fairness we have to seek to the flowers, for all sublimity, to the hills.

The same want of care operates, in another way, by lowering the standard of health, increasing the susceptibility to nervous or sentimental impressions, and thus adding to the other powers of nature over us whatever charm may be felt in her fostering the melancholy fancies of brooding idleness.

It is not, however, only to existing inanimate nature that our want of beauty in person and dress has driven us. The imagination of it, as it was seen in our ancestors, haunts us continually; and while we yield to the present fashions, or act in accordance with the dullest modern principles of economy and utility, we look fondly back to the manners of the ages of chivalry, and delight in painting, to the fancy, the fashions we pretend to despise, and the splendours we think it wise to abandon. The furniture and personages of our romance are sought, when the writer desires to please most easily, in the centuries which we profess to have surpassed in everything; the art which takes us into the present times is considered as both daring and degraded, and while the weakest words please us, and are regarded as poetry, which recall the manners of our forefathers, or of strangers, it is only as familiar and vulgar that we accept the description of our own.

In this we are wholly different from all the races that preceded us. All other nations have regarded their ancestors with reverence as saints or heroes; but have nevertheless thought their own deeds and ways of life the fitting subjects for their arts of painting or of verse. We, on the contrary, regard our ancestors as foolish and wicked, but yet find our chief artistic pleasure in descriptions of their ways of life.

The Greeks and mediævals honoured, but did not imitate their forefathers; we imitate, but do not honour.

With this romantic love of beauty, forced to seek in history, and in external nature, the satisfaction it cannot find in ordinary life, we mingle a more rational passion, the due and just result of newly awakened powers of attention. Whatever may first lead us to the scrutiny of natural objects, that scrutiny never fails of its reward. Unquestionably they are intended to be regarded by us with both reverence and delight; and every hour we give to them renders their beauty more apparent, and their interest more engrossing. Natural science – which can hardly be considered to have existed before modern times – rendering our knowledge fruitful in accumulation, and exquisite in accuracy, has acted for good or evil, according to the temper of the mind which received it; and though it has hardened the faithfulness of the dull and proud, has shown new grounds for reverence to hearts which were thoughtful and humble. The neglect of the art of war, while it has somewhat weakened and deformed the body, has given us leisure and opportunity for studies to which, before, time and space were equally wanting; lives which once were early wasted on the battlefield are now passed usefully in the study; nations which exhausted themselves in annual warfare now dispute with each other the discovery of new planets;[4] and the serene philosopher dissects the plants, and analyses the dust, of lands which were of old only traversed by the knight in hasty march, or by the borderer in heedless rapine.

The elements of progress and decline being thus strangely mingled in the modern mind, we might beforehand anticipate that one of the notable characters of our art would be its inconsistency; that efforts would be made in every direction, and arrested by every conceivable cause and manner of failure; that in all we did, it would become next to impossible to distinguish accurately the grounds for praise or for regret; that all previous canons of practice and methods of thought would be gradually overthrown, and criticism continually defied by successes which no one had expected, and sentiments which no one could define.

Accordingly, while, in our inquiries into Greek and mediæval art, I was able to describe, in general terms, what all men did or felt, I find now many characters in many men; some, it seems to me, founded on the inferior and evanescent principles of modernism, on its recklessness, impatience, or faithlessness; others founded on its science, its new affection for nature, its love of openness and liberty. And among all these characters, good or evil, I see that some, remaining to us from old or transitional periods, do not properly belong to us, and will soon fade away, and others, though not yet distinctly developed, are yet properly our own, and likely to grow forward into greater strength.

For instance . . . the peculiar levity with which natural scenery is regarded by a large number of modern minds cannot be considered as entirely characteristic of the age, inasmuch as it never can belong to its greatest intellects. Men of any high mental power must be serious, whether in ancient or modern days; a certain degree of reverence for fair scenery is found in all our great writers without exception, – even the one who has made us laugh oftenest, taking us to the valley of Chamouni, and to the sea beach, there to give peace after suffering, and change revenge into pity [Dickens, *David Copperfield*, chs. lv, lviii]. It is only the dull, the uneducated, or the worldly, whom it is painful to meet on the hill sides; and levity, as a ruling character, cannot be ascribed to the whole nation, but only to its holiday-making apprentices, and its House of Commons.

We need not, therefore, expect to find any single poet or painter representing the entire group of powers, weaknesses, and inconsistent instincts which govern or confuse our modern life. But we may expect that in the man who seems to be given by Providence as the type of the age (as Homer and Dante were given, as the types of classical and mediæval mind), we shall find whatever is fruitful and substantial to be completely present, together with those of our weaknesses, which are indeed nationally characteristic, and compatible with general greatness of mind, just as the weak love of fences, and dislike of mountains, were found compatible with Dante's greatness in other respects.[b]

---

[b] *The nearest to a great representative modern man, says Ruskin, is Sir Walter Scott in his poetry, to go alongside Turner in painting:*
First, observe Scott's habit of looking at nature neither as dead, or merely material, in the way that Homer regards it, nor as altered by his own feelings, in the way that Keats and Tennyson regard it, but as having an animation and pathos of *its own*, wholly irrespective of human presence or passion, – an animation which Scott loves and sympathises with, as he would with a fellow-creature, forgetting himself altogether, and subduing his own humanity before what seems to him the power of the landscape.

> Yon lonely Thorn, – would he could tell
> The changes of his parent dell,
> Since he, so grey and stubborn now,
> Waved in each breeze a sapling bough:
> Would he could tell, how deep the shade
> A thousand mingled branches made,
> How broad the shadows of the oak,
> How clung the rowan to the rock,
> And through the foliage show'd his head,
> With narrow leaves and berries red!
> [*Marmion*, intro. Canto ii]

Scott does not dwell on the grey stubbornness of the thorn, because he himself is at that moment disposed to be dull or stubborn; neither on the cheerful peeping forth of the rowan, because he himself is at that moment cheerful or curious: but he perceives them both with the kind of interest that he would take in an old man or a climbing boy; forgetting himself, in sympathy with either age or youth.

Farther: as the admiration of mankind is found, in our times, to have in great part passed from men to mountains, and from human emotion to natural phenomena, we may anticipate that the great strength of art will also be warped in this direction; with this notable result for us, that whereas the greatest painters or painter of classical and mediæval periods, being wholly devoted

> And from the grassy slope he sees
> The Greta flow to meet the Tees;
> Where issuing from her darksome
> bed,
> She caught the morning's eastern red,
> And through the softening vale below
> Roll'd her bright waves in rosy glow,
> All blushing to her bridal bed,
> Like some shy maid, in convent bred;
> While linnet, lark, and blackbird gay
> Sing forth her nuptial roundelay.
>
> [*Rokeby*, ii. 16]

Is Scott, or are the persons of his story, gay at this moment? Far from it. Neither Scott nor Risingham is happy, but the Greta is; and all Scott's sympathy is ready for the Greta, on the instant.

Observe, therefore, this is not *pathetic* fallacy; for there is no passion in *Scott* which alters nature. It is not the lover's passion, making him think the larkspurs are listening for his lady's foot; it is not the miser's passion, making him think that dead leaves are falling coins; but it is an inherent and continual habit of thought, which Scott shares with the moderns in general, being, in fact, nothing else than the instinctive sense which men must have of the Divine presence, not formed into distinct belief. In the Greek it created, as we saw, the faithfully believed gods of the elements; in Dante and the mediævals, it formed the faithfully believed angelic presence: in the modern, it creates no perfect form, does not apprehend distinctly any Divine being or operation; but only a dim, slightly credited animation in the natural object, accompanied with great interest and affection for it. This feeling is quite universal with us, only varying in depth according to the greatness of the heart that holds it; and in Scott, being more than usually intense, and accompanied with infinite affection and quickness of sympathy, it enables him to conquer all tendencies to the pathetic fallacy, and, instead of making Nature anywise subordinate to himself, he makes himself subordinate to *her* – follows her lead simply – does not venture to bring his own cares and thoughts into her pure and quiet presence – paints her in her simple and universal truth, adding no result of momentary passion or fancy, and appears, therefore, at first shallower than other poets, being in reality wider and healthier. 'What am I?' he says continually, 'that I should trouble this sincere nature with my thoughts. I happen to be feverish and

to the representation of humanity, furnished us with but little to examine in landscape, the greatest painters or painter of modern times will in all probability be devoted to landscape principally. (MP III, Pt. IV, Ch. XVI, paras. 1–18, 20–2)

depressed, and I could see a great many sad and strange things in those waves and flowers; but I have no business to see such things. Gay Greta! sweet harebells! *you* are not sad nor strange to most people; you are but bright water and blue blossoms; you shall not be anything else to me, except that I cannot help thinking you are a little alive, – no one can help thinking that.' And thus, as Nature is bright, serene, or gloomy, Scott takes her temper, and paints her as she is; nothing of himself being ever intruded, except this far-away Æolian tone, of which he is unconscious; and sometimes a stray syllable or two, like that about Blackford Hill,[5] distinctly stating personal feeling, but all the more modestly for that distinctness, and for the clear consciousness that it is not the chiming brook, nor the cornfields, that are sad, but only the boy that rests by them; so returning on the instant to reflect, in all honesty, the image of Nature, as she is meant by all men to be received; nor that in fine words, but in the first that come; nor with comment of far-fetched thoughts, but with easy thoughts, such as all sensible men ought to have in such places, only spoken sweetly; and evidently also with an undercurrent of more profound reflection, which here and there murmurs for a moment, and which, I think, if we choose, we may continually pierce down to, and drink deeply from, but which Scott leaves us to seek, or shun, at our pleasure.

And in consequence of this unselfishness and humility, Scott's enjoyment of Nature is incomparably greater than that of any other poet I know. All the rest carry their cares to her, and begin maundering in her ears about their own affairs. Tennyson goes out on a furzy common, and sees it is calm autumn sunshine, but it gives him no pleasure. He only remembers that it is

> Dead calm in that noble breast
> Which heaves but with the heaving deep.
> [*In Memoriam* xi]

He sees a thundercloud in the evening, and *would* have 'doted and pored' on it, but cannot, for fear it should bring the ship bad weather. Keats drinks the beauty of nature violently; but has no more real sympathy with her than he has with a bottle of claret. His palate is fine; but he 'bursts joy's grape against it' ['Ode on Melancholy' line 28], gets nothing but misery, and a bitter taste of dregs, out of his desperate draught.

Byron and Shelley are nearly the same, only with less truth of perception, and even more troublesome selfishness. Wordsworth is more like Scott, and understands how to be happy, but yet cannot altogether rid himself of the sense that he is a philosopher, and ought always to be saying something wise. He has also a vague notion that nature would not be able to get on well without

'Of Modern Landscape' – Conclusion

We began our investigation, it will be remembered, in order to determine whether landscape-painting was worth studying or not. We have now reviewed the three principal phases of temper in the civilized human race, and we find that landscape has been mostly disregarded by great men, or cast into a second place, until now; and that now it seems dear to us, partly in consequence of our faults, and partly owing to accidental circumstances, soon, in all likelihood, to pass away: and there seems great room for question still, whether our love of it is a permanent and healthy feeling, or only a healthy crisis in a generally diseased state of mind. If the former, society will for ever hereafter be affected by its results; and Turner, the first great landscape-painter, must take a place in the history of nations corresponding in art accurately to that of Bacon in philosophy; – Bacon having first opened the study of the laws of material nature, when, formerly, men had thought only of the laws of human mind; and Turner having first opened the study of the aspect of material nature, when, before, men had thought only of the aspect of the human form. Whether, therefore, the love of landscape be trivial and transient, or important and permanent, it now becomes necessary to consider. We have, I think, data enough before us for the solution of the question, and we will enter upon it, accordingly, in the following chapter [below]. (MP III, Pt. IV, Ch. XVI, para. 45)

'Of the Moral of Landscape'
(on the mental value of the pleasure to be found in nature)

Is it a safe or a seductive one? May we wisely boast of it, and unhesitatingly indulge it? or is it rather a sentiment to be despised when it is slight, and condemned when it is intense; a feeling which disinclines us to labour, and confuses us in thought; a joy only to the inactive and the visionary, incompatible with the duties of life, and the accuracies of reflection?

Wordsworth; and finds a considerable part of his pleasure in looking at himself as well as at her. But with Scott the love is entirely humble and unselfish. 'I, Scott, am nothing, and less than nothing; but these crags, and heaths, and clouds, how great they are, how lovely, how for ever to be beloved, only for their own silent, thoughtless sake!' (MP III, Pt. IV, Ch. XVI, paras. 36–8)

It seems to me that, as matters stand at present, there is considerable ground for the latter opinion. We saw, [in the preceding chapter,] that our love of nature had been partly forced upon us by mistakes in our social economy, and led to no distinct issues of action or thought. And when we look to Scott – the man who feels it most deeply – for some explanation of its effect upon him, we find a curious tone of apology (as if for an involuntary folly) running through his confessions of such sentiment, and a still more curious inability to define, beyond a certain point, the character of this emotion. He has lost the company of his friends among the hills, and turns to these last for comfort. He says, 'there is a pleasure in the pain' consisting in such thoughts

> As oft awake
> By lone St. Mary's silent lake;

but when we look for some definition of these thoughts, all that we are told is, that they compose

> A mingled sentiment
> 'Twixt resignation and content;
> [*Marmion*, intro. canto ii]

a sentiment which, I suppose, many people can attain to on the loss of their friends, without the help of lakes or mountains; while Wordsworth definitely and positively affirms that *thought* has nothing whatever to do with the matter, and that though, in his youth, the cataract and wood 'haunted him like a passion', it was without the help of any 'remoter charm, by thought supplied'. ['Tintern Abbey'].

There is not, however, any question but that both Scott and Wordsworth are here mistaken in their analysis of their feelings. Their delight, so far from being without thought, is more than half made up of thought, but of thought in so curiously languid and neutralized a condition that they cannot trace it. The thoughts are beaten to a powder so small that they know not what they are; they know only that in such a state they are not good for much, and disdain to call them thoughts . . .

And observe, farther, that this comparative Dimness and Untraceableness of the thoughts which are the sources of our admiration, is not a *fault* in the thoughts, at such a time. It is, on the contrary, a necessary condition of their subordination to the pleasure of Sight. If the thoughts were more distinct we should not *see* so well; and beginning definitely to think, we must comparatively cease to see. In the instance just supposed, as long as we look at the film of mountain or Alp, with only an obscure consciousness of its being the source of mighty rivers, that consciousness adds to our sense of its sublimity; and if we have ever seen the Rhine or the Rhone near their mouths, our knowledge, so long as it is only obscurely suggested, adds to our admiration of the Alp; but once let the idea define itself, – once let us begin to consider seriously *what* rivers flow from that mountain, to trace their source, and to recall determinately our memories of their distant aspect, – and we cease to behold the Alp; or, if we still behold it, it is only as a point in a map which we are painfully designing, or as a subordinate object which we strive to thrust aside, in order to make room for our remembrances of Avignon or Rotterdam.

Again: so long as our idea of the multitudes who inhabit the ravines at the foot remains indistinct, that idea comes to the aid of all the other associations which increase our delight. But let it once arrest us, and entice us to follow out some clear course of thought respecting the causes of the prosperity or misfortune of the Alpine villagers, and the snowy peak again ceases to be visible, or holds its place only as a white spot upon the retina, while we pursue our meditations upon the religion or the political economy of the mountaineers.

It is thus evident that a curiously balanced condition of the powers of mind is necessary to induce full admiration of any natural scene. Let those powers be themselves inert, and the mind vacant of knowledge, and destitute of sensibility; and the external object becomes little more to us than it is to birds or insects; we fall into the temper of the clown. On the other hand, let the reasoning powers be shrewd in excess, the knowledge vast, or sensibility intense, and it will go hard but that the visible object will suggest so much that it shall be soon itself forgotten, or become, at the utmost, merely a kind of keynote to the course of purposeful thought. Newton, probably, did not perceive whether the apple which suggested his meditations on gravity was withered or rosy; nor could John Howard [prison reformer] be affected by the picturesqueness of the architecture which held the sufferers it was his occupation to relieve.

This wandering away in thought from the thing seen to the business of life, is not, however, peculiar to men of the highest reasoning powers, or most active benevolence. It takes place more or less in nearly all persons of average mental endowment. They see and love what is beautiful, but forget their admiration of it in following some train of thought which it suggested, and which is of more personal interest to them. Suppose that three or four persons come in sight of a group of pine-trees, not having seen pines for some time. One, perhaps an engineer, is struck by the manner in which their roots hold the ground, and sets himself to examine their fibres, in a few minutes retaining little more consciousness of the beauty of the trees than if he were a rope-maker untwisting the strands of a cable: to another, the sight of the trees calls up some happy association, and presently he forgets them, and pursues the memories they summoned: a third is struck by certain groupings of their colours, useful to him as an artist, which he proceeds immediately to note mechanically for future use, with as little feeling as a cook setting down the constituents of a newly discovered dish; and a fourth, impressed by the wild coiling of boughs and roots, will begin to change them in his fancy into dragons and monsters, and lose his grasp of the scene in fantastic metamorphosis: while, in the mind of the man who has most the power of contemplating the thing itself, all these perceptions and trains of idea are partially present, not distinctly, but in a mingled and perfect harmony. He will not see the colours of the tree so well as the artist, nor its fibres so well as the engineer; he will not altogether share the emotion of the sentimentalist, nor the trance of the idealist; but fancy, and feeling, and perception, and imagination, will all obscurely meet and balance themselves in him, and he will see the pine-trees somewhat in this manner:

> Worthier still of note
> Are those fraternal Four of Borrowdale,
> Joined in one solemn and capacious grove;
> Huge trunks! and each particular trunk a growth
> Of intertwisted fibres serpentine
> Up-coiling, and inveterately convolved;
> Nor uninformed with Phantasy, and looks
> That threaten the profane; a pillared shade,
> Upon whose grassless floor of red-brown hue,
> By sheddings from the pining umbrage tinged
> Perennially, – beneath whose sable roof
> Of boughs, as if for festal purpose decked
> With unrejoicing berries, ghostly Shapes
> May meet at noontide; Fear and trembling Hope,

Silence and Foresight; Death the Skeleton,
And Time the Shadow; there to celebrate,
As in a natural temple scattered o'er
With altars undisturbed of mossy stone,
United worship.

                          Wordsworth, 'Yew-Trees'

The power, therefore, of thus fully *perceiving* any natural object depends on our being able to group and fasten all our fancies about it as a centre, making a garland of thoughts for it, in which each separate thought is subdued and shortened of its own strength, in order to fit it for harmony with others; the intensity of our enjoyment of the object depending, first, on its own beauty, and then on the richness of the garland. And men who have this habit of clustering and harmonizing their thoughts are a little too apt to look scornfully upon the harder workers who tear the bouquet to pieces to examine the stems. This was the chief narrowness of Wordsworth's mind; he could not understand that to break a rock with a hammer in search of crystal may sometimes be an act not disgraceful to human nature, and that to dissect a flower may sometimes be as proper as to dream over it . . .

We shall at once perceive that the intense love of nature is, in modern times, characteristic of persons not of the first order of intellect, but of brilliant imagination, quick sympathy, and undefined religious principle, suffering also usually under strong and ill-governed passions: while in the same individual it will be found to vary at different periods, being, for the most part, strongest in youth, and associated with force of emotion, and with indefinite and feeble powers of thought; also, throughout life, perhaps developing itself most at times when the mind is slightly unhinged by love, grief, or some other of the passions.

But, on the other hand, while these feelings of delight in natural objects cannot be construed into signs of the highest mental powers, or purest moral principles, we see that they are assuredly indicative of minds above the usual standard of power, and endowed with sensibilities of great preciousness to humanity; so that those who find themselves entirely destitute of them, must make this want a subject of humiliation, not of pride. The apathy which cannot perceive beauty is very different from the stern energy which disdains it; and the coldness of heart which receives no emotion from external nature, is not to be confounded with the wisdom of purpose which represses emotion in action. In the case of most men, it is neither acuteness of the reason, nor breadth of humanity, which shields them from the impressions of natural scenery, but rather low anxieties, vain discontents, and mean pleasures: and for one who is blinded to the works of God by profound abstraction or lofty purpose, tens of thousands have their eyes sealed by vulgar selfishness, and their intelligence crushed by impious care . . .

And we see in this, therefore, that the instinct which leads us thus to attribute life to the lowest forms of organic nature, does not necessarily spring from faithlessness, nor the deducing a moral out of them from an irregular and languid conscientiousness. In this, as in almost all things connected with moral discipline, the same results may follow from contrary causes; and as there are a good and evil contentment, a good and evil discontent, a good and evil care, fear, ambition, and so on, there are also good and evil forms of this sympathy with nature, and disposition to moralize over it.[6] In general, active men, of strong sense and stern principle, do not care to see anything in a leaf, but vegetable tissue, and are so well convinced of useful moral truth, that it does not strike them as a new or notable thing when they find it in any way symbolized by material nature; hence there is a strong presumption, when first we perceive a tendency in any one to regard trees as living, and enunciate moral aphorisms over every pebble they stumble against, that such tendency proceeds from a morbid temperament, like Shelley's, or an inconsistent one, like Jacques's [in *As You Like It*]. But when the active life is nobly fulfilled, and the mind is then raised beyond it into clear and calm beholding of the world around us, the same tendency again manifests itself in the most sacred way: the simplest forms of nature are strangely animated by the sense of the Divine presence; the trees and flowers seem all, in a sort, children of God; and we ourselves, their fellows, made out of the same dust, and greater than they only in having a greater portion of the Divine power exerted on our frame, and all the common uses and palpably visible forms of things, become subordinate in our minds to their inner glory, – to the mysterious voices in which they talk to us about God, and the changeful and typical aspects by which they witness to us of holy truth, and fill us with obedient, joyful, and thankful emotion. (MP III, Pt. IV, Ch. XVII, paras. 1–9, 41)

Modern Painters Vol. V –
'The Dark Mirror'

In the course of our inquiry into the moral of landscape (Vol. III., Chap. XVII.), we promised at the close of our work to seek for some better, or at least clearer, conclusions than were then possible to us. We confined ourselves in that chapter to the vindication of the probable utility of the *love* of natural scenery. We made no assertion of the usefulness of *painting* such scenery. It might be well to delight in the real country, or admire the real flowers and true mountains. But it did not follow that it was advisable to paint them.

Far from it. Many reasons might be given why we should not paint them. All the purposes of good which we saw that the beauty of Nature could accomplish, may be better fulfilled by the meanest of her realities, than by the brightest of imitations. For prolonged entertainment, no picture can be compared with the wealth of interest which may be found in the herbage of the poorest field, or blossoms of the narrowest copse. As suggestive of supernatural power, the passing away of a fitful raincloud, or opening of dawn, are in their change and mystery more pregnant than any pictures. A child would, I suppose, receive a religious lesson from a flower more willingly than from a print of one; and might be taught to understand the nineteenth Psalm, on a starry night, better than by diagrams of the constellations.

Whence it might seem a waste of time to draw landscape at all.

I believe it is; – to draw landscape mere and solitary, however beautiful (unless it be for the sake of geographical or other science, or of historical record). But there *is* a kind of landscape which it is not inexpedient to draw. What kind, we may probably discover by considering that which mankind has hitherto contented itself with painting.

We may arrange nearly all existing landscape under the following heads:—

1 HEROIC – Representing an imaginary world, inhabited by men not perhaps perfectly civilized, but noble, and usually subjected to severe trials, and by spiritual powers of the highest order. It is frequently without architecture; never without figure-action, or emotion. Its principal master is Titian.

2 CLASSICAL – Representing an imaginary world, inhabited by perfectly civilized men, and by spiritual powers of an inferior order.

It generally assumes this condition of things to have existed among the Greek and Roman nations. It contains usually architecture of an elevated character, and always incidents of figure-action, or emotion. Its principal master is Nicolas Poussin.

3 PASTORAL – Representing peasant life and its daily work, or such scenery as may naturally be suggestive of it, consisting usually of simple landscape, in part subjected to agriculture, with figures, cattle, and domestic buildings. No supernatural being is ever visibly present. It does not in ordinary cases admit architecture of an elevated character nor exciting incident. Its principal master is Cuyp.

4 COMTEMPLATIVE – Directed principally to the observance of the powers of Nature, and record of the historical associations connected with landscape, illustrated by, or contrasted with, existing states of human life. No supernatural being is visibly present. It admits every variety of subject, and requires, in general, figure incident, but not of an exciting character. It was not developed completely until recent times. Its principal master is Turner.[7]

These are the four true orders of landscape, not of course distinctly separated from each other in all cases, but very distinctly in typical examples. Two spurious forms require separate note.

(A) PICTURESQUE – This is indeed rather the degradation (or sometimes the undeveloped state) of the contemplative, than a distinct class; but it may be considered generally as including pictures meant to display the skill of the artist, and his powers of composition; or to give agreeable forms and colours, irrespective of sentiment. It will include much modern art, with the street views and church interiors of the Dutch, and the works of Canaletto, Guardi, Tempesta, and the like.

(B) HYBRID – Landscape in which the painter endeavours to unite the irreconcilable sentiment of two or more of the above-named classes. Its principal masters are Berghem and Wouvermans.

Passing for the present by these inferior schools, we find that all true landscape, whether simple or exalted, depends primarily for its interest on connection with humanity, or with spiritual powers. Banish your heroes and nymphs from the classical landscape – its laurel shades will move you no more. Show that the dark clefts of the most romantic mountain are uninhabited and untraversed; it will cease to be romantic. Fields without shepherds and without fairies will have no gaiety in their green, nor will the noblest masses of ground or colours of cloud arrest or raise your thoughts, if the earth has no life to sustain, and the heaven none to refresh.

It might perhaps be thought that, since from scenes in which the figure was principal, and landscape symbolical and subordinate (as in the art of Egypt), the process of ages had led us to scenes in which landscape was principal and the figure subordinate, – a continuance in the same current of feeling might bring forth at last an art from which humanity and its interests should wholly vanish, leaving us to the passionless admiration of herbage and stone. But this will not, and cannot be. For observe the parallel instance in the gradually increasing importance of dress. From the simplicity of Greek design, concentrating, I suppose, its skill chiefly on the naked form, the course of time developed conditions of Venetian imagination which found nearly as much interest, and expressed nearly as much dignity, in folds of dress and fancies of decoration as in the faces of the figures themselves: so that if from Veronese's Marriage in Cana we remove the architecture and the gay dresses, we shall not in the faces and hands remaining, find a satisfactory abstract of the picture. But try it the other way. Take out the faces; leave the draperies, and how then? Put the fine dresses and jewelled girdles into the best group you can; paint them with all Veronese's skill: will they satisfy you?

Not so. As long as they are in their due service and subjection – while their folds are formed by the motion of men, and their lustre adorns the nobleness of men – so long the lustre and the folds are lovely. But cast them from the human limbs; – golden circlet and silken tissue are withered; the dead leaves of autumn are more precious than they.

This is just as true, but in a far deeper sense, of the weaving of the natural robe of man's soul. Fragrant tissue of flowers, golden circlets of clouds, are only fair when they meet the fondness of human thoughts, and glorify human visions of heaven.

It is the leaning on this truth which, more than any other, has been the distinctive character of all my own past work. And in closing a series of Art-studies, prolonged during so many years, it may be perhaps permitted me to point out this specialty – the rather that it has been, of all their characters, the one most denied.

I constantly see that the same thing takes place in the estimation formed by the modern public of the work of almost any true person, living or dead. It is not needful to state here the causes of such error; but the fact is indeed so, that precisely the distinctive root and leading force of any true man's work and way are the things denied concerning him.[8]

And in these books of mine, their distinctive character, as essays on art, is their bringing everything to a root in human passion or human hope.[c] Arising first not in any desire to explain the principles of art, but in the endeavour to defend an individual painter from injustice, they have been coloured throughout, — nay, continually altered in shape, and even warped and broken, by digressions respecting social questions, which had for me an interest tenfold greater than the work I had been forced into undertaking. Every principle of painting which I have stated is traced to some vital or spiritual fact; and in my works on architecture the preference accorded finally to one school over another, is founded on a comparison of their influences on the life

[c] *Thus in architecture, even a wall 'has no business to be dead':*
It was noticed in our account of the divisions of a wall, that there was something in those divisions like the beginning, the several courses, and the close of a human life. And as, in all well-conducted lives, the hard work, and roughing, and gaining of strength comes first, the honour or decoration in certain intervals during their course, but most of all in their close, so, in general, the base of a wall, which is its beginning of labour, will bear least decoration, its body more, especially those epochs of rest called its string courses; but its crown or cornice most of all. (SV I, Ch. XXV, para. 2)

For it is perfectly natural that the different kinds of stone used in its successive courses should be of different colours; and there are many associations and analogies which metaphysically justify the introduction of horizontal bands of colour, or of light and shade. They are, in the first place, a kind of expression of the growth or age of the wall, like the rings in the wood of a tree; then they are a farther symbol of the alternation of light and darkness, which was above noted as the source of the charm of many inferior mouldings: again, they are valuable as an expression of horizontal space to the imagination, space of which the conception is opposed, and gives more effect by its opposition, to the enclosing power of the wall itself (this I spoke of as probably the great charm of these horizontal bars to the Arabian mind): and again they are valuable in their suggestion of the natural courses of rocks, and beds of the earth itself. And to all these powerful imaginative reasons we have to add the merely ocular charm of interlineal opposition of colour. (SV I, Ch. XXVI, para. 1)

of the workman – a question by all other writers on the subject of architecture wholly forgotten or despised.

The essential connection of the power of landscape with human emotion is not less certain, because in many impressive pictures the link is slight or local. That the connection should exist at a single point is all that we need. The comparison with the dress of the body may be carried out into the extremest parallelism. It may often happen that no part of the figure wearing the dress is discernible, nevertheless, the perceivable fact that the drapery is worn by a figure makes all the difference. In one of the most sublime figures in the world this is actually so: one of the fainting Maries in Tintoret's Crucifixion has cast her mantle over her head, and her face is lost in its shade, and her whole figure veiled in folds of gray. But what the difference is between that gray woof, that gathers round her as she falls, and the same folds cast in a heap upon the ground, that difference, and more, exists between the power of Nature through which humanity is seen, and her power in the desert. Desert – whether of leaf or sand – true desertness is not in the want of leaves, but of life. Where humanity is not, and was not, the best natural beauty is more than vain. It is even terrible; not as the dress cast aside from the body; but as an embroidered shroud hiding a skeleton.

And on each side of a right feeling in this matter there lie, as usual, two opposite errors.

The first, that of caring for man only; and for the rest of the universe, little, or not at all, which, in a measure, was the error of the Greeks and Florentines; the other, that of caring for the universe only; – for man, not at all – which, in a measure, is the error of modern science, and of the Art connecting itself with such science.

The degree of power which any man may ultimately possess in landscape-painting will depend finally on his perception of this influence. If he has to paint the desert, its awfulness – if the garden, its gladsomeness – will arise simply and only from his sensibility to the story of life. Without this he is nothing but a scientific mechanist; this, though it cannot make him yet a painter, raises him to the sphere in which he may become one. Nay, the mere shadow and semblance of this have given dangerous power to works in all other respects unnoticeable; and the least degree of its true presence has given value to work in all other respects vain.

The true presence, observe, of sympathy with the spirit of man. Where this is not, sympathy with any higher spirit is impossible.

For the directest manifestation of Deity to man is in His own image, that is, in man.

'In His own image. After His likeness.' *Ad imaginem et Similitudinem Suam* [Genesis i. 26 – Vulgate]. I do not know what people in general understand by those words. I suppose they ought to be understood. The truth they contain seems to lie at the foundation of our knowledge both of God and man; yet do we not usually pass the sentence by, in dull reverence, attaching no definite sense to it at all? For all practical purpose, might it not as well be out of the text?

I have no time, nor much desire, to examine the vague expressions of belief with which the verse has been encumbered. Let us try to find its only possible plain significance.

It cannot be supposed that the bodily shape of man resembles, or resembled, any bodily shape in Deity. The likeness must therefore be, or have been, in the soul. Had it wholly passed away, and the divine soul been altered into a soul brutal or diabolic, I suppose we should have been told of the change. But we are told nothing of the kind. The verse still stands as if for our use and trust. It was only death which was to be our punishment. Not *change*. So far as we live, the image is still there; defiled, if you will; broken, if you will; all but effaced, if you will, by death and the shadow of it. But not changed. We are not made now in any other image than God's. There are, indeed, the two states of this image – the earthly and heavenly, but both Adamite, both human, both the same likeness; only one defiled, and one pure. So that the soul of man is still a mirror, wherein may be seen, darkly, the image of the mind of God [I Corinthians xiii. 12].

These may seem daring words. I am sorry that they do; but I am helpless to soften them. Discover any other meaning of the text if you are able; – but be sure that it *is* a meaning – a meaning in your head and heart; – not a subtle gloss, nor a shifting of one verbal expression into another, both idealess. I repeat that, to me, the verse has, and can have, no other signification than this – that the soul of man is a mirror of the mind of God. A mirror, dark, distorted, broken, use what blameful words you please of its state; yet in the main, a true mirror, out of which alone, and by which alone, we can know anything of God at all.

'How?' the reader, perhaps, answers indignantly. 'I know the nature of God by revelation, not by looking into myself.'

Revelation to what? To a nature incapable of receiving truth? That cannot be; for only to a nature capable of truth, desirous of it, distinguishing it, feeding upon it, revelation is possible. To a being undesirous of it, and hating it, revelation is impossible. There can be none to a brute, or fiend. In so far, therefore, as you love truth, and live therein, in so far revelation can exist for you; – and in so far, your mind is the image of God's.

But consider, farther, not only *to* what, but *by* what, is the revelation. By sight? or word? If by sight, then to eyes which see justly. Otherwise, no sight would be revelation. So far, then, as your sight is just, it is the image of God's sight.

If by words, – how do you know their meanings? Here is a short piece of precious word revelation, for instance. 'God is love' [I John iv. 16].

Love! yes. But what is *that*? The revelation does not tell you that, I think. Look into the mirror, and you will see. Out of your own heart, you may know what love is. In no other possible way, – by no other help or sign. All the words and sounds ever uttered, all the revelations of cloud, or flame, or crystal, are utterly powerless. They cannot tell you, in the smallest point, what love means. Only the broken mirror can.

Here is more revelation. 'God is just!' [Deuteronomy xxii. 4]. Just! What is that? The revelation cannot help you to discover. You say it is dealing equitably or equally. But how do you discern the equality? Not by inequality of mind; not by a mind incapable of weighing, judging, or distributing. If the lengths seem unequal in the broken mirror, for you they are unequal; but if they seem equal, then the mirror is true. So far as you recognize equality, and your conscience tells you what is just, so far your mind is the image of God's; and so far as you do *not* discern this nature of justice or equality, the words 'God is just' bring no revelation to you.

'But His thoughts are not as our thoughts' [Isaiah lv. 8]. No; the sea is not as the standing pool by the wayside. Yet when the breeze crisps the pool, you may see the image of the breakers, and a likeness of the foam. Nay, in some sort, the same foam. If the sea is for ever invisible to you, something you may learn of it from the pool. Nothing, assuredly, any otherwise.

'But this poor miserable Me! Is *this*, then, all the book I have got to read about God in?' Yes, truly so. No other book, nor fragment of book, than that, will you ever find; no velvet-bound missal, nor frankincensed manuscript; — nothing hieroglyphic nor cunei-form; papyrus and pyramid are alike silent on this matter; — nothing in the clouds above, nor in the earth beneath [Exodus xx. 4]. That flesh-bound volume is the only revelation that is, that was, or that can be. In that is the image of God painted; in that is the law of God written; in that is the promise of God revealed. Know thyself; for through thyself only thou canst know God.[d]

[d] *This belief was worked for in the first volume of* The Stones of Venice — *for example, on the human Strength and Beauty expressed in architecture,* '*both of these being less admired in themselves than as testifying the intelligence or imagination of the builder*':

For we have a worthier way of looking at human than at divine architecture; much of the value both of construction and decoration, in the edifices of men, depends upon our being led by the thing produced or adorned, to some contemplation of the powers of mind concerned in its creation or adornment. We are not so led by divine work, but are content to rest in the contemplation of the thing created. I wish the reader to note this especially; we take pleasure, or *should* take pleasure, in architectural construction altogether as the manifestation of an admirable human intelligence; it is not the strength, not the size, not the finish of the work which we are to venerate: rocks are always stronger, mountains always larger, all natural objects more finished; but it is the intelligence and resolution of man in overcoming physical difficulty which are to be the source of our pleasure and subject of our praise. And again, in decoration or beauty, it is less the actual loveliness of the thing produced than the choice and invention concerned in the production, which are to delight us; the love and the thoughts of the workman more than his work; his work must always be imperfect, but his thoughts and affections may be true and deep. (SV I, Ch. II, para. 4)

Divine architecture is of course Nature. And if our architectural work expresses the human, the human should express, even thus in that work, love of the divine:

Is there, then, nothing to be done by man's art? Have we only to copy, and again copy, for ever, the imagery of the universe? Not so. We have work to do upon it; there is not any one of us so simple, nor so feeble, but he has work to do upon it. But the work is not to improve, but to explain. This infinite universe is unfathomable, inconceivable, in its whole; every human creature must slowly spell out, and long contemplate, such part of it as may be possible for him to reach; then set forth what he has learned of it for those beneath him; extricating it from infinity, as one gathers a violet out of grass; one does not improve either violet or grass in gathering it, but one makes the flower visible;

Through the glass, darkly [Corinthians xiii. 12]. But, except through the glass, in nowise.

A tremulous crystal, waved as water, poured out upon the ground; – you may defile it, despise it, pollute it, at your pleasure and at your peril; for on the peace of those weak waves must all the heaven you shall ever gain be first seen; and through such purity as you can win for those dark waves, must all the light of the risen Sun of Righteousness be bent down, by faint refraction. Cleanse them, and calm them, as you love your life.

Therefore it is that all the power of nature depends on subjection to the human soul. Man is the sun of the world; more than the real sun. The fire of his wonderful heart is the only light and heat worth gauge or measure. Where he is, are the tropics; where he is not, the ice-world. (MP V, Pt. IX, Ch. 1, paras. 1–15)

'The Lance of Pallas'

It might be thought that the tenor of the preceding chapter was in some sort adverse to my repeated statement that all great art is the expression of man's delight in God's work, not in *his own*.[e] But observe, he is not himself his own work: he is himself precisely the most wonderful piece of God's workmanship extant. In this best piece not only he is bound to take delight, but cannot, in a right state of thought, take delight in anything else, otherwise than through himself. Through himself, however, as the sun of

---

and then the human being has to make its power upon his own heart visible also, and to give it the honour of the good thoughts it has raised up in him, and to write upon it the history of his own soul. And sometimes he may be able to do more than this, and to set it in strange lights, and display it in a thousand ways before unknown: ways specially directed to necessary and noble purposes, for which he had to choose instruments out of the wide armoury of God. All this he may do: and in this he is only doing what every Christian has to do with the written, as well as the created word, 'rightly *dividing* the word of truth' [2 Timothy ii. 15] (SV I, Ch. XXX, para. 5).

[e] But the requirement in decoration, is that it should show we like the right thing. And the right thing to be liked is God's work, which He made for our delight and contentment in this world. And all noble ornamentation is the expression of man's delight in God's work.

So, then, these are the two virtues of building: first, the signs of man's own good work; secondly, the expression of man's delight in better work than his own. (SV I, Ch. II, paras. 14–15)

creation, not as *the* creation. In himself, as the light of the world [Matthew v. 14]. Not as being the world. Let him stand in his due relation to other creatures, and to inanimate things – know them all and love them, as made for him, and he for them; – and he becomes himself the greatest and holiest of them. But let him cast off this relation, despise and forget the less creation round him, and instead of being the light of the world, he is a sun in space – a fiery ball, spotted with storm.[f]

[f] *Compare Ruskin's unashamedly human insistence that for us God always must be taken literally as a He not an It:*
The expression, 'He bowed the heavens,' (2 Samuel xxii. 10] for instance, is, I suppose, received by most readers as a magnificent hyperbole, having reference to some peculiar and fearful manifestation of God's power to the writer of the Psalm in which the words occur. But the expression either has plain meaning, or it has *no* meaning. Understand by the term 'Heavens' the compass of infinite space around the earth, and the expression, 'bowed the Heavens', however sublime, is wholly without meaning; infinite space cannot be bent or bowed. But understand by the 'Heavens' the veil of clouds above the earth, and the expression is neither hyperbolical nor obscure; it is pure, plain, and accurate truth, and it describes God, not as revealing Himself in any peculiar way to David, but doing what He is still doing before our own eyes day by day. By accepting the words in their simple sense, we are thus led to apprehend the immediate presence of the Deity, and His purpose of manifesting Himself as near us whenever the storm-cloud stoops upon its course; while by our vague and inaccurate acceptance of the words we remove the idea of His presence far from us, into a region which we can neither see nor know: and gradually, from the close realization of a living God Who 'maketh the clouds His Chariot' [Psalms civ. 3], we refine and explain ourselves into dim and distant suspicion of an inactive God, inhabiting inconceivable places, and fading into the multitudinous formalisms of the laws of nature.
All errors of this kind – and in the present day we are in constant and grievous danger of falling into them – arise from the originally mistaken idea that man can, 'by searching, find out God – find out the Almighty to perfection' [Job xi. 7]; that is to say, by help of courses of reasoning and accumulations of science, apprehend the nature of the Deity in a more exalted and more accurate manner than in a state of comparative ignorance; whereas it is clearly necessary, from the beginning to the end of time, that God's way of revealing Himself to His creatures should be a *simple* way, which *all* those creatures may understand. Whether taught or untaught, whether of mean capacity or enlarged, it is necessary that communion with their Creator should be possible to all; and the admission to such communion must be rested, not on their having a knowledge of astronomy, but on their having a human soul. In order to render this communion possible, the Deity has stooped from His

All the diseases of mind leading to fatalest ruin consist primarily in this isolation. They are the concentration of man upon himself, whether his heavenly interests or his worldly interests, matters not; it is the being *his own* interests which makes the regard of them so mortal. Every form of asceticism on one side, of sensualism on the other, is an isolation of his soul or of his body; the fixing his thoughts upon them alone; while every healthy state of nations and of individual minds consists in the unselfish presence of the human spirit everywhere, energizing over all things; speaking and living through all things.

Man being thus the crowning and ruling work of God, it will follow that all his best art must have something to tell about himself, as the soul of things, and ruler of creatures. It must also make this reference to himself under a true conception of his own nature. Therefore all art which involves no reference to man is inferior or nugatory. And all art which involves misconception of man, or base thought of him, is in that degree false and base.

Now the basest thought possible concerning him is, that he has no spiritual nature; and the foolishest misunderstanding of him possible is, that he has or should have, no animal nature. For his nature is nobly animal, nobly spiritual – coherently and irrevocably so; neither part of it may, but at its peril, expel, despise, or defy the other. All great art confesses and worships both.

throne, and has not only, in the person of the Son, taken upon Him the veil of our human *flesh*, but, in the person of the Father, taken upon Him the veil of our human *thoughts*, and permitted *us*, by His own spoken authority, to conceive Him simply and clearly as a loving Father and Friend; – a being to be walked with and reasoned with; to be moved by our entreaties, angered by our rebellion, alienated by our coldness, pleased by our love, and glorified by our labour; and, finally, to be beheld in immediate and active presence in all the powers and changes of creation. This conception of God, which is the child's, is evidently the only one which can be universal, and therefore the only one which *for us* can be true. The moment that, in our pride of heart, we refuse to accept the condescension of the Almighty, and desire Him, instead of stooping to hold our hands, to rise up before us into His glory, – we hoping that by standing on a grain of dust or two of human knowledge higher than our fellows, we may behold the Creator as He rises, – God takes us at our word; He rises, into His own invisible and inconceivable majesty; He goes forth upon the ways which are not our ways, and retires into the thoughts which are not our thoughts; and we are left alone. And presently we say in our vain hearts, 'There is no God.' [Isaiah iv. 8] (MP IV, Pt. V, Ch. VI, paras. 6–7)

The art which, since the writings of Rio and Lord Lindsay,[9] is specially known as 'Christian', erred by pride in its denial of the animal nature of man; – and, in connection with all monkish and fanatical forms of religion, by looking always to another world instead of this. It wasted its strength in visions, and was therefore swept away, notwithstanding all its good and glory, by the strong truth of the naturalist art of the sixteenth century.[g] But that

[g] Let us take one or two instances in order clearly to explain our meaning.

The life of Angelico was almost entirely spent in the endeavour to imagine the beings belonging to another world. By purity of life, habitual elevation of thought, and natural sweetness of disposition, he was enabled to express the sacred affections upon the human coutenance as no one ever did before or since. In order to effect clearer distinction between heavenly beings and those of this world, he represents the former as clothed in draperies of the purest colour, crowned with glories of burnished gold, and entirely shadowless. With exquisite choice of gesture, and disposition of folds of drapery, this mode of treatment gives, perhaps, the best idea of spiritual beings which the human mind is capable of forming. It is, therefore, a true ideal: but the mode in which it is arrived at (being so far mechanical and contradictory of the appearances of nature) necessarily precludes those who practise it from being complete masters of their art. It is always childish, but beautiful in its childishness . . .

I remember another interesting example of ideality on this same root, but belonging to another branch of it, in the works of a young German painter, which I saw some time ago in a London drawing-room. He had been travelling in Italy, and had brought home a portfolio of sketches remarkable alike for their fidelity and purity. Every one was a laborious and accurate study of some particular spot. Every cottage, every cliff, every tree, at the site chosen, had been drawn, and drawn with palpable sincerity of portraiture, and yet in such a spirit that it was impossible to conceive that any sin or misery had ever entered into one of the scenes he had represented; and the volcanic horrors of Radicofani, the pestilent gloom of the Pontines, and the boundless despondency of the Campagna, became, under his hand, only various appearances of Paradise.

It was very interesting to observe the minute emendations or omissions by which this was effected. To set the tiles the slightest degree more in order upon a cottage roof; to insist upon the vine-leaves at the window, and let the shadow which fell from them naturally conceal the rent in the wall; to draw all the flowers in the foreground, and miss the weeds; to draw all the folds of the white clouds, and miss those of the black ones; to mark the graceful branches of the trees, and, in one way or another, beguile the eye from those which were ungainly; to give every peasant-girl whose face was visible the expression of an angel, and every one whose back was turned the bearing of a princess; finally, to give a general look of light, clear organization and serene vitality to every

naturalist art erred on the other side; denied at last the spiritual nature of man, and perished in corruption.

feature in the landscape; – such were his artifices, and such his delights. It was impossible not to sympathise deeply with the spirit of such a painter; and it was just cause for gratitude to be permitted to travel, as it were, through Italy with such a friend. But his work had, nevertheless, its stern limitations and marks of everlasting inferiority. Always soothing and pathetic, it could never be sublime, never perfectly nor entrancingly beautiful; for the narrow spirit of correction could not cast itself fully into any scene; the calm cheerfulness which shrank from the shadow of the cypress and the distortion of the olive, could not enter into the brightness of the sky that they pierced, nor the softness of the bloom that they bore: for every sorrow that his heart turned from, he lost a consolation; for every fear which he dared not confront, he lost a portion of his hardness: the unsceptred sweep of the storm-clouds, the fair freedom of glancing shower and flickering sunbeam, sank into sweet rectitudes and decent formalisms; and, before eyes that refused to be dazzled or darkened, the hours of sunset wreathed their rays unheeded, and the mists of the Apennines spread their blue veils in vain.

To this inherent shortcoming and narrowness of reach the farther defect was added, that this work gave no useful representation of the state of facts in the country which it pretended to contemplate. It was not only wanting in all the higher elements of beauty, but wholly unavailable for instruction of any kind beyond that which exists in pleasurableness of pure emotion. And considering what cost of labour was devoted to the series of drawings, it could not but be matter for grave blame, as well as for partial contempt, that a man of amiable feeling and considerable intellectual power should thus expend his life in the declaration of his own petty pieties and pleasant reveries, leaving the burden of human sorrow unwitnessed, and the power of God's judgments unconfessed; and, while poor Italy lay wounded and moaning at his feet, pass by, in priestly calm, lest the whiteness of his decent vesture should be spotted with unhallowed blood . . .

It is finally to be remembered, therefore, that Purism is always noble when it is *instinctive*. It is not the greatest thing that can be done, but it is probably the greatest thing that the man who does it can do, provided it comes from his heart. True, it is a sign of weakness, but it is not in our choice whether we will be weak or strong; and there is a certain strength which can only be made perfect in weakness. If he is working in humility, fear of evil, desire of beauty, and sincere purity of purpose and thought, he will produce good and helpful things; but he must be much on his guard against supposing himself to be greater than his fellows, because he has shut himself into this calm and cloistered sphere. His only safety lies in knowing himself to be, on the contrary, *less* than his fellows, and in always striving, so far as he can find it in his heart, to extend his delicate narrowness towards the great naturalist ideal. (MP III, Pt. IV, Ch. VI, paras. 2–4, 6–7, 9).

A contemplative reaction is taking place in modern times, out of which it may be hoped a new spiritual art may be developed. The first school of landscape, named, in the foregoing chapter, the Heroic, is that of the noble naturalists. The second (Classical), and third (Pastoral), belong to the time of sensual decline. The fourth (Contemplative) is that of modern revival.

But why, the reader will ask, is no place given in this scheme to the 'Christian' or spiritual art which preceded the naturalists? Because all landscape belonging to that art is subordinate, and in one essential principle false. It is subordinate, because intended only to exalt the conception of saintly or Divine presence: — rather therefore to be considered as a landscape decoration or type, than an effort to paint nature. If I included it in my list of schools, I should have to go still farther back, and include with it the conventional and illustrative landscape of the Greeks and Egyptians.

But also it cannot constitute a real school, because its first assumption is false, namely, that the natural world can be represented without the element of death.

The real schools of landscape are primarily distinguished from the preceding unreal ones by their introduction of this element. They are not at first in any sort the worthier for it. But they are more true, and capable, therefore, in the issue, of becoming worthier.

It will be a hard piece of work for us to think this rightly out, but it must be done.

Perhaps an accurate analysis of the schools of art of all time might show us that when the immortality of the soul was practically and completely believed, the elements of decay, danger, and grief in visible things were always disregarded. However this may be, it is assuredly so in the early Christian schools. The ideas of danger or decay seem not merely repugnant, but inconceivable to them; the expression of immortality and perpetuity is alone possible. I do not mean that they take no note of the absolute fact of corruption. This fact the early painters often compel themselves to look fuller in the front than any other men: as in the way they usually paint the Deluge (the raven feeding on the bodies), and in all the various triumphs and processions of the power of Death, which formed one great chapter of religious teaching and painting, from Orcagna's time to the close of the Purist epoch. But I mean that this external fact of corruption is separated in their minds from the main conditions of their work; and its horror enters no more into their general treatment of landscape than the fear of murder or martyrdom, both of which they had nevertheless continually to represent. None of these things appeared to them as affecting the general dealings of the Deity with His world. Death, pain, and decay were simply momentary accidents in the course of immortality, which never ought to exercise any depressing influence over the hearts of men, or in the life of Nature. God, in intense life, peace, and helping power, was always and everywhere. Human bodies, at one time or another, had indeed to be made dust of, and raised from it; and this becoming dust was hurtful and humiliating, but not in the least melancholy, nor, in any very high degree, important; except to thoughtless persons who needed sometimes to be reminded of it, and whom, not at all fearing the things much himself, the painter accordingly did remind of it, somewhat sharply.

A similar condition of mind seems to have been attained, not unfrequently, in modern times, by persons whom either narrow-ness of circumstance or education, or vigorous moral efforts, have guarded from the troubling of the world, so as to give them firm and childlike trust in the power and presence of God, together with peace of conscience, and a belief in the passing of all evil into some form of good. It is impossible that a person thus disciplined should feel, in any of its more acute phases, the sorrow for any of the phenomena of nature, or terror in any material danger which would occur to another. The absence of personal fear, the consciousness of security as great in the midst of pestilence and storm, as amidst beds of flowers on a summer's morning, and the certainty that whatever appeared evil, or was assuredly painful, must eventually issue in a far greater and enduring good – this general feeling and conviction, I say, would gradually lull, and at last put to entire rest, the physical sensations of grief and fear; so that the man would look upon danger without dread, – expect pain without lamentation.

It may perhaps be thought that this is a very high and right state of mind.

Unfortunately, it appears that the attainment of it is never possible without inducing some form of intellectual weakness.

No painter belonging to the purist religious schools ever mastered his art. Perugino nearly did so; but it was because he was more rational – more a man of the world – than the rest. No literature exists of a high class produced by minds in the pure religious temper. On the contrary, a great deal of literature exists, produced by persons in that temper, which is markedly, and very far, below average literary work.

The reason of this I believe to be, that the right faith of man is not intended to give him repose, but to enable him to do his work. It is not intended that he should look away from the place he lives in now, and cheer himself with thoughts of the place he is to live in next, but that he should look stoutly into this world, in faith that if he does his work thoroughly here, some good to others or himself, with which however he is not at present concerned, will come of it hereafter. And this kind of brave, but not very hopeful or cheerful faith, I perceive to be always rewarded by clear practical success and splendid intellectual power; while the faith which dwells on the future fades away into rosy mist, and emptiness of musical air. That result indeed follows naturally enough on its habit of assuming that things must be right, or must come right, when, probably, the fact is, that so far as we are concerned, they are entirely wrong; and going wrong: and also on its weak and false way of looking on what these religious persons call 'the bright side of things', that is to say, on one side of them only, when God has given them two sides, and intended us to see both.[h]

<hr />

[h] *'The fact is, a man who can see truth at all, sees it wholly, and neither desires nor dares to mutilate it' – hence the naturalistic ideal is not false idealization:*
Herein is the chief practical difference between the higher and lower artists; a difference which I feel more and more every day that I give to the study of art. All the great men *see* what they paint before they paint it, – see it in a perfectly passive manner, – cannot help seeing it if they would; whether in their mind's eye, or in bodily fact, does not matter; very often the mental vision is, I believe, in men of imagination, clearer than the bodily one; but vision it is, of one kind or another, – the whole scene, character, or incident passing before them as in second sight, whether they will or no, and requiring them to paint it as they see it; they not daring, under the might of its presence, to alter one jot or tittle of it as they write it down or paint it down; it being to them in its own kind and degree always a true vision of Apocalypse, and invariably accompanied in their hearts by a feeling correspondent to the words, – 'Write the things *which thou hast seen*, and the things which *are*.' [Revelation i. 19]

And the whole power, whether of painter or poet, to describe rightly what we call an ideal thing, depends upon its being thus, to him, not an ideal, but a

I was reading but the other day, in a book by a zealous, useful, and able Scotch clergyman, one of these rhapsodies, in which he described a scene in the Highlands to show (he said) the goodness of God. In this Highland scene there was nothing but sunshine,

real thing. No man ever did or ever will work well, but either from actual sight or sight of faith; and all that we call ideal in Greek or any other art, because to us it is false and visionary, was, to the makers of it, true and existent. The heroes of Phidias are simply representations of such noble human persons as he every day saw, and the gods of Phidias simply representations of such noble divine persons as he thoroughly believed to exist, and did in mental vision truly behold. Hence I said in the second preface to the *Seven Lamps of Architecture*: 'All great art represents something that it sees or believes in; – nothing unseen or uncredited. [Preface to 2nd editon, para. 7].

And just because it is always something that it sees or believes in, there is the peculiar character above noted, almost unmistakable, in all high and true ideals, of having been as it were studied from the life, and involving pieces of sudden familiarity, and close *specific* painting which never would have been admitted or even thought of, had not the painter drawn either from the bodily life or from the life of faith. For instance, Dante's centaur, Chiron, dividing his beard with his arrow before he can speak, is a thing that no mortal would ever have thought of, if he had not actually seen the centaur do it [*Inferno* xii 77–80]. They might have composed handsome bodies of men and horses in all possible ways, through a whole life of pseudo-idealism, and yet never dreamed of any such thing. But the real living centaur actually trotted across Dante's brain, and he saw him do it.

And on account of this reality it is, that the great idealists venture into all kinds of what, to the pseudo-idealists, are 'vulgarities'. Nay, *venturing* is the wrong word; the great men have no choice in the matter; they do not know or care whether the things they describe are vulgarities or not. They *saw* them; they are the facts of the case. If they had merely composed what they describe, they would have had it at their will to refuse this circumstance or add that. But they did not compose it. It came to them ready fashioned; they were too much impressed by it to think what was vulgar or not vulgar in it. It might be a very wrong thing in a centaur to have so much beard; but so it was. And, therefore, among the various ready tests of true greatness there is not any more certain than this daring reference to, or use of, mean and little things – mean and little, that is, to mean and little minds; but, when used by the great men, evidently part of the noble whole which is authoritatively present before them . . .

'Well, but,' (at this point the reader asks doubtfully,) 'if then your great central idealist is to show all truth, low as well as lovely, receiving it in this passive way, what becomes of all your principles of selection, and of setting in the right place, which you were talking about [earlier[? . . . Why, . . . the vision comes to him in its chosen order. Chosen *for* him, not *by* him, but yet full of visible and exquisite choice, just as a sweet and perfect dream will come to a

and fresh breezes, and bleating lambs, and clean tartans, and all manner of pleasantness. Now a Highland scene is, beyond dispute, pleasant enough in its own way; but, looked close at, has its shadows. Here, for instance, is the very fact of one, as pretty as I can remember – having seen many. It is a little valley of soft turf, enclosed in its narrow oval by jutting rocks and broad flakes of nodding fern. From one side of it to the other winds, serpentine, a clear brown stream, drooping into quicker ripple as it reaches the end of the oval field, and then, first islanding a purple and white rock with an amber pool, it dashes away into a narrow fall of foam under a thicket of mountain-ash and alder. The autumn sun, low but clear, shines on the scarlet ash-berries and on the golden birch-leaves, which, fallen here and there, when the breeze has not caught them, rest quiet in the crannies of the purple rock. Beside the rock, in the hollow under the thicket, the carcase of a ewe, drowned in the last flood, lies nearly bare to the bone, its white ribs protruding through the skin, raven-torn; and the rags of its wool still flickering from the branches that first stayed it as the stream swept it down. A little lower, the current plunges, roaring, into a circular chasm like a well, surrounded on three sides by a chimney-like hollowness of polished rock, down which the foam slips in detached snow-flakes. Round the edges of the pool beneath, the water circles slowly, like black oil; a little butterfly lies on its back, its wings glued to one of the eddies, its limbs feebly quivering; a fish rises, and it is gone. Lower down the stream, I can just see over a knoll, the green and damp turf roofs of four or five hovels, built at the edge of a morass, which is trodden by the cattle into a black Slough of Despond at their doors, and traversed by a few ill-set stepping-stones, with here and there a flat slab on the tops, where they have sunk out of sight, and at the turn of the brook I see a man fishing, with a boy and a dog – a picturesque and pretty group enough certainly, if they had not been there all day starving. I know them, and I know the dog's ribs also, which are nearly as bare as the dead ewe's; and the child's wasted

sweet and perfect person, so that, in some sense, they may be said to have chosen their dream, or composed it; and yet they could not help dreaming it so, and in no otherwise. Thus, exactly thus, in all results of true inventive power, the whole harmony of the thing done seems as if it had been wrought by the most exquisite rules. But to him who did it, it presented itself so, and his will, and knowledge, and personality, for the moment went for nothing; he became simply a scribe; and wrote what he heard and saw. (MP III, Pt. IV, Ch. VII, paras. 5–7, 10)

shoulders, cutting his old tartan jacket through, so sharp are they. We will go down and talk with the man.

Or, that I may not piece pure truth with fancy, for I have none of his words set down, let us hear a word or two from another such, a Scotchman also, and as true-hearted, and in just as fair a scene. I write out the passage, in which I have kept his few sentences, word for word, as it stands in my private diary: – '22nd April (1851). Yesterday I had a long walk up the Via Gellia, at Matlock, coming down upon it from the hills above, all sown with anemones and violets, and murmuring with sweet springs. Above all the mills in the valley, the brook, in its first purity, forms a small shallow pool, with a sandy bottom covered with cresses and other water plants. A man was wading in it for cresses as I passed up the valley, and bade me good-day. I did not go much farther; he was there when I returned. I passed him again, about one hundred yards, when it struck me I might as well learn all I could about watercresses: so I turned back. I asked the man, among other questions, what he called the common weed, something like watercress, but with a serrated leaf, which grows at the edge of nearly all such pools. "We calls that brooklime, hereabouts," said a voice behind me. I turned, and saw three men, miners or manufacturers – two evidently Derbyshire men, and respectable-looking in their way; the third, thin, poor, old, and harder-featured, and utterly in rags. "Brooklime?" I said. "What do you call it lime for?" The man said he did not know; it was called that. "You'll find that in the British 'Erba," said the weak, calm voice of the old man. I turned to him in much surprise; but he went on saying something drily (I hardly understood what) to the cress-gatherer; who contradicting him, the old man said he "didn't know fresh water", he "knew enough of sa't". "Have you been a sailor?" I asked. "I was a sailor for eleven years and ten months of my life," he said, in the same strangely quiet manner. "And what are you now?" "I lived for ten years after my wife's death by picking up rags and bones; I hadn't much occasion afore." "And now how do you live?" "Why, I lives hard and honest, and haven't got to live long," or something to that effect. He then went on, in a kind of maundering way, about his wife. "She had rheumatism and fever very bad; and her second rib growed over her hench-bone. A' was a clever woman, but a' grow'd to be a very little one" (this, with an expression of deep melancholy). "Eighteen years after her first lad she was in the family-way again, and they had doctors up from Lunnon about it. They wanted to rip her open, and take the child out of her side. But I never would give my consent." (Then, after a pause:) "She died twenty-six hours and ten minutes after it. I never cared much what come of me since; but I know that I shall soon reach her; that's a knowledge I would na gie for the king's crown." "You are a Scotchman, are not you?" I asked. "I'm from the Isle of Skye, sir; I'm a McGregor." I said something about his religious faith. "Ye'll know I was bred in the Church of Scotland, sir," he said, "and I love it as I love my own soul: but I think thae Wesleyan Methodists ha' got salvation among them too." '

Truly, this Highland and English hill-scenery is fair enough; but has its shadows; and deeper colouring, here and there, than that of heath and rose. (MP V, Pt. IX, Ch. II, paras. 1–12)

The Naturalist Ideal – seeing the whole of truth fearlessly: (1) The Classical Greeks

Now, as far as I have watched the main powers of human mind, they have risen first from the resolution to see fearlessly, pitifully, and to its very worst, what these deep colours mean, wheresoever they fall; not by any means to pass on the other side, looking pleasantly up to the sky, but to stoop to the horror, and let the sky, for the present, take care of its own clouds. However this may be in moral matters, with which I have nothing here to do,[i] in my

---

[i] *It is worth remembering that while the problem is offered here as an historical question, it could also be registered as a personal one. In 1885 in* Praeterita *Ruskin turned back to Byron rather than to Scott – but behind the artistic question there was, as so often, a personal concern which for once was made explicit:*

here at last I had found a man who spoke only of what he had seen, and known; and spoke without exaggeration, without mystery, without enmity, and without mercy. 'That is so – make what you will of it!' . . .

And in this narrow, but sure, truth, to Byron, as already to me, it appeared that Love was a transient thing, and Death a dreadful one. He did not attempt to console me for Jessie's death, by saying she was happier in Heaven; or for Charles's, by saying it was a Providential dispensation to me on Earth. He did not tell me that war was a just price for the glory of captains, or that the National command of murder diminished its guilt. Of all things within range of human thought he felt the facts, and discerned the natures with accurate justice. (Vol. I, Ch. VIII, para. 173)

Jessie was the daughter of Ruskin's Scottish aunt, a playmate who died

own field of inquiry the fact is so; and all great and beautiful work has come of first gazing without shrinking into the darkness. If, having done so, the human spirit can, by its courage and faith, conquer the evil, it rises into conceptions of victorious and consummated beauty. It is then the spirit of the highest Greek and Venetian Art. If unable to conquer the evil, but remaining in strong though melancholy war with it, not rising into supreme beauty, it is the spirit of the best northern art, typically represented by that of Holbein and Dürer. If, itself conquered by the evil, infected by the dragon breath of it, and at last brought into captivity, so as to take delight in evil for ever, it becomes the spirit of the dark, but still powerful sensualistic art, represented typically by that of Salvator. We must trace this fact briefly through Greek, Venetian, and Düreresque art; we shall then see how the art of decline came of avoiding the evil, and seeking pleasure only; and thus obtain, at last, some power of judging whether the tendency of our own contemplative art be right or ignoble.

The ruling purpose of Greek poetry is the assertion of victory, by heroism, over fate, sin, and death. The terror of these great enemies is dwelt upon chiefly by the tragedians. The victory over them, by Homer . . .

---

suddenly in childhood. Charles was another cousin, who lost his mother, Ruskin's Croydon aunt, at a young age, and was kind to the boy Ruskin during a period when other boys generally were not. Charles was made to learn to swim by being pitched by his elder brother into Croydon Canal, at a time when Ruskin himself was never allowed by his mother even 'to go to the edge of a pond, or be in the same field with a pony' (Vol. I, Ch. V, para. 100). But Charles died at sea, leaping overboard in an attempt to save others. His bereaved father said, '(I can hear the words now), "They caught the cap off his head, and yet they couldn't save him" ' (Vol. I, Ch. VII, para. 158). Who could bear, like Byron, to 'feel the facts'? Down the ages, did people manage anything better than a 'sure' but 'narrow' truth in response?

In his epilogue to Stones of Venice, Vol. III (para. 2) Ruskin wonders if the public's apparent non-acceptance of his teaching of Gothic derived from 'the entire concealment of my own personal feelings throughout', but concludes that if he had told 'as a more egoistic person would, my own impressions, as thinking those, forsooth, and not the history of Venice, the most important business to the world in general', then he would only have encouraged a similar opinionated egoism in his readers.

Now observe that in their dealing with all these subjects the Greeks never shrink from horror; down to its uttermost depth, to its most appalling physical detail, they strive to sound the secrets of sorrow. For them there is no passing by on the other side, no turning away the eyes to vanity from pain. Literally, they have not 'lifted up their souls unto vanity' [Psalms xxiv. 4]. Whether there be consolation for them or not, neither apathy nor blindness shall be their saviour; if, for them, thus knowing the facts of the grief of earth, any hope, relief, or triumph may hereafter seem possible, —well; but if not, still hopeless, reliefless, eternal, the sorrow shall be met face to face. This Hector, so righteous, so merciful, so brave, has, nevertheless, to look upon his dearest brother in miserablest death. His own soul passes away in hopeless sobs through the throat-wound of the Grecian spear. That is one aspect of things in this world, a fair world truly, but having, among its other aspects, this one, highly ambiguous.

Meeting it boldly as they may, gazing right into the skeleton face of it, the ambiguity remains; nay, in some sort gains upon them. We trusted in the gods; – we thought that wisdom and courage would save us. Our wisdom and courage themselves deceive us to our death. Athena had the aspect of Deiphobus – terror of the enemy. She has not terrified him, but left us, in our mortal need.[10]

And beyond that mortality, what hope have we? Nothing is clear to us on that horizon, nor comforting. Funeral honours; perhaps also rest; perhaps a shadowy life – artless, joyless, loveless. No devices in that darkness of the grave [Ecclesiastes ix. 10], nor daring, nor delight. Neither marrying nor giving in marriage [Mark xii. 25], nor casting of spears, nor rolling of chariots, nor voice of fame. Lapped in pale Elysian mist, chilling the forgetful heart and feeble frame, shall we waste on for ever? Can the dust of earth claim more of immortality than this? Or shall we have even so much as rest? May we, indeed, lie down again in the dust: or have not our sins hidden from us even the things that belong to that peace [Luke xix. 42]? May not chance and the whirl of passion govern us there: when there shall be no thought, nor work, nor wisdom, nor breathing of the soul [Odyssey x 495]?

Be it so. With no better reward, no brighter hope, we will be men while we may: men, just, and strong, and fearless, and up to our power, perfect. Athena herself, our wisdom and our strength, may betray us: – Phoebus, our sun, smite us with plague, or hide his face from us helpless; – Jove and all the powers of fate oppress us, or give us up to destruction. While we live, we will hold fast our integrity; no weak tears shall blind us, no untimely tremors abate our strength of arm nor swiftness of limb. The gods have given us at least this glorious body and this righteous conscience; these will we keep bright and pure to the end. So may we fall to misery, but not to baseness; so may we sink to sleep, but not to shame.

And herein was conquest. So defied, the betraying and accusing shadows shrank back; the mysterious horror subdued itself to majestic sorrow. (MP V, Pt. IX, Ch. II, paras 13–14, 18–20)

(2) The Middle Ages

Evil, as we saw, had been fronted by the Greek, and thrust out of his path. Once conquered, if he thought of it more, it was involuntarily, as we remember a painful dream, yet with a secret dread that the dream might return and continue for ever. But the teaching of the Church in the Middle Ages had made the contemplation of evil one of the duties of men. As sin, it was to be duly thought upon, that it might be confessed. As suffering, endured joyfully, in hope of future reward. Hence conditions of bodily distemper which an Athenian would have looked upon with the severest contempt and aversion, were in the Christian Church regarded always with pity, and often with respect: while the partial practice of celibacy by the clergy, and by those over whom they had influence, – together with the whole system of conventual penance and pathetic ritual (with the vicious reactionary tendencies necessarily following), introduced calamitous conditions both of body and soul, which added largely to the pagan's simple list of elements of evil, and introduced the most complicated states of mental suffering and decrepitude.

Therefore the Christian painters differed from the Greek in two main points. They had been taught a faith which put an end to restless questioning and discouragement. All was at last to be well – and their best genius might be peacefully given to imagining the glories of heaven and the happiness of its redeemed. But on the other hand, though suffering was to cease in heaven, it was to be not only endured, but honoured upon earth. And from the Crucifixion, down to a beggar's lameness, all the tortures and maladies of men were to be made, at least in part, the subjects of art. The Venetian was, therefore, in his inner mind, less serious than the Greek: in his superficial temper, sadder. In his heart there was none of the deep horror which vexed the soul of Æschylus or Homer. His Pallas-shield was the shield of Faith, not the shield of the Gorgon. All was at last to issue happily; in sweetest harpings and seven-fold circles of light. But for the present he had to dwell with the maimed and the blind, and to revere Lazarus more than Achilles.

This reference to a future world has a morbid influence on all their conclusions. For the earth and all its natural elements are despised. They are to pass away like a scroll [Revelations vi. 14]. Man, the immortal, is alone revered; his work and presence are all that can be noble or desirable. Men, and fair architecture, temples and courts such as may be in a celestial city, or the clouds and angels of Paradise; these are what we must paint when we want beautiful things. But the sea, the mountains, the forests, are all adverse to us, – a desolation. The ground that was cursed for our sake [Genesis iii. 17]; – the sea that executed judgment on all our race, and rages against us still, though bridled; storm-demons churning it into foam in nightly glare on Lido, and hissing from it against our palaces. Nature is but a terror, or a temptation. She is for hermits, martyrs, murderers, – for [Titian's] St Jerome, and [Tintoretto's] St Mary of Egypt, and the Magdalen in the desert, and [Bellini's] monk Peter, falling before the sword.

But the worst point we have to note respecting the spirit of Venetian landscape is its pride.

It was observed in the course of the third volume how the mediæval temper had rejected agricultural pursuits, and whatever pleasures could come of them.

At Venice this negation had reached its extreme. Though the Florentines and Romans had no delight in farming, they had in gardening. The Venetian possessed, and cared for, neither fields nor pastures ... No simple joy was possible to him. Only stateliness and power; high intercourse with kingly and beautiful humanity, proud thoughts, or splendid pleasures; throned sensualities, and ennobled appetites ...

In all its roots of power, and modes of work; – in its belief, its breadth, and its judgment, I find the Venetian mind perfect.

How, then, did its art so swiftly pass away? How become, what it became unquestionably, one of the chief causes of the corruption of the mind of Italy, and of her subsequent decline in moral and political power?

By reason of one great, one fatal fault; – recklessness in aim. Wholly noble in its sources, it was wholly unworthy in its purposes.

Separate and strong, like Samson, chosen from its youth, and with the spirit of God visibly resting on it [Judges xiii. 24–5], – like him, it warred in careless strength, and wantoned in untimely pleasure. No Venetian painter ever worked with any aim beyond that of delighting the eye, or expressing fancies agreeable to himself or flattering to his nation. They could not be either, unless they were religious. But he did not desire the religion. He desired the delight. (MP V, Pt. IX, Ch. III, paras. 7–11, 31–2)

(3) *The Moderns: 'Of the Turnerian Picturesque'*

On the whole, the first master of the lower picturesque, among our living artists, is Clarkson Stanfield; his range of art being, indeed, limited by his pursuit of this character. I take, therefore, a windmill, forming the principal subject in his drawing of Brittany near Dol (engraved in the Coast Scenery), Plate 26, fig. 1, and beside it I place a windmill, which forms also the principal subject in Turner's study of the Lock, in the Liber Studiorum.[11] At first sight I dare say the reader may like Stanfield's best; and there is, indeed, a great deal more in it to attract liking. Its roof is nearly as interesting in its ruggedness as a piece of the stony peak of a mountain, with a châlet built on its side; and it is exquisitely varied in swell and curve. Turner's roof, on the contrary, is a plain, ugly gable, – a windmill roof, and nothing more. Stanfield's sails are twisted into most effective wrecks, as beautiful as pine bridges over Alpine streams; only they do not look as if they had ever been serviceable windmill sails; they are bent about in cross and awkward ways, as if they were warped or cramped; and their timbers look heavier than necessary. Turner's sails have no beauty about them like that of Alpine bridges; but they have the exact switchy sway of the sail that is always straining against the wind; and the timbers form clearly the lightest possible framework for the canvas, – thus showing the essence of windmill sail. Then the clay wall of Stanfield's mill is as beautiful as a piece of chalk cliff, all worn into furrows by the rain, coated with mosses, and rooted to the ground by a heap of crumbled stone, embroidered with

Plate 26 *The Picturesque of Windmills*

1 *Stanfield*   2 *Turner*

grass and creeping plants. But this is not a serviceable state for a windmill to be in. The essence of a windmill, as distinguished from all other mills, is, that it should turn round, and be a spinning thing, ready always to face the wind; as light, therefore, as possible, and as vibratory; so that it is in no wise good for it to approximate itself to the nature of chalk cliffs.

Now observe how completely Turner has chosen his mill so as to mark this great fact of windmill nature; how high he has set it; how slenderly he has supported it; how he has built it all of wood; how he has bent the lower planks so as to give the idea of the building lapping over the pivot on which it rests inside; and how, finally, he has insisted on the great leverage of the beam behind it, while Stanfield's lever looks more like a prop than a thing to turn the roof with. And he has done all this fearlessly, though none of these elements of form are pleasant ones in themselves, but tend, on the whole, to give a somewhat mean and spiderlike look to the principal feature in his picture; and then, finally, because he could not get the windmill dissected, and show us the real heart and centre of the whole, behold, he has put a pair of old millstones,[12] *lying outside*, at the bottom of it. These – the first cause and motive of all the fabric – laid at its foundation; and beside them the cart which is to fulfil the end of the fabric's being, and take home the sacks of flour.

So far of what each painter chooses to draw. But do not fail also to consider the spirit in which it is drawn. Observe, that though all the ruin has befallen Stanfield's mill, Stanfield is not in the least sorry for it. On the contrary, he is delighted, and evidently thinks it the most fortunate thing possible. The owner is ruined, doubtless, or dead; but his mill forms an admirable object in our view of Brittany. So far from being grieved about it, we will make it our principal light; – if it were a fruit-tree in spring-blossom, instead of a desolate mill, we could not make it whiter or brighter; we illuminate our whole picture with it, and exult over its every rent as a special treasure and possession.

Not so Turner. *His* mill is still serviceable; but, for all that, he feels somewhat pensive about it. It is a poor property, and evidently the owner of it has enough to do to get his own bread out from between its stones. Moreover, there is a dim type of all melancholy human labour in it, – catching the free winds, and setting them to turn grindstones. It is poor work for the winds; better, indeed, than drowning sailors or tearing down forests, but not their proper work of marshalling the clouds, and bearing the wholesome rains to the place where they are ordered to fall, and fanning the flowers and leaves when they are faint with heat. Turning round a couple of stones, for the mere pulverization of human food, is not noble work for the winds. So, also, of all low labour to which one sets human souls. It is better than no labour; and, in a still higher degree, better than destructive wandering of imagination; but yet that grinding in the darkness, for mere food's sake, must be melancholy work enough for many a living creature. All men have felt it so; and this grinding at the mill, whether it be breeze or soul that is set to it, we cannot much rejoice in. Turner has no joy of his mill. It shall be dark against the sky, yet proud, and on the hill-top; not ashamed of its labour, and brightened from beyond, the golden clouds stooping over it, and the calm summer sun going down behind, far away, to his rest.

Now in all this observe how the higher condition of art (for I suppose the reader will feel, with me, that Turner *is* the highest)[j] depends upon largeness of sympathy. It is mainly because the one painter has communion of heart with his subject, and the other only casts his eyes upon it feelinglessly, that the work of the one is greater than that of the other. And, as we think farther over the

---

[j] *Turnerian Picturesque: religion or ruin?*
Religious art, at once complete and sincere, never yet has existed.

It will exist: nay, I believe the era of its birth has come, and that those bright Turnerian imageries, which the European public declared to be 'dotage', and those calm Pre-Raphaelite studies which, in like manner, it pronounced 'puerility', form the first foundation that has been ever laid for true sacred art.
(MP III, Pt. IV, Ch. IV, paras. 22–3)

[But] wherever he looked, [Turner] saw ruin.

Ruin and twilight . . . Fading of the last rays of sunset. Faint breathing of the sorrow of night.

And fading of sunset, note also, on ruin. I cannot but wonder that this difference between Turner's work and previous art-conception has not been more observed. None of the great early painters draw ruins, except compulsorily. The shattered buildings introduced by them are shattered artificially, like models. There is no real sense of decay; whereas Turner only momentarily dwells on anything else than ruin. Take up the Liber Studiorum, and observe how this feeling of decay and humiliation gives solemnity to all its simplest subjects; even to his view of daily labour. I have marked its tendency in examining the design of the Mill and Lock, but observe its continuance through the book. There is no exultation in thriving city, or mart, or in happy rural toil, or harvest gathering. Only the grinding at the mill, and patient striving with hard conditions of life. (MP V, Pt. IX, Ch. XI, paras. 27–8)

matter, we shall see that this is indeed the eminent cause of the difference between the lower picturesque and the higher. For, in a certain sense, the lower picturesque ideal is eminently a *heartless* one; the lover of it seems to go forth into the world in a temper as merciless as its rocks.[k] (MP IV, Pt. V, Ch. I, paras. 10–12)

Turner and Giorgione: 'The Two Boyhoods' –
The first time Turner really got away from London, he found himself 'sitting alone among the Yorkshire hills':

For the first time, the silence of Nature round him, her freedom sealed to him, her glory opened to him. Peace at last; no roll of cart-wheel, nor mutter of sullen voices in the back shop; but curlew-cry in space of heaven, and welling of bell-toned streamlet by its shadowy rock. Freedom at last. Dead-wall, dark railing, fenced field, gated garden, all passed away like the dream of a prisoner; and behold, far as foot or eye can race or range, the moor, and cloud. Loveliness at last. It is here then, among these deserted vales! Not among men. Those pale, poverty-struck, or cruel faces; – that multitudinous, marred humanity – are not the only things that God has made. Here is something He has made which no one has marred. Pride of purple rocks, and river pools of

[k] *Stanfield's picturesqueness is described in* The Seven Lamps of Architecture *as 'Parasitical Sublimity' (Ch. VI, para. 12). Ruskin's dictum is 'what is impossible in reality, is ridiculous in fancy' (MP IV, Pt. V, Ch. XIX, para. 8): the social and political implications of this defence of realistic truth are spelt out in* Modern Painters Vol. IV, Pt. V, Ch. XIX, para. 6:
If all the gold that has gone to paint the simulacra of the cottages, and to put new songs in the mouths of the simulacra of the peasants, had gone to brighten the existent cottages, and to put new songs in the mouths of the existent peasants, it might in the end, perhaps, have turned out better so, not only for the peasant, but for even the audience. For that form of the False Ideal has also its correspondent True Ideal, – consisting not in the naked beauty of statues, nor in the gauze flowers and crackling tinsel of theatres, but in the clothed and fed beauty of living men, and in the lights and laughs of happy homes. Night after night, the desire of such an ideal springs up in every idle human heart; and night after night, as far as idleness can, we work out this desire in costly lies. We paint the faded actress, build the lath landscape, feed our benevolence with fallacies of felicity, and satisfy our righteousness with poetry of justice. The time will come when, as the heavy-folded curtain falls upon our own stage of life, we shall begin to comprehend that the justice we loved was intended to have been done in fact, and not in poetry, and the felicity we sympathized in, to have been bestowed and not feigned.

blue, and tender wilderness of glittering trees, and misty lights of evening on immeasurable hills.

Beauty, and freedom, and peace; and yet another teacher, graver than these. Sound preaching at last here, in Kirkstall crypt, concerning fate and life. Here, where the dark pool reflects the chancel pillars, and the cattle lie in unhindered rest, the soft sunshine on their dappled bodies, instead of priests' vestments; their white furry hair ruffled a little, fitfully, by the evening wind deep-scented from the meadow thyme.

Consider deeply the import to him of this, his first sight of ruin, and compare it with the effect of the architecture that was around Giorgione. There were indeed aged buildings, at Venice, in his time, but none in decay. All ruin was removed, and its place filled as quickly as in our London; but filled always by architecture loftier and more wonderful than that whose place it took, the boy himself happy to work upon the walls of it; so that the idea of the passing away of the strength of men and beauty of their works never could occur to him sternly. Brighter and brighter the cities of Italy had been rising and broadening on hill and plain, for three hundred years. He saw only strength and immortality, could not but paint both; conceived the form of man as deathless, calm with power, and fiery with life.

Turner saw the exact reverse of this. In the present work of men, meanness, aimlessness, unsightliness: thin-walled, lath-divided, narrow-garreted houses of clay; booths of a darksome Vanity Fair, busily base.

But on Whitby Hill, and by Bolton Brook,[13] remained traces of other handiwork. Men who could build had been there; and who also had wrought, not merely for their own days. But to what purpose? Strong faith, and steady hands, and patient souls – can this, then, be all you have left? this the sum of your doing on the earth; – a nest whence the night-owl may whimper to the brook, and a ribbed skeleton of consumed arches, looming above the bleak banks of mist, from its cliff to the sea?

As the strength of men to Giorgione, to Turner their weakness and vileness, were alone visible. They themselves, unworthy or ephemeral; their work, despicable, or decayed. In the Venetian's eyes, all beauty depended on man's presence and pride; in Turner's, on the solitude he had left, and the humiliation he had suffered.

And thus the fate and issue of all his work were determined at once. He must be a painter of the strength of nature, there was no beauty elsewhere than in that; he must paint also the labour and sorrow and passing away of men: this was the great human truth visible to him.

Their labour, their sorrow, and their death. Mark the three. Labour; by sea and land, in field and city, at forge and furnace, helm and plough. No pastoral indolence nor classic pride shall stand between him and the troubling of the world; still less between him and the toil of his country, — blind, tormented, unwearied, marvellous England.

Also their Sorrow; Ruin of all their glorious work, passing away of their thoughts and their honour, mirage of pleasure, FALLACY OF HOPE; gathering of weed on temple step; gaining of wave on deserted strand; weeping of the mother for the children, desolate by her breathless first-born in the streets of the city, desolate by her last sons slain, among the beasts of the field.[14]

And their Death. That old Greek question again;[15] — yet unanswered. The unconquerable spectre still flitting among the forest trees at twilight; rising ribbed out of the sea-sand; — white, a strange Aphrodite, — out of the sea-foam; stretching its gray, cloven wings among the clouds; turning the light of their sunsets into blood. This has to be looked upon, and in a more terrible shape than ever Salvator or Dürer saw it. (MP V, Pt. IX, Ch. IX, paras. 16–22)

Salvator versus Dürer

Up to the time of the Reformation, it was possible for men even of the highest powers of intellect, to obtain a tranquillity of faith, in the highest degree favourable to the pursuit of any particular art . . .

But this possibility ceased at the Reformation. Thenceforward human life became a school of debate, troubled and fearful. Fifteen hundred years of spiritual teaching were called into fearful question, whether indeed it had been teaching by angels or devils? Whatever it had been, there was no longer any way of trusting it peacefully.

A dark time for all men. We cannot now conceive it. The great horror of it lay in this: — that, as in the trial-hour of the Greek, the heavens themselves seemed to have deceived those who had trusted in them.

'We had prayed with tears; we had loved with our hearts. There was no choice of way open to us. No guidance, from God or man, other than this, and behold, it was a lie. "When He, the Spirit of Truth, is come, He shall guide you into all truth" [John xvi. 13]. And he has guided us into *no* truth. There can be no such Spirit. There is no Advocate, no Comforter. Has there been no Resurrection?'

Then came the Resurrection of Death. Never since man first saw him face to face, had his terror been so great. 'Swallowed up in victory' [1 Corinthians xv. 54]: alas! no; but king over all the earth. All faith, hope, and fond belief were betrayed. Nothing of futurity was now sure but the grave.

For the Pan-Athenaic Triumph, and the Feast of Jubilee, there came up, through fields of spring, the Dance of Death.

The brood of weak men fled from the face of him. A new Bacchus and his crew this, with worm for snake and gall for wine. They recoiled to such pleasure as yet remained possible to them – feeble infidelities, and luxurious sciences, and so went their way.

At least, of the men with whom we are concerned – the artists – this was almost the universal fate. They gave themselves to the following of pleasure only; and, as a religious school, after a few pale rays of fading sanctity from Guido, and brown gleams of gipsy Madonnahood from Murillo, came utterly to an end.[16]

Three men only stood firm, facing the new Dionysiac revel, to see what would come of it.

Two in the north, Holbein and Dürer; and, later, one in the south, Salvator . . .

Among this pastoral simplicity and formal sweetness of domestic peace [in Nuremberg], Dürer had to work out his question concerning the grave. It haunted him long; he learnt to engrave death's-heads well before he had done with it; looked deeper than any other man into those strange rings, their jewels lost; and gave answer at last conclusively in his great Knight and Death – of which more presently. But while the Nuremberg landscape is still fresh in our minds, we had better turn south quickly, and compare the elements of education which formed, and of creation which companioned, Salvator.

Born with a wild and coarse nature (how coarse I will show you soon), but nevertheless an honest one, he set himself in youth hotly to the war, and cast himself carelessly on the current, of life. No rectitude of ledger-lines stood in his way; no tender precision of household customs; no calm successions of rural labour. But past his half-starved lips rolled profusion of pitiless wealth; before him glared and swept the troops of shameless pleasure. Above him muttered Vesuvius; beneath his feet shook the Solfatara.

In heart disdainful, in temper adventurous; conscious of power, impatient of labour, and yet more of the pride of the patrons of his youth, he fled to the Calabrian hills, seeking, not knowledge, but freedom. If he was to be surrounded by cruelty and deceit, let them at least be those of brave men or savage beasts, not of the timorous and the contemptible. Better the wrath of the robber, than enmity of the priest; and the cunning of the wolf than of the hypocrite.

We are accustomed to hear the south of Italy spoken of as a beautiful country. Its mountain forms are graceful above others, its sea bays exquisite in outline and hue; but it is only beautiful in superficial aspect. In closer detail it is wild and melancholy. Its forests are sombre-leaved, labyrinth-stemmed; the carubbe, the olive, laurel, and ilex, are alike in that strange feverish twisting of their branches, as if in spasms of half human pain: — Avernus forests; one fears to break their boughs, lest they should cry to us from the rents; the rocks they shade are of ashes, or thrice-molten lava; iron sponge whose every pore has been filled with fire. Silent villages, earthquake shaken, without commerce, without industry, without knowledge, without hope, gleam in white ruin from hillside to hillside; far-winding wrecks of immemorial walls surround the dust of cities long forsaken: the mountain streams moan through the cold arches of their foundations, green with weed, and rage over the heaps of their fallen towers. Far above, in thunder-blue serration, stand the eternal edges of the angry Apennine, dark with rolling impendence of volcanic cloud.

Yet even among such scenes as these, Salvator might have been calmed and exalted, had he been, indeed, capable of exaltation. But he was not of high temper enough to perceive beauty. He had not the sacred sense — the sense of colour; all the loveliest hues of the Calabrian air were invisible to him; the sorrowful desolation of the Calabrian villages unfelt. He saw only what was gross and terrible, — the jagged peak, the splintered tree, the flowerless bank of grass, and wandering weed, prickly and pale. His temper confirmed itself in evil, and became more and more fierce and morose; though not, I believe, cruel, ungenerous, or lascivious. I should not suspect Salvator of wantonly inflicting pain. His constantly painting it does not prove he delighted in it; he felt the horror of it, and in that horror, fascination. Also, he desired fame, and saw that there was an untried field rich enough in morbid excitement to catch the humour of his indolent patrons. But the gloom gained upon him, and grasped him. He could jest, indeed, as men jest in prison-yards (he became afterwards a renowned mime in Florence); his satires are full of good mocking, but his own doom to sadness is never repealed.

Of all men whose work I have ever studied, he gives me most distinctly the idea of a lost spirit. Michelet calls him, 'Ce damné Salvator', perhaps in a sense merely harsh and violent; the epithet to me seems true in a more literal, more merciful sense, – 'That condemned Salvator.' I see in him, notwithstanding all his baseness, the last traces of spiritual life in the art of Europe. He was the last man to whom the thought of a spiritual existence presented itself as a conceivable reality. All succeeding men, however powerful – Rembrandt, Rubens, Vandyck, Reynolds – would have mocked at the idea of a spirit. They were men of the world; they are never in earnest, and they are never appalled. But Salvator was capable of pensiveness, of faith, and of fear. The misery of the earth is a marvel to him; he cannot leave off gazing at it. The religion of the earth is a horror to him. He gnashes his teeth at it, rages at it, mocks and gibes at it. He would have acknowledged religion, had he seen any that was true. Anything rather than that baseness which he did see. 'If there is no other religion than this of pope and cardinals, let us to the robber's ambush and the dragon's den.' He was capable of fear also. The gray spectre, horse-headed, striding across the sky – (in the Pitti Palace) – its bat wings spread, green bars of the twilight seen between its bones; it was no play to him – the painting of it. Helpless Salvator! A little early sympathy, a word of true guidance, perhaps, had saved him. What says he of himself? 'Despiser of wealth and of death.' Two grand scorns; but, oh, condemned Salvator! the question is not for man what he can scorn, but what he can love.[17]

I do not care to trace the various hold which Hades takes on this fallen soul. It is no part of my work here to analyze his art, nor even that of Dürer; all that we need to note is the opposite answer they gave to the question about death.

To Salvator it came in narrow terms. Desolation, without hope, throughout the fields of nature he had to explore; hypocrisy and sensuality, triumphant and shameless, in the cities from which he

Plate 27 *The Knight and Death*

derived his support. His life, so far as any nobility remained in it, could only pass in horror, disdain, or despair . . .

On the contrary, in the sight of Dürer, things were for the most part as they ought to be. Men did their work in his city and in the fields round it. The clergy were sincere. Great social questions unagitated; great social evils either non-existent, or seemingly a part of the nature of things, and inevitable. His answer was that of patient hope . . . The Fortitude, commonly known as the 'Knight and Death', represents a knight riding through a dark valley overhung by leafless trees, and with a great castle on a hill beyond. Beside him, but a little in advance, rides Death on a pale horse. Death is gray-haired and crowned; – serpents wreathed about his crown; (the sting of Death involved in the kingly power). He holds up the hour-glass, and looks earnestly into the knight's face. Behind him follows Sin; but Sin powerless; he has been conquered and passed by, but follows yet, watching if any way of assault remains . . . The knight does not heed him, nor even Death, though he is conscious of the presence of the last.

He rides quietly, his bridle firm in his hand, and his lips set close in a slight sorrowful smile, for he hears what Death is saying; and hears it as the word of a messenger who brings pleasant tidings, thinking to bring evil ones. A little branch of delicate heath is twisted round his helmet. His horse trots proudly and straight; its head high, and with a cluster of oak on the brow where on the fiend's brow is the sea-shell horn. But the horse of Death stoops its head; and its rein catches the little bell which hangs from the knight's horse-bridle, making it toll as a passing-bell.

Dürer's second answer is the plate of 'Melancholia', which is the history of the sorrowful toil of the earth, as the 'Knight and Death' is of its sorrowful patience under temptation.

Salvator's answer, remember, is in both respects that of despair. Death, as he reads, lord of temptation, is victor over the spirit of man; and lord of ruin, is victor over the work of man. Dürer declares the sad but unsullied conquest over Death the tempter; and the sad but enduring conquest over Death the destroyer . . .

I do not know how far Dürer intended to show that labour, in many of its most earnest forms, is closely connected with the morbid sadness or 'dark anger', of the northern nations. Truly some of the best work ever done for man, has been in that dark anger; but I have not yet been able to determine for myself how far this is necessary, or how far great work may also be done with cheerfulness. If I knew what the truth was, I should be able to interpret Dürer better; meantime the design seems to me his answer to the complaint, 'Yet is his strength labour and sorrow.'

'Yes,' he replies, 'but labour and sorrow are his strength.' (MP V, Pt. IX, Ch. IV, paras. 1–4, 10–18)

The Knight of Faith

Thus, as we saw that Unity demanded for its expression what at first might have seemed its contrary, Variety, so Repose demands for its expression the implied capability of its opposite, Energy: and this even in its lower manifestations, in rocks and stones and trees. By comparing the modes in which the mind is disposed to regard the boughs of a fair and vigorous tree, motionless in the summer air, with the effect produced by one of the same boughs hewn square and used for threshold or lintel, the reader will at once perceive the connection of vitality with repose, and the part they both bear in beauty.

But that which in lifeless things ennobles them by seeming to indicate life, ennobles higher creatures by indicating the exaltation of their earthly vitality into a Divine vitality; and raising the life of sense into the life of faith: faith, whether we receive it in the sense of adherence to resolution, obedience to law, regardfulness of promise, in which from all time it has been the test, as the shield, of the true being and life of man; or in the still higher sense of trustfulness in the presence, kindness, and word of God, in which form it has been exhibited under the Christian dispensation. For, whether in one or other form, – whether the faithfulness of men whose path is chosen and portion fixed, in the following and receiving of that path and portion, as in the Thermopylæ camp; or the happier faithfulness of children in the good giving of their Father, and of subjects in the conduct of their King, as in the 'Stand still and see the salvation of God' [Exodus xiv. 13] of the Red Sea shore, there is rest and peacefulness, the 'standing still', in both, the quietness of action determined, of spirit unalarmed, of expectation unimpatient: beautiful even when based only, as of old, on the self-command and self-possession, the persistent dignity or the un-calculating love, of the creature; but more beautiful yet when the rest is one of humility instead of pride, and the trust no more in the resolution we have taken, but in the hand we hold.

The universal instinct of repose,
The longing for confirmed tranquillity
Inward and outward, humble, yet sublime,
The life where hope and memory are as one.
Earth quiet and unchanged; the human soul
Consistent in self-rule; and heaven revealed
To meditation, in that quietness.
                    — Wordsworth, *Excursion*, Book iii.
            (MP II, Pt. III, Sec. I, Ch. VII, paras. 3–4)

Veronese and Hope
— 'the portrait of Veronese's family painted by himself'

He wishes to represent them as happy and honoured [Plate 28]. The best happiness and highest honour he can imagine for them is that they should be presented to the Madonna, to whom, therefore, they are being brought by the three virtues — Faith, Hope, and Charity.

The Virgin stands in a recess behind two marble shafts, such as may be seen in any house belonging to an old family in Venice. She places the boy Christ on the edge of a balustrade before her. At her side are St John the Baptist, and St Jerome. This group occupies the left side of the picture. The pillars, seen sideways, divide it from the group formed by the Virtues, with the wife and children of Veronese. He himself stands a little behind, his hands clasped in prayer.

His wife kneels full in front, a strong Venetian woman, well advanced in years. She has brought up her children in fear of God, and is not afraid to meet the Virgin's eyes. She gazes steadfastly on them; her proud head and gentle, self-possessed face are relieved in one broad mass of shadow against a space of light, formed by the white robes of Faith, who stands beside her — guardian, and companion. Perhaps a somewhat disappointing Faith at the first sight, for her face is not in any special way exalted or refined. Veronese knew that Faith had to companion simple and slow-hearted people, perhaps oftener than able or refined people — does not therefore insist on her being severely intellectual, or looking as if she were always in the best company. So she is only distinguished by her pure white (not bright white) dress, her delicate hand, her golden hair drifted in light ripples across her breast, from which the white robes fall nearly in the shape of a shield — the shield of Faith. A little behind her stands Hope; she also, at first,

Plate 28 *A Family Group*

not to most people a recognizable Hope. We usually paint Hope as young, and joyous. Veronese knows better. The young hope is vain hope – passing away in rain of tears; but the Hope of Veronese is aged, assured, remaining when all else has been taken away. 'For tribulation worketh patience, and patience experience, and experience hope' ; and *that* hope maketh not ashamed [Romans v. 3, 5].

She has a black veil on her head.

(MP V, Pt. IX, Ch. III, paras. 19–20)

Veronese and Peace
– but not the falsest kind of Peace which consists in 'that marvellous thought that we, of all generations of the earth, only know the right'

Another kind of peace I look for than this, though I hear it said of me that I am hopeless.

I am not hopeless, though my hope may be as Veronese's: the dark-veiled.

Veiled, not because sorrowful, but because blind. I do not know what my England desires, or how long she will choose to do as she is doing now; – with her right hand casting away the souls of men, and with her left the gifts of God.

(MP V, Pt. IX, Ch. XII, para. 18)

* * *

Postscript: 'The Mystery of Life and its Arts'

'What is your life? It is even as a vapour that appeareth for a little time, and then vanisheth away.' [James iv. 14].

I suppose few people reach the middle or latter period of their age, without having, at some moment of change or disappointment, felt the truth of those bitter words; and been startled by the fading of the sunshine from the cloud of their life into the sudden agony of the knowledge that the fabric of it was as fragile as a dream, and the endurance of it as transient as the dew. But it is not always that, even at such times of melancholy surprise, we can enter into any true perception that this human life shares in the nature of it, not only the evanescence, but the mystery of the cloud; that its avenues are wreathed in darkness, and its forms and courses no less fantastic, than spectral and obscure; so that not only in the vanity which we cannot grasp, but in the shadow which we cannot pierce, it is true of this cloudy life of ours, that 'man walketh in a vain shadow, and disquieteth himself in vain' [Psalms xxxix. 7].

And least of all, whatever may have been the eagerness of our passions, or the height of our pride, are we able to understand in its depth the third and most solemn character in which our life is like those clouds of heaven; that to it belongs not only their transience, not only their mystery, but also their power; that in the cloud of the human soul there is a fire stronger than the lightning, and a grace more precious than the rain; and that though of the good and evil it shall one day be said alike, that the place that knew them knows them no more [Psalms ciii. 16], there is an infinite separation between those whose brief presence had there been a blessing, like the mist of Eden that went up from the earth to water the garden [Genesis ii. 6], and those whose place knew them only as a drifting and changeful shade, of whom the heavenly sentence is, that they are 'wells without water; clouds that are carried with a tempest, to whom the mist of darkness is reserved for ever' [2 Peter ii. 17].

To those among us, however, who have lived long enough to form some just estimate of the rate of the changes which are, hour by hour in accelerating catastrophe, manifesting themselves in the laws, the arts, and the creeds of men, it seems to me, that now at least, if never at any former time, the thoughts of the true nature of our life, and of its powers and responsibilities, should present themselves with absolute sadness and sternness. And although I know that this feeling is much deepened in my own mind by disappointment, which, by chance, has attended the greater number of my cherished purposes, I do not for that reason distrust the feeling itself, though I am on my guard against an exaggerated degree of it: nay, I rather believe that in periods of new effort and violent change, disappointment is a wholesome medicine; and that in the secret of it, as in the twilight so beloved by Titian, we may see the colours of things with deeper truth than in the most dazzling sunshine. And because these truths about the works of men, which I want to bring to-day before you, are most of them sad ones, though at the same time helpful; and because also I believe that your kind Irish hearts will answer more gladly to the truthful expression of a personal feeling, than to the exposition of an abstract principle, I will permit myself so much unreserved speaking of my own causes of regret, as may enable you to make just allowance for what, according to your sympathies, you will call either the bitterness, or the insight, of a mind which has surrendered its best hopes, and been foiled in its favourite aims.

I spent the ten strongest years of my life, (from twenty to thirty,) in endeavouring to show the excellence of the work of the man [Turner] whom I believed, and rightly believed, to be the greatest painter of the schools of England since Reynolds. I had then perfect faith in the power of every great truth of beauty to prevail ultimately, and take its right place in usefulness and honour; and I strove to bring the painter's work into this due place, while the painter was yet alive. But he knew, better than I, the uselessness of talking about what people could not see for themselves. He always discouraged me scornfully, even when he thanked me – and he died before even the superficial effect of my work was visible. I went on, however, thinking I could at least be of use to the public, if not to him, in proving his power. My books got talked about a little. The prices of modern pictures, generally, rose, and I was beginning to take some pleasure in a sense of gradual victory, when, fortunately or unfortunately, an opportunity of perfect trial undeceived me at once, and for ever. The Trustees of the National Gallery commissioned me to arrange the Turner drawings there, and permitted me to prepare three hundred examples of his studies from nature, for exhibition at Kensington. At Kensington they were, and are, placed for exhibition; but they are not exhibited, for the room in which they hang is always empty.[18]

Well – this showed me at once, that those ten years of my life had been, in their chief purpose, lost. For that, I did not so much care; I had, at least, learned my own business thoroughly, and should be able, as I fondly supposed, after such a lesson, now to use my knowledge, with better effect. But what I did care for was the – to me frightful – discovery, that the most splendid genius in the arts might be permitted by Providence to labour and perish uselessly; that in the very fineness of it there might be something rendering it invisible to ordinary eyes; but that, with this strange excellence, faults might be mingled which would be as deadly as its virtues were vain; that the glory of it was perishable, as well as invisible, and the gift and grace of it might be to us as snow in summer and as rain in harvest [Proverbs xxvi. 1].

That was the first mystery of life to me. But, while my best energy was given to the study of painting, I had put collateral effort, more prudent if less enthusiastic, into that of architecture; and in this I could not complain of meeting with no sympathy. Among several personal reasons which caused me to desire that I might give this, my closing lecture on the subject of art here, in Ireland, one of the chief was, that in reading it, I should stand near the beautiful building, – the engineer's school of your college, –which was the first realization I had the joy to see, of the principles I had, until then, been endeavouring to teach! but which, alas, is now, to me, no more than the richly canopied monument of one of the most earnest souls that ever gave itself to the arts, and one of my truest and most loving friends, Benjamin Woodward . . .

You may perhaps think that no man ought to speak of disappointment, to whom, even in one branch of labour, so much success was granted. Had Mr Woodward now been beside me, I had not so spoken; but his gentle and passionate spirit was cut off from the fulfilment of its purposes, and the work we did together is now become vain. It may not be so in future; but the architecture we endeavoured to introduce is inconsistent alike with the reckless luxury, the deforming mechanism, and the squalid misery of modern cities; among the formative fashions of the day, aided, especially in England, by ecclesiastical sentiment, it indeed obtained notoriety; and sometimes behind an engine furnace, or a railroad bank, you may detect the pathetic discord of its momentary grace, and, with toil, decipher its floral carvings choked with soot. I felt answerable to the schools I loved, only for their injury. I perceived that this new portion of my strength had also been spent in vain; and from amidst streets of iron, and palaces of crystal, shrank back at last to the carving of the mountain and colour of the flower.[19]

And still I could tell of failure, and failure repeated, as years went on; but I have trespassed enough on your patience to show you, in part, the causes of my discouragement. Now let me more deliberately tell you its results. You know there is a tendency in the minds of many men, when they are heavily disappointed in the main purposes of their life, to feel, and perhaps in warning, perhaps in mockery, to declare, that life itself is a vanity. Because it has disappointed them, they think its nature is of disappointment always, or at best, of pleasure that can be grasped by imagination only; that the cloud of it has no strength nor fire within; but is a painted cloud only, to be delighted in, yet despised. You know how beautifully Pope has expressed this particular phase of thought:—

> Meanwhile opinion gilds, with varying rays,
> These painted clouds that beautify our days;
> Each want of happiness by hope supplied,
> And each vacuity of sense, by pride.
> Hope builds as fast as Knowledge can destroy;
> In Folly's cup, still laughs the bubble joy.
> One pleasure past, another still we gain,
> And not a vanity is given in vain.
>   [Pope, *Essay on Man* ii, 283–90]

But the effect of failure upon my own mind has been just the reverse of this. The more that my life disappointed me, the more solemn and wonderful it became to me. It seemed, contrarily to Pope's saying, that the vanity of it *was* indeed given in vain; but that there was something behind the veil of it, which was not vanity. It became to me not a painted cloud, but a terrible and impenetrable one: not a mirage, which vanished as I drew near, but a pillar of darkness, to which I was forbidden to draw near. For I saw that both my own failure, and such success in petty things as in its poor triumph seemed to me worse than failure, came from the want of sufficiently earnest effort to understand the whole law and meaning of existence, and to bring it to noble and due end; as, on the other hand, I saw more and more clearly that all enduring success in the arts, or in any other occupation, had come from the ruling of lower purposes, not by a conviction of their nothingness, but by a solemn faith in the advancing power of human nature, or in the promise, however dimly apprehended, that the mortal part of it would one day be swallowed up in immortality [2 Corinthians v. 4]; and that, indeed, the arts themselves never had reached any vital strength or honour, but in the effort to proclaim this immortality, and in the service either of great and just religion, or of some unselfish patriotism, and law of such national life as must be the foundation of religion.

Nothing that I have ever said is more true or necessary – nothing has been more misunderstood or misapplied – than my strong assertion that the arts can never be right themselves, unless their motive is right. It is misunderstood this way: weak painters, who have never learned their business, and cannot lay a true line, continually come to me, crying out – 'Look at this picture of mine; it *must* be good, I had such a lovely motive. I have put my whole heart into it, and taken years to think over its treatment.' Well, the only answer for these people is – if one had the cruelty to make it – 'Sir, you cannot think over *any*thing in any number of years, – you haven't the head to do it; and though you had fine motives, strong enough to make you burn yourself in a slow fire, if only first you could paint a picture, you can't paint one, nor half an inch of one; you haven't the hand to do it.'

But, far more decisively we have to say to the men who *do* know their business, or may know it if they choose – 'Sir, you have this gift, and a mighty one; see that you serve your nation faithfully with it. It is a greater trust than ships and armies: you might cast *them* away, if you were their captain, with less treason to your people than in casting your own glorious power away, and serving the devil with it instead of men. Ships and armies you may replace if they are lost, but a great intellect, once abused, is a curse to the earth for ever.'

This, then, I meant by saying that the arts must have noble motive. This also I said respecting them, that they never had prospered, nor could prosper, but when they had such true purpose, and were devoted to the proclamation of divine truth or law. And yet I saw also that they had always failed in this proclamation – that poetry, and sculpture, and painting, though only great when they strove to teach us something about the gods, never had taught us anything trustworthy about the gods, but had always betrayed their trust in the crisis of it, and, with their powers at the full reach, became ministers to pride and to lust. And I felt also, with increasing amazement, the unconquerable apathy in ourselves and hearers, no less than in these the teachers; and that while the wisdom and rightness of every act and art of life could only be consistent with a right understanding of the ends of life, we were all plunged as in a languid dream – our hearts fat, and our eyes heavy, and our ears closed, lest the inspiration of hand or voice should reach us – lest we should see with our eyes, and understand with our hearts and be healed [Isaiah vi. 10].

This intense apathy in all of us is the first great mystery of life; it stands in the way of every perception, every virtue. There is no making ourselves feel enough astonishment at it. That the occupations or pastimes of life should have no motive, is understandable; but – That life itself should have no motive – that we neither care to find out what it may lead to, nor to guard against its being for ever taken away from us – here is a mystery indeed. For just suppose I were able to call at this moment to any one in this audience by name, and to tell him positively that I knew a large estate had been lately left to him on some curious conditions; but that though I knew it was large, I did not know how large, nor even where it was – whether in the East Indies or the West, or in England, or at the Antipodes. I only knew it was a vast estate, and that there was a chance of his losing it altogether if he did not soon find out on what terms it had been left to him. Suppose I were able to say this positively to any single man in this audience, and he knew that I did not speak without warrant, do you think that he would rest content with that vague knowledge, if it were anywise possible to obtain more? Would he not give every energy to find some trace of the facts, and never rest till he had ascertained where this place was, and what it was like? And suppose he were a young man, and all he could discover by his best endeavour was that the estate was never to be his at all, unless he persevered, during certain years of probation, in an orderly and industrious life; but that, according to the rightness of his conduct, the portion of the estate assigned to him would be greater or less, so that it literally depended on his behaviour from day to day whether he got ten thousand a year, or thirty thousand a year, or nothing whatever – would you not think it strange if the youth never troubled himself to satisfy the conditions in any way, nor even to know what was required of him, but lived exactly as he chose, and never inquired whether his chances of the estate were increasing or passing away? Well, you know that this is actually and literally so with the greater number of the educated persons now living in Christian countries. Nearly every man and woman in any company such as this, outwardly professes to believe – and a large number unquestionably think they believe – much more than this; not only that a quite unlimited estate is in prospect for them if they please the Holder of it, but that the infinite contrary of such a possession – an estate of perpetual misery – is in store for them if they displease this great Land-Holder, this great Heaven-Holder. And yet there is not one in a thousand of these human souls that cares to think, for ten minutes of the day, where this estate is or how beautiful it is, or what kind of life they are to lead in it, or what kind of life they must lead to obtain it.

You fancy that you care to know this: so little do you care that, probably, at this moment many of you are displeased with me for talking of the matter! You came to hear about the Art of this world, not about the Life of the next, and you are provoked with me for talking of what you can hear any Sunday in church. But do not be afraid. I will tell you something before you go about pictures, and carvings, and pottery, and what else you would like better to hear of than the other world. Nay, perhaps you say, 'We want you to talk of pictures and pottery, because we are sure that you know something of them, and you know nothing of the other world.' Well – I don't. That is quite true. But the very strangeness and mystery of which I urge you to take notice, is in this – that I do not; – nor you either. Can you answer a single bold question unflinchingly about that other world? – Are you sure there is a heaven? Sure there is a hell? Sure that men are dropping before your faces through the pavements of these streets into eternal fire, or sure that they are not? Sure that at your own death you are going to be delivered from all sorrow, to be endowed with all virtue, to be gifted with all felicity, and raised into perpetual companionship with a King, compared to whom the kings of the earth are as grasshoppers, and the nations as the dust of His feet? [Isaiah xl. 15, 22; Nahum iii. 17, i. 3]. Are you sure of this? or, if not sure, do any of us so much as care to make it sure? and, if not, how can anything that we do be right – how can anything we think be wise? what honour can there be in the arts that amuse us, or what profit in the possessions that please?

Is not this a mystery of life? . . .

You sent for me to talk to you of art; and I have obeyed you in coming. But the main thing I have to tell you is, – that art must not be talked about. The fact that there is talk about it at all, signifies that it is ill done, or cannot be done. No true painter ever speaks, or ever has spoken, much of his art. The greatest speak nothing. Even Reynolds is no exception, for he wrote of all that he could not himself do, and was utterly silent respecting all that he himself did.

The moment a man can really do his work[1] he becomes speechless about it. All words become idle to him – all theories.

---

[1] *On the real meaning of 'doing' a thing*:

It will, perhaps appear to you, after a little farther thought, that to create anything in reality is to put life into it.

A poet, or creator, is therefore a person who puts things together, not as a watchmaker steel, or a shoemaker leather, but who puts life into them.

Does a bird need to theorize about building its nests, or boast of it when built? All good work is essentially done that way – without hesitation, without difficulty, without boasting; and in the doers of the best, there is an inner and involuntary power which approximates literally to the instinct of an animal – nay, I am certain that in the most perfect human artists, reason does *not* supersede instinct, but is added to an instinct as much more divine than that of the lower animals as the human body is more beautiful than theirs; that a great singer sings not with less instinct than the nightingale, but with more – only more various, applicable, and governable; that a great architect does not build with less instinct than the beaver or the bee, but with more – with an innate cunning of proportion that embraces all beauty, and a divine ingenuity of skill that improvises all construction. But be that as it may – be the instinct less or more than that of inferior animals – like or unlike theirs, still the human art is dependent on that first, and then upon an amount of practice, of science, – and of imagination disciplined by thought, which the true possessor of it knows to be incommunicable, and the true critic of it, inexplicable, except through long process of laborious years. That journey of life's conquest, in which hills over hills, and Alps on Alps arose [Pope, *Essay on Criticism* ii. 32], and sank, – do you think you can make another trace it painlessly, by talking? Why, you cannot even carry us up an Alp, by talking. You can guide us up it, step by step, no otherwise – even so, best silently. You girls, who have been among the hills, know how the bad guide chatters and gesticulates, and it is 'Put your foot here'; and 'Mind how you balance yourself there'; but the good guide walks on quietly, without a word, only with his eyes on you when need is, and his arm like an iron bar, if need be.

In that slow way, also, art can be taught – if you have faith in your guide, and will let his arm be to you as an iron bar when need is. But in what teacher of art have you such faith? Certainly not in me; for, as I told you at first, I know well enough it is only because you think I can talk, not because you think I know my business, that you let me speak to you at all. If I were to tell you anything

His work is essentially this: it is the gathering and arranging of material by imagination, so as to have in it at last the harmony or helpfulness of life, and the passion or emotion of life. Mere fitting, and adjustment of material is nothing; that is watchmaking. (MP V, Pt. VIII, Ch. I, para. 20)

that seemed to you strange you would not believe it, and yet it would only be in telling you strange things that I could be of use to you. I could be of great use to you – infinite use – with brief saying, if you would believe it; but you would not, just because the thing that would be of real use would displease you. You are all wild, for instance, with admiration of Gustave Doré. Well, suppose I were to tell you, in the strongest terms I could use, that Gustave Doré's art was bad – bad, not in weakness, – not in failure, – but bad with dreadful power – the power of the Furies and the Harpies mingled, enraging, and polluting; that so long as you looked at it, no perception of pure or beautiful art was possible for you. Suppose I were to tell you that! What would be the use? Would you look at Gustave Doré less? Rather, more, I fancy. On the other hand, I could soon put you into good humour with me, if I chose. I know well enough what you like, and how to praise it to your better liking. I could talk to you about moonlight, and twilight, and spring flowers, and autumn leaves, and the Madonnas of Raphael – how motherly! and the Sibyls of Michael Angelo – how majestic! and the Saints of Angelico – how pious! and the Cherubs of Correggio – how delicious! Old as I am, I could play you a tune on the harp yet, that you would dance to. But neither you nor I should be a bit the better or wiser; or, if we were, our increased wisdom could be of no practical effect. For, indeed, the arts, as regards teachableness, differ from the sciences also in this, that their power is founded not merely on facts which can be communicated, but on dispositions which require to be created. Art is neither to be achieved by effort of thinking, nor explained by accuracy of speaking. It is the instinctive and necessary result of power, which can only be developed through the mind of successive generations, and which finally burst into life under social conditions as slow of growth as the faculties they regulate. Whole æras of mighty history are summed, and the passions of dead myriads are concentrated, in the existence of a noble art; and if that noble art were among us, we should feel it and rejoice; not caring in the least to hear lectures on it; and since it is not among us, be assured we have to go back to the root of it, or, at least, to the place where the stock of it is yet alive, and the branches began to die . . .

And now, returning to the broader question, what these arts and labours of life have to teach us of its mystery, this is the first of their lessons – that the more beautiful the art, the more it is essentially the work of people who *feel themselves wrong*; – who are striving for the fulfilment of a law, and the grasp of a loveliness, which they have not yet attained, which they feel even farther and farther from attaining the more they strive for it. And yet, in still deeper sense, it is the work of people who know also that they are right. The very sense of inevitable error from their purpose marks the perfectness of that purpose, and the continued sense of failure arises from the continued opening of the eyes more clearly to all the sacredest laws of truth.

This is one lesson. The second is a very plain, and greatly precious one: namely – that whenever the arts and labours of life are fulfilled in this spirit of striving against misrule, and doing whatever we have to do, honourably and perfectly, they invariably bring happiness, as much as seems possible to the nature of man.[m] In all other paths by which that happiness is pursued

[m] *Ruskin had put it thus with regard to human work in his introduction to* The Seven Lamps of Architecture:

There is no branch of human work whose constant laws have not close analogy with those which govern every other mode of man's exertion. But, more than this, exactly as we reduce to greater simplicity and surety any one group of these practical laws, we shall find them passing the mere condition of connection or analogy, and becoming the actual expression of some ultimate nerve or fibre of the mighty laws which govern the moral world. However mean or inconsiderable the act, there is something in the well doing of it, which has fellowship with the noblest forms of manly virtue; and the truth, decision, and temperance, which we reverently regard as honourable conditions of the spiritual being, have a representative or derivative influence over the works of the hand, the movements of the frame, and the action of the intellect.

And as thus every action, down even to the drawing of a line or utterance of a syllable, is capable of a peculiar dignity in the manner of it, which we sometimes express by saying it is truly done (as a line or tone is true), so also it is capable of dignity still higher in the motive of it. For there is no action so slight, nor so mean, but it may be done to a great purpose, and ennobled therefore; nor is any purpose so great but that slight actions may help it, and may be so done as to help it much, most especially that chief of all purposes, the pleasing of God. Hence George Herbert—

> A servant with this clause
> Makes drudgery divine;
> Who sweeps a room, *as for Thy laws*,
> Makes that and the action fine.   'The Elixir'

(SL, 'Introductory' paras. 4–5)

there is disappointment, or destruction: for ambition and for passion there is no rest – no fruition; the fairest pleasures of youth perish in a darkness greater than their past light . . .

And out of such exertion in plain duty all other good will come; for in this direct contention with material evil, you will find out the real nature of all evil; you will discern by the various kinds of resistance, what is really the fault and main antagonism to good; also you will find the most unexpected helps and profound lessons given, and truths will come thus down to us which the speculation of all our lives would never have raised us up to. You will find nearly every educational problem solved, as soon as you truly want to do something; everybody will become of use in their own fittest way, and will learn what is best for them to know in that use. (*Sesame*, Lecture III, paras. 98–109, 120–2, 127–8, 131)

CHAPTER 7

Epilogue: Ruskin the Man

So much of Ruskin went into his work that the meaning of his life is inseparable from it. Nonetheless this chapter offers a last view of Ruskin from a position just outside the work: above it and after it. It is a view of that 'personal character' detectable all along: 'which, without endeavour to conceal, I yet have never taken pains to display' (preface to Praeterita, *C&W XXXV, p. 11).*

A position above *the work refers to those moments in prefaces and lectures when Ruskin, surfacing for a moment, detaches himself from the immersed detail of his concerns and re-asserts the anterior principles deeply implicit in his investigations. This is Ruskin speaking out, offering his own brave provocatively puckish voice. For he sought to draw out equivalent innerly responding voices from his audience, in the lecture hall or study, in the effort to establish some community of belief in England.*

For a sense of Ruskin after *his work, the crucial document is his autobiography,* Praeterita *(1885–9). Written in the midst of weariness as at the end of a strained life,* Praeterita *is about decay and failure, and physical and spiritual dying – composed in a quiet style, itself the remains of the decay it describes. By the time of its writing, Ruskin felt himself to be a man from yesterday:*

> The reader of 'to-day' who has been accustomed to hear me spoken of by the artists of to-day as a super-annuated enthusiast, and by the philosophers of to-day as a delirious visionary, will scarcely believe with what serious interest the appearance of the second volume of *Modern Painters* was looked for, by more people than my father and mother, – by people even belonging to the shrewdest literary circles, and highest artistic schools, of the time. (Vol. II, Ch. IX, para. 164)

He was a disappointed man who felt he had lived in a society that seemed more and more to have judged both him and what he cared for to be useless:

> I used to fancy that everybody would like clouds and rocks as well as I did, if once to look at them; whereas, after fifty years of trial, I

find that is not so, even in modern days; having long known that, in ancient ones, the clouds and mountains which have been life to me, were mere inconvenience and horror to most of mankind. (Vol. II, Ch. I, para. 1)

Many and many an hour of precious time and perfect sight was spent, during these years, in thus watching skies; much was written which would be useful – if I took a year to put it together, – to myself; but, in the present smoky world, to no other creature: and much was learned, which is of no use now to anybody; for to me it is only sorrowful memory, and to others, an old man's fantasy. (Vol. II, Ch. V, para. 94)

Ruskin had now to give up his universalist ambitions and be no more than a partial and mortal person, eschewing violent or painful memories for the sake of his remaining mental health. The lost potential of the past – the 'might-have-beens' and 'if-onlys' – settle into something residually and resignedly factual. Praeterita is a sort of writing off or signing off.

Yet amidst this decay Praeterita is also, for all its account of failures and even because of the weaknesses, itself a success in the very act of writing. As such, it is the very last of Ruskin's ambiguities and contradictions.

The weak only child, 'the little floppy and soppy tadpole' (Vol. II, Ch. III, para. 42), managed to champion Turner strongly. 'Looking out of myself, I saw farther than Kings of Naples or Cardinals of Rome' (Vol. II, Ch. IV, para. 79). The son, who felt choked by the puritanical narrowness of his home and antipathetic to his father's business interests, still depended on his father for the money to travel abroad, to study and to buy Turners. Later he even thought that the very disadvantages of his evangelical background had helped him 'feel by contrast the divine wildness of Jura forest' (Vol. I, Ch. IX, para. 190). But the human relationship with his father ironically deteriorated in a dispute over Ruskin's study of architecture, just when that study was teaching him more than ever about the human meaning of art. This then is a man whose personal, family and sexual life seems so small. Yet he himself believed that his most real life could not be described merely in terms of time or personal history but belonged instead to the great spaces and places of the world. This was a writer who put his whole life into art while believing in art only for the sake of human life. These are the matters that the excerpts from Praeterita finally touch upon. They are arranged in

*four subsections: Ruskin as only child, the relationship with his
father, love and women, the central places of his life.*

Finally, all the apparent inconsistencies may not be signs that
Ruskin's belief in one whole life was simply a grievous error. The
wish not to disguise the contradictions but to invite and interro-
gate them, the pained readiness to consider how far they were
merely personal failings, are themselves testimony to the power of
Ruskin's continuing belief in the unity of things – even down to
the last paragraph of Praeterita itself.

On Speaking Out
'Too keenly to be silent'

The memoranda which form the basis of the following Essay have
been thrown together during the preparation of one of the sections
of the third volume of *Modern Painters*. I once thought of giving
them a more expanded form; but their utility, such as it may be,
would probably be diminished by farther delay in their publication, more than it would be increased by greater care in their
arrangement. Obtained in every case by personal observation,
there may be among them some details valuable even to the
experienced architect; but with respect to the opinions founded
upon them I must be prepared to bear the charge of impertinence
which can hardly but attach to the writer who assumes a
dogmatical tone in speaking of an art he has never practised.
There are, however, cases in which men feel too keenly to be
silent, and perhaps too strongly to be wrong; I have been forced
into this impertinence; and have suffered too much from the
destruction or neglect of the architecture I best loved, and from
the erection of that which I cannot love, to reason cautiously
respecting the modesty of my opposition to the principles which
have induced the scorn of the one or directed the design of the
other. And I have been the less careful to modify the confidence of
my statements of principles, because, in the midst of the
opposition and uncertainty of our architectural systems, it seems
to me that there is something grateful in any *positive* opinion,
though in many points wrong, as even weeds are useful that grow
on a bank of sand. (SL, Preface to the first edition [1849], para. 1
[C&W VIII, p. 3])

'Positive Opinion'

As the statements briefly made in the chapters on Construction
involve questions so difficult and so general . . . I cannot hope that
every expression referring to them will be found free from error:
and as the conclusions to which I have endeavoured to lead the
reader are thrown into a form the validity of which depends on
that of each successive step, it might be argued, if fallacy or
weakness could be detected in one of them, that all the subsequent
reasonings were valueless. The reader may be assured, however,
that it is not so; the method of proof used in the following essay
being only one out of many which were in my choice, adopted
because it seemed to me the shortest and simplest, not as being the
strongest. In many cases, the conclusions are those which men of
quick feeling would arrive at instinctively; and I then sought to
discover the reasons of what so strongly recommended itself as
truth. Though these reasons could every one of them, from the
beginning to the end of the book, be proved insufficient, the truth
of its conclusions would remain the same. I should only regret that
I had dishonoured them by an ill-grounded defence; and endeavour to repair my error by a better one. (SVI, Preface to first
edition [1851], para. 4 [C&W IX, p. 7])

'Do it'

Some years ago, in conversation with an artist [William
Mulready] whose works, perhaps, alone, in the present day, unite
perfection of drawing with resplendence of colour, the writer
made some inquiry respecting the general means by which this
latter quality was most easily to be attained. The reply was as
concise as it was comprehensive – 'Know what you have to do,
and do it' – comprehensive, not only as regarded the branch of art
to which it temporarily applied, but as expressing the great
principle of success in every direction of human effort; for I
believe that failure is less frequently attributable to either
insufficiency of means or impatience of labour, than to a confused
understanding of the thing actually to be done; and therefore,
while it is properly a subject of ridicule, and sometimes of blame,
that men propose to themselves a perfection of any kind, which
reason, temperately consulted, might have shown to be impossible with the means at their command, it is a more dangerous

error to permit the consideration of means to interfere with our conception, or, as is not impossible, even hinder our acknowledgment of goodness and perfection in themselves. And this is the more cautiously to be remembered; because, while a man's sense and conscience, aided by Revelation, are always enough, if earnestly directed, to enable him to discover what is right, neither his sense, nor conscience, nor feeling, is ever enough, because they are not intended, to determine for him what is possible. He knows

APHORISM

We may always know what is right: but not always what is possible.

neither his own strength nor that of his fellows, neither the exact dependence to be placed on his allies nor resistance to be expected from his opponents. These are questions respecting which passion may warp his conclusions, and ignorance must limit them; but it is his own fault if either interfere with the apprehension of duty, or the acknowledgment of right. And, as far as I have taken cognizance of the causes of the many failures to which the efforts of intelligent men are liable, more especially, in matters political, they seem to me more largely to spring from this single error than from all others, that the inquiry into the doubtful, and in some sort inexplicable, relations of capability, chance, resistance, and inconvenience, invariably precedes, even if it do not altogether supersede, the determination of what is absolutely desirable and just. Nor is it any wonder that sometimes the too cold calculation of our powers should reconcile us too easily to our shortcomings, and even lead us into the fatal error of supposing that our conjectural utmost is in itself well, or, in other words, that the necessity of offences renders them inoffensive. (SL, 'Introductory', para. 1 [C&W VIII, pp. 19–20])

'Say what you like truly'

For to what shall we trust for our distinction from the beasts that perish [Psalms xlix. 12,20]? To our higher intellect? – yet are we not bidden to be wise as the serpent [Matthew x. 16], and to consider the ways of the ant [Proverbs vi. 6]? Or to our affections? nay; these are more shared by the lower animals than our intelligence: – Hamlet leaps into the grave of his beloved, and leaves it, – a dog would have stayed. Humanity and immortality consist neither in reason, nor in love; not in the body, nor in the animation of the heart of it, nor in the thoughts and stirrings of the brain of it, – but in the dedication of them all to Him who will raise them up at the last day [John vi. 40, 44, 54].

It is not, therefore, that the signs of his affections, which man leaves upon his work, are indeed more ennobling than the signs of his intelligence; but it is the balance of both whose expression we need, and the signs of the government of them all by Conscience; and Discretion, the Daughter of Conscience. So, then, the intelligent part of man being eminently, if not chiefly, displayed in the structure of his work, his affectionate part is to be shown in its decoration; and, that decoration may be indeed lovely, two things are needed: first, that the affections be vivid, and honestly shown; secondly, that they be fixed on the right things.

You think, perhaps, I have put the requirements in wrong order. Logically I have; practically I have not: for it is necessary first to teach men to speak out, and say what they like, truly; and, in the second place, to teach them which of their likings are ill set, and which justly. If a man is cold in his likings and dislikings, or if he will not tell you what he likes, you can make nothing of him. Only get him to feel quickly and to speak plainly, and you may set him right. And the fact is, that the great evil of all recent architectural effort has not been that men liked wrong things; but that they either cared nothing about any, or pretended to like what they did not. . . .

Of common buildings, built in common circumstances, it is very possible for every man, or woman, or child, to form judgment both rational and rapid. Their necessary, or even possible, features are but few; the laws of their construction are as simple as they are interesting. The labour of a few hours is enough to render the reader master of their main points; and from that moment he will find in himself a power of judgment which can neither be escaped nor deceived, and discover subjects of interest where everything before had appeared barren. For though the laws are few and simple, the modes of obedience to them are not so.[a] Every

[a] *On laws and commandments:*
The law is fixed and everlasting; uttered once, abiding for ever, as the sun, it may not be moved. It is 'perfect, converting the soul': the whole question about the soul being, whether it has been turned from darkness to light, acknowledged this law or not, – whether it is godly or ungodly? But the commandment is given momentarily to each man, according to the need. It does not convert: it guides. It does not concern the entire purpose of the soul: but it enlightens the

building presents it own requirements and difficulties: and every good building has peculiar appliances or contrivances to meet them. Understand the laws of structure, and you will feel the special difficulty in every new building which you approach; and you will know also, or feel instinctively, whether it has been wisely met or otherwise. And an enormous number of buildings, and of styles of building, you will be able to cast aside at once, as at variance with these constant laws of structure, and therefore unnatural and monstrous.

Then, as regards decoration, I want you only to consult your own natural choice and liking. There is a right and wrong in it; but you will assuredly like the right if you suffer your natural instinct to lead you. Half the evil in this world comes from people not knowing what they do like; – not deliberately setting themselves to find out what they really enjoy. All people enjoy giving away money, for instance: they don't know *that*, – they rather think they like keeping it; – and they *do* keep it, under this false impression, often to their great discomfort. Everybody likes to do good; but not one in a hundred finds *this* out. Multitudes think they like to do evil; yet no man ever really enjoyed doing evil since God made the world.

So in this lesser matter of ornament. It needs some little care to try experiments upon yourself; it needs deliberate question and upright answer. But there is no difficulty to be overcome, no abstruse reasoning to be gone into; only a little watchfulness needed, and thoughtfulness, and so much honesty as will enable you to confess to yourself, and to all men, that you enjoy things, though great authorities say you should not.

This looks somewhat like pride; but it is true humility, a trust that you have been so created as to enjoy what is fitting for you, and a willingness to be pleased, as it was intended you should be. It is the child's spirit, which we are most happy when we most recover; remaining wiser than children in our gratitude that we can still be pleased with a fair colour, or a dancing light. And,

eyes, respecting a special act. The law is, 'Do this always'; the commandment, 'Do *thou* this *now*': often mysterious enough, and through the cloud; chilling, and with strange rain of tears; yet always pure (the law converting, but the commandment cleansing): a rod not for guiding merely, but for strengthening, and tasting honey with. 'Look how mine eyes have been enlightened, because I tasted a little of this honey' [I Samuel xiv. 29] (MP V, Pt. VII, Ch. IV, para. 32] above all, do not try to make all these pleasures reasonable, nor to connect the delight which you take in ornament with that which you take in construction or usefulness. (SV I, Ch. II, paras. 10–12, 15–17)

'What we like . . . what we are' – 'Of Traffic'

My good Yorkshire friends, you asked me down here among your hills that I might talk to you about this Exchange you are going to build: but, earnestly and seriously asking you to pardon me, I am going to do nothing of the kind. I cannot talk, or at least can say very little, about this same Exchange. I must talk of quite other things, though not willingly; – I could not deserve your pardon, if, when you invited me to speak on one subject, I *wilfully* spoke on another. But I cannot speak, to purpose, of anything about which I do not care; and most simply and sorrowfully I have to tell you, in the outset, that I do *not* care about this Exchange of yours.

If, however, when you sent me your invitation, I had answered, 'I won't come, I don't care about the Exchange of Bradford,' you would have been justly offended with me, not knowing the reasons of so blunt a carelessness. So I have come down, hoping that you will patiently let me tell you why, on this, and many other such occasions, I now remain silent, when formerly I should have caught at the opportunity of speaking to a gracious audience.

In a word, then, I do not care about this Exchange – because *you* don't; and because you know perfectly well I cannot make you. Look at the essential conditions of the case, which you, as business men, know perfectly well, though perhaps you think I forget them. You are going to spend £30,000, which to you, collectively, is nothing; the buying a new coat is, as to the cost of it, a much more important matter of consideration to me, than building a new Exchange is to you. But you think you may as well have the right thing for your money. You know there are a great many odd styles of architecture about; you don't want to do anything ridiculous; you hear of me, among others, as a respectable architectural man-milliner; and you send for me, that I may tell you the leading fashion; and what is, in our shops, for the moment, the newest and sweetest thing in pinnacles.

Now, pardon me for telling you frankly, you cannot have good architecture merely by asking people's advice on occasion. All good architecture is the expression of national life and character;

and it is produced by a prevalent and eager national taste, or desire for beauty. And I want you to think a little of the deep significance of this word 'taste'; for no statement of mine has been more earnestly or oftener controverted than that good taste is essentially a moral quality.[b] 'No,' say many of my antagonists,

[b] *This word 'taste'*:

Meanwhile, the art of sculpture, less capable of ministering to mere amusement, was more or less reserved for the affectations of taste; and the study of the classical statues introduced various ideas on the subjects of 'purity', 'chastity', and 'dignity', such as it was possible for people to entertain who were themselves impure, luxurious, and ridiculous. It is a matter of extreme difficulty to explain the exact character of this modern sculpturesque ideal; but its relation to the true ideal may be best understood by considering it as in exact parallelism with the relation of the word 'taste' to the word 'love'. Wherever the word 'taste' is used with respect to matters of art, it indicates either that the thing being spoken of belongs to some inferior class of objects, or that the person speaking has a false conception of its nature. For, consider the exact sense in which a work of art is said to be 'in good or bad taste'. It does not mean that it is true or false; that it is beautiful or ugly: but that it does or does not comply either with the laws of choice, which are enforced by certain modes of life, or the habits of mind produced by a particular sort of education. It does not mean merely fashionable, that is, complying with a momentary caprice of the upper classes; but it means agreeing with the habitual sense which the most refined education, common to those upper classes at the period, gives to their whole mind. Now, therefore, so far as that education does indeed tend to make the senses delicate, and the perceptions accurate, and thus enables people to be pleased with quiet instead of gaudy colour, and with graceful instead of coarse form; and, by long acquaintance with the best things, to discern quickly what is fine from what is common; – so far, acquired taste is an honourable faculty, and it is true praise of anything to say it is 'in good taste'. But so far as this higher education has a tendency to narrow the sympathies and harden the heart, diminishing the interest of all beautiful things by familiarity, until even what is best can hardly please, and what is brightest hardly entertain; – so far as it fosters pride, and leads men to found the pleasure they take in anything, not on the worthiness of the thing, but on the degree in which it indicates some greatness of their own (as people build marble porticoes, and inlay marble floors, not so much because they like the colours of marble, or find it pleasant to the foot, as because such porches and floors are costly, and separated in all human eyes from plain entrances of stone and timber); – so far as it leads people to prefer gracefulness of dress, manner, and aspect, to value of substance and heart, liking a well *said* thing better than a true thing, and a well-trained manner better than a sincere one, and a delicately formed face better than a good-natured one, and in all other ways and things setting custom and semblance above everlasting truth; – so far, finally, as it induces a sense of 'taste is one thing, morality is another. Tell us what is pretty: we shall be glad to know that; but we need no sermons – even were you able to preach them, which may be doubted.'

Permit me, therefore, to fortify this old dogma of mine somewhat. Taste is not only a part and an index of morality; – it is the ONLY morality. The first, and last, and closest trial question to any living creature is, 'What do you like?' Tell me what you like, and I'll tell you what you are. Go out into the street, and ask the first man or woman you meet, what their 'taste' is; and if they

inherent distinction between class and class, and causes everything to be more or less despised which has no social rank, so that the affection, pleasure, and grief of a clown are looked upon as of no interest compared with the affection and grief of a well-bred man; – just so far, in all these several ways, the feeling induced by what is called a 'liberal education' is utterly adverse to the understanding of noble art; and the name which is given to the feeling, – Taste, Goût, Gusto, – in all languages indicates the baseness of it, for it implies that art gives only a kind of pleasure analogous to that derived from eating by the palate. (MP III, Pt. IV, Ch. V, para. 6)

Compare Ruskin on the word 'urbane' in a discussion of trees:
Being thus prepared for us in all ways, and made beautiful, and good for food, and for building, and for instruments of our hands, this race of plants, deserving boundless affection and admiration from us, becomes, in proportion to their obtaining it, a nearly perfect test of our being in right temper of mind and way of life; so that no one can be far wrong in either who loves the trees enough, and every one is assuredly wrong in both who does not love them, if his life has brought them in his way. It is clearly possible to do without them, for the great companionship of the sea and sky are all that sailors need; and many a noble heart has been taught the best it had to learn between dark stone walls. Still if human life be cast among trees at all, the love borne to them is a sure test of its purity. And it is a sorrowful proof of the mistaken ways of the world that the 'country', in the simple sense of a place of fields and trees, has hitherto been the source of reproach to its inhabitants, and that the words 'countryman, rustic, clown, paysan, villager', still signify a rude and untaught person, as opposed to the words 'townsman' and 'citizen'. We accept this usage of words, or the evil which it signifies, somewhat too quietly; as if it were quite necessary and natural that country-people should be rude, and townspeople gentle. Whereas I believe that the result of each mode of life may, in some stages of the world's progress, be the exact reverse; and that another use of words may be forced upon us by a new aspect of facts, so that we may find ourselves saying: 'Such and such a person is very gentle and kind – he is quite rustic; and such and such another person is very rude and ill-taught – he is quite urbane.' (MP V, Pt. VI, Ch. I, para. 4)

and on the word 'gentleman':
And, though rightness of moral conduct is ultimately the great purifier of race,

answer candidly, you know them, body and soul. 'You, my friend in the rags, with the unsteady gait, what do *you* like?' 'A pipe, and a quartern of gin.' I know you. 'You, good woman, with the quick step and tidy bonnet, what do you like?' 'A swept hearth, and a clean tea-table; and my husband opposite me, and a baby at my breast.' Good, I know you also. 'You, little girl with the golden hair and the soft eyes, what do you like?' 'My canary, and a run among the wood hyacinths.' 'You, little boy with the dirty hands, and the low forehead, what do you like?' 'A shy at the sparrows, and a game at pitch farthing.' Good; we know them all now. What more need we ask?

'Nay,' perhaps you answer; 'we need rather to ask what these people and children do, than what they like. If they *do* right, it is no matter that they like what is wrong; and if they *do* wrong, it is no matter that they like what is right. Doing is the great thing; and it does not matter that the man likes drinking, so that he does not drink; nor that the little girl likes to be kind to her canary, if she will not learn her lessons; nor that the little boy likes throwing stones at the sparrows, if he goes to the Sunday school.' Indeed, for a short time, and in a provisional sense, this is true. For if, resolutely, people do what is right, in time to come they like doing it. But they only are in a right moral state when they *have* come to like doing it; and as long as they don't like it, they are still in a vicious state. The man is not in health of body who is always thinking of the bottle in the cupboard, though he bravely bears his thirst; but the man who heartily enjoys water in the morning, and

the sign of nobleness is not in this rightness of moral conduct, but in sensitiveness. When the make of the creature is fine, its temptations are strong, as well as its perceptions; it is liable to all kinds of impressions from without in their most violent form; liable therefore to be abused and hurt by all kinds of rough things which would do a coarser creature little harm, and thus to fall into frightful wrong if its fate will have it so. Thus David, coming of gentlest as well as royalest race, of Ruth as well as of Judah, is sensitiveness through all flesh and spirit; not that his compassion will restrain him from murder when his terror urges him to it; nay, he is driven to the murder all the more by his sensitiveness to the shame which otherwise threatens him. But when his own story is told under a disguise, though only a lamb is now concerned, his passion about it leaves him no time for thought. 'The man shall die' – note the reason – 'because he had no pity' [2 Samuel xii, 5, 6]. He is so eager and indignant that it never occurs to him as strange that Nathan hides the name. This is true gentleman. A vulgar man would assuredly have been cautious, and asked who it was. (MP V, Pt. IX, Ch. VII, para. 6)

wine in the evening, each in its proper quantity and time. And the entire object of true education is to make people not merely *do* the right things, but *enjoy* the right things: — not merely industrious, but to love industry — not merely learned, but to love knowledge —not merely pure, but to love purity — not merely just, but to hunger and thirst after justice [Matthew v. 6] . . .

And it is not an indifferent nor optional thing whether we love this or that; but it is just the vital function of all our being. What we *like* determines what we *are*, and is the sign of what we are; and to teach taste is inevitably to form character.

I notice that among all the new buildings which cover your once wild hills, churches and schools are mixed in due, that is to say, in large proportion, with your mills and mansions; and I notice also that the churches and schools are almost always Gothic, and the mansions and mills are never Gothic. May I ask the meaning of this? for, remember, it is peculiarly a modern phenomenon. When Gothic was invented, houses were Gothic as well as churches; and when the Italian style superseded the Gothic, churches were Italian as well as houses. If there is a Gothic spire to the cathedral of Antwerp, there is a Gothic belfry to the Hôtel de Ville at Brussels; if Inigo Jones builds an Italian Whitehall, Sir Christopher Wren builds an Italian St Paul's. But now you live under one school of architecture, and worship under another. What do you mean by doing this? Am I to understand that you are thinking of changing your architecture back to Gothic; and that you treat your churches experimentally, because it does not matter what mistakes you make in a church? Or am I to understand that you consider Gothic a pre-eminently sacred and beautiful mode of building, which you think, like the fine frankincense, should be mixed for the tabernacle only, and reserved for your religious services? For if this be the feeling, though it may seem at first as if it were graceful and reverent, at the root of the matter, it signifies neither more nor less than that you have separated your religion from your life. . . .

Now, you feel, as I say this to you — I know you feel — as if I were trying to take away the honour of your churches. Not so; I am trying to prove to you the honour of your houses and your hills; not that the Church is not sacred — but that the whole Earth is. I would have you feel what careless, what constant, what infectious sin there is in all modes of thought, whereby, in calling your churches only 'holy', you call your hearths and homes 'profane';

and have separated yourselves from the heathen by casting all your household gods to the ground, instead of recognizing, in the places of their many and feeble Lares, the presence of your One and Mighty Lord and Lar.

'But what has all this to do with our Exchange?' you ask me, impatiently. My dear friends, it has just everything to do with it; on these inner and great questions depend all the outer and little ones; and if you have asked me down here to speak to you, because you had before been interested in anything I have written, you must know that all I have yet said about architecture was to show this. The book I called *The Seven Lamps* was to show that certain right states of temper and moral feeling were the magic powers by which all good architecture, without exception, had been produced. *The Stones of Venice* had, from beginning to end, no other aim than to show that the Gothic architecture of Venice had arisen out of, and indicated in all its features, a state of pure national faith, and of domestic virtue; and that its Renaissance architecture had arisen out of, and in all its features indicated, a state of concealed national infidelity, and of domestic corruption. And now, you ask me what style is best to build in, and how can I answer, knowing the meaning of the two styles, but by another question – do you mean to build as Christians or as infidels? And still more – do you mean to build as honest Christians or as honest Infidels? as thoroughly and confessedly either one or the other? You don't like to be asked such rude questions. I cannot help it; they are of much more importance than this Exchange business; and if they can be at once answered, the Exchange business settles itself in a moment. But before I press them farther, I must ask leave to explain one point clearly.

In all my past work, my endeavour has been to show that good architecture is essentially religious – the production of a faithful and virtuous, not of an infidel and corrupted people. But in the course of doing this, I have had also to show that good architecture is not *ecclesiastical*. People are so apt to look upon religion as the business of the clergy, not their own, that the moment they hear of anything depending on 'religion', they think it must also have depended on the priesthood; and I have had to take what place was to be occupied between these two errors, and fight both, often with seeming contradiction. . . .

I hope, now, that there is no risk of your misunderstanding me when I come to the gist of what I want to say to-night; – when I repeat, that every great national architecture has been the result and exponent of a great national religion. You can't have bits of it here, bits there – you must have it everywhere or nowhere. It is not the monopoly of a clerical company – it is not the exponent of a theological dogma – it is not the hieroglyphic writing of an initiated priesthood; it is the manly language of a people inspired by resolute and common purpose, and rendering resolute and common fidelity to the legible laws of an undoubted God . . .

It is long since you built a great cathedral; and how you would laugh at me if I proposed building a cathedral on the top of one of these hills of yours, to make it an Acropolis! But your railroad mounds, vaster than the walls of Babylon: your railroad stations, vaster than the temple of Ephesus, and innumerable; your chimneys, how much more mighty and costly than cathedral spires! your harbour-piers; your warehouses; your exchanges! – all these are built to your great Goddess of 'Getting-on'; and she has formed, and will continue to form, your architecture, as long as you worship her; and it is quite vain to ask me to tell you how to build to *her*; you know far better than I.

There might, indeed, on some theories, be a conceivably good architecture for Exchanges – that is to say, if there were any heroism in the fact or deed of exchange, which might be typically carved on the outside of your building. For, you know, all beautiful architecture must be adorned with sculpture or painting; and for sculpture or painting, you must have a subject. And hitherto it has been a received opinion among the nations of the world that the only right subjects for either, were *heroisms* of some sort . . . The Master of Christians not only left His followers without any orders as to the sculpture of affairs of exchange on the outside of buildings, but gave some strong evidence of His dislike of affairs of exchange within them [Matthew xxi. 12–13]. And yet there might surely be a heroism in such affairs; and all commerce become a kind of selling of doves, not impious. The wonder has always been great to me, that heroism has never been supposed to be in anywise consistent with the practice of supplying people with food, or clothes, but rather with that of quartering one's self upon them for food, and stripping them of their clothes. Spoiling of armour is an heroic deed in all ages; but the selling of clothes, old, or new, has never taken any colour of magnanimity. Yet one does not see why feeding the hungry and clothing the naked should ever become base businesses, even when engaged in on a large scale. If one could contrive to attach the notion of conquest to them anyhow! so that, supposing there were anywhere an obstinate race, who refused to be comforted, one might take some pride in giving them compulsory comfort! and, as it were, '*occupying* a country' with one's gifts, instead of one's armies? If one could only consider it as much a victory to get a barren field sown, as to get an eared field stripped; and contend who should build villages, instead of who should 'carry' them! Are not all forms of heroism conceivable in doing these serviceable deeds?

('Traffic', a lecture delivered in the Town Hall, Bradford, in *The Crown of Wild Olive*, paras. 52–6, 61, 64–7, 73–4.)

On the Voice of Books
The alternative society

The first use of education was to enable us to consult with the wisest and greatest men on all points of earnest difficulty. That to use books rightly, was to go to them for help: to appeal to them, when our own knowledge and power of thought failed: to be led by them into wider sight, – purer conception, – than our own, and receive from them the united sentence of the judges and councils of all time, against our solitary and unstable opinion.

Let us do this now . . .

Granting, that we had both the will and the sense to choose our friends well, how few of us have the power! or, at least, how limited, for most, is the sphere of choice! Nearly all our associations are determined by chance or necessity; and restricted within a narrow circle. We cannot know whom we would; and those whom we know, we cannot have at our side when we most need them. All the higher circles of human intelligence are, to those beneath, only momentarily and partially open. We may, by good fortune, obtain a glimpse of a great poet, and hear the sound of his voice; or put a question to a man of science, and be answered good-humouredly. We may intrude ten minutes' talk on a cabinet minister, answered probably with words worse than silence, being deceptive; or snatch, once or twice in our lives, the privilege of throwing a bouquet in the path of a princess, or arresting the kind glance of a queen. And yet these momentary chances we covet; and spend our years, and passions, and powers, in pursuit of little more than these; while, meantime, there is a society continually open to us, of people who will talk to us as long as we like, whatever our rank or occupation; – talk to us in the best words they can choose, and of the things nearest their hearts. And this society, because it is so numerous and so gentle, and can be kept waiting round us all day long, – kings and statesmen lingering patiently, not to grant audience, but to gain it! – in those plainly furnished and narrow ante-rooms, our bookcase shelves, – we make no account of that company, – perhaps never listen to a word they would say, all day long! . . .

The apathy with which we regard this company of the noble, who are praying us to listen to them; and the passion with which we pursue the company, probably of the ignoble, who despise us, or who have nothing to teach us! . . . Life is short. You have heard as much before; – yet have you measured and mapped out this short life and its possibilities? Do you know, if you read this, that you cannot read that – that what you lose to-day you cannot gain to-morrow? Will you go and gossip with your housemaid, or your stable-boy, when you may talk with queens and kings; or flatter yourself that it is with any worthy consciousness of your own claims to respect, that you jostle with the hungry and common crowd for *entrée* here, and audience there, when all the while this eternal court is open to you, with its society, wide as the world, multitudinous as its days, the chosen, and the mighty, of every place and time? Into that you may enter always; in that you may take fellowship and rank according to your wish; from that, once entered into it, you can never be outcast but by your own fault; by your aristocracy of companionship there, your own inherent aristocracy will be assuredly tested, and the motives with which you strive to take high place in the society of the living, measured, as to all the truth and sincerity that are in them, by the place you desire to take in this company of the Dead.

'The place you desire', and the place you *fit yourself for*, I must also say; because, observe, this court of the past differs from all living aristocracy in this: – it is open to labour and to merit, but to nothing else. No wealth will bribe, no name overawe, no artifice deceive, the guardian of those Elysian gates. In the deep sense, no vile or vulgar person ever enters there. At the portières of that silent Faubourg St Germain, there is but brief question: – 'Do you deserve to enter? Pass. Do you ask to be the companion of nobles? Make yourself noble, and you shall be. Do you long for the conversation of the wise? Learn to understand it, and you shall hear it. But on other terms? – no. If you will not rise to us, we cannot stoop to you. The living lord may assume courtesy, the living philosopher explain his thought to you with considerate pain; but here we neither feign nor interpret; you must rise to the level of our thoughts if you would be gladdened by them, and share our feelings, if you would recognise our presence.'

This, then, is what you have to do, and I admit that it is much. You must, in a word, love these people, if you are to be among them. No ambition is of any use. They scorn your ambition. You must love them, and show your love in these two following ways.

(1) First, by a true desire to be taught by them, and to enter into their thoughts. To enter into theirs, observe; not to find your own expressed by them. If the person who wrote the book is not wiser than you, you need not read it; if he be, he will think differently from you in many respects.

(2) Very ready we are to say of a book, 'How good this is – that's exactly what I think!' But the right feeling is, 'How strange that is! I never thought of that before, and yet I see it is true; or if I do not now, I hope I shall, some day.' But whether thus submissively or not, at least be sure that you go to the author to get at *his* meaning, not to find yours. Judge it afterwards if you think yourself qualified to do so; but ascertain it first. And be sure, also, if the author is worth anything, that you will not get at his meaning all at once; – nay, that at his whole meaning you will not for a long time arrive in any wise. Not that he does not say what he means, and in strong words too; but he cannot say it all; and what is more strange, *will* not, but in a hidden way and in parables, in order that he may be sure you want it. I cannot quite see the reason of this, nor analyse that cruel reticence in the breasts of wise men which makes them always hide their deeper thought. They do not give it you by way of help, but of reward; and will make themselves sure that you deserve it before they allow you to reach it. . . .

And, therefore, first of all, I tell you earnestly and authoritatively (I *know* I am right in this), you must get into the habit of looking intensely at words, and assuring yourself of their meaning, syllable by syllable – nay, letter by letter . . . the kind of word-by-word examination of your author which is rightly called 'reading'; watching every accent and expression, and putting ourselves always in the author's place, annihilating our own personality, and seeking to enter into his, so as to be able assuredly to say, 'Thus Milton thought', not 'Thus *I* thought, in mis-reading Milton'. And by this process you will gradually come to attach less weight to your own 'Thus I thought' at other times. You will begin to perceive that what *you* thought was a matter of no serious importance; – that your thoughts on any subject are not perhaps the clearest and wisest that could be arrived at thereupon: – in fact, that unless you are a very singular person, you cannot be said to have any 'thoughts' at all; that you have no materials for them, in any serious matters; – no right to 'think', but only to try to learn more of the facts. Nay, most probably all your life (unless, as I said, you are a singular person) you will have no legitimate right to an 'opinion' on any business, except that instantly under your hand. What must of necessity be done, you can always find out, beyond question, how to do. Have you a house to keep in order, a commodity to sell, a field to plough, a ditch to cleanse? There need be no two opinions about these proceedings; it is at your peril if you have not much more than an 'opinion' on the way to manage such matters. And also, outside of your own business, there are one or two subjects on which you are bound to have but one opinion. That roguery and lying are objectionable, and are instantly to be flogged out of the way whenever discovered; – that covetousness and love of quarrelling are dangerous dispositions even in children, and deadly dispositions in men and nations; – that, in the end, the God of heaven and earth loves active, modest, and kind people, and hates idle, proud, greedy, and cruel ones; – on these general facts you are bound to have but one, and that a very strong, opinion. For the rest, respecting religions, governments, sciences, arts, you will find that, on the whole, you can know NOTHING, – judge nothing; that the best you can do, even though you may be a well-educated person, is to be silent, and strive to be wiser every day, and to understand a little more of the thoughts of others, which so soon as you try to do honestly, you will discover that the thoughts even of the wisest are very little more than pertinent questions. To put the difficulty into a clear shape, and exhibit to you the grounds for *in*decision, that is all they can generally do for you! – and well for them and for us, if indeed they are able 'to mix the music with our thoughts and sadden us with heavenly doubts'. . . . [1]

Having then faithfully listened to the great teachers, that you may enter into their Thoughts, you have yet this higher advance to make; – you have to enter into their Hearts. As you go to them first for clear sight, so you must stay with them, that you may share at last their just and mighty Passion. Passion, or 'sensation'. I am not afraid of the word; still less of the thing. You have heard many outcries against sensation lately; but, I can tell you, it is not less sensation we want, but more...

My friends, I do not know why any of us should talk about reading. We want some sharper discipline than that of reading; but, at all events, be assured, we cannot read. No reading is possible for a people with its mind in this state. No sentence of any great writer is intelligible to them. It is simply and sternly impossible for the English public, at this moment, to understand any thoughtful writing, – so incapable of thought has it become in its insanity of avarice. (*Sesame* I, 'Of Kings' Treasuries', paras. 5, 6–7, 11–13, 15, 25, 27, 31)

A real book

All books are divisible into two classes, the books of the hour, and the books of all time. Mark this distinction – it is not one of quality only. It is not merely the bad book that does not last, and the good one that does. It is a distinction of species. There are good books for the hour, and good ones for all time; bad books for the hour, and bad ones for all time. I must define the two kinds before I go farther.

The good book of the hour, then, – I do not speak of the bad ones, – is simply the useful or pleasant talk of some person whom you cannot otherwise converse with, printed for you. Very useful often, telling you what you need to know; very pleasant often, as a sensible friend's present talk would be. These bright accounts of travels; good-humoured and witty discussions of question; lively or pathetic story-telling in the form of novel; firm fact-telling, by the real agents concerned in the events of passing history; – all these books of the hour, multiplying among us as education becomes more general, are a peculiar possession of the present age: we ought to be entirely thankful for them, and entirely ashamed of ourselves if we make no good use of them. But we make the worst possible use if we allow them to usurp the place of true books: for, strictly speaking, they are not books at all, but merely letters or newspapers in good print. Our friend's letter may be delightful, or necessary, to-day: whether worth keeping or not, is to be considered. The newspaper may be entirely proper at breakfast time, but assuredly it is not reading for all day. So, though bound up in a volume, the long letter which gives you so pleasant an account of the inns, and roads, and weather, last year at such a place, or which tells you that amusing story, or gives you the real circumstances of such and such events, however valuable for occasional reference, may not be, in the real sense of the word, a 'book' at all, nor, in the real sense, to be 'read'. A book is essentially not a talking thing, but a written thing; and written, not with a view of mere communication, but of permanence. The book of talk is printed only because its author cannot speak to thousands of people at once; if he could, he would – the volume is mere *multiplication* of his voice. You cannot talk to your friend in India; if you could, you would; you write instead: that is mere *conveyance* of voice. But a book is written, not to multiply the voice merely, not to carry it merely, but to perpetuate it. The author has something to say which he perceives to be true and useful, or helpfully beautiful. So far as he knows, no one has yet said it; so far as he knows, no one else can say it. He is bound to say it, clearly and melodiously if he may; clearly at all events. In the sum of his life he finds this to be the thing, or group of things, manifest to him; – this, the piece of true knowledge, or sight, which his share of sunshine and earth has permitted him to seize. He would fain set it down for ever; engrave it on rock, if he could; saying, 'This is the best of me; for the rest, I ate, and drank, and slept, loved, and hated, like another; my life was as the vapour [James iv. 14], and is not; but this I saw and knew: this, if anything of mine, is worth your memory.' That is his 'writing'; it is, in his small human way, and with whatever degree of true inspiration is in him, his inscription, or scripture. That is a 'Book'.

Perhaps you think no books were ever so written?

But, again, I ask you, do you at all believe in honesty, or at all in kindness, or do you think there is never any honesty or benevolence in wise people? None of us, I hope, are so unhappy as to think that. Well, whatever bit of a wise man's work is honestly and benevolently done, that bit is his book or his piece of art. It is mixed always with evil fragments – ill-done, redundant, affected work. But if you read rightly, you will easily discover the true bits, and those *are* the book.

(*Sesame* I, 'Of Kings' Treasuries', paras 9–10.)

*   *   *

Praeterita
'His book, his piece of art'

The only child –

I had a bunch of keys to play with, as long as I was capable only of pleasure in what glittered and jingled; as I grew older, I had a cart, and a ball; and when I was five or six years old, two boxes of well-cut wooden bricks. With these modest, but, I still think, entirely sufficient possessions, and being always summarily whipped if I cried, did not do as I was bid, or tumbled on the stairs, I soon attained serene and secure methods of life and motion; and could pass my days contentedly in tracing the squares and comparing the colours of my carpet; – examining the knots in the wood of the floor, or counting the bricks in the opposite houses; with rapturous intervals of excitement during the filling of the water cart, through its leathern pipe, from the dripping iron post at the pavement edge; or the still more admirable proceedings of the turncock, when he turned and turned till a fountain sprang up in the middle of the street. But the carpet, and what patterns I could find in bed covers, dresses, or wall-papers to be examined, were my chief resources, and my attention to the particulars in these was soon so accurate, that when at three and a half I was taken to have my portrait painted by Mr Northcote, I had not been ten minutes alone with him before I asked why there were holes in his carpet. (Vol. I, Ch. I, para. 14)

The first seven years:

I will first count my blessings ... And for best and truest beginning of all blessings, I had been taught the perfect meaning of Peace, in thought, act, and word.

I never had heard my father's or mother's voice once raised in any question with each other; nor seen an angry, or even slightly hurt or offended, glance in the eyes of either. I had never heard a servant scolded; nor even suddenly, passionately, or in any severe manner, blamed. I had never seen a moment's trouble or disorder in any household matter; nor anything whatever either done in a hurry, or undone in due time. I had no conception of such a feeling as anxiety; my father's occasional vexation in the afternoons, when he had only got an order for twelve butts after expecting one for fifteen, ... was never manifested to *me* ... I had never done any wrong that I knew of – beyond occasionally delaying the commitment to heart of some improving sentence, that I might watch a wasp on the window pane, or a bird in the cherry tree; and I had never seen any grief.

Next to this quite priceless gift of Peace, I had received the perfect understanding of the natures of Obedience and Faith. I obeyed word, or lifted finger, of father or mother, simply as a ship her helm; not only without idea of resistance, but receiving the direction as a part of my own life and force, and helpful law, as necessary to me in every moral action as the law of gravity in leaping. And my practice in Faith was soon complete: nothing was ever promised me that was not given; nothing ever threatened me that was not inflicted, and nothing ever told me that was not true.

Peace, obedience, faith; these three for chief good; next to these, the habit of fixed attention with both eyes and mind – on which I will not further enlarge at this moment, this being the main practical faculty of my life, causing Mazzini to say of me, in conversation authentically reported, a year or two before his death, that I had 'the most analytic mind in Europe'. An opinion in which, so far as I am acquainted with Europe, I am myself entirely disposed to concur.

Lastly, an extreme perfection in palate and all other bodily senses, given by the utter prohibition of cake, wine, comfits, or, except in carefullest restriction, fruit; and by fine preparation of what food was given me. Such I esteem the main blessings of my childhood; – next, let me count the equally dominant calamities.

First, that I had nothing to love.

My parents were – in a sort – visible powers of nature to me, no more loved than the sun and the moon: only I should have been annoyed and puzzled if either of them had gone out; (how much, now, when both are darkened!) – still less did I love God; not that I had any quarrel with Him, or fear of Him; but simply found what people told me was His service, disagreeable; and what people told me was His book, not entertaining. I had no companions to quarrel with, neither; nobody to assist, and nobody to thank. Not a servant was ever allowed to do anything for me, but what it was their duty to do; and why should I have been grateful to the cook for cooking, or the gardener for gardening, – when the one dared not give me a baked potato without asking leave, and the other would not let my ants' nests alone, because they made the walks untidy? The evil consequence of all this was not, however, what might perhaps have been expected, that I grew up selfish or unaffectionate; but that, when affection did come, it came with violence utterly rampant and unmanageable, at least by me, who never before had anything to manage.

For (second of chief calamities) I had nothing to endure. Danger or pain of any kind I knew not: my strength was never exercised, my patience never tried, and my courage never fortified. Not that I was ever afraid of anything, – either ghosts, thunder, or beasts; and one of the nearest approaches to insubordination which I was ever tempted into as a child, was in passionate effort to get leave to play with the lion's cubs in Wombwell's menagerie.

Thirdly. I was taught no precision nor etiquette of manners; it was enough if, in the little society we saw, I remained unobtrusive, and replied to a question without shyness: but the shyness came later, and increased as I grew conscious of the rudeness arising from the want of social discipline, and found it impossible to acquire, in advanced life, dexterity in any bodily exercise, skill in any pleasing accomplishment, or ease and tact in ordinary behaviour.

Lastly, and chief of evils. My judgment of right and wrong, and powers of independent action, were left entirely undeveloped; because the bridle and blinkers were never taken off me. Children should have their times of being off duty, like soldiers; and when once the obedience, if required, is certain, the little creature should be very early put for periods of practice in complete command of itself; set on the bare-backed horse of its own will, and left to break it by its own strength. But the ceaseless authority exercised over my youth left me, when cast out at last into the world, unable for some time to do more than drift with its vortices . . . My mother saw this herself, and but too clearly, in later years; and whenever I did anything wrong, stupid, or hard-hearted, – (and I have done many things that were all three,) – always said, 'It is because you were too much indulged.'

(Vol. I, Ch. II, paras. 48–54)

The Discovery of Turner

(Henry Telford, a business partner of Ruskin's father, gave the young Ruskin, aged thirteen, the illustrated edition of Rogers's Italy)

This book was the first means I had of looking carefully at Turner's work: and I might, not without some appearance of reason, attribute to the gift the entire direction of my life's energies. But it is the great error of thoughtless biographers to attribute to the accident which introduces some new phase of character, all the circumstances of character which gave the accident importance. The essential point to be noted, and accounted for, was that I could understand Turner's work, when I saw it; – not by what chance, or in what year, it was first seen. Poor Mr Telford, nevertheless, was always held by papa and mamma primarily responsible for my Turner insanities. (Vol. I, Ch. I, para. 28)

The undergraduate at Oxford

I count it is just a little to my credit that I was not ashamed, but pleased, that my mother came to Oxford with me to take such care of me as she could. Through all three years of residence, during term time, she had lodging in the High Street (first in Mr Adams's pretty house of sixteenth-century wood-work), and my father lived alone all through the week at Herne Hill, parting with wife and son at once for the son's sake. On the Saturday, he came down to us, and I went with him and my mother, in the old domestic way, to St Peter's, for the Sunday morning service: otherwise, they never appeared with me in public, lest my companions should laugh at me, or any one else ask malicious questions concerning vintner papa and his old-fashioned wife. . . .

The reader will please also note that my mother did not come to Oxford because she could not part with me, – still less, because she distrusted me. She came simply that she might be at hand in case of accident or sudden illness. (Vol. I, Ch. XI, para. 226)

The sickly youth taken away from Oxford, *1841*

We stopped at Albano for the Sunday, and I went out in the morning for a walk through its ilex groves with my father and mother and Mary. For some time back, the little cough bringing blood had not troubled me, and I had been taking longer walks and otherwise counting on comparative safety, when here suddenly, in the gentle morning saunter through the shade, the cough came back – with a little darker stain on the handkerchief than usual. I sat down on a bank by the roadside, and my father's face was very grave.

We got quietly back to the inn, where he found some sort of light carriole disposable, and set out, himself, to fetch the doctor from Rome.

It has always been one of the great shadows of thought to me, to fancy my father's feelings as he was driven that day those eighteen miles across the Campagna.

Good Dr Gloag comforted him, and returned with him. But there was nothing new to be done, nor said. Such chance attack was natural in the spring, he said, only I must be cautious for a while. My mother never lost her courage for an instant. Next day we went on to Rome, and it was the last time the cough ever troubled me. (Vol. II, Ch. III, para. 52)

Ruskin's first visit abroad on his own, to Florence and Pisa, 1845 – ironically opposed by Turner himself as family friend

How papa and mamma took this new vagary, I have no recollection; resignedly, at least: perhaps they also had some notion that I might think differently, and it was to be hoped in a more orthodox and becoming manner, after another sight of the Tribune [Uffizi Gallery]. At all events, they concluded to give me my own way entirely this time; and what time I chose. My health caused them no farther anxiety; they could trust my word to take care of myself every day, just the same as if I were coming home to tea: my mother was satisfied of Couttet's skill as a physician, and care, if needed, as a nurse; – he was engaged for the summer in those capacities, – and, about the first week in April, I found myself dining on a trout of the Ain, at Champagnole; with Switzerland and Italy at my feet – for to-morrow.

Curiously, the principal opposition to this unprincipled escapade had been made by Turner. He knew that one of my chief objects was to see the motives of his last sketches on the St Gothard; and he feared my getting into some scrape in the then disturbed state of the cantons... Every time Turner saw me during the winter, he said something to dissuade me from going abroad; when at last I went to say good-bye, he came down with me into the hall in Queen Anne Street, and opening the door just enough for me to pass, laid hold of my arm, gripping it strongly. 'Why *will* you go to Switzerland – there'll be such a fidge about you, when you're gone.'

I am never able to collect myself in a moment, and am simply helpless on any sudden need for decision like this; the result being, usually, that I go on doing what I meant to do. If I say anything, it is sure to be wrong. I made no answer, but grasped his hand closely, and went. I believe he made up his mind that I was heartless and selfish; anyhow he took no more pains with me. (Vol. II, Ch. VI, paras. 105–6)

Ruskin and his father

The twenty-first birthday present, Turner's drawing of Winchelsea, 'a curious choice, and an unlucky one'

The thundrous sky and broken white light of storm round the distant gate and scarcely visible church, were but too true symbols of the time that was coming upon us; but neither he nor I were given to reading omens, or dreading them. I suppose he had been struck by the power of the drawing, and he always liked soldiers. I was disappointed, and saw for the first time clearly that my father's joy in Rubens and Sir Joshua could never become sentient of Turner's microscopic touch. But I was entirely grateful for his purpose, and very thankful to have any new Turner drawing whatsoever; and as at home the 'Gosport,' so in St Aldate's the 'Winchelsea', was the chief recreation of my fatigued hours. (Vol. II, Ch. I, para. 13)

The allowance to spend – especially on Turner's paintings

But [father] had always the most curious suspicion of my taste for minerals, and only the year before, was entirely vexed and discomfited at my giving eleven shillings for a piece of Cornish chalcedony. That I never thought of buying a mineral without telling him what I had paid for it, besides advising him duly of the fact, curiously marks the intimate confidence between us; but alas, my respect for his judgment was at this time by these littlenesses gradually diminished; and my confidence in my own painfully manifested to him a very little while after he had permitted me the above measure of independence. The Turner drawings hitherto bought, – Richmond, Gosport, Winchelsea, – were all supplied by Mr Griffith, an agent in whom Turner had perfect confidence, and my father none. Both were fatally wrong. Had Turner dealt straight with my father, there is no saying how much happiness might have come of it for all three of us; had my father not been always afraid of being taken in by Mr Griffith, he might at that time have bought some of the loveliest drawings that Turner ever made, at entirely fair prices. But Mr Griffith's art-salesmanship entirely offended my father from the first, and the best drawings were always let pass, because Mr Griffith recommended them, while Winchelsea and Gosport were both bought – among other reasons – because Mr Griffith said they were not drawings which we ought to have!

Among those of purest quality in his folios at this time was one I especially coveted, the Harlech . . . The private view day of the Old Water Colour came; and, arm in arm with my father, I met Mr Griffith in the crowd. After the proper five minutes of how we liked the exhibition, he turned specially to me. 'I have some good news for you, the Harlech is ready for sale.' 'I'll take it then,' I replied, without so much as a glance at my father, and without asking the price. Smiling a little ironically, Mr Griffith went on, 'And – seventy,' – implying that seventy was a low price, at once told me in answer to my confidence. But it was thirty above the 'Winchelsea', twenty-four above 'Gosport', and my father was of course sure that Mr Griffith had put twenty pounds on at the instant.

The mingled grief and scorn on his face told me what I had done; but I was too happy on pouncing on my 'Harlech' to feel for him. All sorts of blindness and error on both sides, but, on his side, inevitable, – on mine, more foolish than culpable; fatal every way, beyond words.

I can scarcely understand my eagerness and delight in getting the 'Harlech' at this time, because, during the winter, negotiations had been carried on in Paris for Adèle's marriage; and, it does not seem as if I had been really so much crushed by that event [see p. 374 ff.] as I expected to be. There are expressions, however, in the foolish diaries I began to write, soon after, of general disdain of life, and all that it could in future bestow on me, which seem inconsistent with extreme satisfaction in getting a water-colour drawing, sixteen inches by nine. But whatever germs of better things remained in me, were then all centred in this love of Turner ... It was not a piece of painted paper, but a Welsh castle and village, and Snowdon in blue cloud, that I bought for my seventy pounds. (Vol. II, Ch. I, paras. 14–16)

Touring together – 1844

A six, morning, I had visisted Signór Zanetti, and reviewed his collection of pictures on Isola dei Pescatori; walked up most of the defile of Gondo; and the moment we got to the Simplon village, dashed off to catch the sunset from the col; five miles up hill against time, (and walk against time up a regular slope of eight feet in the hundred is the most trying foot-work I know,) five miles back under the stars, with the hills not *under* but *among* them, and careful entry, of which I have only given a sentence, make up a day which shows there was now no farther need to be alarmed about my health. My good father, who was never well in the high air, and hated the chills from patches of melting snow, stayed nevertheless all next day at the village, to let me climb the long-coveted peak west of the Simplon col ...

On the 29th July I went up the Buet, and down to Sixt, where I found myself very stiff and tired, and determined that the Alps were, on the whole, best seen from below. And after a walk to the Fer-à-cheval, considering the wild strawberries there to taste of slate, I went rather penitently down to Geneva again.

Feeling also a little ashamed of myself before papa – in the consciousness that all his pining in cold air, and dining on black bread, and waiting, day after day, not without anxiety, while I rambled he knew not whither, had not in the least advanced the object nearest his heart, – the second volume of *Modern Painters*. I had, on the contrary, been acutely and minutely at work in quite other directions – felt tempted now to write on Alpine botany, or devote myself to painting myrtilles and mica-slate for the rest of my days. The Turner charm was indeed as potent as ever; but I felt that other powers were now telling on me besides his, – even beyond his; not in delight, but in vital strength; and that no word could be written of him, till I had tried the range of these ...

The summer's work of 1844, so far from advancing the design of *Modern Painters*, had thrown me off it – first into fine botany, then into difficult geology, and lastly ... into a fit of figure study which meant much.[2] It meant, especially, at last some looking into ecclesiastical history, – some notion of the merit of fourteenth-century painting, and the total abandonment of Rubens and Rembrandt for the Venetian school. Which, the reader will please observe, signified not merely the advance in sense of colour, but in perception of truth and modesty in light and shade. And on getting home, I felt that in the cyclone of confused new knowledge, this was the thing first to be got firm. (Vol. II, Ch. V, paras. 96, 100; Ch. VI, para. 104)

Touring on his own 1845 – at Lucca

Hitherto, all architecture, except fairy-finished Milan, had depended with me for its delight on being partly in decay. I revered the sentiment of its age, and I was accustomed to look for the signs of age in the mouldering of its traceries, and in the interstices deepening between the stones of its masonry. This looking for cranny and joint was mixed with the love of rough stones themselves, and of country cottages built like Westmoreland cottages.

Here in Lucca I found myself suddenly in the presence of twelfth century buildings, originally set in such balance of masonry that they could all stand without mortar; and in material so incorruptible, that after six hundred years of sunshine and rain, a lancet could not now be put between their joints.

Absolutely for the first time I now saw what medieval builders were, and what they meant . . . and thereon literally *began* the study of architecture . . .

I began showing to my father all my new discoveries in architecture and painting. But there now began to assert itself a difference between us I had not calculated on . . . And I was the more viciously stubborn in taking my own way, just because everybody was with him in these opinions; and I was more and more persuaded every day, that everybody was wrong.

Often in my other books, – and now, once for all, and finally here, – I have to pray my readers to note that this continually increasing arrogance was not founded on vanity in me, but on sorrow. There is a vast difference – there is all the difference – between the vanity of displaying one's own faculties, and the grief that other people do not use their own . . . I had no thought but of learning more, and teaching what truth I knew, – assuredly then, and ever since, for the student's sake, not my own fame's;

however sensitive I may be to the fame, also, afterwards. (Vol. II,
Ch. VI, para. 115; Ch. X, para. 188)

Touring together – 1846

My father and I did not get on well in Italy at all, and one of the
worst, wasp-barbed, most tingling pangs of my memory is yet of a
sunny afternoon at Pisa, when, just as we were driving past my pet
La Spina chapel, my father, waking out of a reverie, asked me
suddenly, 'John, what shall I give the coachman?' Whereupon, I,
instead of telling him what he asked me, as I ought to have done
with much complacency at being referred to on the matter, took
upon me with impatience to reprove, and lament over, my father's
hardness of heart, in thinking at that moment of sublunary affairs.
And the spectral Spina of the chapel has stayed in my own heart
ever since. (Vol. II, Ch. X, para. 189)

Ruskin in love
The first time – Adèle

As my adverse stars would have it, that year [1836], my father's
partner, Mr Domecq, thought it might for once be expedient that
he should himself pay a complimentary round of visits to his
British customers, and asked if meanwhile he might leave his
daughters at Herne Hill to see the lions at the Tower, and so on.
How we got them all into Herne Hill corners and cupboards
would be inexplicable but with a plan of the three stories! The
arrangements were half Noah's ark, half Doll's house, but we got
them all in: Clotilde, a graceful oval-faced blonde of fifteen;
Cécile, a dark, finely-browed, beautifully-featured girl of thirteen;
Elise, again fair, round-faced like an English girl, a treasure of
good nature and good sense; Caroline, a delicately quaint little
thing of eleven. They had all been born abroad, Clotilde at Cadiz,
and of course convent-bred; but lately accustomed to be much in
society during vacation at Paris. Deeper than any one dreamed,
the sight of them in the Champs Élysées had sealed itself in me, for
they were the first well-bred and well-dressed girls I had ever seen
– or at least spoken to. I mean of course, by well-dressed, perfectly
simply dressed, with Parisian cutting and fitting. They were all
'bigoted' – as Protestants would say; quietly firm, as they ought to
say – Roman Catholics; spoke Spanish and French with perfect

grace, and English with broken precision: were all fairly sensible, Clotilde sternly and accurately so, Elise gaily and kindly, Cécile serenely, Caroline keenly. A most curious galaxy, or southern cross, of unconceived stars, floating on a sudden into my obscure firmament of London suburb.

How my parents could allow their young novice to be cast into the fiery furnace of the outer world in this helpless manner the reader may wonder, and only the Fates know; but there was this excuse for them, that they had never seen me the least interested or anxious about girls – never caring to stay in the promenades at Cheltenham or Bath, or on the parade at Dover; on the contrary, growling and mewing if I was ever kept there, and off to the sea or the fields the moment I got leave; and they had educated me in such extremely orthodox English Toryism and Evangelicalism that they could not conceive their scientific, religious, and George the Third revering youth, wavering in his constitutional balance towards French Catholics. And I had never *said* anything about the Champs Élysées! Virtually convent-bred more closely than the maids themselves, without a single sisterly or cousinly affection for refuge or lightning rod, and having no athletic skill or pleasure to check my dreaming, I was thrown, bound hand and foot, in my unaccomplished simplicity, into the fiery furnace, or fiery cross, of these four girls, – who of course reduced me to a mere heap of white ashes in four days. Four days, at the most, it took to reduce me to ashes, but the *Mercredi des cendres* [Ash-Wednesday] lasted four years . . .

Clotilde (Adèle Clotilde in full, but her sisters called her Clotilde, after the queen-saint, and I Adèle, because it rhymed to shell, spell, and knell) was only made more resplendent by the circlet of her sisters' beauty; while my own shyness and unpresentableness were farther stiffened, or rather sanded, by a patriotic and Protestant conceit, which was tempered neither by politeness nor sympathy; so that, while in company I sate jealously miserable like a stock fish (in truth, I imagine, looking like nothing so much as a skate in an aquarium trying to get up the glass), on any blessed occasion of tête-à-tête I endeavoured to entertain my Spanish-born, Paris-bred, and Catholic-hearted mistress with my own views upon the subjects of the Spanish Armada, the Battle of Waterloo, and the doctrine of Transubstantiation.

To these modes of recommending myself, however, I did not

fail to add what display I could make of the talents I supposed myself to possess. I wrote with great pains, and straining of my invention, a story about Naples (which I had never seen), and 'the Bandit Leoni', whom I represented as typical of what my own sanguinary and adventurous disposition would have been had I been brought up a bandit; and 'the Maiden Giuletta', in whom I portrayed all the perfections of my mistress. Our connection with Messrs. Smith & Elder enabled me to get this story printed in *Friendship's Offering*; and Adèle laughed over it in rippling ecstasies of derision, of which I bore the pain bravely, for the sake of seeing her thoroughly amused.

I dared not address any sonnets straight to herself; but when she went back to Paris, wrote her a French letter seven quarto pages long, descriptive of the desolations and solitudes of Herne Hill since her departure. This letter, either Elise or Caroline wrote to tell me she had really read, and 'laughed immensely at the French of'. Both Caroline and Elise pitied me a little, and did not like to say she had also laughed at the contents.

The old people, meanwhile, saw little harm in all this . . .

Under these indulgent circumstances, – bitterly ashamed of the figure I had made, but yet not a whit dashed back out of my daily swelling foam of furious conceit, supported as it was by real depth of feeling, and (note it well, good reader) by a true and glorious sense of the newly revealed miracle of human love, in its exaltation of the physical beauty of the world I had till then sought by its own light alone, – I set myself in that my seventeenth year, in a state of majestic imbecility, to write a tragedy on a Venetian subject, in which the sorrows of my soul were to be enshrined in immortal verse . . . The entirely inscrutable thing to me, looking back on myself, is my total want of all reason, will, or design in the business: I had neither the resolution to win Adèle, the courage to do without her, the sense to consider what was at last to come of it all, or the grace to think how disagreeable I was making myself at the time to everybody about me. There was really no more capacity nor intelligence in me than in a just fledged owlet, or just open-eyed puppy, disconsolate at the existence of the moon. (Vol. I, Ch. X, paras. 205–10)

Charlotte Withers

A little incident which happened, I fancy in the beginning of '38, shows that I had thus recovered some tranquillity and sense, and might at that time have been settled down to simple and healthy life, easily enough, had my parents seen the chance.

I forgot to say, when speaking of Mr and Mrs Richard Gray, that, when I was a child, my mother had another religious friend, who lived just at the top of Camberwell Grove, or between it and the White Gate, – Mrs Withers; an extremely amiable and charitable person, with whom my mother organized, I imagine, such schemes of alms-giving as her own housekeeping prevented her seeing to herself. Mr Withers was a coal-merchant, ultimately not a successful one. Of him I remember only a reddish and rather vacant face; of Mrs Withers, no material aspect, only the above vague but certain facts; and that she was a familiar element in my mother's life, dying out of it however without much notice or miss, before I was old enough to get any clear notion of her.

In this spring of '38, however, the widowed Mr Withers, having by that time retired to the rural districts in reduced circumstances, came up to town on some small vestige of carboniferous business, bringing his only daughter with him to show my mother; – who, for a wonder, asked her to stay with us, while her father visited his umquhile clientage at the coal-wharves. Charlotte Withers was a fragile, fair, freckled, sensitive slip of a girl about sixteen; graceful in an unfinished and small wild-flower sort of a way, extremely intelligent, affectionate, wholly right-minded, and mild in piety. An altogether sweet and delicate creature of ordinary sort, not pretty, but quite pleasant to see, especially if her eyes were looking your way, and her mind with them.

We got to like each other in a mildly confidential way in the course of a week. We disputed on the relative dignities of music and painting; and I wrote an essay nine foolscap pages long, proposing the entire establishment of my own opinions, and the total discomfiture and overthrow of hers, according to my usual manner of paying court to my mistresses. Charlotte Withers, however, thought I did her great honour, and carried away the essay as if it had been a school prize.

And, as I said, if my father and mother had chosen to keep her a month longer, we should have fallen quite melodiously and quietly in love; and they might have given me an excellently pleasant little wife, and set me up, geology and all, in the coal business, without any resistance or farther trouble on my part. I don't suppose the idea ever occurred to them; Charlotte was not the kind of person they proposed for me. So Charlotte went away at the week's end, when her father was ready for her. I walked with her to Camberwell Green, and we said good-bye, rather sorrowfully, at the corner of the New Road; and that possibility of meek happiness vanished for ever. A little afterwards, her father 'negotiated' a marriage for her with a well-to-do Newcastle trader, whom she took because she was bid. He treated her pretty much as one of his coal sacks, and in a year or two she died.

Very dimly, and rather against my own will, the incident showed me what my mother had once or twice observed to me, to my immense indignation, that Adèle was not the only girl in the world; and my enjoyment of our tour in the Trossachs was not described in any more Byronian heroics; the tragedy also having been given up . . . (Vol. I, Ch. XII, paras. 247–9)

Georgina Tollemache, 1840

There was another practical chance for me in life at this crisis, – I might have made the most precious records of all the cities in Italy. But all my chances of being anything but what I am were thrown away, or broken short, one after another. An entirely mocking and mirage-coloured one, as it seemed then, yet became, many a year later, a great and beautiful influence on my life.

Between my Protestantism and, as Tom Richmond rightly called it, Proutism, I had now abjured Roman shows altogether, and was equally rude and restive, whether I was asked to go to a church, a palace, or a gallery, – when papa and mamma began to perceive some dawn of docility in me about going to hear musical church services. This they naturally attributed to my native taste for Gregorian chants, and my increasing aptitude for musical composition. But the fact was, that at services of this kind there was always a chance of seeing, at intervals, above the bowed heads of the Italian crowd, for an instant or two before she also stooped – or sometimes, eminent in her grace above a stunted group of them, – a fair English girl, who was not only the admitted Queen of beauty in the English circle of that winter in Rome, but was so, in the kind of beauty which I had only hitherto dreamed of as possible, but never yet seen living: statuesque severity with womanly sweetness joined. I don't think I ever succeeded in getting nearer than within fifty yards of her; but she was the light and solace of all the Roman winter to me, in the mere chance glimpses of her far away, and the hope of them.[3] (Vol. II, Ch. II, paras. 38–9)

30 December 1840

There was a girl walking up and down with some children, her light cap prettily set on very well dressed hair: of whose country I had no doubt; long before I heard her complain to one of her charges, who was jabbering English as fast as the fountain tinkled on the other side of the road, 'Qu'elle n'en comprenait pas un mot.' This girl after two or three turns sat down beside another *bonne*. There they sat laughing and chattering, with the expression of perfect happiness on their faces, thinking no more of the Alpine heights behind them, or the city beneath them, than of Constantinople; while I, with every feeling raised, I should think to a great degree above theirs, was in a state of actually severe mental pain, because I could perceive materials of the highest pleasure around me, and felt the time hang heavy on my hands. Here is the pride, you perceive, good reader and the sullens – *dum pituita molesta est* – both plain enough. But it is no lofty pride in which I say my '*feelings*' were raised above the French *bonne's*. Very solemnly, I did not think myself a better creature than she, nor so good; but only I knew there was a link between far Soracte and me, – nay, even between unseen Voltur and me, – which was not between her and them; and meant a wider earthly, if not heavenly, horizon, under the birth-star.[4]

Meantime, beneath the hill, my mother knitted, as quietly as if she had been at home, in the corner of the great Roman room in which she cared for nothing but the cleanliness, as distinguishing it from the accommodation of provincial inns. (Vol. II, Ch. III, paras. 46–7)

The Tomb of Ilaria di Caretto, Lucca 1845

And here, suddenly, in the sleeping Ilaria, was the perfectness of these [standards of womanhood], expressed with harmonies of line which I saw in an instant were under the same laws as the river wave, and the aspen branch, and the stars' rising and setting; but treated with a modesty and severity which read the laws of nature by the light of virtue. (Vol. II, Ch. VI, para. 114)

The statue of Ilaria became at once, and has ever since

Plate 29 *Tomb of Ilaria di Caretto, Lucca*

remained, my ideal of Christian sculpture. It is, I will venture to say, after these forty years of further study, the most beautiful extant marble-work of the middle-ages, – faultless, as far as human skill and feeling can or may be so. And beside it, I partly then felt, partly vowed, that my life must no more be spent only in the study of rocks and clouds.[5]

(MP II, 'Epilogue' [1883], para. 6 [C&W IV, pp. 347–8])

'Nobody thinking of me'

In the beginning of the Carlyle-Emerson correspondence, edited with too little comment by my dear friend Charles Norton, I find at page 18 this – to me entirely disputable, and to my thought, so far as undisputed, much blameable and pitiable, exclamation of my master's: 'Not till we can think that here and there one is thinking of us, one is loving us, does this waste earth become a peopled garden.' My training, as the reader has perhaps enough perceived, produced in me the precisely opposite sentiment. *My* times of happiness had always been when *nobody* was thinking of me; and the main discomfort and drawback to all proceedings and designs, the attention and interference of the public – represented by my mother and the gardener. The garden was no waste place to me, because I did not suppose myself an object of interest either to the ants or the butterflies; and the only qualification of the entire delight of my evening walk at Champagnole or St Laurent was the sense that my father and mother *were* thinking of me, and would be frightened if I was five minutes late for tea.

I don't mean in the least that I could have done without them. They were, to me, much more than Carlyle's wife to him; and if Carlyle had written, instead of that he wanted Emerson to think of him in America, that he wanted his father and mother to be thinking of him at Ecclefechan, it had been well. But that the rest of the world was waste to him unless he had admirers in it, is a sorry state of sentiment enough; and I am somewhat tempted, for once, to admire the exactly opposite temper of my own solitude. My entire delight was in observing without being myself noticed, – if I could have been invisible, all the better. I was absolutely interested in men and their ways, as I was interested in marmots and chamois, in tomtits and trout. If only they would stay still and let me look at them, and not get into their holes and up their

heights! The living inhabitation of the world – the grazing and
nesting in it, – the spiritual power of the air, the rocks, the waters,
to be in the midst of it, and rejoice and wonder at it, and help it if I
could, – happier if it needed no help of mine, – this was the
essential love *of Nature* in me, this the root of all that I have
usefully become, and the light of all that I have rightly learned.
(Vol. I, Ch. IX, para. 192)

Pivotal Times and Central Places
'The Centres'

I must here, in advance, tell the general reader that there have
been, in sum, three centres of my life's thought: Rouen, Geneva,
and Pisa. All that I did at Venice was bye-work because her history
had been falsely written before, and not even by any of her own
people understood; and because, in the world of painting,
Tintoret was virtually unseen, Veronese unfelt, Carpaccio not so
much as named, when I began to study them; something also was
due to my love of gliding about in gondolas. But Rouen, Geneva,
and Pisa have been tutresses of all I know, and were mistresses of
all I did, from the first moments I entered their gates.

In this journey of 1835 I first saw Rouen and Venice – Pisa not
till 1840; nor could I understand the full power of any of those
great scenes till much later. But for Abbeville, which is the preface
and interpretation of Rouen, I was ready on that 5th of June, and
felt that here was entrance for me into immediately healthy labour
and joy.

For here I saw that art (of its local kind), religion, and present
human life, were yet in perfect harmony. There were no dead six
days and dismal seventh in those sculptured churches; there was
no beadle to lock me out of them, or pew-shutter to shut me in.
(Vol. I, Ch. IX, paras. 180–1)

'The Holy Land' – The Alps

Whether we slept at St Laurent or Morez, the morning of the next
day was an eventful one. In ordinarily fine weather, the ascent
from Morez to Les Rousses, walked most of the way, was mere
enchantment; so also breakfast, and fringed-gentian gathering, at
Les Rousses. Then came usually an hour of tortured watching the
increase of the noon clouds; for, however early we had risen, it

was impossible to reach the Col de la Faucille before two o'clock, or later if we had bad horses, and at two o'clock, if there are clouds above Jura, there will be assuredly clouds on the Alps.

It is worth notice, Saussure himself not having noticed it, that this main pass of Jura, unlike the great passes of the Alps, reaches its traverse-point very nearly under the highest summit of that part of the chain. The col, separating the source of the Bienne, which runs down to Morez and St Claude, from that of the Valserine, which winds through the midst of Jura to the Rhone at Bellegarde, is a spur of the Dôle itself, under whose prolonged masses the road is then carried six miles farther, ascending very slightly to the Col de la Faucille, where the chain opens suddenly, and a sweep of the road, traversed in five minutes at a trot, opens the whole Lake of Geneva, and the chain of the Alps along a hundred miles of horizon.

I have never seen that view perfectly but once – in this year 1835; when I drew it carefully in my then fashion, and have been content to look back to it as the confirming sequel of the first view of the Alps from Schaffhausen. Very few travellers, even in old times, saw it at all; tired of the long posting journey from Paris, by the time they got to the col they were mostly thinking only of their dinners and rest at Geneva; the guide books said nothing about it; and though, for everybody, it was an inevitable task to ascend the Righi, nobody ever thought there was anything to be seen from the Dôle.

Both mountains have had enormous influence on my whole life; – the Dôle continually and calmly; the Righi at sorrowful intervals, as will be seen. But the Col de la Faucille, on that day of 1835, opened to me in distinct vision the Holy Land of my future work and true home in this world. My eyes had been opened, and my heart with them, to see and to possess royally such a kingdom! Far as the eye could reach— (Vol. I, Ch. IX, paras. 192–3)

'The entrance into life' (1833)

Difficult enough for you to imagine, that old travellers' time when Switzerland was yet the land of the Swiss, and the Alps had never been trod by foot of man. Steam, never heard of yet, but for short fair weather crossing at sea (were there paddle-packets across Atlantic? I forget). Any way, the roads by land were safe; and entered once into this mountain Paradise, we wound on through its balmy glens, past cottage after cottage on their lawns, still glistering in the dew.

The road got into more barren heights by the mid-day, the hills arduous; once or twice we had to wait for horses, and we were still twenty miles from Schaffhausen at sunset; it was past midnight when we reached her closed gates. The disturbed porter had the grace to open them – not quite wide enough; we carried away one of our lamps in collision with the slanting bar as we drove through the arch. How much happier the privilege of dreamily entering a mediæval city, though with the loss of a lamp, than the free ingress of being jammed between a dray and a tramcar at a railroad station!

It is strange that I but dimly recollect the following morning; I fancy we must have gone to some sort of church or other; and certainly, part of the day went in admiring the bow-windows projecting into the clean streets. None of us seem to have thought the Alps would be visible without profane exertion in climbing hills. We dined at four, as usual, and the evening being entirely fine, went out to walk, all of us, – my father and mother and Mary and I.

We must have still spent some time in town-seeing, for it was drawing towards sunset, when we got up to some sort of garden promenade – west of the town, I believe; and high above the Rhine, so as to command the open country across it to the south and west. At which open country of low undulation, far into blue, – gazing as at one of our own distances from Malvern of Worcestershire, or Dorking of Kent, – suddenly – behold – beyond!

There was no thought in any of us for a moment of their being clouds. They were clear as crystal, sharp on the pure horizon sky, and already tinged with rose by the sinking sun. Infinitely beyond all that we had ever thought or dreamed, – the seen walls of lost Eden could not have been more beautiful to us; not more awful, round heaven, the walls of sacred Death.

It is not possible to imagine, in any time of the world, a more blessed entrance into life, for a child of such a temperament as mine. True, the temperament belonged to the age: a very few years, – within the hundred, – before that, no child could have been born to care for mountains, or for the men that lived among them, in that way. Till Rousseau's time, there had been no 'sentimental' love of nature; and till Scott's, no such apprehensive love of 'all sorts and conditions of men' [Book of Common Prayer], not in the soul merely, but in the flesh. St Bernard of La Fontaine, looking out to Mont Blanc with his child's eyes, sees above Mont Blanc the Madonna; St Bernard of Talloires, not the Lake of Annecy, but the dead between Martigny and Aosta. But for me, the Alps and their people were alike beautiful in their snow, and their humanity; and I wanted, neither for them nor myself, sight of any thrones in heaven but the rocks, or of any spirits in heaven but the clouds.

Thus, in perfect health of life and fire of heart, not wanting to be anything but the boy I was, not wanting to have anything more than I had; knowing of sorrow only just so much as to make life serious to me, not enough to slacken in the least its sinews; and with so much of science mixed with feeling as to make the sight of the Alps not only the revelation of the beauty of the earth, but the opening of the first page of its volume, – I went down that evening from the garden-terrace of Schaffhausen with my destiny fixed in all of it that was to be sacred and useful. To that terrace, and the shore of the Lake of Geneva, my heart and faith return to this day, in every impulse that is yet nobly alive in them, and every thought that has in it help or peace. (Vol. I, Ch. VI, paras. 132–5)

1841 – the lows and the highs

Diary entry 9 January

I was quite tired as it grew dark, fragments of blue and amber sky showing through colossal thunder clouds, and two or three pure stars labouring among the dark masses. It lightened fast as we got into Naples, and we were stopped again, first by Dogana, and then at passport office, till I lost temper and patience, and could have cried like a girl, for I was quite wearied with the bad roads, and disappointed with the approach to Naples, and cold. I could not help wondering at this. How little could I have imagined, sitting in my home corner, yearning for a glance of the hill snow, or the orange leaf, that I should, at entering Naples, be as thoroughly out of humour as ever after a monotonous day in London. More so!

The sight of the Alps

I woke from a sound tired sleep in a little one-windowed room at

Lans-le-bourg, at six of the summer morning, June 2nd, 1841; the red aiguilles on the north relieved against pure blue – the great pyramid of snow down the valley in one sheet of eastern light. I dressed in three minutes, ran down the village street, across the stream, and climbed the grassy slope on the south side of the valley, up to the first pines.

I had found my life again; – all the best of it.[c] What good of

---

[c] *False and True Life*:

Now in all other kind of energies except that of man's mind, there is no question as to what is life, and what is not. Vital sensibility, whether vegetable or animal, may, indeed, be reduced to so great feebleness, as to render its existence a matter of question, but when it is evident at all, it is evident as such: there is no mistaking any imitation or pretence of it for the life itself; no mechanism nor galvanism can take its place; nor is any resemblance of it so striking as to involve even hesitation in the judgment; although many occur which the human imagination takes pleasure in exalting, without for an instant losing sight of the real nature of the dead things it animates; but rejoicing rather in its own excessive life, which puts gesture into clouds, and joy into waves, and voices into rocks.

But when we begin to be concerned with the energies of man, we find ourselves instantly dealing with a double creature. Most part of his being seems to have a fictitious counterpart, which it is his peril if he do not cast off and deny. Thus he has a true and false (otherwise called a living and dead, or a feigned or unfeigned) faith. He has a true and a false hope, a true and a false charity, and, finally, a true and a false life. His true life is like that of lower organic beings, the independent force by which he moulds and governs external things; it is a force of assimilation which converts everything around him into food, or into instruments; and which, however humbly or obediently it may listen to or follow the guidance of superior intelligence, never forfeits its own authority as a judging principle, as a will capable either of obeying or rebelling. His false life is, indeed, but one of the conditions of death or stupor, but it acts, even when it cannot be said to animate, and is not always easily known from the true. It is that life of custom and accident in which many of us pass much of our time in the world; that life in which we do what we have not proposed, and speak what we do not mean, and assent to what we do not understand; that life which is overlaid by the weight of things external to it, and is moulded by them, instead of assimilating them; that, which instead of growing and blossoming under any wholesome dew, is crystallised over with it, as with hoar-frost, and becomes to the true life what an aborescence is to a tree, a candied agglomeration of thoughts and habits foreign to it, brittle, obstinate, and icy, which can neither bend nor grow, but must be crushed and broken to bits, if it stand in our way. All men are liable to be in some degree frost-bitten in this sort; all are partly encumbered and crusted over with idle matter; only, if religion, love, admiration or hope, had ever been taught me, or felt by my best nature, rekindled at once; and my line of work, both by my own will and the aid granted to it by fate in the future, determined for me. I went down thankfully to my father and mother, and told them I was sure I should get well. (Vol. II, Ch. III, para. 57)

To see – as a Stranger

I wish in general to avoid interference with the reader's judgment on the matters which I endeavour serenely to narrate; but may, I think, here be pardoned for observing to him the advantage, in a certain way, of the contemplative abstraction from the world which, during this early continental travelling, was partly enforced by our ignorance, and partly secured by our love of comfort. There is something peculiarly delightful – nay, delightful

they have real life in them, they are always breaking this bark away in noble rents, until it becomes, like the black strips upon the birch tree, only a witness of their own inward strength. But, with all the efforts that the best men make, much of their being passes in a kind of dream, in which they indeed move, and play their parts sufficiently, to the eyes of their fellow dreamers, but have no clear consciousness of what is around them, or within them; blind to the one, insensible to the other, νωθροὶ [sluggish, stupid]. I would not press the definition into its darker application to the dull heart and heavy ear; I have to do with it only as it refers to the too frequent condition of natural existence, whether of nations or individuals, settling commonly upon them in proportion to their age. The life of a nation is usually, like the flow of a lava stream, first bright and fierce, then languid and covered, at last advancing only by the tumbling over and over of its frozen blocks. And that last condition is a sad one to look upon. All the steps are marked most clearly in the arts, and in Architecture more than in any other; for it, being especially dependent, as we have just said, on the warmth of the true life, is also peculiarly sensible of the hemlock cold of the false: and I do not know anything more oppressive, when the mind is once awakened to its characteristics, than the aspect of a dead architecture. The feebleness of childhood is full of promise and of interest, – the struggle of imperfect knowledge full of energy and continuity, – but to see impotence and rigidity settling upon the form of the developed man; to see the types which once had the die of thought struck fresh upon them, worn flat by over use; to see the shell of the living creature in its adult form, when its colours are faded, and its inhabitant perished, – this is a sight more humiliating, more melancholy, than the vanishing of all knowledge, and the return to confessed and helpless infancy. (SL, Ch. V, ['The Lamp of Life'], paras. 2–3)

inconceivably by the modern German-plated and French-polished tourist, in passing through the streets of a foreign city without understanding a word anybody says! One's ear for all sound of voices then becomes entirely impartial; one is not diverted by the meaning of syllables from recognizing the absolute guttural, liquid, or honeyed quality of them: while the gesture of the body and the expression of the face have the same value for you that they have in a pantomime; every scene becomes a melodious opera to you, or a picturesquely inarticulate Punch. Consider, also, the gain in so consistent tranquillity. Most young people nowadays, or even lively old ones, travel more in search of adventures than of information. One of my most valued records of recent wandering is a series of sketches by an amiable and extremely clever girl, of the things that happened to her people and herself every day that they were abroad. Here it is brother Harry, and there it is mamma, and now paterfamilias, and now her little graceful self, and anon her merry or remonstrant sisterhood, who meet with enchanting hardships, and enviable misadventures; bind themselves with fetters of friendship, and glance into sparklings of amourette, with any sort of people in conical hats and fringy caps: and it is all very delightful and condescending, and, of course, things are learnt about the country that way which can be learned in no other way, but only about that part of it which interests itself in you, or which you have pleasure in being acquainted with. Virtually, you are thinking of yourself all the time; you necessarily talk to the cheerful people, not to the sad ones; and your head is for the most part vividly taken up with very little things. I don't say that our isolation was meritorious, or that people in general should know no language but their own. Yet the meek ignorance has these advantages. We did not travel for adventures, nor for company, but to see with our eyes, and to measure with our hearts. If you have sympathy, the aspect of humanity is more true to the depths of it than its words; and even in my own land, the things in which I have been least deceived are those which I have learned as their Spectator. (Vol. I, Ch. VI, para. 138)

From 'Fontainebleau'

And so the year 1842 dawned for me, with many things in its

morning cloud.[d] In the early spring of it, a change came over Turner's mind. He wanted to make some drawings to please himself; but also to be paid for making them. He gave Mr Griffith fifteen sketches for choice of subject by any one who would give him a commission. He got commissions for nine, of which my father let me choose at first one, then was coaxed and tricked into letting me have two. Turner got orders, out of all the round world besides, for seven more. With the sketches, four finished drawings were shown for samples of the sort of thing Turner meant to make of them, and for immediate purchase by anybody.

Among them was the 'Splügen', which I had some hope of obtaining by supplication, when my father, who was travelling, came home. I waited dutifully till he should come. In the meantime it was bought, with the loveliest Lake Lucerne, by Mr Munro of Novar.

The thing became to me grave matter for meditation. In a story by Miss Edgeworth, the father would have come back in the nick of time, effaced Mr Munro as he hesitated with the 'Splügen' in his hand, and given the dutiful son that, and another. I found, after meditation, that Miss Edgeworth's way was not the world's, nor Providence's. I perceived then, and conclusively, that if you do a foolish thing, you suffer for it exactly the same, whether you do it piously or not. I knew perfectly well that this drawing was the best Swiss landscape yet painted by man; and that it was entirely proper for *me* to have it, and inexpedient that anybody else should. I ought to have secured it instantly, and begged my father's pardon, tenderly. He would have been angry, and surprised, and grieved; but loved me none the less, found in the end I was right, and been entirely pleased. I should have been very uncomfortable and penitent for a while, but loved my father all the more for having hurt him, and, in the good of the thing itself, finally satisfied and triumphant. As it was, the 'Splügen' was a thorn in both our sides, all our lives. My father was always trying

---

[d] *On the intermingled nature of a life in time*:
Whether in the biography of a nation, or of a single person, it is alike impossible to trace it steadily through successive years. Some forces are failing while others strengthen, and most act irregularly, or else at uncorresponding periods of renewed enthusiasm after intervals of lassitude. For all clearness of exposition, it is necessary to follow first one, then another, without confusing notices of what is happening in other directions. (Vol. I, Ch. X, para. 195)

to get it; Mr Munro, aided by dealers, always raising the price on him, till it got up from 80 to 400 guineas. Then we gave it up, – with unspeakable wear and tear of best feelings on both sides.

And how about 'Thou shalt not covet', etc.? Good reader, if you ask this, please consult my philosophical works. Here, I can only tell you facts, whether of circumstance or law. It is a law that if you do a foolish thing you suffer for it, whatever your motive. I do not say the motive itself may not be rewarded or punished on its own merits. In this case, nothing but mischief, as far as I know, came of the whole matter.

In the meantime, bearing the disappointment as best I could, I rejoiced in the sight of the sketches, and the hope of the drawings that were to be. And they gave me much more to think of than my mischance. I saw that these sketches were straight impressions from nature, – not artificial designs, like the Carthages and Romes. And it began to occur to me that perhaps even in the artifice of Turner there might be more truth than I had understood. I was by this time very learned in *his* principles of composition; but it seemed to me that in these later subjects Nature herself was composing with him.

Considering of these matters, one day on the road to Norwood, I noticed a bit of ivy round a thorn stem, which seemed, even to my critical judgment, not ill 'composed'; and proceeded to make a light and shade pencil study of it in my grey paper pocket-book, carefully, as if it had been a bit of sculpture, liking it more and more as I drew. When it was done, I saw that I had virtually lost all my time since I was twelve years old, because no one had ever told me to draw what was really there! All my time, I mean, given to drawing as an art; of course I had the records of places, but had never seen the beauty of anything, not even of a stone – how much less of a leaf!

I was neither so crushed nor so elated by the discovery as I ought to have been, but it ended the chrysalid days. Thenceforward my advance was steady, however slow.

This must have been in May, and a week or two afterwards I went up for my degree, but find no entry of it. I only went up for a pass, and still wrote Latin so badly that there was a chance of my *not* passing! but the examiners forgave it because the divinity, philosophy, and mathematics were all above the average; and they gave me a complimentary double-fourth.

When I was sure I had got through, I went out for a walk in the fields north of New College, (since turned into the Parks,) happy in the sense of recovered freedom, but extremely doubtful to what use I should put it. There I was, at two and twenty, with such and such powers, all second-rate except the analytic ones, which were as much in embryo as the rest, and which I had no means of measuring; such and such likings, hitherto indulged rather against conscience; and a dim sense of duty to myself, my parents, and a daily more vague shadow of Eternal Law.

What should I be, or do? my utterly indulgent father ready to let me do anything; with my room always luxuriously furnished in his house, – my expenses paid if I chose to travel. I was not heartless enough, yet, to choose to do that, alone. Perhaps it may deserve some dim praise that I never seriously thought of leaving my father and mother to explore foreign countries; and certainly the fear of grieving them was intermingled more or less with all my thoughts; but then, I did not much *want* to explore foreign countries. I had not the least love of adventure, but liked to have comfortable rooms always ordered, and a three-course dinner ready by four o'clock. Although no coward under circumstances of accidental danger, I extremely objected to any vestige of danger as a continuous element in one's life. I would not go to India for fear of tigers, nor to Russia for fear of bears, nor to Peru for fear of earthquakes; and finally, though I had no rightly glowing or grateful affection for either father or mother, yet as they could not well do without me, so also I found I was not altogether comfortable without *them*.

So for the present, we planned a summer-time in Switzerland, not of travelling, but chiefly stay in Chamouni, to give me mountain air, and the long coveted power of examining the Mont Blanc rocks accurately. My mother loved Chamouni nearly as much as I; but this plan was of severe self-denial to my father, who did not like snow, nor wooden-walled rooms.

But he gave up all his own likings for me, and let me plan the stages through France as I chose, by Rouen, Chartres, Fontainebleau, and Auxerre. A pencil-sketch or two at first show only want of faith in my old manner, and more endeavour for light and shade, futile enough. The flat cross-country between Chartres and Fontainebleau, with an oppressive sense of Paris to the north, fretted me wickedly; when we got to the Fountain of Fair Water I lay feverishly wakeful through the night, and was so heavy and ill in the morning that I could not safely travel, and fancied some bad sickness was coming on. However, towards twelve o'clock the inn people brought me a little basket of wild strawberries; and they refreshed me, and I put my sketch-book in pocket and tottered out, though still in an extremely languid and woe-begone condition; and getting into a cart-road among some young trees, where there was nothing to see but the blue sky through thin branches, lay down on the bank by the roadside to see if I could sleep. But I couldn't, and the branches against the blue sky began to interest me, motionless as the branches of a tree of Jesse on a painted window.

Feeling gradually somewhat livelier, and that I wasn't going to die at this time, and be buried in the sand, though I couldn't for the present walk any farther, I took out my book; and began to draw a little aspen tree, on the other side of the cart-road, carefully . . .

And, to-day, I missed rocks, palace, and fountain all alike, and found myself lying on the bank of the cart-road in the sand, with no prospect whatever but that small aspen tree against the blue sky.

Languidly, but not idly, I began to draw it; and as I drew, the languor passed away: the beautiful lines insisted on being traced, – without weariness. More and more beautiful they became, as each rose out of the rest, and took its place in the air. With wonder increasing every instant I saw that they 'composed' themselves, by finer laws than any known of man. At last, the tree was there, and everything that I had thought before about trees, nowhere . . .

'He hath made everything beautiful in his time', [Ecclesiastes iii.11] became for me thenceforward the interpretation of the bond between the human mind and all visible things. (Vol. II, Ch. IV, paras. 71–5, 77)

Human regrets

Homewards, from wherever we had got to, the moment the sun was down, and the last clouds had lost their colour. I avoided marshy places, if I could, at all times of the day, because I didn't like them; but I feared neither sun nor moon, dawn nor twilight, malaria nor anything else malefic, in the course of work, except only draughts and ugly people. I never would sit in a draught for half a minute, and fled from some sorts of beggars; but a crowd of the common people round me only made me proud, and try to draw as well as I could; mere rags or dirt I did not care an atom for.

As early as 1835, and as late as 1841, I had been accustomed, both in France and Italy, to feel that the crowd behind me was interested in my choice of subjects, and pleasantly applausive of the swift progress under my hand of street perspectives, and richness of surface decoration, such as might be symbolized by dextrous zigzags, emphatic dots, or graceful flourishes. I had the better pleasure, now, of feeling that my really watchful delineation, while still rapid enough to interest any stray student of drawing who might stop by me on his way to the Academy, had a quite unusual power of directing the attention of the general crowd to points of beauty, or subjects of sculpture, in the buildings I was at work on, to which they had never before lifted eyes, and which I had the double pride of first discovering for them, and then imitating – not to their dissatisfaction.

And well might I be proud; but how much more ought I to have been pitiful, in feeling the swift and perfect sympathy which the 'common people' – companion-people I should have said, for in Italy there is no commonness – gave me, in Lucca, or Florence, or Venice, for every touch of true work that I laid in their sight. How much more, I say, should it have been pitiful to me, to recognize their eager intellect, and delicate senses, open to every lesson and every joy of their ancestral art, far more deeply and vividly than in the days when every spring kindled them into battle, and every autumn was red with their blood: yet left now, alike by the laws and lords set over them, less happy in aimless life than of old in sudden death; never one effort made to teach them, to comfort them, to economize their industries, animate their pleasures, or guard their simplest rights from the continually more fatal oppression of unprincipled avarice, and unmerciful wealth.

But all this I have felt and learned, like so much else, too late. The extreme seclusion of my early training left me long careless of sympathy for myself; and that which I gave to others never led me into any hope of being useful to them, till my strength of active life was past. Also, my mind was not yet catholic enough to feel that the Campo Santo belonged to its own people more than to me; and indeed, I had to read its lessons before I could interpret them. The world has for the most part been of opinion that I entered on the task of philanthropy too soon rather than too late: at all events, my conscience remained at rest during all those first times at Pisa, in mere delight in the glory of the past, and in hope for the future of Italy, without need of my becoming one of her demagogues. (Vol. II, Ch. VI, paras. 122–4)

The last paragraph of Praeterita

How things bind and blend themselves together! The last time I saw the Fountain of Trevi, it was from Arthur's father's room – Joseph Severn's, where we both took Joanie to see him in 1872, and the old man made a sweet drawing of his pretty daughter-in-law, now in her schoolroom; he himself then eager in finishing his last picture of the Marriage in Cana, which he had caused to take place under a vine trellis, and delighted himself by painting the crystal and ruby glittering of the changing rivulet of water out of the Greek vase, glowing into wine. Fonte Branda I last saw with Charles Norton, under the same arches where Dante saw it. We drank of it together, and walked together that evening on the hills above, where the fireflies among the scented thickets shone fitfully in the still undarkened air. How they shone! moving like fire-broken starlight through the purple leaves. How they shone! through the sunset that faded into thunderous night as I entered Siena three days before, the white edges of the mountainous clouds still lighted from the west, and the openly golden sky calm behind the Gate of Siena's heart, with its still golden words, 'Cor magis tibi Sena pandit,' and the fireflies everywhere in the sky and cloud rising and falling, mixed with the lightning, and more intense than the stars.[6]

Brantwood, June 19th, 1889 (Vol. III, Ch. IV, para. 86)

Afterword

We are not sent into this world to do any thing into which we cannot put our hearts. We have certain work to do for our bread, and that is to be done strenuously; other work to do for our delight, and that is to be done heartily: neither is to be done by halves and shifts, but with a will; and what is not worth this effort is not to be done at all. Perhaps all that we have to do is meant for nothing more than an exercise of the heart and of the will, and is useless in itself; but, at all events, the little use it has may well be spared if it is not worth putting our hands and our strength to. (SL, Ch. V, para. 24)

APHORISM

'Whatsoever thy hand findeth to do, do it with thy might;' and no other might.

NOTES

Chapter 3

1. (p. 45) Ruskin writes in a footnote: 'Observe, I do not speak thus of metaphysics, because I have no pleasure in them ... I have strong inclination that way, which would, indeed, have led me far astray long ago, if I had not learned also some use of my hands, eyes, and feet.'

2. (p. 49) Ecclesiastes, iii. 11. For the references above to 'the meat more than life', see Matthew, vi. 25; and for 'hewers of wood and drawers of water', Joshua, ix. 21. The whole passage is a good example of Ruskin's use of Biblical phrases.

3. (p. 52) See Hooker, *Of the Laws of Ecclesiastical Polity* (1593), Book II, chap. II, para. 2. Hooker's vision of a universe full of laws was deeply important to Ruskin.

4 (p. 52) Ruskin's footnote in 1883: ' "Taint" is a false word. The entire system of useful and contemplative knowledge is one; equally pure and holy; its only "taints" are in pride, and subservience to avarice or destruction.'

5. (p. 58) Ruskin's 1883 footnote: 'This quite true conclusion reaches farther than I then knew, or at least felt clearly enough to express. Not only light *in* the sky, but light *from* it, is essential to the greatest work; the diffused light of heaven on all sides, as distinguished from chiaroscuro in a room.'

6. (p. 64) In Jowett's translation:

> Are we right in saying that there is one heaven, or shall we rather say that there are many and infinite? There is one, if the created heaven is to accord with the pattern. For that which includes all other intelligible creatures cannot have a second or companion; in that case there would be no need of another living being which would include these two, and of which they would be parts, and the likeness would be more truly said to resemble not those two, but that other which included them.

7. (p. 65) Ruskin's 1883 footnote: 'The words I have now put in parenthesis are false. Heaven itself may be as changeable as a kaleidoscope, for aught we know.'

8. (p. 65) Hooker, *Ecclesiastical Polity*, Book I, Ch. XI, para. 3. In 1883 Ruskin wrote in a footnote, 'Hooker, I think, by the sound of it: to whom

Pope would have quietly and rightly answered – "Why *wish* to persist, then, when God says you have done enough?"'

9.   (p. 85) Dante's *Purgatorio* xxxvi.4. Cary translates:

> 'The sun
> Now all the western clime irradiate changed
> From azure tinct to white; and, as I passed.
> My passing shadow made the umber'd flame
> Burn ruddier.'

10.   (p. 85) Pholas, a sea-animal of the molluscous kind that makes holes in stone.

11.   (p. 86) Dante, *Inferno*, v. 138 ('That day we read no farther'); Shakespeare, *Macbeth*, iv. iii. 217.

Chapter 4

1.   (p. 102) Ruskin's footnote:

As here, for the first time, I am obliged to use the terms Truth and Beauty in a kind of opposition, I must therefore stop for a moment to state clearly the relation of these two qualities of art; and to protest against the vulgar and foolish habit of confusing truth and beauty with each other. People with shallow powers of thought, desiring to flatter themselves with the sensation of having attained profundity, are continually doing the most serious mischief by introducing confusion into plain matters, and then valuing themselves on being confounded. Nothing is more common than to hear people who desire to be thought philosophical, declare that 'beauty is truth', and 'truth is beauty'. I would most earnestly beg every sensible person who hears such an assertion made, to nip the germinating philosopher in his ambiguous bud; and beg him, if he really believes his own assertion, never henceforward to use two words for the same thing. The fact is, truth and beauty are entirely distinct, though often related, things. One is a property of statements, the other of objects. The statement that 'two and two make four' is true, but it is neither beautiful nor ugly, for it is invisible; a rose is lovely, but it is neither true nor false, for it is silent. That which shows nothing cannot be fair, and that which asserts nothing cannot be false. Even the ordinary use of the words false and true, as applied to artificial and real things, is inaccurate. An artificial rose is not a 'false' rose, it is not a rose at all. The falseness is in the person who states, or induces the belief, that it *is* a rose.

Now, therefore, in things concerning art, the words true and false are only to be rightly used while the picture is considered as a statement of facts. The painter asserts that this which he has painted is the form of a dog, a man, or a tree. If it be *not* the form of a dog, a man, or a tree, the painter's statement is false; and, therefore, we justly speak of a false line, or false colour; not that any lines or colours can in themselves be false, but they become so when they convey a statement that they resemble something which they do *not* resemble. But the beauty of the lines or colours is wholly independent of any such statement. They may be beautiful lines, though quite inaccurate, and ugly lines though quite faithful. A picture may be frightfully ugly, which represents with fidelity some base circumstance of daily life; and a painted window may be exquisitely beautiful, which represents men with eagles' faces, and dogs with blue heads and crimson tails (though, by the way, this is not in the strict sense *false* art, as we shall see hereafter, inasmuch as it means no assertion that men ever *had* eagles' faces). If this were not so, it would be impossible to sacrifice truth to beauty; for to attain the one would always be to attain the other. But unfortunately, this sacrifice is exceedingly possible and it is chiefly this which characterizes the false schools of high art, so far as high art consists in the pursuit of beauty. For although truth and beauty are independent of each other, it does not follow that we are at liberty to pursue whichever we please. They are indeed separable, but it is wrong to separate them; they are to be sought together in the order of their worthiness; that is to say, truth first, and beauty afterwards. High art differs from low art in possessing an excess of beauty in addition to its truth, not in possessing excess of beauty inconsistent with truth.

2.   (p. 108) That is to say, Imagination Associative, Imagination Penetrative and Imagination Contemplative. The last of these is concerned with a certain 'indistinctness of conception' as when 'we do not usually recall . . . one part at a time only of a pleasant scene, one moment only of a happy day; but together with each single object we summon up a kind of crowded and involved shadowing forth of all the other glories with which it was associated, and into every moment we concentrate an epitome of the day' (MP II, Pt. III, Ch. IV, para. 3). Art is always a form of realization, but this sort of contemplation is of things that are not limited to a definite shape: Imagination Contemplative therefore forges a subject's abstract qualities anew into a particular ideal image or symbol – as when Milton says that Satan 'is like a comet burned'.

3.   (p. 109) In a footnote to MP III, Ch. 1, para. 14, on 'The Grand Style', Ruskin compares a stanza from Wordsworth's 'Affliction of Margaret' (beginning 'I look for ghosts, but none will force/Their way to me') with Saussure's prose account in *Voyages dans les Alps* (about a bereaved woman of Argentiere) to distinguish genuine poetical feeling in the latter from the image-making power that in the former goes into the making of true poetry.

4.   (p. 118) Lombardic: meaning, here, in the style of Pietro and Tullio Lombardo in the fifteenth century (not Lombard).

5.   (p. 125) The Napoleon is Turner's *War: the Exile and the Rock Limpet*, now at the Tate Gallery.

6.   (p. 138) In the former passage Ruskin is arguing against illusions such as trompe d'oeil, preferring painterly signs which 'have no pretence, nor hypocrisy, nor legerdemain about them' but 'bear their message simply and clearly and it is that message which the mind takes from them, regardless of the language in which it is delivered'. In the latter, Ruskin rails again against 'the power of the painter to *deceive*', 'to trick the

spectator into a belief of reality', to employ 'jugglery', and he urges painters to ignore the examples of Claude, Salvator and Poussin and rise above the aim of the daguerrotype (one of the earliest photographic processes, invented in 1839).

7. (p. 138) Compare Ruskin on necessary imperfection in *The Stones of Venice* (Chapter 5, and Chapter 4, pp. 165–6).

8. (p. 140). For Turner 'he is the only painter', see Chapter 2, pp. 26–7; for Wordsworth's daisy, Chapter 4, p. 113.

9. (p. 141) See excerpt on Imagination Penetrative, Chapter 3, p. 84ff.

10. (p. 147) Ruskin's diary for June 1849 in the Alps is cited C&W V, pp. xix–xx: 'marvellous blocks of granite and pines beside me, and yet with all this I enjoyed it no more than a walk on Denmark Hill'; but 'when I confined myself to one thing – as to the grass or stones . . . I began to enjoy it directly'. The lesson Ruskin drew in his diary was 'how the majesty of nature depends on the force of human spirit, and how each spirit can only embrace at a time so much of what has been appointed for its food, and may therefore rest contented with little, knowing that if it throws its full energy into that little, it will be more than enough; and that an over-supply of food would only be an over-tax upon its energies.'

11. (p. 153) Lectures on Architecture and Painting, delivered at Edinburgh in November 1853, C&W XII, p. 161, para. 138.

12. (p. 153) See no. 9 of *The Tatler*. Van Eyck was placed by Ruskin, with Dürer as an active resister of mountain gloom.

13. (p. 155) The first version of this passage occurs in the MS. of Ch. IX and is as follows:

> Observe, in the first place, this great fact. You never see anything Plainly. It is with sight as with knowledge. It is written: 'If any man think that he knoweth anything, he knoweth nothing yet as he ought to know.' And in the same sense: if any man think that he seeth, he seeth nothing yet as he ought to see. Whatever we look at is full of mystery. Everything that we look at, be it large or small, near or distant, has an infinite quantity of details still too small to be seen: and the only question is not how much mystery there is, but at what point the mystery begins. For instance, I suppose most people think they can see their own hand clearly. If they do, let them try to count the small furrows, or the lines of the light down which give its texture to the skin, and to trace the course of the fine veins through the shadows of the fingers. You suppose you see the ground under your feet clearly; but if you try to number its grains of dust, you will find that it is as full of confusion and difficulty as the distance; only the confusion on the horizon is of trees and houses, here, of pebbles and of dust. You cannot count the fibres of the cloth stuff, and if you try to draw all the fibres and threads that you see, you will find the work as infinite as if you were drawing a distant forest. Pope asked ironically why man has not a microscopic eye, but man's eyes are just as microscopic as any other creature's; he sees the things that bear a certain proportion to himself with a certain degree of intelligibility, and a fly can do no more. It sees less things than a man, but it does not see them more clearly; infinity is as much beyond a

fly's sight, as beyond our own, only the fly stops at a different point in the infinity. So, then, whenever in drawing any object – be it large or small – we have represented it perfectly distinct, there is something wrong. Our work is either unfinished, or false. Distinct drawing is certainly bad drawing in one way or another, and we must not think we have approached perfection until we have got our work into confusion.

[The Biblical reference is to 1 Corinthians viii. 2; that to Pope, *Essay on Man*, line 193; the lines are quoted again in *Deucalion*, ch. ii.]

14.   (p. 156) Ruskin made these observations originally in his diary for 12 September 1854.

15.   (p. 159) Stanfield's drawing of the Isola Bella and the St Gothard, 'Lago Maggiore', was the vignette on the title-page of Heath's *Picturesque Annual* for 1832.

Chapter 5

1.   (p. 186) Ruskin's footnote in the 1879 revision:

A great deal of this talk is flighty, and some of it fallacious; I should have to rewrite it all, or must leave it alone. Aquileia, not Torcello, was the true mother of Venice; but the sentimental and essential truth of general principle in the chapter induce me to reprint the available part of it in this edition.

2.   (p. 195) Cook and Wedderburn cite here George Herbert, 'The Church Porch', 56:

Sink not in spirit; who aimeth at the sky
Shoots higher much than he that means tree.

and Browning, 'A Grammarian's Funeral':

That low man seeks a little thing to do,
    Sees it and does it:
This high man with a great thing to pursue,
    Dies ere he knows it.

3.   (p. 198) Cook and Wedderburn point out that 'at the time Ruskin wrote, agrarian crime had been prevalent in Ireland. In 1847 a Coercion Act was passed; in 1848 the "Young Ireland" rebellion broke out, and the Habeas Corpus Act was suspended; in 1850 the Irish Tenant-Right League was formed; in the same year "several landlords were murdered by discontented tenants".'

4.   (p. 198) A story told by Sir Walter Scott in the preface to *Fair Maid of Perth*, in which a foster father and seven sons sacrificed themselves for Sir Hector Maclean of Duart.

5.   (p. 198) Ruskin was opposed to political economy: the phrase 'the division of labour' was first used at the beginning of Adam Smith's *The Wealth of Nations* (1776).

6.   (p. 200) The abolition of the slave trade in 1807, the abolition of

slavery in British colonies in 1833 and the extension of the anti-slavery movement into the forming of treaties with other countries, such as Brazil in 1845, in order to prevent the trade.

7.   (p. 202) SV I, Ch. XXI, para. 11: 'The purest architectural abstractions . . . are the deep and laborious thoughts of the greatest men, put into such easy letters that they can be written by the simplest.'

8.   (p. 202) MP III, Pt. IV, Ch. III, para. 21, reprinted in Chapter 4 above (p. 108ff.), on invention as one of the characteristics of original work.

9.   (p. 214) triglyph: three-grooved tablet in the Doric frieze, always the same. 'Them that wake and them that sleep': 1 Thessalonians, v. 10.

10.   (p. 220) 'Design' means 'the power to arrange lines and colours nobly.' Ruskin also notes that 'facts' here are such as are genuinely 'perceived by the eye and mind', not facts accumulated by mere knowledge as in the Roman Renaissance.

11.   (p. 225) See SL, Ch. II, para. 21.

12.   (p. 229) 'Where Giotto planted/His campanille like an unperplexed/Fine question Heavenward': Elizabeth Barrett Browning, *Casa Guidi Windows* (1851).

13.   (p. 240) St Bernard: 'After having passed a whole day in riding along its shore, in the evening when his companions were asking about the Lake, he enquired, "What Lake?"'

14.   (p. 255) Sir Joshua Reynolds in his general manner is here contrasted with the over-particularizations of Hobbima (1638–1709) of the seventeenth-century Dutch realist school.

Chapter 6

1.   (p. 275) The Bible references in this paragraph are: Exodus, iii.12; Deuteronomy, xxxiii. 2; 1 Kings, xvii. 5; Deuteronomy, xxxiv. 5; Numbers, xx. 28; Judges, xi. 37; Matthew, iv. 1–4, v–vii. 27, xvii. 1–2; Luke, ix. 28–36; Matthew, xxvi. 30; Luke, xxii. 39.

2.   (p. 281) Ruskin's footnote: 'Pre-Raphaelitism, of course, excepted, which is a new phase of art, in no wise considered in this chapter. Blake was sincere, but full of wild creeds, and somewhat diseased in brain.'

3.   (p. 282) See Chapter 5, p. 207, footnote b, on the connection between MP and SV.

4.   (p. 284) The Crimean War saw the alliance of the British and the French in 1854, until the end of the war in 1856, during which time discoveries of various minor planets were claimed and contested in both countries.

5.   (p. 287) Earlier in the chapter (para. 34) Ruskin had quoted, as an example of the modern weakness of melancholy even amidst sweet home landscapes, 'Blackford, on whose uncultured breast . . .' *Marmion*, iv. 24:

> Naught do I see unchanged remain
>> Save the rude cliffs and chiming brook;
> To me they make a heavy moan
> Of early friendships past and gone.

6. (p. 293) Ruskin here added a note:

Compare what is said before in various places of good and bad finish, good and bad mystery etc. If a man were disposed to system-making, he could easily throw together a counter-system to Aristotle's, showing that in all things there were two extremes which exactly resembled each other, but of which one was bad, the other good; and a mean, resembling neither, but better than the one, and worse than the other.

7. (p. 295) Ruskin's footnote:

I have been embarrassed in assigning the names to these orders of art, the term 'Contemplative' belonging in justice nearly as much to the romantic and pastoral conception as to the modern landscape. I intended, originally, to call the four schools – Romantic, Classic, Georgic, and Theoretic – which would have been more accurate; and more consistent with the nomenclature of the second volume; but would not have been pleasant in sound, nor, to the general reader, very clear in sense.

8. (p. 297) The manuscript continues:

Thus in Turner, the distinctive mark which separated him from all other painters of this time, so far as method went, was his perpetual use to the end of his life of the Pencil point instead of the brush in drawing from nature, and his consequent power of Drawing more subtly than any contemporary painter. It was precisely *this* which the public mainly denied concerning him. He might do everything else well – but he could not Draw!

9. (p. 305) Alexis Francois Rio, in *De la Poesie Chretienne dansson principe, dans sa matière et dans ses formes* (1836), praised the early Italian masters – Fra Angelico, Giotto etc. Lord Lindsay's *Sketches of the History of Christian Art* (1847) was reviewed by Ruskin.

10. (p. 315) See Homer's *Iliad*, xxii, 236ff, where Athena takes the form of Hector's brother Deiphobus in order to encourage him to fight Achilles, who remains unafraid in the midst of their combat. 'The spear thrown in vain by Hector is taken up by Athena and given to Achilles. Hector calls in vain upon Deiphobus for help, but no Deiphobus is there. It is by the Lance of Pallas that Hector goes bravely to death. In the first draft the title of the chapter was "The Spear of Deiphobus" ' (C&W).

11. (p. 319) From 1807 to 1819 Turner published the 70 plates of his *Liber Studiorum* consisting of landscape compositions.

12. (p. 320) C&W comment: 'In one of his own copies Ruskin here notes "Compare Deuteronomy xxiv. 6" – "No man shall take the nether or the upper millstone to pledge." '

13. (p. 323) Turner's *Bolton Abbey*, sketched in 1800, was published in 1827.

14.   (p. 324) The *Fallacy of Hope* was the title of Turner's manuscript poems, from which he quoted many lines as mottos for his paintings. 'The weeping of the mother' for the first-born refers to the Tenth Plague of Egypt; for her last sons is a reference to Rizpah, daughter of Aiah and concubine of Saul whose two sons were hanged by David (2 Samuel xxi. 8–10).

15.   (p. 324) The old Greek question – 'what hope have we?' – was raised in MP. V, Pt. IX, Ch. II, para. 19 above, p. 315.

16.   (p. 325) The sensual debasement of religion that relates Guido Reni (1575–1642) and Bartolome Esteban Murillo (1617–82) to Salvator, in Ruskin's view, is discussed in MP II, Pt. III, Sec. I, Ch. X, para. 4; Ch. XIV, para. 14.

17.   (p. 327) Michelet, *Du Prêtre, de la Femme, de la Famille* (1845). The painting that shows Salvator to be capable of fear is 'Temptation of St Anthony'. According to C&W, the inscription 'Despiser of Wealth and of Death' was engraved beneath Salvator's etching known as *The Genius of Salvator Rosa*, in which in a wooded spot of ruin the painter, lying at the feet of a Roman philosopher and a satyr, a dead dove on his bosom, rejects the wealth of wisdom.

18.   (p. 335) 'But the public never stops a moment in the room at Kensington where they hang; and the damp, filth, and gas (under the former management of that institution) soiled their frames and warped the drawings' (C&W, XIII, pp. 341–2). Much of Turner's work had been left decaying in parcels in the National Gallery.

19.   (p. 336) A building of iron and glass, similar to the Crystal Palace, had been constructed for the Dublin International Exhibition in 1864, and here it was that Ruskin delivered this lecture – at a time when geology and botany were his main points of recourse.

Chapter 7

1.   (p. 362) From Emerson's lines 'To Rhea':

> He mixes music with her thoughts,
> And saddens her with heavenly doubts.

2.   (p. 372) Especially studies of the Madonna.

3.   (p. 379) Identified as Miss Georgiana Tollemache, afterwards Mrs Cowper Temple (Lady Mount Temple). When *Sesame and Lilies* was reissued in 1871, Ruskin dedicated it to her. 'Proutism' is a reference to Samuel Prout (1783–1852), watercolourist and architectural draughtsman.

4.   (p. 379) 'Dum pituita molesta est': Horace, *Epistles*, i, 1, 108: 'while the phlegm, a morbid discharge, is troublesome'. C&W point out that Ruskin, looking out across the Campagna to Mount Soracte, knew his feelings to be akin to Byron's: 'All, save the lone Soractes's height

display'd, / Not now in snow, which asks the lyric Roman's aid / For our remembrance' (*Childe Harold's Pilgrimage*, IV, 74ff).

5.   (p. 381) See *Fors Clavigera*, Letter 45, where Ruskin says that this statue turned him 'from the study of landscape to that of life'.

6.   (p. 394) Joseph Severn (1793–1879), painter, was a friend of Keats who attended him at his death. On the death of Ruskin's father in 1864, seventeen-year-old Joan Agnew came to help the bereaved mother, her aunt, and stayed seven years, marrying Arthur Severn, a Ruskin devotee and Joseph's son, in 1871. Ruskin gave the couple the Herne Hill house as a wedding present. The Severns looked after Ruskin increasingly at both Herne Hill and Brantwood (which Ruskin had purchased for himself after his mother's death in December 1871). Charles Eliot Norton (1827–1908) was a literary man, translator of Dante, editor of works by Carlyle and Emerson, and Harvard professor. 'Cor magis tibi Sena pandit' was inscribed over the north gate: 'more than her gates, Siena opens her heart to you'.

BIOGRAPHICAL GLOSSARY

Angelico, Fra (1387–55). Dominican friar in the convent of S Marco, Florence, admired by Ruskin not so much as an artist but as an inspired saint with all the strengths and weaknesses of Purist Idealism (MP III, Pt. IV, Ch. VI, paras. 3–7, in Chapter 6 above, pp. 305–6).

Bellini, Giovanni (1430–1516). Was of the family that had a major influence in the development of Venetian painting; Ruskin held his *Madonna with Saints*, in its colour and light and pure contemplative calm, to be one of the three most beautiful pictures in the world and admired his 'profound religious peace' as a landscape painter (see SV I, Appendix 11).

Berghem, Nicolaes (1620–83). Dutch painter of landscapes in the Italianate manner, with golden haze.

Canaletto, Antonio (1697–1768). Ruskin spoke of his 'servile and mindless imitation ... He professes nothing but coloured daguerrotypeism' (MP I, Pt. I, Sec. I, Ch. VII, para. 30).

Caravaggio, Michelangelo (1571–1610). Was criticized by Ruskin for perpetually seeking horror and ugliness.

Cima de Conegliano (1459–1517). One of the early religious painters in Italy whose ideal landscape Ruskin praised for 'entire, exquisite, and humble realization of those objects [he] selects' (MP I, Pt. II, Sec. I, Ch. VII, para. 9).

Claude Lorrain (1600–82). Though to a degree admired by Ruskin, was chiefly criticized as a contrast to Turner, because Claude 'never felt the truth enough to sacrifice supposed propriety, or habitual method to it' (MP V, Pt. IX, Ch. V, para. 10).

Constable, John (1776–1837). Ruskin praised his simplicity and earnestness but thought him, even in his independent devotion to what he really saw, to be erring too much on the other side: too uneducatedly individual as a drawer and too attracted to subjects of a low order – 'There are then two dangerous extremes to be shunned ... slavery on the one hand, and free-thinking on the other' (preface to second edition of *Modern Painters* vol. I, C&W III, p. 45, footnote, and also see MP I, Pt. II, Sec. I, Ch. VII, para. 18).

Correggio, Antonio (1489–1534). Painted mainly in Parma: while criticizing his inherent sensuality, Ruskin nonetheless admired the mysterious power of his drawing and brushwork (MP IV, Pt. V, Ch. IV, para. 9).

De Wint, Peter (1784–1849). Was praised by Ruskin only for a limited pursuit of truth, for 'accuracy of eye and experience of colour' rather than for 'exercise of thought' (MP I, Pt. II, Sec. I, Ch. VII, para. 23).

Doré, Gustave (1823–83). French book illustrator, especially of Dante's *Inferno, Don Quixote*, the Bible and *The Pilgrim's Progress*, and whom Ruskin saw as an example of debased grotesque.

Dow, Gerard (1613–75). Portrait painter also of the Dutch school of realism with (what Ruskin took to be) its over-detailed finish.

Dürer, Albrecht (1471–1528). German painter and engraver, is in many ways the hero of MP V for his landscape painting and his spiritual struggle with gloom and doubt.

Francia, Francesco (1450–1517). An example of those early Italian painters who in their purity loved what they saw beneath the open sky.

Fuseli, Henry (1741–1825). Extravagant visionary painter.

Giorgione (1475–1510). Venetian painter: the fading and loss of so many of his frescoes was a source of deep regret to Ruskin, for by Giorgione, Titian, Tintoret and Veronese 'the walls of Venice were lighted with human life' (MP I, Pt. II, Sec. I, Ch. VII, para. 30).

Ghiberti, Lorenzo (1378–1455). Florentine sculptor, famed for his work on the Baptistery, Florence.

Ghirlandaio, Domenico (1449–94). In Vasari's *Lives* he is said to have resisted household cares, leaving them to his brother David, saying that now that he was in the spirit of his art, he wished he could paint the whole circuit of Florence's walls with stories. Ruskin considered him to have consummate grandeur but without definite knowledge (MP I, Pt. II, Sec. I, Ch. VII, para. 25).

Giotto di Bondone (1267–1337). For Ruskin's extraordinarily high estimate of him as a painter, see SV III, Ch. IV, para. 8 (in Chapter 5, pp. 251–2, above). In architecture Ruskin particularly admired the Campanile (Giotto's tower, though his original design was later altered) in Florence.

Gozzoli, Benozzo (1421–97). Painter of frescoes in Florence and Pisa, assistant to Fra Angelico.

Guardi, Francesco (1712–93). Venetian painter, especially of town scenes.

Helps, Sir Arthur (1813–1875). Published four series of *Friends in Council* (1847–59). His influence was acknowledged by Ruskin in the same breath as that of Thomas Carlyle and Wordsworth.

Holbein, Hans (1497–1543). Was described by Ruskin as the most accurate of portrait painters but as with Dürer, the other great exponent of northern art, the realism was in the service of a clear-eyed struggle against evil (MP V, Pt. IX, Ch. II, para. 13, Ch. IV, para. 4 – quoted in Chapter 6).

Hunt, William Holman (1827–1910). The Pre-Raphaelite who painted *The Light of the World* (1854), which Ruskin so much admired; his *Claudio and Isabella*, taken from Shakespeare's *Measure for Measure*, was noticed by Ruskin at the Royal Academy exhibition in 1853.

Leonardo da Vinci (1452–1519). Criticized by Ruskin in *The Stones of Venice* for attempting perfection.

Leslie, C. R. (1794–1859). The biographer of Constable, was praised by Ruskin for his depiction of the delicate expressions of the human face.

Masaccio 1401–28). To Ruskin the greatest of the fifteenth-century Florentine masters, 'getting always vital truth out of the vital present' (MP III, Pt. IV, Ch. VIII, para. 19).

Michelangelo, Buonarotti (1475–1564). Ruskin largely exempted Michelangelo, like Leonardo, from his general censure of the Renaissance.

Orcagna, Andrea (1308–68). Successor to Giotto in Florence, Ruskin admired the severe grandness of his work in the Campo Santo, including his *Triumph of Death*.

Overbeck, Johann Friedrich (1789–1869). Leader of the modern religious movement in nineteenth-century German art.

Perugino (1445–1523). Ruskin admired the finish of his work in Florence, where finish was itself an act of spiritual devotion (MP II, Pt. III, Sec. I, Ch. X, para. 2).

Phidias. An Athenian sculptor of the mid-fifth century BC.

Poussin, Gaspard (or Gaspard Dughet) (1615–75). Brother-in-law and pupil of Nicolas Poussin who took his teacher's name. His *Landscape with Abraham and Isaac approaching the Place of Sacrifice* was criticized by Ruskin in 'Of Truth of Colour' for its 'murky browns and melancholy greens' as being hardly representative of the tint of leaves under full noonday sun.

Poussin, Nicholas (1594–1665). Thought of by Ruskin as the principal French master, with Claude, of classical landscape, 'representing an imaginary world, inhabited by perfectly civilized men, and by spiritual powers of an inferior order' (MP V, Pt. IX, Ch. I, para. 2). His brother-in-law and pupil was Gaspard Poussin (1615–75).

Raphael (1483–1520). The painter whose very skill made Ruskin want art to get away from his influence and be as if before he had ever happened – hence Pre-Raphaelitism.

Rembrandt van Ryn (1606–69). Ruskin disliked his darkness, except in so far as he favoured a Rembrandtism of shadow in architecture (see Chapter 5).

Retsch (or Retzsch), Friedrich August Moritz (1779–1857). German engraver of Goethe's *Faust* and the *Gallery of Shakespeare*.

Reynolds, Sir Joshua (1723–92). At the beginning of MP III Ruskin quotes from the *Idler* essays that Reynolds wrote for Samuel Johnson; Reynolds's *Discourses on Art* are referred to in MP I (at the beginning of Ch. II, Pt. I, Sec. I and of Pt. II, Sec. I, Ch. I), but in MP III Ruskin says that 'nearly every word that Reynolds wrote was contrary to his own practice' (Pt. IV, Ch. III, para. 2).

Rubens, Sir Peter Paul (1577–1640). The Flemish master, amazed and disappointed Ruskin by his coldness of vision, for all his skill as a painter and his rectitude and kindliness as a person (MP V, Pt. IX, Ch. VI, paras. 8–11).

Salvator Rosa 1615–73). Italian Romantic school: 'he saw only what was gross and terrible . . . I should not suspect Salvator of wantonly inflicting pain. His constantly painting it does not prove he delighted in it; he felt the horror of it, and in that horror fascination' (MP V, Pt. IX, Ch. IV, para. 13).

Stanfield, Clarkson (1793–1867). Nineteenth-century English realist and definer whom Ruskin both praised and criticized.

Tempesta, Antonio (1555–1630). Florentine painter best remembered for hunting and battle scenes.

Teniers, David II (1610–90). Seen by Ruskin as typical of seventeenth-century Dutch painters in his depiction of low subjects, substituting imitative skills for high spiritual thought.

Tintoretto, Jacopo (1518–94). Venetian painter who after the fires in the Doge's Palace in 1574 and 1577 was commissioned with Veronese to renew the interior.

Turner, Joseph Mallord William (1775–1851). Son of a barber, born in Covent Garden, London. He was heavily supported by the Royal Academy during the early part of his career, elected as a full member in

1802, becoming Professor of Perspective in 1807. Up to 1796 Turner was almost exclusively a watercolourist, thereafter turning increasingly to oils. Critical attacks on his oil paintings, led by Sir George Beaumont and the Classicists on the grounds of alleged lack of formal organization, induced Turner to publish between 1807 and 1819 seventy plates of his *Liber Studiorum* in defence of his conception of landscape painting. In his will Turner left nearly 300 paintings and nearly 20,000 watercolours and drawings to the nation, to be carefully preserved and housed in one gallery. The conditions of his will were not met until 1987, when a special Turner Gallery (Clore) was opened at the Tate. Among the Turner paintings that Ruskin most admired are *Ulysses deriding Polythemus* (1829), *Long Ships Lighthouse, Land's End* (1834–5), *Llanthony Abbey* (1835), *Juliet and her Nurse* (1836), *The Fighting Téméraire, tugged to her last berth to be broken up* (1839), *Slavers, throwing overboard the dead and dying – Typhoon coming on* (1841), *The Pass of Faido, St Gothard* (1843), *Goldau* (1843).

Veronese, Paul (1528–88). Ruskin's revelatory appreciation of his sensuous work contributed towards his so-called unconversion from strict Evangelical Protestantism in 1858.

Verrocchio, Andrea del (1435–88). Florentine painter and sculptor, carried out much work for the Medici.

Vitruvius. His *De Architectura* (27 BC) became the gospel for Renaissance architects.

Webster, Thomas (1800–86). Member of the British Academy, a painter of modest range of the realist school.

Woodward, Benjamin (1815–61). Between 1845 and 1861 the Irish architectural firm of Deane and Woodward was the principal nineteenth-century exponent of Ruskinian Gothic in the building in Dublin of Trinity College Museum, the Oxford Museum, Crown Life Assurance Company Office and the Kildare Street Club.

Wouverman(s), Philips (1619–68). Dutch painter, especially of battle-scenes, contrasted in his insensitive and carnal work with Angelico (MP V, Pt. IX, Ch. VIII, paras. 7–13).

RUSKIN AND HIS CRITICS

Marcel Proust (1871–1922) took Ruskin as his first major mentor. In the early 1900s he translated *The Bible of Amiens* and *Sesame and Lilies* into French, using his annotation of Ruskin's work as a means of getting inside the master's mind:

> Mediocre people generally believe that to let oneself be guided by books one admires takes away some of one's independence of judgment. 'What is it to you how Ruskin feels: feel for yourself.' Such an opinion rests on a psychological error ... There is no better way of becoming aware of one's feelings than to try to recreate in oneself what a master has felt ... Actually the only times when we truly have all our powers of mind are those when we do not believe ourselves to be acting with independence, when we do not arbitrarily choose the goal of our efforts.

For Proust, what reconciled all Ruskin's apparent contradictions was his religious purpose – a purpose so big as to include almost everything within it. Ruskin was above all a religious writer:

> At first he was called a realist. And, indeed, he has often repeated that the artist must adhere to the pure imitation of nature, 'without rejecting, despising, choosing anything'. [*Modern Painters, CW* 3:624]
> But it has also been said that he was an intellectual, because he wrote that the best painting was the one that contained the loftiest thoughts. Speaking of a group of children who, in the foreground of Turner's *Building of Carthage*, play with toy sailing boats, he concluded: 'The exquisite choice of this incident, as expressive of the ruling passion which was to be the source of future greatness, is quite as appreciable when it is told as when it is seen, it has nothing to do with the technicalities of painting; a scratch of the pen would have conveyed the idea and spoken to the intellect as much as the elaborate realizations of colour. Such a thought is something far above all art: it is epic poetry of the highest order.' [*Modern Painters, CW* 3:113] 'Likewise,' adds [Joseph-Antoine] Milsand,[1]

[1] (1817–86), critic and philosopher. One of the first Frenchmen to write about Ruskin.

who quotes this passage in analyzing the *Holy Family* by
Tintoretto, 'the features which allowed Ruskin to recognize the
great master are a ruined wall and the beginning of a new structure,
by which the artist symbolically makes us understand that the birth
of Christ was the end of the Jewish order and the coming of the new
covenant.' In a composition by the same Venetian, a *Crucifixion*,
Ruskin sees a masterpiece of painting because the author, by
means of the apparently insignificant incident of an ass feeding on
palm leaves in the background of Calvary [cf. *Modern Painters,
CW* 4:271; *Stones of Venice, CW* 11:385], knew how to assert the
profound idea that 'it was Jewish materialism, with its expectation
of a wholly temporal Messiah, and with the confounding of its
hopes at the time of the entry into Jerusalem, that had been the
cause of the hatred unleashed against the Savior and hence of his
death'.

It has been said that he suppressed the role of imagination in art
by giving too large a share to science. Did he not say that 'every
class of rock, every kind of earth, every form of cloud, must be
studied and rendered with equal precision? . . . Every geological
formation has features entirely peculiar to itself; definite lines of
fracture, giving rise to fixed resultant forms of rocks and earth;
peculiar vegetable products, among which still farther distinctions
are wrought out by climate and elevation. In the plant, the painter
observes every character of colour and form, . . . seizes on its lines
of rigidity or repose, . . . observes its local habits, its love or fear of
peculiar places, its nourishment or destruction by particular
influences; he associates it . . . with all the features of the situation
it inhabits . . .' [*Modern Painters, CW* 3:34–48] He must 'render
the delicate fissure, and descending curve, and undulating shadow
of the mouldering soil with gentle and fine finger, like the touch of
the rain itself . . .' [*Ibid., CW* 3:483] 'The greatest picture is that
which conveys to the mind of the spectator the greatest number of
the greatest ideas.' [*Ibid., CW* 3:92]

It has been said on the other hand that he ruined science by
giving imagination too large a part in it. In fact, one cannot help
but think of the naïve finalism of Bernardin de Saint-Pierre, who
said that God had divided melons into segments so that men could
eat them more easily, when one reads such pages as this: 'God has
employed colour in His creation as the unvarying accompaniment
of all that is purest and most precious; while for things precious
only in material uses, or dangerous, common colours are reserved.
Look at a dove's neck, and compare it with the grey back of a viper.
The crocodile and alligator are grey, but the innocent lizard green
and beautiful.' [*Ibid., VI*, 68]

If it has been said that he reduced art to be but a vassal of science, because he put forth the theory that a work of art should be considered as information on the nature of things, so far as to declare that 'a Turner discovers more on the nature of rocks than any academy will ever know', and 'a Tintoretto has but to let his hand go to reveal on the play of muscles a multitude of truths that will baffle all the anatomists on earth', it has also been said that he humiliated science before art [*Eagle's Nest, CW* 22:211 and *Stones of Venice, CW* 11:49–50].

Finally, it has been said that he was a pure aesthetician and that Beauty was his sole religion, because in fact he loved it all his life.

But on the other hand, it has been said that he was not even an artist, because he introduced into his appreciation of beauty considerations which were perhaps superior, but at any rate foreign to aesthetics. The first chapter of *The Seven Lamps of Architecture* prescribes to the artist the use of the most precious and durable material, and makes this duty derive from the sacrifice of Jesus, and the long-standing conditions for the sacrifice well-pleasing to God, conditions which must not be considered as abrogated, since God never informed us expressly that they were [cf. *The Seven Lamps, CW* 8:30–4]. And in *Modern Painters*, to settle the question of who is right, the partisans of color or the adepts of chiaroscuro, here is one of the arguments: 'Take a wider view of nature, and compare generally rainbows, sunrises, roses, violets, butterflies, birds, goldfish, rubies, opals, and corals, with alligators, hippopotami, lions, wolves, bears, swine, sharks, slugs, bones, fungi, fogs, and corrupting, stinging, destroying things in general, and you will feel then how the question stands between the colourists and chiaroscurists, – which of them have nature and life on their side, and which have sin and death.' [*Modern Painters, CW* 6:69]

And since so many contrary things have been said about Ruskin, it has been concluded that he was himself contradictory.

Of so many aspects of Ruskin's character, the one that is most familiar to us, because it is the one of which we possess (if one may so put it) the most beautiful portrait, the most studied and the most effective one, the most striking and the most famous, and in fact thus far the only one, is the Ruskin who during his whole life knew but one religion: that of Beauty.

That the adoration of Beauty was, in fact, the perpetual act of Ruskin's life may be true literally; but I think the aim of that life, its profound, secret, and constant intention, was something else . . .

For reasons whose metaphysical nature exceeds the bounds of a simple study of art, Beauty cannot be loved fruitfully if it is loved only for the pleasure it gives. Just as the pursuit of happiness for happiness' sake leads but to ennui, and as in order to find it we must look for something else, so too aesthetic pleasure is given to us in addition if we love Beauty for itself as something real existing outside of us, and infinitely more important than the joy it gives us. Far from having been a dilettante or an aesthete, Ruskin was precisely the opposite, one of those men who, like Carlyle, were warned by their genius of the vanity of pleasure and, at the same time, of the presence near them of an eternal reality, intuitively perceived by inspiration. Talent is given them as a power to relate this reality to the all-powerful and eternal to which, with enthusiasm and as if obeying a command of conscience, they dedicate their ephemeral life in order to give it some value. Such men, attentive to and eager about the universe to be explored, are made aware of the parts of reality which their special gifts provide them with a particular understanding of, by a kind of demon that guides them, a voice they hear, the eternal inspiration of men of genius. Ruskin's special gift was the feeling for beauty, in nature as in art. It was in Beauty that his nature led him to seek reality, and his entirely religious life received from it an entirely aesthetic use. But this Beauty to which he thus happened to dedicate his life was not conceived of by him as an object of enjoyment made to charm, but as a reality infinitely more important than life, for which he would have given his own life. From this, as you will see, the whole aesthetic system of Ruskin follows. First, you will understand that the years when he became acquainted with a new school of architecture or of painting were the principal landmarks in the development of his ethics. He would speak of the years when Gothic art presented itself to him with the same gravity, the same emotional nostalgia, the same serenity with which a Christian speaks of the day the truth was revealed to him. The events of his life are intellectual and the important dates are those on which he comprehends a new form of art: the year he understands Abbeville, the year he understands Rouen, the day Titian's painting and the shadows in Titian's painting appear to him as nobler than Rubens's painting, than the shadows in Rubens's painting.

You will then understand that, the poet being for Ruskin, as for Carlyle, a sort of scribe writing at nature's dictation a more or less important part of its secret, the artist's first duty is to add nothing of his own to the sublime message. From this eminence you will see vanish, like low-lying mists, the accusations of realism as well as of intellectualism levelled at Ruskin. If these objections are off the mark, it is because they do not aim high enough . . .

Let us pause here as at a fixed point, at the center of gravity of Ruskinian aesthetics. It is thus that his religious feeling directed his aesthetic feeling. To begin with, let us reply to those who might believe that his religious feeling altered his aesthetic feeling, that to the artistic appreciation of monuments, statues, and paintings he added religious considerations that had no business there, by asserting that the case was, in fact, quite to the contrary. That something of the divine which Ruskin felt was the basis of the feeling which works of art inspired in him was precisely what was profound and original in this feeling and which imposed itself on his taste without being susceptible to modification. And the religious veneration with which he expressed this feeling, his fear of distorting it in the slightest degree when translating it, prevented him, contrary to what has often been thought, from ever mixing any artifice of reasoning that would be foreign to his impression when faced with works of art. So that those who see in him a moralist and an apostle enjoying in art what is not art are as mistaken as those who, neglecting the profound essence of his aesthetic feeling, confuse it with a voluptuous dilettantism. So that, in short, his religious fervor, which had been the sign of his aesthetic sincerity, strengthened it further and protected him from any foreign encroachment. Whether some of these conceptions of his supernatural aesthetics be false is a matter which, in our opinion, is of no importance. All those who have any understanding of the laws governing the development of genius know that its force is measured more by the force of its beliefs than by what may be satisfying to common sense in the object of those beliefs. But, since Ruskin's Christianity resulted from the very essence of his intellectual nature, his artistic preferences, equally profound, must have had some relation to it. Therefore, just as the love of Turner's landscapes corresponded in Ruskin to that love of nature which gave him the greatest joys, so to the thoroughly Christian nature of his thinking corresponded his permanent attraction, which dominates his whole life and work, to what one may call Christian art: French medieval architecture and sculpture, Italian medieval architecture, sculpture, and painting . . .

In fact, he could pass thus from one country to another, for the same soul he had adored in the stones of Pisa was also the one that had given to the stones of Chartres their immortal form. No one has felt as he did the unity of Christian art during the Middle Ages, from the banks of the Somme to those of the Arno, and he realized in our hearts the dream of the great popes of the Middle Ages: 'Christian Europe.' If, as has been said, his name must remain attached to Pre-Raphaelitism, one should understand by that not what followed Turner, but what preceded Raphael. Today we may forget the services he rendered to Hunt, to Rossetti, to Millais, but what he has done for Giotto, for Carpaccio, for Bellini, we cannot. His sublime work was not to rouse the living, but to raise the dead.

Even so, Proust was also disturbed by his youthful admiration for Ruskin – as if he had needed to *use* worship of Ruskin as a means of learning, through Ruskin, worship of life:

> Infatuation for living creatures sometimes has a base origin which is later purified. A man becomes acquainted with a woman because she may help him reach a goal other than herself. Then once he knows her, he loves her for herself and sacrifices to her without hesitation that goal which it was merely her function to help him attain. Likewise, with my love for Ruskin's books was mingled, in the beginning, something of a selfish interest, the joy of the intellectual benefit I was going to draw from them. It is certain that when I read the first pages, feeling their power and their charm, I tried not to resist them, not to argue too much within myself, because I felt that if one day the charm of Ruskin's thought should, for me, permeate everything it had touched upon, in a word, if I were entirely captivated by his thought, the universe would become enriched by all that I had not known until then, Gothic cathedrals and innumerable paintings of England and Italy, which had not yet roused in me that longing without which there is never true knowledge. For Ruskin's thought is not like that of Emerson, for example, which is entirely contained in a book, that is to say, an abstract thing, a pure sign of itself. The object to which thought such as Ruskin's is applied, and from which it is inseparable, is not immaterial, it is scattered here and there over the surface of the earth. One must seek it where it is, in Pisa, Florence, Venice, the National Gallery, Rouen, Amiens, the mountains of Switzerland. Such thought which has an object other than itself, which has materialized in space, which is no longer infinite and free, but limited and subdued, which is incarnated in bodies of sculptured marble, in snowy mountains, in painted countenances, is perhaps less sublime than pure thought. But it makes the universe more beautiful for us, or at least certain individual parts, certain specifically named parts of the universe, because it touched upon them, and because it introduced us to them by obliging us, if we want to understand it, to love them.
>
> And so it was, in fact; all at once the universe regained an infinite value in my eyes. And my admiration for Ruskin gave such an importance to the things he had made me love that they seemed to be charged with a value greater even than that of life.

Proust achieved liberation from his idolatry of Ruskin, precisely by seizing on Ruskin's own anxieties about idolatry – the aesthetic substitution of reading for doing, of letter for spirit, of art for the very religion it depicts. Idolatry: 'the serving with the best of our hearts and minds some dear and sad fantasy which we have made for ourselves, while we disobey the present call of the Master, who is not dead, and who is not fainting upon His cross, but requiring us to take up ours'; Idolatry: 'the apprehension of a healing sacredness in the act of reading the Book whose primal commands we refuse to obey' (C&W XX, pp. 66, 240). The influence of Ruskin drove Proust to conclude thus of the use of art and books, in preparing himself for the writing of *A la Recherche du Temps Perdu*:

> And there, indeed, is one of the great and marvelous features of beautiful books (and one which will make us understand the role, at once essential and limited, that reading can play in our spiritual life) which for the author could be called 'Conclusions' and for the reader 'Incitements'. We feel quite truly that our wisdom begins where that of the author ends, and we would like to have him give us answers, when all he can do is give us desires. And these desires he can arouse in us only by making us contemplate the supreme beauty which the last effort of his art has permitted him to reach. But by a singular and, moreover, providential law of mental optics (a law which perhaps signifies that we can receive the truth from nobody, and that we must create it outselves), that which is the end of their wisdom appears to us as but the beginning of ours, so that it is at the moment when they have told us all they could tell us that they create in us the feeling that they have told us nothing yet . . . Reading is at the threshold of spiritual life; it can introduce us to it; it does not constitute it. (*On Reading Ruskin*, translated and edited by J. Autret, W. Burford and P. J. Wolfe (Yale, 1987), pp. 60, 29–34, 36–8, 58–9, 114–16)

George Eliot (1819–1880), reviewing *Modern Painters* Vol. III [*Westminster Review* April 1856, vol. 9 n.s. 625–33], saw the force of Ruskin's universalism:

> The critic of art, as he tells us, 'has to take *some* note of optics, geometry, geology, botany, and anatomy; he must acquaint himself with the works of all great artists, and with the temper and history of the times in which they lived; he must be a fair metaphysician, and a careful observer of the phenomena of natural scenery'. And when a writer like Mr. Ruskin brings these varied studies to bear on one great purpose, when he has to trace their common relation to a grand phase of human activity, it is obvious that he will have a great deal to say which is of interest and importance to others besides painters. The fundamental principles of all just thought and beautiful action or creation are the same,

and in making clear to ourselves what is best and noblest in art, we are making clear to ourselves what is best and noblest in morals.

Although George Eliot praised Ruskin's defence of realism, her own sense of the meaning of realism was, at least initially, probably closer to the spirit of seventeenth-century Dutch painting – which Ruskin despised but which George Eliot celebrated in chapter 17 of *Adam Bede* – rather than to the religious vision of Ruskin's Turner:

> The truth of infinite value that he teaches is *realism* – the doctrine that all truth and beauty are to be attained by a humble and faithful study of nature, and not by substituting vague forms, bred by imagination on the mists of feeling, in place of definite, substantial reality. The thorough acceptance of this doctrine would remould our life; and he who teaches its application to any one department of human activity with such power as Mr. Ruskin's, is a prophet for his generation. It is not enough simply to teach truth; that may be done, as we all know, to empty walls, and within the covers of unsaleable books; we want it to be so taught as to compel men's attention and sympathy.

Thomas Hardy (1840–1928) shows evidence of the influence of *Modern Painters* and 'The Nature of Gothic' in diary entries.

> January 1887. After looking at the landscape ascribed to Bonington in our drawing-room I feel that Nature is played out as a Beauty, but not as a Mystery ... The simply 'natural' is interesting no longer. The much decried, mad, late-Turner rendering is now necessary to create my interest. The exact truth as to material fact ceases to be of importance in art – it is a student's style – the style of a period when the mind is serene and unawakened to the tragical mysteries of life; when it does not bring anything to the object that coalesces with and translates the qualities already there, – half-hidden it may be – and the two united are depicted as the All.

> 9 January 1889. At the Old Masters, Royal Academy. Turner's water-colours; each is a landscape *plus* a man's soul ... What he paints chiefly is *light as modified by objects*. He first recognizes the impossibility of really producing on canvas all that is in a landscape; then gives for that which cannot be reproduced a something else which shall have upon the spectator an approximative effect to that of the real. He said, in his maddest and greatest days: 'What pictorial drug can I dose a man with, which shall affect his eyes somewhat in the manner of this reality which I cannot carry to him?' – and set to make such strange mixtures as he was

tending towards in 'Rain, Steam and Speed', 'The Burial of Wilkie', 'Agrippina landing with the ashes of Germanicus', 'Approach to Venice', 'Snowstorm and a Steamboat', etc. Hence, one may say, Art is the secret of how to produce by a false thing the effect of a true.

1898. [Hardy] knew that in architecture cunning irregularity is of enormous worth, and it is obvious that he carried on into his verse, perhaps in part unconsciously, the Gothic art-principle in which he had been trained – the principle of spontaneity, found in mouldings, tracery, and such like – resulting in the 'unforeseen' . . .

1906. I prefer late Wagner, as I prefer late Turner, to early (which I suppose is all wrong in taste), the idiosyncrasies of each master being more strongly shown in these strains. When a man not contented with the grounds of his success goes on and on, and tries to achieve the impossible, then he gets profoundly interesting to me.

Eve of Good Friday 1907. Critics can never be made to understand that the failure may be greater than the success. It is their particular duty to point this out; but the public points it out to them. To have strength to roll a stone weighing a hundredweight to the top of the mount is a success, and to have the strength to roll a stone of ten hundredweight only half-way up that mount is a failure. But the latter is two or three times so strong a deed.

[F. E. Hardy, *The Life of Thomas Hardy* (London, 1972) pp. 185, 216, 301, 329, 333–4]

Tony Tanner is a contemporary critic, familiar with structuralism and deconstruction. His account of Ruskin in *Venice Desired* implicitly takes up Proust's charge of idolatry and ponders it in twentieth-century terms. In the following excerpts he deploys the critical ideas of modern scepticism – beliefs deconstructed into fictions, writing interpreted as self-referential even when the writer thinks it is directed towards the world outside – while scrupulously also acknowledging the force of Ruskin's resistance to such interpretations:

Before we try to read the stones of Venice – and *The Stones of Venice* – Ruskin wants to prepare us, educate us, train us. He wants to establish 'canons of judgement' and hopes 'in making the Stones of Venice [capital letters but not capitalized words – neither and both city and book] touchstones, and detecting, by the mouldering of her marble, poison more subtle than ever was betrayed by the rending of her crystal' (CW 9, 57). Canons and touchstones – very Arnoldian and high Victorian: the overt and announced polemical intent is to show up the 'baseness' of the last three centuries (no less) of European architecture. But his real urge is to look into how you build a temple, a cathedral, a palace, and to this end he feels he has to go, indeed, right back to the quarry. The first volume is accurately and comprehensively entitled *The Foundations*.

'All European architecture . . . is derived from Greece through Rome, and coloured and perfected from the East' (*CW* 9, 34). The apodictic, universalizing, generalizing which brooks no possibility of denial or question is characteristic of Ruskin and is part of a strategy and a need. Somehow he wants to hold everything – *everything* – together; contain it, control it, relate it. This opening generalization is, he says, a 'great connecting clue, you may string all the types of successive architectural invention upon it like so many beads'. Immediately after, he informs us that the Greeks probably received their 'shaft system' – the original pillar of all architecture –from Egypt; but the possibly earlier derivation does not matter to the reader. 'It is only necessary that he should be able to refer to a fixed point of origin.' The search for such a point of origin is indeed the 'quarry' of many Victorian thinkers – be it of species, societies, religions, words. And the need for some 'connecting clue' goes along with this. To the extent that things are disoriginated, there is the danger that they may reveal themselves to be unrelated – and that things and people should be properly and significantly and harmoniously related is very important to Ruskin: 'we may also permit men or cities, to gather themselves into companies, or constellate themselves into clusters, but not to fuse themselves into mere masses of nebulous aggregation' (*CW* 9, 134). This permission or prescription informs both his politics (no democratic masses) and his writing, which constantly seeks to resist aggregation and produce constellation.

But from the start he has admitted that the 'point of origin' is not in fact finally determinable, so he establishes it by his own fiat, which means that all the subsequent connections and constellations which are directly or indirectly based on it are of his own making. Which in turn means that his prose has to have tremendous constructive and carrying power: to raise his own Venice he must build slowly and firmly and make his foundations sure.

> Do not think that Nature rusticates her foundations. Smooth sheets of rock, glistening like sea waves, and that ring under the hammer like a brazen bell, – that is her preparation for her first *stories*. She does rusticate sometimes: crumbly sandstones, with their ripple marks filled with red mud; dusty limestones, which the rains wash into labyrinthine

cavities; spongy lavas, which the volcano blast drags hither and thither into ropy coils and bubbling hollows; – these she rusticates, indeed, when she wants to make oyster-shells and magnesia of them; but not when she needs to lay *foundations* with them. Then she seeks the polished surface and iron heart, not rough looks and incoherent substance. (CW 9, 350–1)

Volume II will be called *The Sea Stories*, but before that Ruskin has to write his *Foundations*. For that, there must be no crumbly, dusty, spongy writing, but, like nature, something firm and glistening which will ring under the hammer like a bell – polished, iron-like, coherent. And that is what we get. Though, as always with Ruskin, we get something more as well: that unconfinable surplus which – it is part of his greatness as a writer – he is helpless to exclude and compelled to inscribe.

Since he has to start from the beginning – or a beginning – he is resolved to take us with him on what he announces will be a long journey: 'I shall endeavour so to lead the reader from the foundation upwards, as that he may find out for himself the best way of doing everything, and having so discovered it, never forget it' (CW 9, 73). And so we go right back to basics, down in the etymology of building as it were (Ruskin is very keen on etymology): the wall (and what is a wall? 'an even and united fence, whether of wood, earth, stone or metal') and, from the wall, the pier, then the shaft; the capital, the arch, the arch load, the roof, the buttress, and then on to ornamentation – he is trying to reconstruct the reader as apprentice medieval craftsman. 'Now as I gave the reader the ground and the stones, that he might for himself find out how to build his wall, I shall give him the block of marble, and the chisel, that he may himself find out how to shape the column'; 'The reader is now master of all he need know respecting construction of capitals'; 'The reader has now some knowledge of every feature of all possible architecture.' As a reward we move on to ornament: 'We have no more to do with heavy stones and hard lines; we are going to be happy' (CW 9, 253) – and enjoy ourselves in decorating architecture in ways derived from whatever gives us pleasure in the forms and movements in the natural world . . .

Of the designs in St Michele of Lucca, Ruskin writes:

Geometry seems to have acted as a febrifuge, for beautiful geometrical designs are introduced among the tumult of the hunt; and there is no more seeing double, nor ghastly monstrosity of conception; no more ending of everything in something else; no more disputing for spare legs among bewildered bodies; no more setting on of heads wrong side foremost. *The fragments have come together*: we are out of the Inferno with its weeping down the spine; we are in the fair hunting fields of the Lucchese mountains. (CW 9, 430)

The italicized words point to an ongoing need and search for Ruskin, until at the end on the verge of his last madness he found that 'things bind and blend themselves together': how do you make the fragments come together? How avoid the Inferno and keep yourself in the fair hunting fields? (This was to be Ezra Pound's – one might even say modernism's – problem.) It might be argued that this Inferno is a cultural nightmare and that, for Ruskin, Nature is still to be perceived as sweetly and serenely self-administering. Usually so indeed, and he often turns to Nature to see 'with what imagery she will fill our thoughts'. Yet it is not always the desired or needed model. 'But we want no cold and careful imitation of catastrophe; no calculated mockery or convulsion; no delicate recommendation of ruin. We are to follow the labour of nature, but not her disturbance; to imitate what she has deliberately ordained, not what she has violently suffered, or strangely permitted' (CW 9, 270). But how can you tell the labour from the disturbance, the difference between the permitted and the ordained? Ruskin needs his confident lists and classifications, his almost obsessive systematizations, at the same time as he reveals that they depend on arbitrary, if impetuous exclusions, just as his work is based on an origin which is deemed rather than discovered. While 'proving four laws' governing the ways in which capitals may change according to changes in proportion, he admits, or marvels, 'infinity of infinities in the sum of possible change' (CW 9, 142). Infinity is always seeping into Ruskin's writing, as his writing everywhere acknowledges: constantly arborescently reaching out for the not-yet-included, even while numbering, listing and generally seeking to bring to rule. 'This infinite universe is unfathomable, inconceivable, in its whole.' It is matched by 'the infinity of the written word' (CW 9, 410). Ruskin wrote in and between, and in the fullest possible knowledge of, these two infinities. For the purposes of perception and description, a key strategy is finding the appropriate distance. As an example, he cites the case of looking at a mountain. If you want to see 'its great harmonies of form' you 'don't climb up it where, seen close to, all is disorder and accident.' Rather, you draw away and, as you see more and more, 'dim sympathies begin to busy themselves in the disjointed mass; line binds itself into stealthy fellowship with line; group by group, the helpless fragments gather themselves into ordered companies . . . until the powerless chaos is seen risen up with girded loins, and not one piece of all the unregarded heap could now be spared from the mystic whole' (CW 9, 294–5). This is a kind of polity of vision whereby you retire to the point at which reality begins to form groups, fellowships, companies, with sympathies and bindings and gatherings gradually becoming visible. It is a form of perspectivism. It is a matter of finding the right way of looking, the right standpoint from which to look (and seeing is everything in Ruskin), which can transform the 'powerless' (or perhaps potentially all too powerful) 'chaos' into a 'mystic whole'. For Ruskin's immediate purpose it will be a matter of retiring from the contemporary stones of Venice, lying indeed in 'disorder and accident', until, deploying his civics of vision, he can see it as some part of a 'mystic whole' . . .

But his main 'quarry', and the climax of his 'story', is the DUCAL PALACE, writ large to indicate its pre-eminence, since it is 'the building which at once consummates and embodies the entire system of the Gothic architecture in Venice' (CW 10, 327). Before embarking on his account of that edifice Ruskin feels it necessary, as usual, to go back – back to first principles and basics, and establish 'The Nature of Gothic'. He is in pursuit of 'Gothicness'. It is a justly famous chapter, and the sustained passage in which he imagines what a bird sees as its flies over the changing landscape from south to north is one of his most impressive imaginative *tours de force*. From this passage one would sense that his sympathies were drawn northward. The south is seen as serene (later as 'languid', even 'listless') – 'a great peacefulness of light, Syria and Greece, Italy and Spain, laid like pieces of a golden pavement into the sea-blue'. But Ruskin's prose is more energized – galvanized – as the landscape gets rougher: 'and then, farther north still to see the earth heave into mighty masses of leaden rock and heathy moor, bordering with a broad waste of gloomy purple that belt of field and wood, and splintering into irregular and grisly islands midst the northern seas, beaten by storm, and chilled by ice-drift, and tormented by furious pulse of contending tide' (CW 10, 186–7). Ruskin's prose heaves and splinters with the land. Similarly when he imagines the generic or ur-craftsman in each sphere:

> Let us watch him with reverence as he sets side by side the burning gems, and smooths with soft sculpture the jasper pillars, that are to reflect a ceaseless sunshine, and rise into a cloudless sky: but not with less reverence let us stand by him, when, with rough strength and hurried stroke, he smites an uncouth animation out of the rocks which he has torn from among the moss of the moorland, and heaves into the darkened air the pile of iron buttress and rugged wall, instinct with a work of an imagination as wild and wayward as the northern sea; creations of ungainly shape and rigid limb, but full of wolfish life; fierce as the winds that beat, and changeful as the clouds that shade them. (CW 10, 187–8)

Not with less reverence indeed, and, it would seem, with a good deal more excitement, and attracting more of Ruskin's prose by a factor of three to one.

Ruskin's moralized or aestheticized geography is all his own, and we should not be concerned with cartographic accuracy or consistency. Venice as the midway, intersecting or meeting point of all directions, tendencies, forces, energies, styles must be the place where the Gothic touches and pauses on a moment of perfection. But one can feel Ruskin's imagination pulling northward. Here is one of his most striking formulations of the nature of Gothic, which he rather oddly calls 'the *only rational* architecture': 'it can shrink into a turret, expand into a hall, coil into a staircase, or spring into a spire, with undegraded grace and unexhausted energy' (CW 10, 212). This is what draws him, and his own expanding, coiling, springing writing; and rationality is, really, little to the point. His prose does not much like to 'bask in dreamy benignity of sunshine' (the south) but tends more to 'wilderness of thought, and roughness of work' (the north) (CW 10, 188). Two of the features of Gothic which seem most important for him are excess and unfinishedness, unfinishableness. His list of the six 'moral elements' of Gothic commences with 'Savageness' and concludes with 'Redundance', which he will amplify as 'the uncalculating bestowal of the wealth of its labour'. One can everywhere detect Ruskin's impatience and dissatisfaction with any art, or work, which seems to aim for and be content with 'finish', closure, perfection – 'to banish imperfection is to destroy expression, to check exertion, to paralyse vitality'. He likes the 'perpetual change both in design and execution' that he finds in Gothic work ('the workman must have been altogether set free'); he esteems 'the infringement of every servile principle'; he cherishes forms which were '*capable of perpetual novelty*' and celebrates the proportions of the pointed arch because they are 'changeable to infinity'. You can feel his prose warming to Gothic ornament which 'stands out in prickly independence, and frosty fortitude, jutting into crockets and freezing into pinnacles; here starting up into a monster, there germinating into a blossom, anon knitting itself into a branch, alternately thorny, bossy, and bristly, or writhed into every form of nervous entanglement' (CW 10, 203–4, 208, 240). Whatever else it is describing, this is writing that is describing itself. For clearly this is where Ruskin is at home, is indeed making his home . . .

We must note that he is seeking to constitute an 'image of the *lost* city' – Ruskin is one of the great writers of loss, and his writing has, correspondingly, incomparable regaining powers. 'I do not wonder at what men suffer, but I wonder often at what they Lose' (CW 10, 178). Ruskin writes always to rescue, to preserve, to bring things back. It is no wonder – and a matter for wonder – that he inspired Proust to set out to retrieve lost time. Ruskin, for the moment, is after the Venice which lost itself. (*Venice Desired* (Blackwells, Oxford, 1992) pp. 82–4, 86–7, 102–3, 91.)

Robert Hewison is a modern academic Ruskinian. In his essay he quotes Ruskin in 1875, on the fortieth anniversary of his matriculation from Oxford: 'Looking back, it seems to me as if I had been rebelling in the Wilderness forty years, and were now only received again by the University as her prodigal son' (C&W XXXVII, p. 166). Ruskin returned to his *alma mater* to become its first Slade Professor in 1869, but resigned in 1879, was re-appointed in 1882 and resigned again. He felt he was never accepted at Oxford, and Hewison sees this as part of Ruskin's courageous but unhappy 'refusal to respect categories and the institutions that enforce them'. The rebel in the wilderness still:

'No true disciple of mine will ever be a "Ruskinian"! (C&W XXIV p. 371). When Ruskin wrote these words he could not know that a hundred years later students of his work would be calling themselves Ruskinians, nor that they would savour this additional irony. His words, in their context, paradox and meaning, are a direct challenge to any would-be explicator of Ruskin, for this typically Ruskinian statement follows typically Ruskinian procedures, and demands a typically Ruskinian method of analysis. And if we are to be logical about Ruskin's paradox, we should reverse its terms, and admit that to be truly Ruskinian, we must at all costs avoid discipleship . . .

> I imagine the sorrowfulness of these feelings [of being a dismissed schoolboy] must be abated, in the minds of most men, by a pleasant vanity in their hope of being remembered as the discoverers, at least, of some important truth, or the founders of some exclusive system called after their own names. But I have never applied myself to discover anything, being content to praise what had already been discovered; and the only doctrine or system peculiar to me is the abhorrence of all that is doctrinal instead of demonstrable, and of all that is systematic instead of useful: so that no true disciple of mine will ever be a 'Ruskinian'! – he will follow, not me, but the instincts of his own soul, and the guidance of its Creator. Which, though not a sorrowful object of contemplation in itself, leaves me none of the common props and crutches of halting pride. I know myself to be a true master, because my pupils are well on the way to do better than I have done; but there is not always a sense of extreme pleasure in watching their advance, where one has no more strength, though more than ever the will, to companion them. (C&W XXIV, p. 371)

In this broad context – and the necessity of long quotation is emblematic of the need for long reading when studying Ruskin – Ruskin's key phrase is only one paradox among several. He denies – he, the tireless investigator, list-maker, collector and rearranger –ever trying to discover anything; he dogmatically states that his one dogma is absence of dogma. He makes himself humble, and congratulates himself on being a true master. He says that he has given up, but he wants to go on. Such use of paradox requires a special method of interpretation . . .

Ruskin's disrespect for categories makes him as hard to fit into a University course as it was to accommodate the first Slade Professor of Art . . . The teaching of Art may be 'the teaching of all things' (C&W XXIX, p. 86), but the teaching of art history is another matter, and art historians are wary of his wayward methodology and misattributions. Literary critics are faced with an imaginative writer who wrote no fiction other than a fairy tale, and his literary judgments are no more straightforward than his artistic ones. Analysis of his prose style for its own sake is only narrowly rewarding, and there is the daunting fact that Ruskin, to be read at all, must be read at length. (This is written at a time when most of his work is out of print, and the once ubiquitous second-hand volumes are hard to come by.) According to the categories he is neither philosopher, scientist nor economist. Only the vague genre 'cultural history', of which Ruskin was a pioneer, can accommodate all the facets of his work, but that genre is so vague, and its methodology so unestablished, that Ruskin may yet escape academic institutionalization.

As a Ruskinian, I am delighted that this should be so . . . ('Ruskin and the Institutions' in *New Approaches to Ruskin* (Routledge, London, 1981), pp. 214–16, 228–9)

John Berger has, during the course of his career as writer and critic, expressed something of what is at stake in the late twentieth century in seeking increasingly to relate his left-wing socio-political and ecological concerns with spiritual forms of serious-ness. The following, apart perhaps from the word 'aesthetic', could also have been written by Ruskin himself – or at least may be said to give a reader some sense of what a Ruskin might sound like today:

There seem to be certain constants which all cultures have found 'beautiful': among them – certain flowers, trees, forms of rock, birds, animals, the moon, running water . . .

One is obliged to acknowledge a coincidence or perhaps a congruence. The evolution of natural forms and the evolution of human perception have coincided to produce the phenomenon of a potential recognition: what *is* and what we can see (and by seeing also feel) sometimes meet at a point of affirmation. This point, this coincidence, is two-faced: what has been seen is recognized and affirmed and, at the same time, the seer is affirmed by what he sees. For a brief moment one finds oneself – without the pretensions of a creator – in the position of God in the first chapter of Genesis . . . And he saw that it *was* good. The aesthetic emotion before nature derives, I believe, from this double affirmation.

Yet we do not live in the first chapter of Genesis. We live – if one follows the biblical sequence of events – after the Fall. In any case, we live in a world of suffering in which evil is rampant, a world whose events do not confirm our Being, a world that has to be resisted. It is in this situation that the aesthetic moment offers hope. That we find a crystal or a poppy beautiful means that we are less alone, that we are more deeply inserted into existence than the course of a single life would lead us to believe. I try to describe as accurately as possible the experience in question; my starting point is phenomenological, not deductive; its form, perceived as such, becomes a message that one receives but cannot translate because, in it, all is instantaneous. For an instant, the energy of one's perception becomes inseparable from the energy of the creation.

The aesthetic emotion we feel before a man-made object . . . is a derivative of the emotion we feel before nature . . . All the languages of art have been developed as an attempt to transform the instantaneous into the permanent. Art supposes that beauty is not an exception – is not *in despite of* – but is the basis for an order.

Several years ago, when considering the historical face of art, I wrote that I judged a work according to whether or not it helped men in the modern world claim their social rights. I hold to that. Art's other, transcendental face raises the question of man's ontological right.

The notion that art is the mirror of nature is one that only appeals in periods of scepticism. Art does not imitate nature, it imitates a creation, sometimes to propose an alternative world, sometimes simply to amplify, to confirm, to make social the brief hope offered by nature. Art is an organized response to what nature allows us to glimpse occasionally. Art sets out to transform the potential recognition into an unceasing one. It proclaims man in the hope of receiving a surer reply . . . the transcendental face of art is always a form of prayer. (*The White Bird* (Chatto, London, 1985) pp. 8–9)

SUGGESTIONS FOR FURTHER READING

My main suggestion is to read Ruskin's *Praeterita* (Oxford University Press) in full. For Ruskin's socio-political writings, the Penguin selection, *Unto This Last and Other Writings*, edited by Clive Wilmer, is admirable.

For those who wish to consult biographical accounts there is John Dixon-Hunt, *The Wider Sea* (Dent, 1982), and Tim Hilton, *John Ruskin: The Early Years* (Yale, 1985).

On Ruskin's architectural writings, John Unrau, *Looking at Architecture with John Ruskin* (Thames and Hudson, 1978) is excellent. Paul Walton's *The Drawings of John Ruskin* (Oxford, 1972) is especially good on Ruskin as an artist in his own right.

Those readers who wish to know more about Turner's work might consult first of all Andrew Wilton, *J. M. W. Turner: His Life and Art* (Academy Editions, 1979), and John Gage, *Colour in Turner, Poetry and Truth* (Studio Vista, 1969).

For the thinking implicit in the selection in this volume, see Philip Davis, *Memory and Writing: from Wordsworth to Lawrence* (Liverpool University Press, 1983); also 'Arnold or Ruskin?' in *Literature and Theology*, vol., 6 no. 4, December 1992, pp. 320–44. For the Victorian context, David De Laura's *Hebrew and Hellene in Victorian England: Newman, Arnold, Pater* (Austin, Texas, 1969), though not specifically about Ruskin's Hebraism, is nonetheless suggestive.

Ruskin's best critic is Marcel Proust in *On Reading Ruskin* translated and edited by J. Autret, W. Burford and P. J. Wolfe (Yale, 1987). Probably the best introduction to Ruskin's work is still J. D. Rosenberg, *The Darkening Glass* (Routledge, 1962). The reader will also find comprehensive accounts in Elizabeth K. Helsinger, *Ruskin and the Art of the Beholder* (Harvard University Press, 1982); Robert Hewison, *John Ruskin: The Argument of the Eye* (Thames and Hudson, 1976); and George P. Landow, *The Aesthetic and Critical Theories of John Ruskin* (Princeton, 1971). Peter Fuller's *Theoria* (Chatto and Windus, 1988) has been influential on the study of Ruskin in relation to ecology, modern art and religion. On *The Stones of Venice* in particular, Tony Tanner's *Venice Desired* (Blackwells, 1992) is engaging and impressive. Two collections of essays, Robert Hewison (ed.), *New Approaches to Ruskin* (Routledge, 1981), and Robert Rhodes and Del Ivan Janik (eds) *Studies in Ruskin* (Ohio University Press, 1982), are useful for those who prefer essay-length criticism: Helsinger, Hewison, Landow, and Unrau are to be found in these collections. In *New Approaches to Ruskin*, John Hayman's 'Towards the Labyrinth' is particularly helpful: it may be supplemented by Jay Fellowes' difficult but stimulating book, *The Failing Distance* (Johns Hopkins University Press, 1978) and his *Ruskin's Maze* (Princeton University Press, 1981).

ACKNOWLEDGEMENTS

The publishers and editor wish to thank the following for permission to use copyright material:

Blackwell Publishers for material from Tony Tanner, *Venice Desired*, 1992;

Macmillan Ltd for material from F. E. Hardy, *The Life of Thomas Hardy*, 1972;

Peters, Fraser & Dunlop Group Ltd on behalf of the author for material from Robert Hewison, 'Ruskin and the Institutions' in *New Approaches to Ruskin*, Routledge, 1981;

Random House UK Ltd and Pantheon Books, a division of Random House, Inc. for material from John Berger, *The White Bird*, Chatto & Windus, 1985, known also as *The Sense of Sight*, Pantheon Books. Copyright © 1985 by John Berger;

Yale University Press for material from Marcel Proust, *On Reading Ruskin*, trans. and ed. by J. Autret, W. Burford and P. J. Wolfe, 1987;

The Tate Gallery, London, for the reproduction of *Caudebec* by J. M. W. Turner, the Turner Collection, Tate Gallery;

The Trustees of The British Museum, London, for the reproduction of *Jason*, by J. M. W. Turner, copyright The British Museum;

The William Morris Gallery, Walthamstow, London, for the reproduction of *West Porch of Rouen Cathedral* by John Ruskin;

The National Gallery for the reproduction of *A Man Washing His Feet*, attributed to Nicolas Poussin;

The Victoria & Albert Museum for the reproduction of *Christ's Charge to St Peter* by Raphael;

The Mansell Collection for the reproduction of *San Giovanni Fuorcivitas*, Pistoia;

The Conway Library, Courtauld Institute of Art for the reproduction of *West Front, Pisa Cathedral*.

Every effort has been made to trace all the copyright holders, but if any have been inadvertently overlooked the publishers will be pleased to make the necessary arrangement at the first opportunity.

PHILOSOPHY AND RELIGIOUS WRITING IN EVERYMAN

A SELECTION

Ethics
SPINOZA
Spinoza's famous discourse on the power of understanding **£4.99**

Critique of Pure Reason
IMMANUEL KANT
The capacity of the human intellect examined **£6.99**

A Discourse on Method, Meditations, and Principles
RENÉ DESCARTES
Takes the theory of mind over matter into a new dimension **£4.99**

Philosophical Works including the Works on Vision
GEORGE BERKELEY
An eloquent defence of the power of the spirit in the physical world **£4.99**

Utilitarianism, On Liberty, Considerations on Representative Government
J. S. MILL
Three radical works which transformed political science **£5.99**

Utopia
THOMAS MORE
A critique of contemporary ills allied with a visionary ideal for society **£3.99**

An Essay Concerning Human Understanding
JOHN LOCKE
A central work in the development of modern philosophy **£5.99**

Hindu Scriptures
The most important ancient Hindu writings in one volume **£6.99**

Apologia Pro Vita Sua
JOHN HENRY NEWMAN
A moving and inspiring account of a Christian's spiritual journey **£5.99**

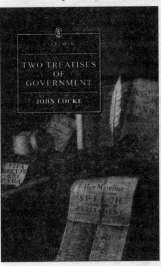

£3.99

AVAILABILITY

All books are available from your local bookshop or direct from
Littlehampton Book Services Cash Sales, 14 Eldon Way, Lineside Estate, Littlehampton, West Sussex BN17 7HE. PRICES ARE SUBJECT TO CHANGE.

To order any of the books, please enclose a cheque (in £ sterling) made payable to Littlehampton Book Services, or phone your order through with credit card details (Access, Visa or Mastercard) on 0903 721596 (24 hour answering service) stating card number and expiry date. Please add £1.25 for package and postage to the total value of your order.

In the USA, for further information and a complete catalogue call 1-800-526-2778.

ESSAYS, CRITICISM AND HISTORY IN EVERYMAN

A SELECTION

The Embassy to Constantinople and Other Writings
LIUDPRAND OF CREMONA
An insider's view of political machinations in medieval Europe **£5.99**

Speeches and Letters
ABRAHAM LINCOLN
A key document of the American Civil War **£4.99**

Essays
FRANCIS BACON
An excellent introduction to Bacon's incisive wit and moral outlook **£3.99**

Puritanism and Liberty: Being the Army Debates (1647-49) from the Clarke Manuscripts
A fascinating revelation of Puritan minds in action **£7.99**

Biographia Literaria
SAMUEL TAYLOR COLERIDGE
A masterpiece of criticism, marrying the study of literature with philosophy **£4.99**

Essays on Literature and Art
WALTER PATER
Insights on culture and literature from a major voice of the 1890s **£3.99**

Chesterton on Dickens: Criticisms and Appreciations
A landmark in Dickens criticism, rarely surpassed **£4.99**

Essays and Poems
R. L. STEVENSON
Stevenson's hidden treasures in a new selection **£4.99**

£3.99

POETRY
IN EVERYMAN

A SELECTION

Silver Poets of the Sixteenth Century

EDITED BY

DOUGLAS BROOKS-DAVIES
A new edition of this famous
Everyman collection **£6.99**

Complete Poems

JOHN DONNE
The father of metaphysical verse in
this highly-acclaimed edition **£6.99**

Complete English Poems, Of Education, Areopagitica

JOHN MILTON
An excellent introduction to
Milton's poetry and prose **£6.99**

Selected Poems

JOHN DRYDEN
A poet's portrait of Restoration
England **£4.99**

Selected Poems and Prose

PERCY BYSSHE SHELLEY
'The essential Shelley' in one
volume **£3.50**

Women Romantic Poets 1780-1830: An Anthology

Hidden talent from the Romantic era
rediscovered **£5.99**

Poems in Scots and English

ROBERT BURNS
The best of Scotland's greatest lyric
poet **£4.99**

Selected Poems

D. H. LAWRENCE
A new, authoritative selection
spanning the whole of Lawrence's
literary career **£4.99**

The Poems

W. B. YEATS
Ireland's greatest lyric poet
surveyed in this ground-breaking
edition **£7.99**

£5.99

DRAMA
IN EVERYMAN

A SELECTION

Everyman and Medieval Miracle Plays

EDITED BY A. C. CAWLEY
A selection of the most popular medieval plays **£3.99**

Complete Plays and Poems

CHRISTOPHER MARLOWE
The complete works of this fascinating Elizabethan in one volume **£5.99**

Complete Poems and Plays

ROCHESTER
The most sexually explicit – and strikingly modern – writing of the seventeenth century **£6.99**

Restoration Plays

Five comedies and two tragedies representing the best of the Restoration stage **£7.99**

Female Playwrights of the Restoration: Five Comedies

Rediscovered literary treasures in a unique selection **£5.99**

Poems and Plays

OLIVER GOLDSMITH
The most complete edition of Goldsmith available **£4.99**

Plays, Poems and Prose

J. M. SYNGE
The most complete edition of Synge available **£6.99**

Plays, Prose Writings and Poems

OSCAR WILDE
The full force of Wilde's wit in one volume **£4.99**

A Doll's House/The Lady from the Sea/The Wild Duck

HENRIK IBSEN
A popular selection of Ibsen's major plays **£4.99**

£6.99

ANCIENT CLASSICS IN EVERYMAN

A SELECTION

The Republic
PLATO
The most important and enduring of
Plato's works **£5.99**

The Education of Cyrus
XENOPHON
A fascinating insight into the culture
and politics of ancient Greece **£6.99**

Juvenal's Satires with the Satires of Persius
JUVENAL AND PERSIUS
Unique and acute observations of
contemporary Roman society **£5.99**

The Odyssey
HOMER
A classic translation of one of the
greatest adventures ever told **£5.99**

History of the Peloponnesian War
THUCYDIDES
The war that brought to an end a
golden age of democracy **£5.99**

The Histories
HERODOTUS
The earliest surviving work of
Greek prose literature **£7.99**

£5.99

SAGAS AND OLD ENGLISH LITERATURE IN EVERYMAN

A SELECTION

Egils saga
TRANSLATED BY
CHRISTINE FELL
A gripping story of Viking exploits
in Iceland, Norway and Britain **£4.99**

Edda
SNORRI STURLUSON
TRANSLATED BY
ANTHONY FAULKES
The first complete English transla-
tion **£5.99**

The Fljotsdale Saga and
The Droplaugarsons
TRANSLATED BY
ELEANOR HAWORTH
AND JEAN YOUNG
A brilliant portrayal of life and
times in medieval Iceland **£3.99**

The Anglo-Saxon Chronicle
TRANSLATED BY
G. N. GARMONSWAY
A fascinating record of events in
ancient Britain **£4.99**

Anglo-Saxon Poetry
TRANSLATED BY
S. A. J. BRADLEY
A widely acclaimed collection **£6.99**

Fergus of Galloway:
Knight of King Arthur
GUILLAUME LE CLERC
TRANSLATED BY
D. D. R. OWEN
Essential reading for students of
Arthurian romance **£3.99**

£4.99
